ELEVATED

The Global Rise of the N.B.A.

By the Staff of
The New York Times

•

Edited and Annotated
by Harvey Araton

TRIUMPH
BOOKS

TRIUMPHBOOKS.COM

The articles on which this book is based originally appeared in *The New York Times*. Inquiries concerning permission to reprint any article or portion thereof should be directed to The New York Times Company, c/o Pars International, 253 West 35th Street, 7th Floor, New York, N.Y. 10001, or NYTPermissions@Parsintl.com.

Library of Congress Catalog-in-Publication Data

Names: Araton, Harvey, editor.
Title: Elevated : the global rise of the N.B.A. / by the staff of the New York Times ; edited and annotated by Harvey Araton.
Other titles: New York times.
Description: Chicago, Illinois : Triumph Books, [2019]
Identifiers: LCCN 2018056205 | ISBN 9781629376509 (hardcover)
Subjects: LCSH: National Basketball Association—History. | Basketball--United States--History.
Classification: LCC GV885.515.N38 E55 2019 | DDC 796.323/6406—dc23 LC record available at https://lccn.loc.gov/2018056205

This book is available in quantity at special discounts for your group or organization. For further information, contact:

Triumph Books LLC
814 North Franklin Street
Chicago, Illinois 60610
(312) 337-0747
www.triumphbooks.com

Printed in U.S.A.

ISBN: 978-1-62937-792-6

Design by Sue Knopf

*For Jay Schreiber, who drove us crazy
but steered us right.*

Contents

Foreword

No professional sports league appeals to a broad base of fans quite like the N.B.A., which cuts across many demographic groups on a global scale, in large part due to its many great, marketable stars.

It wasn't always this way.

Back in the late 1970s, the future of the league looked bleak, until Larry Bird and Magic Johnson came along. With great casts alongside them, they empowered the most historically successful teams — the Boston Celtics and Los Angeles Lakers — on opposite coasts across the 1980s, electrifying fans everywhere in between.

The sport's popularity soared even more during the 1990s, which was dominated by Michael Jordan and the Chicago Bulls. That decade also launched the N.B.A. game as a smashing success beyond U.S. borders. By the fall of 2004, as coach of the Houston Rockets, I saw first-hand how this uniquely American game had penetrated foreign cultures in faraway lands.

Led by Yao Ming, we went to Shanghai for the first N.B.A. games on Chinese soil, a homecoming for a groundbreaking player and national hero in a country where basketball was the fastest-growing participation sport.

Never will I forget Yao's countrymen — who had become instant Rockets fans — literally rocking our team bus as we left the hotel. In the three years I was privileged to coach Yao, there were more reporters from China covering our team than from the U.S. Role players on the Rockets scored endorsement deals in China just by being teammates of Yao's.

Having previously worked in New York with the Knicks for a dozen years as an assistant and head coach, and at a time when we became blood rivals to Jordan and the Bulls (among others), I was already well aware of how captivating the N.B.A. game could be. On so many spring nights, it seemed all that mattered in the city was how Patrick Ewing and the Knicks would do.

In New York, the media was a major part of the N.B.A. phenomenon. The tabloid newspapers raised the temperature around the team but *The New York Times* provided the most balanced coverage. Throughout my years in New York, *The Times* had a Murderers' Row of sports reporters and columnists weighing in from Madison Square Garden.

Harvey Araton was one of them. A 2017 Curt Gowdy Award winner at the Naismith Memorial Basketball Hall of Fame, he has been front and center for the N.B.A.'s resurgence and glory years that have carried on into the 21st century.

The modern game has changed, faster and more wide open than ever. It speaks to its fan base better than any other sport, and without the inherent problems facing its main competitors — baseball (too slow) and football (too many injuries). The league's popularity and growth show no signs of slowing.

In *Elevated: The Global Rise of the N.B.A.*, Araton has selected the most important and trend-setting stories published by *The Times* during his 40-plus years of covering the sport. This expansive compilation by *Times* reporters and columnists provides a nuanced view of the league and a look into the complexities of its most intriguing personalities and issues.

Bird. Dr. J. Magic. Michael. LeBron. Durant. Curry. They're all here, and many more who may be less famous but are no less a part of the N.B.A. developmental fabric. These in-depth features and incisive commentary — enhanced by Araton's chapter introductions and multiple reporter postscripts telling the story behind the stories — are playfully and passionately chronicled by the staff of a truly global newspaper that has covered the sport across all borders crossed by the N.B.A.

Enjoy the journey.

— Jeff Van Gundy
ESPN N.B.A. analyst, 2017 FIBA AmeriCup gold medal–winning coach,
and former coach of the New York Knicks and Houston Rockets

Godfathers of the Modern Game

As N.B.A. Godfathers go, Danny Biasone was by reputation, compared to Red Auerbach, more of the whacky uncle. Auerbach, the Celtics' imperious smoker of victory cigars, was indisputably the dominant coach and team architect of the league's early decades. But Biasone was its most inventive visionary.

Biasone ran the old Syracuse Nationals out of a bowling alley in that frosty upstate New York outpost and inspired the adoption of a 24-second shot clock that became — according to Maurice Podoloff — the "salvation of professional basketball."

A Russian-born and Yale-educated lawyer, Podoloff was the league's first president (now commissioner). In a *New York Times* story by Louis Effrat on Dec. 11, 1955, he claimed no credit for the rule change that, when implemented for the 1954–55 season, increased scoring by 13.6 points per game. Biasone, Podoloff said, had passionately advocated for the shot clock during owners' meetings.

Auerbach had actually been one of the more aggressive manipulators of the pre–shot clock game, as Bob Cousy dribbled figure eights around dazed opponents, putting games to bed and fans to sleep. In one 1953 playoff snoozer against Syracuse, an incensed Biasone watched as 106 fouls were called, 128 free throws were taken, and Cousy alone scored 30 points from the line.

"There was danger that the fans, disgusted by the continual stalling and intentional fouling throughout the final four minutes of a game, were losing interest," Podoloff told Effrat.

Life, unfortunately, doesn't always reward the most deserving. Nobody benefited more from the shot clock than Auerbach, whose Bill Russell–led Celtics would soon embark on a run of 11 titles in 13 years.

Brilliant a tactician as he was, Auerbach was certainly no prophet. Much later, sizing up the shift in leverage between owners and players following pro-labor decisions in federal courts, he forecast difficult times for the sport in a 1977 story that he wrote for *The Times*. Then Larry Bird happened. So much for Auerbach's career as a columnist.

MAY 28, 1992

Biasone as Visionary Is N.B.A. Loss

BY HARVEY ARATON

The last call Dolph Schayes would make to the old man was not unlike countless others over four decades. The subject, as always, was basketball, a game invented by James Naismith and reinvented into its current popular form by an irascible fellow named Daniel Biasone.

"They won't give me a television," Biasone complained to Schayes last Sunday from the intensive care unit of University Hospital in Syracuse.

His 83-year-old body having surrendered to cancer, his life into its final 24 hours, Biasone wanted only to watch the Portland Trail Blazers play the Utah Jazz and the Cleveland Cavaliers play the Chicago Bulls.

"Oh, Danny never stopped following the game," said Schayes, the longtime star of Biasone's great love, the Syracuse Nationals, whom Biasone outlived by 29 years.

Just a couple of weeks before Biasone's death on Memorial Day, in fact, Schayes and Paul Seymour, another former Nat, visited Biasone at his bowling alley, the Eastwood Sports Center. This was the very building in which Biasone's players would drink and be merry, or melancholy, long into the night after their games at the State Fair Coliseum and later the Syracuse War Memorial.

It was there, in 1951, that Biasone began to complain, to anyone who would listen, that professional basketball needed a clock to limit time of possession. It took three years before the rest of the National Basketball Association's owners acknowledged Biasone, saving their sport until Magic Johnson and Larry Bird could carry it prime time two and a half decades later.

Time stood still inside the Eastwood Sports Center, especially on the picture-filled walls and trophy-laden shelves of Biasone's tiny office. History reached a dead end there in 1963, when Biasone sold the Nationals and they were moved to Philadelphia. Over lunch, three basketball guys who never left

Syracuse — Biasone, Schayes and Seymour — talked of the league that left them and their central New York city far behind.

"We were talking about how big and successful the league has gotten," said Schayes. "Danny had these favorite expressions, and one of them was: 'The bubble's going to burst.' He always felt that the league shouldn't grow on the back of the average fan, but that's exactly what happened. Danny was saying that the average guy can't even afford to go to a game anymore. That really bothered him. Danny was always for the little guy."

That is understandable, as Biasone, an Italian immigrant to the United States at the age of 10, stood about 5 feet 6 inches, although perhaps more important to the shaping of his conviction was the manner in which he and his Nationals were treated by the rest of the N.B.A.

Nobody liked going to Syracuse, a cold winter outpost, the last of the league's small markets, like Fort Wayne, Ind., and Rochester. When the Lakers moved from Minneapolis to Los Angeles in 1961, teams like Boston and New York pushed Biasone to move west, to San Francisco, the way baseball's Giants followed its Dodgers. Biasone burned when Ned Irish of the Knicks would say: "What does Syracuse versus New York look like on the Madison Square Garden marquee?"

From his office in the bowling alley, Biasone turned a deaf ear on all pleas to surrender Syracuse. He held on as long as he could. He continued to sit on the bench at home games, appointing himself assistant coach when the league ruled it off limits to owners, while suffering the sport's nightly highs and lows.

Johnny Kerr, the onetime Nationals center and now a broadcaster for the Bulls, remembers returning to Syracuse in the wee hours by plane in a snowstorm from a losing road game. As the players descended the stairs, they came upon Biasone, his face frosted, his hat and coat covered with snow.

"Can't we beat anybody?" the owner mumbled as the players trudged past.

Inadvertently, Biasone may have defeated himself in his crusade for the little guy and the little market. The formula used to create the 24-second clock — the 2,880 seconds of a 48-minute game divided by the average number of shots a game over the previous three seasons (120) — was actually devised by Biasone's general manager, Leo Ferris. But the man with the vision, the member of the rules committee who badgered his contemporaries at almost every meeting between 1951 and 1954, was unquestionably Biasone.

Will he be proved right about the modern N.B.A., the league of sky boxes and $300 front-row seats, and the direction in which it is going?

"Danny knew basketball and he loved basketball," said Schayes, who named his son, the Milwaukee Bucks' center, after Biasone.

Today, Schayes, Seymour and other former Nationals like Larry Costello and Earl Lloyd will be pallbearers. Biasone's wife, Rachel, told Schayes that's what he wanted.

"They never had children," said Schayes. "I guess we were like his kids."

APRIL 3, 1977

Pride and Integrity: Pro Basketball Has Changed

BY RED AUERBACH

Toward the end of my new book, "Red Auerbach: An Autobiography," I'm asked hypothetically whether I could return to the bench and coach the way I did during my 20-year career.

I replied yes, even though conditions have changed so much since I retired in 1966. No, the game hasn't changed that much. The people in it have changed — the players, the owners, the agents.

I'm not making a blanket indictment. But by and large, we're seeing an erosion of basic values — things like pride and integrity and dedication — and this upsets me tremendously. You can talk all you want about new breeds and changing lifestyles and the rest of it, but, damn it, some things should never change. They should not be allowed to change.

A Talk With Rizzuto

Fans booed me when I coached. They threw things at me — snowballs, eggs, you name it. I was controversial. But anyone who ever dealt with me will tell you — and this means more to me than all of the honors and accolades — that my word was good.

I'm not saying I was a saint. Anyone who saw me on the sidelines knows better. But I ran my Celtics organization with two constant guidelines — pride and integrity.

Let me explain what I mean.

In the early 1940s, when I was in the Navy, I met Phil Rizzuto, and we talked about the way Joe McCarthy ran those great Yankee clubs. Phil told me how Joe would take rookies from the farms and teach them little things like tipping properly in restaurants and acting properly in hotel lobbies. Joe was vitally concerned with the image of the Yankees. He believed the way you acted off the field had a great deal to do with the way you performed on it.

I decided that any club I ever coached would be imbued with this philosophy: Dress like a champion, act like a champion and you'll play like champion. Did you ever see a Celtic player looking sloppy or bawling out a teammate or throwing a tantrum when he was taken out of a game? No, you didn't, because it never happened.

We carried ourselves like champions, and we were doing that long before we began winning titles in 1957. Before you laugh at that, let me assure you that any man who ever wore our famous green jersey — Bob Cousy, Bill Russell, John Havlicek, any of them — will tell you Celtics Pride was no myth, no fairy tale.

But pride was only a part of what made us what we were. For a player to feel good about his team and teammates, he must also feel good about his role in the team's success.

Nothing can kill a great club any quicker than egos, jealousies and dissension, so I dealt with these threats head on every time I sat down with a player to sign a contract. I had a standard opening statement:

"Don't bring me your statistics, because I'm not interested in them. I don't want to see them. Just tell me what you've done to make us a better club."

Winning Matters Most

The only statistic that mattered to me was winning, so I paid every player on the basis of what he did to help us win. That meant the man who set the pick was as important as the man who scored from behind it; the man whose tough defense got us the ball was as important as the man who ended up with the easy bucket a few seconds later.

Some of my greatest stars — Satch Sanders, K. C. Jones, Jim Loscutoff — never had to score a point to be valuable players in my eyes. Everybody on the team understood and accepted this, so there was no reason to envy another's man's statistics if you were doing your job well because you knew your contributions were fully appreciated, too. Our payroll reflected that appreciation.

I had another policy regarding contracts, and I think this is important today. A contract, I'd tell my players, is a two-way deal. If a player got hurt, I'd continue to pay him. But if he had a super season, that was a plus for me. I never wanted to hear talk about renegotiating upward after a good season, then why shouldn't he be willing to renegotiate downward after a bad one. But suggest that to a ballplayer or an agent and you'll get horrified looks.

So just before signing any contract, I'd look across the desk and say:

"Are you sure you're satisfied? Be certain, because I intend to honor my end of this agreement and I expect you to honor your end, too."

Now, some kids are guaranteed lifetime security before they do anything to help their clubs. That's ridiculous. We've created a system that works against motivation, desire and discipline.

But I still think a smart coach can stress these values today if he presents them properly. Every athlete loves to win, even the ones with millions of dollars in the bank. There's no substitute for the joy and fulfillment that come with winning.

But wanting to win isn't sufficient. You must know how to win.

And the answer is the same as always. It lies in the old-fashioned values like pride and integrity. And teamwork.

They still work, and they're the surest route to success in basketball or any other business.

2

Darkness Before Dawn

Over the course of his storied 40-year run as commissioner, David Stern liked to take measure of his league's ascendant prosperity by recalling a more troubled time when, as he said on many occasions, much of America viewed the N.B.A. as "too black and drug-infested."

That loaded assessment peaked in 1980 when the *Los Angeles Times* reported estimates of "40 to 75 percent" of the league's players were cocaine users or abusers. No doubt drug-use was fairly common around the league, but as several astute players of the day confided to me, then a young reporter for the *New York Post*: What was so different about them from other young professionals with disposable income?

Simon Gourdine, then the league's outgoing deputy commissioner and its highest-ranking black official, laid bare the underlying bias.

"Seventy-five percent happens to be the proportion of blacks in the N.B.A.," he told *The Times*'s Jane Gross in a 1981 interview. "If someone chose to, they could have concluded that 100 percent of the black players were involved with drugs. Any time there are social problems like drugs and alcohol, the perception is that it's black players involved."

White stars were already increasingly rare. In a couple of markets, there were no white players at all. In October 1979, the Knicks broke training camp with their first all-black roster, prompting a request from my *Post* editor to write about it in depth. Sonny Werblin, the president of Madison Square

Garden, contributed a quote that would, within a few years, sound quite prescient.

"Are there people who are upset by that?" he said. "Why, certainly. There are bigots in every walk of life. Even so, I haven't received one phone call or letter — not one — about the team being all-black. Perhaps in some other cities it might be a factor. I would think in a city like Boston it would be."

But not to worry, Mr. Auerbach, suddenly forced to fill Boston Garden for the first time in order to compete for talent in the nascent era of free agency. A hick from French Lick was on his way.

OCT. 25, 1979

About the All-Black Knicks

BY DAVE ANDERSON

To anyone aware of the racial mix of the National Basketball Association in recent years, it was inevitable that the Knicks would be an all-black team sooner or later. Now that it's happened, some white basketball aficionados in New York appear surprised or offended, or both. That's only natural. Race, like sex and religion, inspires an awareness in virtually everybody whenever there is change. For the Knicks to comprise all black players indeed is change. Not a drastic change, however. During recent seasons the Knicks' white players were benchwarmers. Even so, some white Knick followers suddenly are annoyed, some black Knick loyalists suddenly are proud. But those are strictly short-term reactions. For the long-term, the game is bigger than the genes. Pro basketball at Madison Square Garden will depend on the success of the Knicks as a team, not on the racial makeup of the roster.

Some of those offended by the all-black roster have been quick to use that as the reason for the Knicks' small crowds in three of their four Garden games this season. But that's a false argument.

True, the crowd of 7,911 that the Knicks announced Tuesday night during their 136–112 victory over the Indiana Pacers was their lowest in the 11½-year history of the new Garden; the previous low had been 8,373 for the previous Tuesday night game with the Houston Rockets. And the Knicks had attracted only 10,798 for their season opener against the Washington Bullets on a Saturday night.

But last Saturday night they drew 16,900 against the Philadelphia 76ers with Julius Erving.

The Season-Ticket Situation

True, the Knicks' sale of season tickets has dwindled to about 6,500, a drop of about 1,600 from last season, after the team failed to qualify for the playoffs for the third time in the last four years. But the primary reason for the drop was the Knicks' fourth-place finish in the Atlantic Division last season. Those 1,600 season tickets had been abandoned long before the all-black roster developed.

In their glory years, the Knicks once sold a high of about 13,000 season tickets. Those teams had two white forwards whom white followers could identify with, Bill Bradley and Dave DeBusschere, but those 1973 and 1970 teams also had more blacks than whites.

Three of those blacks — Willis Reed, Walt Frazier and Earl Monroe — were folk heroes along with Bradley and DeBusschere, the five symbols of success and style that all Knick followers still cling to. But in those years, none of those five were thought of as black or white. They were thought of simply as a winning team, as basketball players should be. If the current Knicks eventually are thought of as a winning team, virtually no one will be concerned that they're all black. They'll simply be folk heroes. But now Coach Red Holzman is the only link to those glory years. None of the new young Knicks has accomplished enough to be acclaimed yet. Except for an unusual rookie, such as Larry Bird of the Boston Celtics and Earvin (Magic) Johnson of the Los Angeles Lakers, new young names never sell tickets. That is the Knicks' problem now — new names and new hope for success without a superstar.

If the Knicks had Glen Gondrezick and John Rudd, their two white players from last season, their current attendance would not have improved. Gondrezick averaged 5 points a game last season, Rudd only 3.2. Nobody went to the Garden to see them last season. Nobody would have gone to see them this season.

"When it came down to our last cuts," says Eddie Donovan, the Knicks' general manager, "Red and I felt we had to keep the best players. If we had kept Gondo and Rudd just because they were white, we would have lost the respect of our other players. The players know who can play and who can't. I've had a couple of calls from fans about our decision, but when I asked them if they would have wanted us to keep Gondo or Rudd as tokens, they said of course not."

Not that the Knicks are committed to an all-black roster forevermore. They need quality players — black or white. Yes, a white star, such as Larry Bird, surely would be a drawing card at the Garden, but so would a black star on a winning team. And a black star is easier to find.

Bird, Walton and Maravich

Only three white drawing cards exist in the N.B.A. now — Larry Bird, if he is as flashy as he was in college; Bill Walton, if he's healthy; and Pete Maravich, if he's healthy. Several quality white players contribute to their team's being a drawing card — Jack Sikma with the champion Seattle SuperSonics; Doug Collins with the Philadelphia 76ers; Dave Cowens with the Celtics; Paul Westphal, Alvan Adams and Don Buse with the Phoenix Suns; Rick Barry and Rudy Tomjanovich with the Houston Rockets and Dan Issel with the Denver Nuggets. But for the most part, the N.B.A. depends on black drawing cards. And each year it must depend on them more and more. When this season started, of the 273 players on the 22 rosters, 198 were black — 73 percent. Of the 110 usual starters, 89 were black — 76 percent. Of the first 11 players selected in the opening round of last June's college draft, all were black; of the 22 players chosen in the first round, 18 were black — 81 percent.

Yes, the N.B.A. is predominantly a black league now. It's taken time for some people to adjust to that. It always does.

Back when Jackie Robinson broke baseball's color barrier three decades ago, it was fashionable to count the increasing number of blacks on the Brooklyn Dodgers' roster. Some people still count the blacks and the whites in baseball, pro football and pro basketball. But boxing appears to have outgrown the quota systems. Years ago a boxing promoter often used a black fighter only against a white fighter. But now nobody even thinks twice about it.

The best fight in recent years, perhaps in history, was the "Thrilla in Manila" in 1975, when Muhammad Ali and Joe Frazier concluded their five-year war. Nobody even mentioned that their title fight was all black.

AUG. II, 1979

Basketball's Image Crisis

BY STEVE CADY

From the splendor of their sixth-floor headquarters on Columbus Circle, members of the National Basketball Players' Association get an appropriately privileged view of the world.

Through the Venetian blinds along one side of the office suite, they can look down onto the fashionable greenery of Central Park South. Below the front windows, plumes of water leap from an elegant ring of fountains surrounding a statue of Christopher Columbus. The view is soothing, a comfortable reminder that salaries for pro basketball's 240 players average $158,000 year. But it's a long way from the marble, glass and steel of the 43-story Gulf and Western Building to the asphalt playgrounds of Harlem, Bedford-Stuyvesant and other depressed areas where underprivileged inner-city youngsters dream of basketball gold and glory. Starting today, though, the lavishly paid pros hope to narrow that gap through a collective effort.

They call it "Give Something Back," and they will bounce the idea onto the court with what they describe as a people-to-people "day of fun" at the National Tennis Center in Flushing Meadows Corona Park, Queens. There will be tennis matches at 5:00 P.M., a basketball clinic at 6:00, an old-timers basketball game at 7:00 and an all-star basketball game at 8:30 P.M. Tickets for today's charity program are scaled from $7 to $20, with half the seats going for the lowest price.

Walt Frazier, Dave DeBusschere, Willis Reed and other former New York Knicks, possibly including Senator Bill Bradley, will be there. So will Connie Hawkins, Oscar Robertson and John Havlicek, along with present stars of the National Basketball Association such as Wes Unseld, Bernard King, David Thompson, Maurice Lucas, Julius Erving and Nate Archibald. Some of them will play. Others will go into the stands, mingling with the fans, signing autographs and trying to explain that pro basketball athletes aren't really the selfish money-grubbers they are sometimes accused of being.

The promotion goes beyond an effort by N.B.A. players, 75 percent of whom are black, to give something back to the inner-city communities where many of them began their basketball climb. Their collective venture reflects concern over basketball's eroded image. After years of unbroken prosperity, attendance slumped last season in New York, Boston, Los Angeles and other major markets. Television ratings tumbled, and higher ticket prices stirred resentment among fans against what they consider excessive player salaries. In the N.B.A., annual earnings range from the minimum of $30,000 to about $1 million. The median salary is $130,000.

"The image of the game itself is suffering," said Paul Silas, president of the players association. "We're concerned with TV ratings, attendance, fan interest. We want to put some zest back into the game. And, of course, we want to show people we haven't forgotten the communities we came from. A lot of us have always been involved, but it never gets written up. Now we're involved as a group. That's the difference."

Working closely with Larry Fleisher, general counsel for the players' group, Silas has been providing the same kind of forceful leadership for "Give Something Back" as he shows under the basket. The 6-foot-7-inch forward for the champion Seattle SuperSonics is particularly concerned about improving the usefulness of pro stars as role models for deprived youngsters who pour an inordinate amount of time and energy into basketball.

For years, black educators have criticized the playground pattern as a potential ripoff. They note that the chances of becoming a pro are infinitesimal, and that those who don't make it are frequently left without the skills to be anything more than economic and social derelicts. From a pool of several million, the N.B.A. drafts only 200 players each year. Fewer than 40 of those stay with an N.B.A. team for an entire season.

"First and foremost," Silas said, "our message to the young people will be that the foundation for anything is education. We want them to know there's something positive about having these sports aspirations."

Silas, a playground alumnus who did his early dreaming at DeFremery Park in Oakland, Calif., and later went to Creighton University, regards the high N.B.A. salaries as normal consequence of supply and demand.

"There are 240 of us," said the 36-year-old survivor of 16 N.B.A. seasons, "and close to 240 million in the United States. So we feel we're one in a million."

At the same time, he feels that fan interest is being eroded by higher ticket prices and a growing resentment by the sport's predominantly white customers about so many black players making so much money.

"You hear talk about the league having too many blacks," Silas said, "but I don't think that's the problem. The main cause of the erosion is how the white public perceives black stars making this type of money. Our image is suffering."

Will new white superstars such as Larry Bird, last season's college player of the year at Indiana State, help the 22-team league sell tickets?

"I would venture to say," Silas conceded, "that when Larry Bird goes around the league with the Celtics it's going to help. But how many Larry Birds are out there? They're just not available. So we're going to have to create a better image for the game."

Meanwhile, four good tickets to an N.B.A. game will continue to cost somewhere around $50, not to mention the extras for parking, a couple of beers and a bite to eat.

"It's a lot of money just for one night," said Silas. "If the buying public stops coming to games, then I guess the owners will have to decide what they want to do about the big salaries."

That, of course, is the other side of the supply-and-demand coin.

3

Showdown in Salt Lake

Magic Johnson was a smiling showman from the moment he hit the national consciousness. Larry Bird was an enigma wrapped inside an introvert. Nowhere in the run-up to a 1979 N.C.A.A. championship game that would serve as a nationally televised marketing bonanza for the college and pro games was there any hint that these two would end up as Siamese basketball twins, the best of frenemies.

Johnson's Michigan State coach, Jud Heathcote, had some intuitive sense of the stylistic similarities — both were players whose talent transcended position and whose teammates had to play off them in order to succeed. In rehearsals for Bird and Indiana State, Heathcote had Johnson play the role of Bird for a Spartans defense that would focus on ball denial and result in more pressure on the other Sycamores and a 75–64 Indiana State defeat.

Having covered Bird in an early-round victory over Virginia Tech and Johnson in a regional final takedown of Notre Dame, I already had a pretty good idea of how opposite their public personas were. In Johnson, I had never been around an athlete so charismatically evolved. Bird was a reticent mystery man from an obscure school.

How much so became more obvious after the title game. As Malcolm Moran reported in *The Times* the next day on the postgame scene, "Notes were passed around that [Bird teammates] Bob Heaton and Brad Miley would be available after the game for interviews. Bird would not. He dictated a statement, which was typed, copied and distributed. He said that Michigan State had a 'real tough defense,' that he hated to lose, that his team 'just didn't hit the shots tonight,' that he would like to play Michigan State again."

That's how Bird rolled upon entry into the N.B.A., where he would get his wish to challenge Magic over and over — and on sides even more diametrically opposed.

MARCH 26, 1979

Johnson: Magical by Nature

BY MALCOLM MORAN

SALT LAKE CITY — Earvin Magic Johnson. It is as if the name appeared just that way on the birth certificate, almost 20 years ago, like John Cameron Swayze, or Norman Vincent Peale. That is the way he is introduced by Jud Heathcote, the basketball coach at Michigan State University, and it is the way Johnson signs autographs when other students ask for them in class. "I have to," he said. "That's a request." You can call him Magic, and you can call him Earvin. You don't have to call him Johnson.

He has been Magic for several years, going back to the days at Everett High School in Lansing, where hundreds of people once welcomed him at the airport, some of them carrying signs that pleaded for him to go to Michigan State. Terry Donnelly was already a starting guard at Michigan State when Johnson was a senior at Everett, and Donnelly knew all about him. He had heard the stories and he had seen him play. And yet, Donnelly really didn't know much at all.

"It didn't really hit me until I got in the backcourt with him, on the first day of practice," Donnelly said. "You're running down the floor and you're open and most people can't get the ball to you through two or three people, and all of a sudden the ball's in your hands and you've got a layup."

Before last season, when Johnson enrolled at Michigan State, the basketball team finished more than two games above .500 in just one of the previous 10 seasons. Last season, the Spartans were 25-5, and reached the Mideast regional championship game, where they lost to Kentucky, the eventual national champion. This season, the Spartans (25-6) are one game away, the championship game tomorrow night against Indiana State.

Johnson's passes are so quick, and sometimes so startling, that they have been known to loosen teeth and make mouths bleed. "I didn't mean it," he said. He handles the ball well enough to be a point guard, yet at 6 feet 8 inches and 207 pounds, he is bigger than some college centers and able to force smaller guards close to the basket. Nine times this season, including the victory over Pennsylvania in the semifinals of the National Collegiate Athletic Association tournament, Johnson has led the Spartans, or tied for the lead, in rebounds. He has averaged 16.5 points and 7.2 rebounds this season, second in both categories to Greg Kelser. Those numbers, he says, are not important to him.

"I'll take zero," he said, "as long as I get the assists."

Numbers are just numbers. "When you can make a pass that leads to a basket," Heathcote said, "where a receiver has to do nothing other than put it in the basket, the pass is more important than the basket. Earvin has proved that."

Even more than the numbers or the concept, his personality has made him magic. He was the leader as a freshman, setting up his team, shouting instructions, leading celebrations. "He gets the team going," Donnelly said. "He's got a personality that's like Muhammad Ali. It's classy, not conceited or anything. He would be running down the floor, and he's telling jokes. He's always smiling, always laughing. Never a frown on his face. Everyone likes a guy like that."

"We needed something like this," said Kelser, a senior. "I don't think it took any adjustment, because he was the new guy. He was so far advanced than any freshman in the country. We understood this. We needed it."

Loves to Talk

It is difficult to tell what Johnson enjoys more — watching Kelser leap for a perfect lob pass, inches from the rim, and jam it through, or talking about it later.

"I'm lovin' it," Johnson said. "Every minute of it. It's exciting. I'm really having a good time. I'm having a ball. It's like a kid going to a birthday party. Being in the Final Four, to get all the attention, to have your name in all the newspapers in the country. You gotta love it. All the parents from California to Germany know about it."

He smiles when he thinks about each question. He tugs on the tiny hairs on his chin, and his big, brown eyes look up, and then he'll talk about his dream last night, or the mind games he played as a child. He would go to the Main Street playground by himself, and go up and down the court, playing an imaginary game. He was always the Philadelphia 76ers, and he was always playing the Knicks, his brother's team. "I loved Philadelphia, see, and I always made sure they won the game," he said. "I'd make sure I missed a last-second shot and then Wilt Chamberlain would come down and dunk it. Except I'd lay it up."

He will smile even at the questions that are becoming annoying — the comparisons of his personality with Larry Bird's, which he thinks are unfair, and the criticism of his shooting, which he says is incorrect. He is a 45 percent shooter. It is merely good, the only unspectacular part of his game, and so it stands out. "People say, 'You can't shoot,'" he said. "I don't even care about that, as long as we win. I know deep inside myself I can shoot."

The most annoying question is whether or not this will be his last game at Michigan State, whether or not he will become a professional. "How could I think about it when I have a chance for the national championship?" he said. "That's what everyone's been asking me. Pro, pro, pro, pro. What about pro? Maybe after Monday night."

— POSTSCRIPT —

MALCOLM MORAN, 2018: "As *The Times*'s national college reporter, I was supposed to do profiles that season of Bird and Magic. Bird was going to be first, but I got a call from the sports information director telling me that Larry had shut it down, no more one-on-one interviews, because the narrative had become too much about his father's suicide. So now I'm going to do Magic, it's all set up for me to go to East Lansing. But Al Menendez, who was scouting for the Nets, tells Tony Kornheiser, who's also on our staff, that he didn't understand what the fuss was over this Magic kid — he couldn't shoot. Tony tells that to the sports editor, who decides to cancel the assignment. I said, 'Hold on, Magic is the hottest player in the country.' He said, 'No, we're done.' So I didn't get to write about Magic until the day before the final — along with every other reporter in Salt Lake City."

MARCH 26, 1979

Herb Shriner With a Jumper

BY DAVE ANDERSON

SALT LAKE CITY, Utah — In the morning yesterday, Larry Bird was supposed to appear at a brunch honoring him as the college basketball player of the year. But when the Indiana State coach, Bill Hodges, woke him up at 9 o'clock, he said, "Coach, I'm dead — can I stay in bed?" The coach agreed.

Bill Hodges likes to say that his primary contribution to the Sycamores this season has been "not messing up Larry Bird." And with Indiana State hoping to complete a 34–0 won-lost record tomorrow night against Michigan State in the National Collegiate Athletic Association championship game, the coach was not about to mess up Larry Bird's sack time. Larry Bird scored 35 points against De Paul in Saturday's 76–74 victory. If the 6-foot-9-inch forward wanted to stay in bed until halftime tonight, Bill Hodges would have shrugged and considered it in the best interests of the team.

But by noon, Larry Bird was up and about and strolling into the Salt Lake Hilton for a tournament news conference. Just his appearance was news.

Throughout the season, Larry Bird had fulfilled his virtual vow of silence. He had talked on TV a few times, he had traveled to New York last week to receive an award. "And when you receive an award," Bill Hodges had told him, "you talk." And after Saturday's game, he had answered a few questions about it. But mostly, he had been the Silent Sycamore, a country bumpkin who apparently didn't know what to say.

And when he arrived for the news conference, Larry Bird was dressed for the occasion — a sleepy look, a blue warmup jacket over a white T-shirt, jeans and sneakers.

But from the beginning, it was apparent that Larry Bird was willing to answer questions. And slowly he created a new image of himself, the image of a hayseed with humor, a Herb Shriner with a jump shot. That was apparent when he was asked what he remembered about playing with Earvin (Magic) Johnson of Michigan State in a series of all-star games a year ago.

"Yeah," he said with a straight face, "Earvin passed the ball to me."

"How did you develop your style as both a shooter and a passer?"

"In high school I was a guard my sophomore year; I was little then. I had to get the ball in to the big guys. I found out that a two-foot shot by the basket is better than a 14-foot shot any day."

"How's your thumb?"

"Broke," he said of the hairline fracture of his left thumb. "It's still tender, but the doctor told me to go ahead and play."

"People who have seen you play in person for the first time think you're better than when they saw you on television."

"Yeah, they know what they're talking about."

"You seem to have a great feeling for passing."

"My feeling about passing is that it don't matter who's doing the scoring as long as it's us. I just think when a man is open, he should get the ball whether it's 30 feet out on the wing or underneath. We had guys last year who didn't care about passing. They thought scoring was more important, but passing is more important."

"Earvin Johnson gives the impression he's having fun during a game, but you don't."

"He's probably laughing at the opponents," Larry Bird said. "But you can't have fun when the game's tied with two seconds to go and they got the ball. If you got a 1-point lead, it's different, but I got to do what I do. I can't be laughing out there. Earvin's different. I just hope he's not laughing at me."

"Ray Meyer [the De Paul coach] said you must have given some of your teammates bloody noses with your passes. Have you?"

"No, but I knocked a few out," he said. "I've bounced 'em off their legs or their knees, on their heads. But no bloody noses."

"Ray Meyer also said your hands were as big as toilet seats."

"I heard him," he said, smiling. "But it's a shame I have a broken thumb. I don't usually have 11 turnovers in a game like I did yesterday."

"For somebody who has avoided interviews, you seem be enjoying yourself."

"That's wrong," he replied with another smile. "Where all this started out was my first year I had all the pressure. My first year all they wanted to do was talk to me. That's the way it should be. But we got seven guys who play. They deserve to be talked to, too. It got so it was taking up two or three hours a day so I decided not to do interviews. If all of you were paying me, I'd enjoy it, but I know that's coming. I don't mind interviews. I can handle any situation if it's all about me, but I don't like it when I'm asked about my family."

Larry Bird is divorced, with a child; his father was a suicide, his mother works in a French Lick, Ind., restaurant.

"But what changed your mind," he was asked, "about doing this interview after you have avoided them throughout the season?"

"Everybody wants publicity," Larry Bird said. "I just thought the other guys on the team weren't getting it but now they are, so it's time to come back. We didn't expect to be here."

"You didn't expect to be here?"

"Did you," Larry Bird said with a smile, "expect us to be here?"

4

Julius Erving, Ph.D.

Across the decades, powerfully symbolic scenes remain as vivid in the mind's eye as the moment in which they were recorded. One of mine is from the 1996 finals — Bulls over Sonics, Jordan's triumphant return from his season-and-a-half hiatus to flail at breaking balls.

After the Bulls had won Game 2 at the United Center, Jordan finished his postgame press conference and made his way through the corridor, followed by an entourage of security and friends. By chance he came face-to-face with Denzel Washington, actor extraordinaire, in a chance meeting between two men so successfully famous that they transcended most black typecasting.

They spent a few minutes basking in each other's glory, arms on one another's shoulders, until another instantly recognizable figure approached — tall, distinguished, gray. But the basketball legend nicknamed Dr. J turned no heads, drew no adoring gazes. He stood quietly on the perimeter watching, a mere mortal, ostensibly, in the presence of the divine.

Just the day before, at a press conference to promote the league's 50th anniversary, Erving had been asked, in effect, how he felt about being born about a decade too soon — before the shoe-company partnerships, the Dream Team adoration, the explosion of revenue, the global stage.

"I'm not offended by it," he said. "I always had the philosophy that if someone recognized me, it didn't make my day. So someone who doesn't recognize me doesn't break it."

But that day, he advocated including A.B.A. stats in the N.B.A. record book, and pleaded his case to the point of audience discomfort. Erving might well have had regret for having been pro basketball's poster player during leaner times.

He was accompanied into the establishment N.B.A. by other thrill-a-minute stars — George Gervin, David Thompson — but the newly expanded league was not yet on the launch pad and in several places wasn't doing well at all.

In Philadelphia with the 76ers, Erving routinely played to thousands of empty seats, though without ceding the spotlight. In the early '80s, practically speaking, he was as much a rival to Magic and Bird as they were to each other. He reached three N.B.A. finals (four overall) and co-starred with Moses Malone as the Sixers swept the Lakers for the ring in 1983. Historians and documentarians rarely remember it that way. Dr. J is typically recalled as a legend who flew across 1970s skies, when pro basketball stars were not nearly as enlightening.

MAY 29, 1983

Erving Is Keeping Things in Persepective

BY ROY S. JOHNSON

The feeling was there, just as he expected it would be. It was a fluttering in the pit of his stomach, a gentle gnawing, reflecting the anticipation, the anxiety and the nervousness of the unusual moment.

Julius Erving had sensed the feeling more than a few times before. It was the one that came when he was about to launch a last-second shot in a game with his Philadelphia 76ers down by 1 point. Or the one that came when he made a key rebound or critical steal. Yet, somehow, with all his illustrious experiences to draw on, this feeling was something else entirely.

"I was just standing there trying to keep my breathing together," Erving recalled. "There was this tingling all over, and it was different than anything I've felt. I just kept breathing 'cause I knew I didn't want to pass out. Not here."

"Here" was not where Erving was accustomed to being — a dank, cluttered locker room or a basketball court, the kinds of places he has used to contemplate and to create so many moments of almost disbelieving joy for those who have seen him play. Nor was he in the company of his peers, those within the confines of the game who can most appreciate the level of his art.

Instead, he was standing tall — indeed conspicuously tall — amid an ocean of black, yet colorfully trimmed gowns near the front of the stage at Civic Center Convention Hall in Philadelphia, about to address the 5,800 graduates, dignitaries and their families in attendance at Temple University's 97th commencement exercises last Thursday.

Erving was there to receive an honorary Doctor of Arts — his first degree — for "adding an entirely new dimension to his profession, transcending the human condition through a new dimension of fine art."

Julius Winfield Erving II, the incomparable Doctor J, was now Dr. Doctor J.

Fighting back the feelings within him, he stepped forward to the podium, shook the hand of Dr. Peter J. Liacouras, the university president, and addressed the now quiet crowd, which had given him a standing ovation and had been shouting, "Beat L.A., Beat L.A."

He began with a story that he often tells — of how he once responded to a reporter's question about how his career had reached such legendary stature, saying "because I dared to be great."

"Take a look at the stars," he told the graduates, "and label them your limit. God instilled in me a desire to explore the boundaries of His wonderful gift to me… and I seek the light of creative exploration as all artists do."

During his formative years, there were no stars that Julius Erving could label his limit. His father was killed in an automobile accident when Julius — "June" for Junior as his mother, Mrs. Callie Mae Lindsey, calls him — was only 11 years old. And his brother Marvin, the first person whom young Erving idolized, died from lupus erythematosus, a disease that destroys the ability to fight diseases, when Erving was 19 and in his second year at the University of Massachusetts.

Marvin, three years younger than Julius, was the antithesis of his older brother. He was an extrovert — the class president, a drum player. He was in awe of Julius for his basketball skills, but Julius admired his brother's strong leadership abilities. Marvin's death, Julius said, was the last time he cried and the time when he became Doctor J.

Erving's education began to manifest itself during the following year. He outgrew the simple confines of his Roosevelt, L.I., home, emerging as a player of national prominence. As a junior, he was among the top scorers in college basketball, averaging almost 27 points, grabbing 20 rebounds a game and becoming only the seventh 20-20 player in the history of the National Collegiate Athletic Association.

That, he decided, was worth much more than an academic degree. (He would not know just how much more until later.) He signed a four-year contract with the American Basketball Association's Virginia Squires worth $500,000.

"There is too much emphasis," he said afterward, "on the end result. Degrees. Grades. And as a result, too many take as many shortcuts as they can, such as cheating. Amidst all of the games being played, the meat of the matter is often overlooked. That without disappointments, hard work and sacrifice, there can be no gain."

In sports, much of that same sort of emphasis is placed on, as Erving put it, the end result. In football, there's the Super Bowl. In baseball, the World Series. And in pro basketball, the National Basketball Association title. The N.B.A. degree. Erving was a member of two championship teams — the New York Nets in 1974 and 1976 — during his five A.B.A. seasons.

Erving has not yet gained his N.B.A. degree. In six previous seasons, he has been in the final series three times — in 1977, 1980 and again last year. But his name has yet to be called as a champion of the N.B.A.

Obtaining that elusive N.B.A. degree was a passion for him, a force behind each of his creative acts of basketball artistry. That changed this season.

"Winning has to be a goal," he said. "As the end result, it can't be denied. But the thing that must be most enjoyable is the work itself. The end result cannot be your only joy. If it was and you played on a losing team, you wouldn't be getting anything out of it. The game is the thing.

"Those experiences with the 76ers helped me grow. In looking back, maybe some of them were necessary for me. If they hadn't happened, I'd be a different person. I wouldn't be as prepared to handle some of the other things I wanted to do. I've accomplished a lot I can be proud of. So instead of feeling sorry for myself, it's a matter of setting an example. There can be satisfaction in that."

Erving did not stop feeling sorry for himself until the end of last season when the 76ers were defeated in the finals, four games to two, by the Los Angeles Lakers. "Getting to the brink and not making it was very hard to accept in my first three seasons," he said. "But when I looked at it last year, it was clear that rebounding was a real weakness for us. Harold Katz, our owner, committed himself to changing that. Now, we are a new creation and we must carry on."

The new creation will take a two-games-to-none lead over the Lakers into the third game of the final series today (Channel 2 in New York at 3:30 P.M.) at the Forum in Inglewood, Calif.

Most critical in the new creation was Moses Malone, the game's most dominating center, whom Katz signed to a six-year, $13.2-million contract during the off-season. Skeptics who believed the marriage of the two stars — Malone, the workhorse, and Erving, the artist — was destined for failure were soon silenced. The 76ers raced to a record of 50–7 by March. "It was proof enough for me," Erving said, "that we were one helluva team. All the questions that I had were answered. I was convinced."

With convincing victories in the first two games of the championship series, the 76ers have put the Lakers at a disadvantage that only two teams in N.B.A. history have surmounted. One team was the Portland Trail Blazers, who, in 1977, emerged from a 2–0 deficit to win the title with four consecutive victories over Erving and the 76ers.

Should the 76ers lose again, Erving will persevere. "My life, and the enjoyment of it, is not based on the ups and downs of my profession. That's a very unstable way to live," he said.

Erving has abided by that edict away from the basketball court, too. Although he did not complete his degree at Massachusetts, Erving, who majored in personnel management, has established a financial empire worth more than $10 million. There have been a few disappointments. Such as The Doctor's Shoe Salon, a high-fashion shop that was in Philadelphia's elite Society Hill section. It lasted 18 months before going bankrupt. Nonetheless, there aren't many blemishes on Erving's estate, which is testimony to his self-teaching.

"I'm educated to a point," he declared. "I think I might've thrived on life's experiences a bit more than I did on book knowledge to stay on my path. I thrive more on instinct and experience than knowledge.

"Take basketball. It's a smart-man's sport. Now, that may be street-wise or academic, but it's necessary." And in this discipline, Erving's N.B.A. degree is in sight. "We have a new feeling about ourselves," he said of this team, his best ever. "When we're at the top of our game, certain things happen that we can't bottle, uncork and put out on the floor at any time. But the potential for it is always there. I hope everything goes right, but I realize that it could all go wrong. For us, though, the downside isn't that far down, and the upside is way, way up there."

As for his academic degree, Erving said that he does not regret not obtaining it. "My educational process was extremely accelerated," he said, confidently. But his wife, Turquoise, says that he often speaks of returning to college, although a hectic off-season schedule does not permit it. For now, an honorary doctorate will suffice for Julius Erving. But for Doctor J, a championship ring will do nicely, too.

5

Descendants of Havlicek

Of the three great steals in Celtics history, Gerald Henderson's pinching of James Worthy's pass to Byron Scott in Game 2 of the 1984 finals is easily the most historically significant. That has long been my claim and I'm sticking with it.

John Havlicek famously stole Hal Greer's inbounds pass from under the basket in the dying seconds of Game 7 of the 1965 Eastern Conference finals — but that instinctive act of thievery merely preserved a lead.

Larry Bird's pilfering of Isiah Thomas's sideline entry was the most visually striking, given the ensuing dime — to an alert Dennis Johnson rushing to the rim — while falling out of bounds. The Celtics survived the Pistons in the 1987 conference finals but still required a grueling Game 7 victory, and they eventually lost to the Lakers in the finals.

Henderson not only angled his way to the ball as Worthy floated it toward the rookie Scott but also swooped in for a layup that tied Game 2, sending it to overtime, where the Celtics prevailed and avoided a two-game deficit on the way to playing Games 3 and 4 in Los Angeles.

As Scott, who always regretted not coming back to the ball, told me years later, "If not for that pass, they never would have beaten us head-to-head."

In other words, Bird would never have beaten Magic.

The final tally was Magic 3 (including their N.C.A.A. showdown), Larry 1. Bird was the first to admit he owed Henderson, who was traded to Seattle at the outset of the next season after a bitter contract dispute. The 1986 first-round draft pick Red Auerbach brought back in return never played for the Celtics.

His name was Len Bias.

JUNE 3, 1984

Henderson Stole the Ball

BY GEORGE VECSEY

BOSTON — John Havlicek thought of it right away. He was watching from the sky boxes in Boston Garden Thursday night, staring down at the parquet floor, where once upon a time he, too, had stolen a basketball.

"As soon as it happened, I knew it would bring up memories of another steal, 19 years ago," Havlicek says. "They're similar, but they're also very different."

Havlicek's interception of a pass by Hal Greer has become one of the epic moments in a glorious history of Boston Celtics basketball. He was not the only one who compared Gerald Henderson's steal of a James Worthy pass to his play.

Thousands of loyal Celtic fans have worn out their records of Johnny Most shouting, "Havlicek stole the ball." One of the most rabid of those fans, Jonathan Schwartz, the novelist and WNEW radio personality, immediately flashed upon the similarities when Henderson stole his ball.

Schwartz, getting his play-by-play information in a telephone booth at the airport, also flashed back to April 15, 1965, in Boston Garden when Havlicek made his one giant step.

"I have seen seven final games in Boston," says Jonathan Schwartz, "but this Eastern final was the best. I distinctly remember Red Auerbach supine on the bench. Absolutely supine."

The Havlicek game came against the Philadelphia 76ers of Wilt Chamberlain & Co. in the seventh game of the Eastern finals. The Celtics, with Bill Russell, had taken a 110–107 lead and allowed Chamberlain to score an uncontested layup with five seconds remaining, to avoid a 3-point play.

Russell was to pass the ball inbounds, but he attempted to throw it over the outstretched hands of Chamberlain, forcing the ball into the guy wires attached to the basket. Therefore, the ball turned over to Philadelphia with no time having elapsed.

"I'll never forget that moment," Schwartz says. "I was in agony, sure I would see a shot going in the air. I saw Greer take the ball out. I feared Greer more than Baylor, more than West. He terrorized the Celtics. He terrorized me. I only hoped they had enough sense to foul Chamberlain. I saw the pass and I saw Havlicek's body and I was sure he was going to make contact with somebody, and there would be two foul shots, and we would lose."

Schwartz has spent a hundred lifetimes fretting in similar moments for Boston teams. Sometimes Ted Williams or Carl Yastrzemski would let him down, as he slumped in a bleacher seat or listened in his car radio in Manhattan. But not that night in Boston Garden. Havlicek moved in front of Chet Walker and picked off the pass cleanly.

"Mine was just a defensive play," Havlicek says. "Except that you knew within a few seconds someone was going to live and someone was going to die."

The Celtics lived, 110–109, and it was bedlam. After the Celtics went on to their eighth playoff championship, the Fleetwood Record Company of Revere, Mass., issued a record of the highlights of that championship season. The title of the record was, of course, "Havlicek Stole the Ball" — featuring the dulcet tones of Johnny Most, softly reciting the plain facts.

"It sold 80,000 units in the first six months," reports Chris Eichner, who recently purchased Fleetwood, but knows that ancient success story by heart. "And it has sold around 115,000 copies. There are still some copies around. It's a big collector's item."

Jonathan Schwartz has a copy. Oh, yes. Jonathan Schwartz has a copy. There was a night at his apartment in the late '60s when he insisted that all his guests listen, at least a dozen times, to the cut on the album that went "Havlicek stole the ball." Johnny Most was louder than The Doors; he was louder than Jimi Hendrix; he was louder than Dylan.

Havlicek-Stole-the-Ball himself knew it was a bad pass even before James Worthy released it Thursday night. Havlicek says: "As a player, you try to prevent the cross-court pass in a game that's pretty well won. You want to advance it. I saw the pass being made and I'm sure Worthy wanted it back right away.

"The difference between my play and Gerald's was that he also had to make a layup at the end. But you know they're both special. I remarked about the steal to the guy sitting with me, but nobody really said much to me after the game. It was so late, I just sort of went home. I'm just sorry I missed Johnny Most on the radio. I bet he went bonkers.

"You know, it's funny how things turn out. A few years before that, one of the Celtics made a bad pass and Jerry West slipped in and stole it to win a game. This time the Celtics hung on to win. Two years ago, James Worthy stole a pass against Georgetown to help win the N.C.A.A. final. This time he has a pass stolen. So it balances out, in the long run."

For Jonathan Schwartz, there will never be enough steals by Havlicek and Henderson, never enough banners in the rafters — and never an end to the agony of a Celtics fan. On a "perfect desert Sunday morning in Palm Springs," he watched the Celtics lose the opening game ("Maxwell charged Magic twice; I have no patience for a man who doesn't pass off in a spot like that"). Schwartz planned his Thursday evening to avoid the anxiety of watching.

"I took a plane to New York and planned its arrival late in the game," he says. "I got to a phone booth and called my friend David McClintick, who wrote the book 'Indecent Exposure' and is known for his accuracy in reporting. But David is a baseball man, not a basketball man, and he had just turned on the television set, so he was not in the flow of the game.

"In our telephone conversation, he repeatedly got things wrong. He told me 'the Celtics stole the ball' and I yelled, 'Who was it, Henderson?' because I figured it had to be Henderson. Who else is that quick? He also told me somebody blocked Magic Johnson's shot, and I tried to figure out in my mind who could have blocked Magic.

"I was prepared for overtime. I had collected 20 quarters at the Palm Springs Airport just for this moment. I knew there are pay-television sets at Kennedy, and I took the last set, surrounded by kitchen and maintenance workers. I asked one man, 'Who blocked Magic?' and he looked at me as if I were crazy. 'Nobody blocked Magic, man. Magic ran out the clock.'

"By the way, the television costs only a quarter for 15 minutes," Schwartz says. "I was so delighted with the game, I left the other 19 quarters all lined up on a table as a present for my companions. When I left the airport, they were divvying them up."

For his companions, Thursday night may be remembered as the night of the 19 quarters. For Celtic fans and for John Havlicek and Gerald Henderson, Thursday night will always be the night Henderson Stole the Ball.

— POSTSCRIPT —

GEORGE VECSEY, 2018: "Sports columnists wrote three or four a week back then. We were always thinking of a new way to inform, entertain, infuriate. Columnists had a lot of freedom to be creative, think for ourselves. I was not actually at this game but was always plugged into the N.B.A. playoffs — and particularly in the grand old hoops city of Boston. I knew that Jonathan Schwartz — a popular FM radio personality, author and rabid Boston sports fan — had lived there and had an old record of the great John Havlicek call by Johnny Most. I somehow reached Havlicek to talk about his famous steal and then I reached out to Schwartz. Using lore familiar to sports fans, I put together a column that united the ages. I loved playing with myth and memory and current events — what sports is viscerally all about."

May 27, 1987

Bird Stole the Ball

by George Vecsey

BOSTON — Dennis Rodman did the boogaloo, a snazzy little two-step, with both arms pumping at midcourt. That's how happy he was. Then there was a noise behind him, and he wasn't happy anymore. Just as the Detroit Pistons were doing a bit of premature celebrating on the parquet floor of Boston Garden, Larry Bird staged a quick-minded robbery that may rank along with the famous "Havlicek Stole the Ball" incident of the 1965 Celtics' championship season.

Bird stole a dangerous inbounds pass by Isiah Thomas near the Celtics' basket and whipped it to Dennis Johnson, who alertly cut for a spinning layup with one second left to give the Celtics a 108–107 victory and put them a game ahead in the Eastern Conference finals.

The Garden had not seen quite such a bit of larceny since John Havlicek took the pass from Hal Greer in the closing seconds of a playoff game on April 15, 1965, prompting Johnny Most, the Celtics' longtime announcer, to issue his famous rasping call of "Havlicek stole the ball," now incorporated into sports memory records and chanted late at night wherever Celtics fans congregate. The Celtics might not have been that close to the Pistons if the officials had chosen to see three quick punches thrown by Robert Parish late in the first half.

The punches hit the face of Bill Laimbeer, the Pistons' center, who was fined $5,000 for throwing a hockey-style wrestling hold on Bird last Saturday.

There have been moments when this series resembled a hockey game, but no one has started a fight 15 minutes before game time — at least not yet — the way the Philadelphia Flyers did in their Stanley Cup playoff against Montreal.

The president of the National Hockey League, John Ziegler, banned the Flyers' designated brawler, Ed Hospodar, from the finals, and the Flyers promptly went into a tailspin without Hospodar's menacing presence in the pregame warmups.

Hospodarism is contagious, apparently, as Laimbeer and Bird staged their brawl in Michigan on Saturday. In hockey, that kind of grappling might be worth only a two-minute penalty — depending upon the period in which it occurred, what the score was, and whether it was a playoff game — but in basketball, it is considered an unfriendly abnormal act, and Bird responded in force. It cost him $2,000.

Bird and Laimbeer do not get along. In a sample of tall Boston Celtics a while back, Bill Walton, Robert Parish and Larry Bird were all willing to say they did not like Laimbeer, an All-Star center with a suburban jump shot and a truck-stop elbow.

Bird wouldn't even shake hands with Laimbeer at the start of Sunday's fourth game, making Bird the basketball version of Billy Smith, the blunt hockey goalie of the New York Islanders, who refuses to join the ritual reception line at the end of every Stanley Cup series.

The Michigan fans did not appreciate Bird's snub on Sunday and roasted him with full-throated contempt in the Silverdome in Pontiac, Mich. Bird declined to stick out his hand in friendship last night, also. He was saving that hand for the crucial steal a few hours later.

The rabid fans in Boston arrived last night displaying "Wanted" posters of Laimbeer, as the Celtics tried to regroup from the worst two games a Boston team has had on the road since a certain Boston baseball team had its pocket picked in Fun City last October.

In their two victories in Michigan, the Pistons seemed to be getting better and more confident minute by minute, while the Celtics — in the recent words of Stan Kasten, the general manager of the Atlanta Hawks — were "getting older with every minute."

With injuries and old age catching up, the Celtics presented the image of Shoeless Joe Hardy suddenly turning gray and wrinkled and slow in the play "Damn Yankees."

The Celtics revived in their home building last night, taking a lead in the first half before Parish threw his quick punches that, had they been landed by

Massachusetts' own Marverlous Marvin Hagler, might have defeated Sugar Ray Leonard in their recent outing.

Parish tossed his punches after some very tepid leaning and shoving under the basket. Basically, he just hauled off and punched Laimbeer three times. That might have been worth a couple of fouls — a technical, and an ejection — if either Jess Kersey or Jack Madden had seen it, or chosen to see it, as the case may be.

The sight of Laimbeer lying on the floor seemed not to disturb the officials. After all, those "Wanted" banners did refer to Laimbeer as "A/K/A Cry Baby," and Madden and Kersey may have believed the posters.

"I said to the officials, 'I assume you ejected him,' and they said they didn't see it," Laimbeer said. The three punches hurt less than the ball Laimbeer never touched with three seconds left in the game. Isiah Thomas had scored a 16-foot jump shot with 17 seconds left, perhaps a bit too soon with 13 seconds left on the shot clock.

The Celtics had time for Bird to have his shot smothered by three swarming Pistons, and then to stage his revenge. The ball went out, and Thomas took it as a few Pistons danced on the court.

Chuck Daly, the Pistons' coach, said later that he was trying to signal a timeout but Thomas said, "I never saw any signal, and besides, I was trying to get it in and get fouled."

But Thomas threw a looping pass toward the basket, and the two old pals from Saturday, Bird and Laimbeer, were together again. Bird anticipated perfectly and stepped in front of Laimbeer, catching the ball and flicking it to Johnson for the driving layup that hurt worse than the punches. As Johnson's layup went in, Laimbeer and Kevin McHale collided, and all four arms went up, but Hospodarism did not rear its ugly head.

Game 6 is tomorrow night.

6

Race in the '80s

In 1991, Filip Bondy and I co-wrote a book titled "The Selling of the Green: The Financial Rise and Moral Decline of the Boston Celtics." (Don't look for it — it's long out of print, perhaps residing peacefully somewhere in a 99-cent bin.) It could be the idea was planted in our brains by the aforementioned Sonny Werblin quotation suggesting that the racial makeup of a team mattered in a city as historically segregated as was Boston.

Let's just say the book didn't go over well in Boston, where we were falsely accused of calling Red Auerbach a racist — as opposed to, and as intended, a marketing opportunist.

Years later, Bird essentially agreed with the book's premise and Magic asserted that the league could use "a few more LBs." But the aging Bird-lovers in Boston never could acknowledge how profitable it had been for Auerbach to have transformed the Celtics from the black team in a white sport in the '60s to the white team in a black sport by the '80s, by which time free agency had empowered players and he could no longer afford to be the third most popular team in his market.

"No matter what they'd say for the record, it was always assumed there had to be a certain amount of whites on the team," Jo Jo White, a 1970s mainstay, said in the book. "You'd start with the blacks you knew would make it and figure everyone else would be white."

Such claims by White and others long denied a voice also fell on the deaf loyalist ears of those who would not consider the possibility that certain qualities — work ethic, dedication, team orientation — were generally ascribed more readily to white players than to blacks. This issue raged in the aftermath of Bird's steal of Isiah Thomas's inbounds pass and resentful comments by the young Dennis Rodman and Isiah in the aftermath of crushing defeat.

For a sport that was on the verge of having an African-American leading man carry it to once-unimaginable heights in the '90s, the '80s were a bridge to progress, built with the immensely likable Magic partnered with Bird, the greatest of all white hopes.

June 2, 1987

The Coloring of Bird

by Ira Berkow

On the eve of this championship series that makes the basketball fan tingle with expectation — another in the enduring, bruising Laker-Celtic series, the clash of Magic and Bird, the hobbling Parish and McHale who maybe should be in traction versus the quadragenarian Jabbar, the numerous Coopers who seem to reproduce themselves on the court versus D. J., of whom there is only one, and who is rarely anywhere except in the right place at the right time — with all this, an unfortunate note has been raised.

It is the matter of racism, concerning the white star in a predominantly — 75 percent — black league.

The controversy created here was lit after the seventh and final game of the Eastern Conference championship, in which the Celtics beat the Pistons, 117–114, and earned the right to meet the Lakers in the finals for the 10th time in N.B.A. history.

In the visiting and losing team's locker room Saturday afternoon in Boston Garden, Isiah Thomas, the Detroit guard, said he didn't want it to sound like sour grapes, and that there was no question that his team got beat, and that they came up short, but he harbored a resentment.

In regard to Bird, he said, "I think Larry is a very, very good basketball player. An exceptional talent, but I'd have to agree with Rodman. If Bird was black, he'd be just another good guy."

Dennis Rodman, the teammate to whom Thomas had referred, had said that Bird was "overrated," and that the only reason he had won three straight league most valuable player awards (until this year, that is), "is because he's white. That's the only reason."

The nation, however, whether in the Garden or in their living rooms, observed the kind of player Bird is.

He led — no, drove — Boston to victory Saturday afternoon — scoring 37 points, more than anyone else in the game, adding nine rebounds and nine assists and playing all 48 minutes (the only one to do so) in an arena so hot it was more suitable for roasting chickens than for playing basketball. It was also Bird who made the play in the fifth game that turned defeat for the Celtics into victory, by stealing an inbounds pass from Thomas with five seconds left, then passing to Dennis Johnson, who made the layup. It provided the Celtics with the 1-point margin of triumph.

If Bird hadn't made that play, the Pistons and not the Celtics would be here competing in the N.B.A. finals.

And it is Bird who has contributed mightily to three Celtic championships — and possibly a fourth — in the eight seasons he has been there.

"What I was referring to," said Thomas, by telephone yesterday, "was not so much Larry Bird, but the the perpetuation of stereotypes about blacks.

"When Bird makes a great play, it's due to his thinking, and his work habits. It's all planned out by him. It's not the case for blacks. All we do is run and jump. We never practice or give a thought to how we play. It's like I came dribbling out of my mother's womb.

"You hear it on television, you see it in the papers. I remember watching the N.C.A.A. finals between Syracuse and Indiana. I listened to Billy Packer, who I like, and who I think likes me, and he said when Indiana was sending in [Dean] Garrett and [Keith] Smart, 'Well, here come the athletes into the game.' The word 'athletes.' I think that that's an unconscious statement concerning race. I don't like it.

"Magic and Michael Jordan and me, for example, we're playing only on God-given talent, like we're animals, lions and tigers, who run around wild in a jungle, while Larry's success is due to intelligence and hard work.

"Blacks have been fighting that stereotype about playing on pure instinct for so long, and basically it still exists — regardless of whether people want to believe it or not.

"And maybe I noticed it more during this series. I listened to Tommy Heinsohn on tapes of the games, and he kept going over plays by Bird, like that left-handed bank shot, where he might not with someone else. And maybe I was more sensitive to it because Boston has more white players than any other pro team, and maybe because it's so hard to win in Boston Garden. I feel that it's not so much the fouls that the referees call there, but the ones they don't call.

"Like the punches that Parish hit Laimbeer with. I guarantee you that if it was in Atlanta, and Tree Rollins did that to Laimbeer, Rollins is thrown out of the game so fast you wouldn't believe it." Parish, who was fined and suspended for one game after that game, was not even called for a foul at the time. About Bird's steal in Game 5, Thomas said: "It was a great basketball play. I didn't put enough zip on the ball, and Laimbeer didn't step up to get it. Meanwhile, this white guy on the other team who is supposed to be very slow, with little coordination, who can't jump, all of a sudden appears out of nowhere, jumps in, grabs the ball, leaps up in the air as he's falling out of bounds, looks over the court in the space of two or three seconds, picks out a player cutting for the basket and hits him with a dead-bullet, picture-perfect pass to win the game. You tell me this white guy — Bird — did that with no God-given talent?"

Thomas is on target in regard to his views of stereotyping blacks. When you hear "athlete" these days, it often means "black," and in the context Thomas stated. The referees' disappearance in the Parish incident was nothing but deplorable.

In the case of Larry Bird, though, his record — both personal and in regard to team performance — speaks with eloquence for him. Black, white or fuchsia, Larry Bird must be considered not just "another good guy," but one of the best players to ever tuck in a jersey. It says here, the best.

— POSTSCRIPT —

IRA BERKOW, 2018: "After Isiah won the national championship at Indiana, I went to Bloomington to do a story about whether he was going to turn pro. He was hiding out at an apartment in town — he already knew he was leaving but he was afraid of Bob Knight, who wanted him to stay. I found out where he was, knocked on the door. He opened up when he found out I was from the same neighborhood on the west side of Chicago, played ball in the same parks. I wrote a story about how his mother scared off gang members from her porch with a shotgun and subsequently developed a trust with Isiah. So when I called him after he and Dennis Rodman were quoted about Bird, he was willing to talk. He knew he had screwed up, given the time and place, after a crushing defeat in Boston. But at the same time Isiah is a really smart guy and what he had to say about the stereotyping of black and white athletes rang true. I also believe his famous quote — 'It's like I came dribbling out of my mother's womb' — did resonate and have a positive effect on the commentary going forward."

7

Sky's the Limit

The pairing of Magic Johnson and Kareem Abdul-Jabbar was fascinatingly awkward from the very first game they played with the Lakers. On Oct. 12, 1979, they trailed by a point with seconds remaining on the road against the San Diego Clippers. As if scripted by the basketball gods and not the coach, Kareem took an inbounds pass on the left side of the free-throw line, turned and drained a trademark sky hook for a 103–102 victory.

And nearly had his neck separated from his shoulders by the wildly celebrating Magic.

Really? Kareem said afterward. *Such histrionics for winning Game 1 of 82?* But such was the essence of the league's newest and most formidable pairing, arguably the greatest of all time: smiling, unbridled passion meeting moody, subdued perfection.

Kareem's sky hook was possibly the greatest individual weapon in the history of *any* sport. But because it was executed with such natural fluidity, along with most things he did on the floor, the complaint that he wasn't trying hard enough was not uncommon — criticism hilariously summed up when he played a co-pilot getting into it with a boy named Joey in the 1980 spoof *Airplane!*

Joey: "I think you're the greatest, but my dad says you don't work hard enough on defense. And he says that lots of times, you don't even run down court. And that you don't really try, except during the playoffs."

Murdock: "The hell I don't! [grabs Joey by collar] Listen, kid! I've been hearing that crap ever since I was at U.C.L.A. I'm out there busting my buns every night. Tell your old man to drag Walton and Lanier up and down the court for 48 minutes."

The only better casting than having the 7-foot-2 creator of the sky hook in that would have been having Magic, even as a rookie, as his co-pilot.

June 10, 1987

Johnson's Right Hook Is a Real Knockout

by Roy S. Johnson

BOSTON — Finally, it became the series everyone wanted to see. It took three complete games, three quarters and numerous gallant performances by players, both well-known and unheralded. But when it came time for one team to take the boldest step toward controlling the series, it was as if no one was on the court except Earvin (Magic) Johnson and Larry Bird.

This is the fourth occasion in nine years in which the two players have faced each another for a championship, beginning with the national collegiate championship game in 1979. But through two impressive Laker routs and a physical Celtic victory in the third game of this series, it looked as if this renewal of their rivalry — actually, it is more a respectful relationship — would never emerge as a test of two great talents and wills.

That changed dramatically tonight during the Lakers' stunning 107–106 comeback victory in Boston Garden, strangely after the two players had merged accidentally. With the Celtics struggling to hang on to a lead that had been 16 points, Bird's knee accidentally jolted Johnson on the side of his already tender left knee and sent the Laker guard to the parquet floor.

There were 9 minutes 22 seconds remaining and the Lakers trailed 89–84. And as Johnson, in pain, was helped off the floor, it seemed as if the Celtics had once again received an unlikely boost in their aged arena.

But Johnson quickly recuperated by jogging lightly on the sideline.

"It was like when you hit your elbow," he said. "The pain goes away, only it comes back to grab you sometimes."

All told, only 50 seconds elapsed and the scoring margin didn't change. That set the stage. First, with the score tied at 95-all, Bird sandwiched 17-footers around two surprising Celtic fast breaks. Suddenly, Boston was in control by 103–95 with 3:30 remaining.

"I felt right then that one of us would win it," Bird said. "But I thought it was going to be me."

It probably would have been, had not Bird committed three costly errors over the next three minutes — a missed jump shot, a lazy pass to Kevin McHale that rolled out of bounds and an errant forced shot over the outstretched arm of Kareem Abdul-Jabbar.

"We made the mistakes," Bird said. "So we have nobody to blame but ourselves."

Johnson still had not scored in the period. But if there has been one staple to his game, it is that he, like Bird, has never had to score to be effective. And that was never more apparent than when he completed a 9–0 spurt with a pass to Abdul-Jabbar, who caught the ball above the rim and slammed it through for a 104–103 lead with 29 seconds left.

Their final efforts were their best. Seventeen seconds later, Bird swished a 3-pointer to put Boston ahead, 106–104. "That's Larry," Johnson shrugged.

In the end it was the Laker guard's moment to celebrate as he scored the winning basket with only two seconds left with a shot he borrowed from Abdul-Jabbar — the sky hook. It was his only basket following the minor knee injury, and his only points of the final period.

"We both do what we have to do to win," said Johnson, referring to Bird and himself. "He takes his shots, I take mine. That's the difference between him and myself and a lot of people."

"It was both of our games to win or lose," said Bird. "This time, I lost."

MARCH 8, 1988

The Shot That Reigns Over the Rim

BY JOHN NIELSEN

Sometime during the game Wednesday night against the Knicks, Kareem Abdul-Jabbar of the Los Angeles Lakers will take a pass near the basket, fake to his left, swing to his right and shoot the most potent and feared shot in the history of basketball.

"It might be the most awesome weapon in the history of any sport," said Pat Riley, coach of the Lakers. "The fact that Kareem is the only one who shoots it makes it that much more amazing."

The shot, called the sky hook, has terrorized Abdul-Jabbar's National Basketball Association opponents for the better part of 19 years. In a game marked increasingly by speed, power and improvisation near the basket, this complicated, almost scientific move characterizes an era unto itself.

Awards, Rings and Records

Because of it, Abdul-Jabbar holds six most valuable player awards, five N.B.A. championship rings and virtually all of the N.B.A.'s career-scoring records. Only three active N.B.A. players have scored half as many as Jabbar's 37,000-plus points in their careers.

At the age of 40, Abdul-Jabbar admits he is not the player he once was. He is slower and quicker to tire now, with uneven skills as a defender and rebounder. He ended a 787-game streak of double-figure scoring performances in December. In recent weeks, while recovering from the flu, he has played quite poorly in some games.

But no one on the Lakers seems greatly worried by this, and the reason is probably the hook. To stop it, opposing teams still double- and triple-team the aging center, leaving other Lakers open for easy shots. In the clutch, his teammates still lob those passes inside, where Abdul-Jabbar remains convinced that the shot will continue to drop.

"If I can take that shot with one-on-one coverage, I'm very confident that I can make it most of the time," Abdul-Jabbar said in the Lakers' dressing room before a recent game.

At the least, it is strange that a shot this great has no rivals or successors. There are several possible explanations, most of them related to broad changes in the nature of the game, like more complex defenses.

Abdul-Jabbar himself thinks it might be simpler than that. "One main reason is the kids growing up today all want to be like Michael Jordan and Dr. J and Dominique," he said, referring to Julius Erving and Dominique Wilkins. "They want to show great and obvious athletic ability and jump high and shoot jumpers and throw the ball down."

For Abdul-Jabbar, it was different. In 1956, before most of the players in the N.B.A. were born, he shot his first sky hook in a junior high school game, acting out of what he said was a mixture of fear and confusion at having the ball in the first place. He missed the shot, but the coach was pleased, so Abdul-Jabbar kept trying.

A Common Shot

In those days, the plain hook shot was far more common than it is in the game today. In the pros, George Mikan of the Minneapolis Lakers shot hooks with either hand near the basket, and in the early 1950s, players like Bob Houbregs of the University of Washington sent sweeping, long-range hook shots in from the corners of the court.

Those maneuvers, like the two-handed set shot, began to fade with the refinement of the jump shot and the advent of the dunk. "I used to practice some of Mikan's drills, but there never has been much of a tradition," Abdul-Jabbar said. "Bill Russell shot this shot sometimes, and Cliff Hagan would shoot it, but it wasn't really something they relied on."

Then, as now, the sky hook began with Abdul-Jabbar turning his back on the defender and the basket, then stretching his arm to signal for the ball. Once he got it, he would step to the left and kick his right knee high into the air, pivoting on his left foot, then twirl and jump in one motion. With his left elbow in the face of his defender, Abdul-Jabbar would extend his right arm over his head and, snapping his wrist, loop the ball toward the net.

This motion is strikingly different from the head-on explosiveness of the dunk or the abruptness of the jumper.

"It's almost a ballet-type shot," said Oscar Robertson, who was a teammate of Abdul-Jabbar's on the Milwaukee Bucks. "There's so much rhythm and balance in it… it's almost like a pirouette."

Improvement at U.C.L.A.

At U.C.L.A., where Abdul-Jabbar's teams were 88–2 and won three consecutive national championships, the shot improved immensely, said John Wooden, who was his coach there. To prevent players from blocking the hook from behind, Wooden said, he encouraged Abdul-Jabbar to abandon the sweeping motion favored by the likes of Houbregs, instead keeping the ball in close to the body and shooting with a straighter trajectory.

The shot improved further in Abdul-Jabbar's junior year, when an N.C.A.A. ban on the dunk forced the use of more touch around the basket. Abdul-Jabbar believes that the ban was designed specifically to reduce his dominance of the game. Instead, it probably increased it.

In his final years in college, Abdul-Jabbar was deadly with his sky hook, often letting it go from several feet above the rim of the basket. The only way to block it was to jump up and over the body of an agile 7-foot-2-inch player, which was virtually impossible. To deny him the ball, opposing teams packed players around him, leaving him with the choice of a pass to an open teammate or a game of one-on-five.

"People tried everything," said Pete Newell, who coached an N.C.A.A. championship team at the University of California, and who today is known as a guru to the game's best centers and forwards. "He'd get pushed, punched, poked in the eye, all kinds of things like that. But people underrated his passing skills, and his inside moves to the basket."

Teamed With Fine Passers

They did not underrate his hook. In the pros with the Bucks, Abdul-Jabbar was teamed with Robertson, whose passing talents were legendary. After the Bucks won the 1972 N.B.A. championship, Abdul-Jabbar was traded to the Lakers, where Robertson's shoes were eventually filled by Earvin (Magic) Johnson.

The result has been an even worse nightmare for defenders. Nate Thurmond, a former center for the then–San Francisco Warriors, and the player cited by Abdul-Jabbar as the best defender he has faced, said guarding against the sky hook was a "sickening" experience.

"When he got into his rhythm, it was over," Thurmond said. "You could have fallen out of the ceiling and never blocked that shot."

While the sky hook was tearing up the pros, the use of zone defenses in college became more or less universal in the 1970s, making it extremely hard for centers to move freely near the basket. So, centers like Ralph Sampson shot outside jumpers instead of inside hooks, using the sky hook rarely.

"Somewhere along the line, a lot of coaches started telling their players the hook shot was a terrible shot," Riley said. "It was obsolete. It disappeared."

Robertson, among others, finds little logic in that trend. "For centers not to emulate what Kareem has done is just stupid," he said. "Today you've got 7-footers who fool around and shoot shots from 30 feet outside the basket. That's really just stupidity. It's not what a big man should be doing."

Premature Obituary

Though the shot was said by some to be gone at the end of 1984, when the Lakers lost to the Boston Celtics in the N.B.A. championship series, it helped Abdul-Jabbar to win the most valuable player trophy in the 1985 championships, which the Lakers won.

In 1987, after Abdul-Jabbar's scoring totals fell off considerably during the regular season, his performance improved steadily in each round of the playoffs, ending with a season high in the final game. Saturday, after having scored only 2 points in a loss to Seattle, he went 10 for 13 in a nationally televised game against the Dallas Mavericks, dominating play.

Abdul-Jabbar says his shot has stayed with him because it is not based on power. Without the sky hook, he might not be planning to start an unprecedented 20th season next fall.

"But I think I can make this shot drop for one more season," he said.

Bad Boys

Any Pistons fans from the city of Detroit fortunate enough to be sitting inside a sweltering Joe Louis Arena for the decisive fifth game of the Knicks-Pistons first-round playoff series in 1984 would recall it as a historically symbolic night. Just not necessarily because Isiah Thomas and Bernard King left everyone with their jaws practically in their laps with performances for the ages.

I covered that game for the *New York Daily News* and still chuckle at the thought of a perspiration-soaked, raving Hubie Brown prowling the sideline for the Knicks. But the real story, in contextual retrospect, was that the game, by a quirk of scheduling conflict, was actually played within city limits, and not in the sterile football dome the Pistons had fled to during the late '70s on their way to the basketball-specific Palace of Auburn Hills.

This was always one of the great N.B.A. betrayals, the abandonment of a troubled urban and majority African-American landscape while the N.H.L.'s Red Wings — a *hockey* team — stayed behind to flourish at, of all places, an arena named for Joe Louis. Pitiful excuses were made by Pistons executives, by league officials, who argued that upscale suburbanites would not venture into Detroit, even as hockey fans did. These suburban schemers were the actual Bad Boys.

Outside of Michigan, the Chuck Daly–coached Pistons of Thomas and Joe Dumars were seldom given their proper due, resented as they were for supplanting the Celtics as the Eastern Conference power and, even more so, their pugnacious play that did, on occasion, cross the line.

Yet nothing those Pistons hyperaggressively did on the court ever came remotely close to the 2004 Malice at the Palace that was foisted upon the sport, in large part by the very suburban fan base the franchise had once deemed so desirable. It would take nearly four decades for the Pistons to join baseball's Tigers, hockey's Red Wings and even football's Lions in a resurgent downtown Detroit. Not a moment too soon.

FEB. 11, 1993

A King Performance Daly Can't Forget

BY HARVEY ARATON

There are games people don't forget. For Chuck Daly, one was played on April 27, 1984.

Not that he could remember it by the month, the date, or even the year. He can't tell you the final score or which player scored what, and he didn't even recall that it happened to be his first season as head coach in Detroit. Daly — and he is far from alone here — primarily recalls this night as simply: Game 5 at Joe Louis Arena.

"One of the all-time great games," he said last night, before his new team, the Nets, took care of his old team, the Pistons, 109–86, at Byrne Meadowlands Arena. "It's in the archives."

Where were you on the steamy, exhausting night when Bernard King scored 44 points and the Knicks beat the Isiah Thomas–led Pistons, 127–123, in overtime to win a five-game first-round playoff series that was the Knicks' most memorable achievement between their winning the 1973 championship and taking the Bulls to seven games last spring?

At the zenith of his game, King averaged 43 points for those five games, leaving Daly in awe, believing that King's lightning release on his turnaround jumper was somewhere beyond the physical laws of nature.

"It was as if the ball was going right through his hands and into the basket without him even shooting it," said Daly.

Daly was asked if he remembered King's offensive rebound in the fourth quarter that night.

"Oh yeah, the one where he comes from nowhere, catches it with one hand and throws it down," he said.

Did Daly remember that King played that game after a three-day bout with the flu?

"Oh, I don't doubt it," he said.

It is not a reach to think that that indelible performance helped persuade Daly to sign King last week, to take the risk of upsetting his young forward, Chris Morris, among others, the rationale being: If Morris is that fragile, where is Daly going with him anyway?

Nine years can be an athletic lifetime, many successes and failures and torn ligaments under the bridge. Daly's Pistons took that experience and later matured into a two-time champion. King had another great year in him with the Knicks before his right knee crumbled. He eventually recovered, but Hubie Brown, his coach that night, didn't survive the loss of his one-man post-up offense.

The principals from Game 5, Joe Louis Arena, happened to be in the building last night. Brown was barking out the commentary for cable TV and then sitting down to interview King. King, at 36, was home with the franchise that drafted him in 1977. Daly was working King into his rotation for 21 fluid minutes and realizing right off that he has a go-to scorer for his second unit. Thomas was denying reports that he was seeking to follow Daly's lead and go someplace where another championship might be won.

"I want to finish in Detroit," said Thomas. "I have a lot of history there."

Thomas was 23 in 1984, reopening doors in the N.B.A. to the electric 6-foot point guard and remaking the position for those who could dominate the game in a variety of ways. Perhaps on April 27 that year, when Game 5 was moved downtown because the building in the suburbs was previously booked, Kevin Johnson or Tim Hardaway or Mark Price were watching somewhere as Thomas single-handedly lifted the Pistons out of the grave King had dug for them, an 8-point deficit with less than two minutes to play.

When Thomas was reminded of the 16 points he somehow scored in 1 minute 33 seconds, he shook his head.

"It's like something that happened in a dream," he said. "It was so hot that night, like a summer league game where everyone is crammed into the gym, and it was a two-man shootout between me and Bernard.

"First it looked like the game was lost, then the plays started happening so fast. I shot a 3. I stole the ball. I got in this zone. I remember going to the bench for a timeout, it was so hot and noisy. I had, like, tears in my eyes."

With 23 seconds left in the fourth quarter, Thomas's 3-pointer tied the game. The Knicks lost the ball. Thomas went for the win. Darrell Walker stripped him of the ball. After King dominated the overtime, Thomas said he was so upset that he jumped into his car, still in uniform, and drove home to Chicago.

"I got about an hour and a half into the trip and I said, 'What the hell am I doing?'"

He was trying to get King out of his mind, but couldn't.

"In all the years I've watched pro basketball, two guys, Bernard and George Gervin, could score with more ease, and less shots, than anyone."

In Game 5, he was reminded, King got 44 points despite sitting out the last 8:55 of the third quarter in foul trouble.

"See what I mean?" said Thomas.

It was no surprise to him that Daly fought off the dissent within his organization and brought in King. What are nine years and torn ligaments when an impression as powerful as Game 5, Joe Louis Arena, has been made?

"After what Bernard did to us," said Thomas, "who should know what he's capable of more than Chuck?"

JUNE 15, 1989

Detroit Hopes Pistons Help To Improve City's Image

BY WILLIAM E. SCHMIDT

DETROIT — Nearly 2,000 fans waited in rain at nearby Willow Run Airport today to welcome home the champion Detroit Pistons, whose triumph as the "bad boys" of professional basketball is making this working-class city feel positively good about itself.

By sweeping the Los Angeles Lakers in four games in the National Basketball Association finals, the Pistons not only brought home Detroit's first basketball championship ever, but touched off delirium among defiant fans who say the Pistons, like Detroit itself, are long overdue for some respect.

"Face it, Detroit has a bad image it doesn't deserve, and neither did the Pistons," said Tim Allison, a refrigeration worker who stood in line this afternoon with hundreds of other people outside the Palace, the Pistons' stadium, in suburban Auburn Hills, to buy a $15 souvenir T-shirt. "Now look who the good guys are. The Detroit Pistons are, because they are the best in the world."

Another fan, Debrah Hayes of Oak Park, put it another way: "Detroit never gets credit for anything. But the Pistons did it their way. Detroit is the champion."

First Championship

By beating the Lakers, 105–97, Tuesday night, the franchise, which began in Fort Wayne, Ind., in 1948 and moved to Detroit in 1957, won the championship for the first time.

The championship was the first professional title for the city since 1984, when the Detroit Tigers won the World Series. But many fans boasted that the Pistons' victory now made the state of Michigan the nation's basketball capital, because the University of Michigan won the national collegiate title in April.

It is a measure of the affection the team commands in the nation's sixth-largest city that more than 21,500 people — 4,000 more than were inside the Forum in Los Angeles — paid $3 apiece Tuesday night to jam the Palace in order to watch the game on the arena's television system.

The crowd noise inside the Palace equaled what it is during an ordinary game, but arena officials took no chances on the crowd turning rowdy: They lowered the baskets at either end of the court at halftime, so fans couldn't climb on them later.

Many Turned Away

Many others were turned away outside the arena. After being chased from the surrounding parking lots by the police, they parked along nearby roads, turned on car radios and sat on their roofs to listen to the game.

Thousands more poured into streets of Detroit following the victory, blocking traffic in celebrations that continued in several parts of the city until nearly dawn. The police said some arrests were made as a result of vandalism, including some brick and bottle throwing aimed at police cars and one city bus.

But there were no injuries, and the demonstrations were not nearly on the scale they were following the 1984 World Series, when fans battled the police and set a police car afire outside Tiger Stadium.

Fans, including some who had been waiting all night, knocked down barricades and rushed to surround team members today when the team's private plane, Roundball One, touched down in drizzle at Willow Run Airport, about 25 miles west of Detroit. The team's arrival was carried live on three Detroit television stations.

Official Celebration Today

The city's official celebration will be Thursday, when the Pistons will ride through downtown. Later, there will be a rally outside the Palace.

The Pistons, like many of the most successful sports franchises, have a visceral link with their fans, who seemed to revel in the team's tough, hard-knuckled style of play.

In a characterization popular here in recent days, a commentator on Detroit radio station WWJ described the team as "a tough-as-nails bunch in a tough-as-nails shot-and-beer city."

"Detroit deserves this," said Jacques Demers, the coach of the Detroit Red Wings, who watched the game Tuesday. "So many negative things are said about Detroit."

Earlier Tuesday, *The Detroit News* ran a front-page story that recalled various insults inveighed against the Pistons in recent days by national television sports commentators and others, including Bryant Gumbel, the *Today* show host, who used the terms "mugging" and "thuggery" to refer to the Pistons' style of play earlier this week.

The "Bad Boys" image grew in part out of the Pistons' aggressive style and some clever marketing, which will net the team an estimated $3 million this year in "Bad Boy" hats, scarves and other paraphernalia, including T-shirts which are now being produced at the rate of about 15,000 a day.

June 5, 1990

Thomas Heard the Oracles

by Ira Berkow

There was a time when Isiah Thomas's greatest goal was to prove that a little man could make it in the National Basketball Association. It was a personal goal, and a personal struggle, though it had another layer to it, one of universality for an underdog.

There were times when Thomas, the second pick in the N.B.A. draft in 1981 as a sophomore out of Indiana University, drove inside against the big guys, and sometimes sank the shot, but other times forced it and had the ball stuffed like a sandwich between his teeth. There were times when, coming down the stretch of a game, he was convinced that only he could save the day for the Pistons, or should, and so he launched a shot amid two and three defenders that sometimes went in, sometimes didn't.

But Thomas got inside successfully enough times, and hit the clutch shot enough times, that he indeed proved that a little man can make it — little, that is, in terms of his profession, since Thomas is listed as standing 6 feet 1 inch in his basketball suit. He was one of the high scorers in the league, one of the assists leaders and one of the steals leaders. He was regularly a first- or second-team All-Pro. And he received munificent financial rewards for these deeds and this acclaim.

As Thomas grew in stature, he also grew in maturity. He began to understand that although personal goals were splendid, they were at bottom insufficiently gratifying. What was left was a yearning, a hole in the soul. And Thomas took out after a new goal: to win a championship. But he wasn't quite sure how to go about achieving this thing.

The Pistons did not make the playoffs in his first two seasons in the league, got knocked out of the playoffs early in the next three years, and then, in 1987, when it seemed they were going to beat Larry Bird and the Celtics in six games and advance to the N.B.A. finals, the Celtics suddenly rose up and smote them in seven games.

This was mightily disturbing to Thomas. The year before, he had gone to Magic Johnson and to Bird, and sat with both, more or less like a supplicant to the Oracle of Delphi, to learn the secrets of winning a championship. In those days, Magic's team won the title one year and Bird's won it the next, and then they reversed it, like a two-sided jacket.

What they told Thomas was: Basketball is a team game, and the greatest player does not necessarily make the greatest team. He must want to win above all personal and statistical considerations.

Thomas recalled yesterday a talk he'd had with Johnson:

"Earvin said: 'When you're the best player on your team, none of your teammates can play at the level you are capable of playing at. Therefore, in order to get the most out of your team, you have to moderate your skills. In that way, everybody rises.'"

He comprehended that, as the point guard, the general of the army, the commander of the tub, he had to make the players around him better players, nailing them, for example, with passes at the most opportune moments, playing a kind of selfless defense that only your teammates and canny observers might appeciate, as well as, dismayingly, the enemy.

While the Pistons made changes and got an improved cast of characters around Thomas, Thomas also helped improve the cast. He was the team leader on the court as well as off.

The team went to the N.B.A. finals in 1988, but lost in seven games to the Lakers, with Thomas hobbling on a sprained ankle in Game 7.

And when his friend Mark Aguirre was traded from Dallas to Detroit the following season, Thomas initiated a welcoming party that included a few of the other standout Pistons, and explained to Aguirre, a sometimes pouty operative, that he was joining a team, with a capital T, that lusted for a title.

Aguirre, like Thomas, would underplay his particular figures for the overall play of the team. And all of them went merrily on to win the 1989 N.B.A. championship, beating the Lakers in four consecutive games.

After the final game, he walked out of the locker room alone, and quietly. "How do you feel, Isiah?" someone asked. Isiah smiled. No words were necessary. But it wasn't the end. There was next year — that is, this year.

And to return to the N.B.A. finals, against Portland starting tonight, the Pistons had to beat the Bulls on Sunday in Game 7 of the Eastern Conference finals. Thomas had perhaps his best game of the playoffs, scoring 21 points, with 8 rebounds, 11 assists and a significant block of an Air Jordan jump shot, in Detroit's 93–74 victory.

"Now I know," Thomas said later, "how tough it was for Earvin and Larry to try to repeat as champions."

To repeat is a new goal. And Thomas knows the answer to achieving it. All that is left, of course, is a little matter called execution.

9

Death and Survival

Generally speaking, basketball stars have been the most commercially success-ful of all American team-sport athletes, largely thanks to their on-stage visi-bility. Their faces are not hidden behind helmets, or shielded by caps, and they are flamboyantly individualistic within a group effort. For those reasons, we can easily conjure up their images. And when tragedy strikes a player of even limited renown, his death becomes a remember-where-you-were moment, fixed in time and often a prompt for a social discussion on what went wrong.

I was boarding a plane to Phoenix for Game 1 of the 1993 finals when I flipped over to the back page of the *New York Post* to learn that Drazen Petrovic, the great Croatian marksman, had died in a car crash on a German autobahn. A column written later that day explored the issue of whether xenophobic attitudes within the league during the early stages of the European invasion had soured Petrovic on returning the following season.

I was checking in on Bernard King's secret workouts — actually hiding in the bushes, peeking through a window, before he caught me — in his monumental effort to become the first N.B.A. player to return whole from major knee surgery when I heard that Len Bias had died. Wait, *what?* It was one day after he had been chosen by the Celtics with their first pick of the 1986 draft.

Under such extraordinary circumstances, Bias's death following a celebratory cocaine binge became as powerful an antidrug message as any.

And when the Celtics lost Reggie Lewis to heart failure during the summer of 1993, revelations that loopholes in the N.B.A.'s drug policy might have contributed to his death ignited an angry debate about an individual's rights to privacy versus a league's right to police its players.

When Bobby Phills was killed while drag-racing his Porsche against a car driven by his Charlotte Hornets teammate David Wesley in early 2000, it was a teaching moment for young men too much fascinated with speed. Wesley's survival also became a lesson in coping with guilt.

"What you eventually find out in a situation like the one this young man is in is that there are so many people who have been there — they are out there, complete strangers, and what I found is that they want to these share these stories," Bobby Ojeda told me for a column before Wesley made his return to the Hornets at Madison Square Garden two weeks later.

A former Mets and Indians pitcher, Ojeda had been the lone survivor of a boating accident that claimed the lives of two Cleveland teammates. In the darkened water, he crouched before the boat hit the pier. Serendipity can determine one's fate — as can the tough love of an unexpected savior.

JUNE 21, 1986

Death of a Young Star

BY IRA BERKOW

Len Bias was born Nov. 18, 1963, four days before John Fitzgerald Kennedy was shot to death at age 46. On Thursday morning, Bias died suddenly at age 22, with no clues or alarms or history of any physical problems.

Hearing of the death of Bias — he was gloriously in the headlines just the day before as the Celtics' first pick in the National Basketball Association draft, and the second selection over all — was as shocking in its way as hearing of the murder of President Kennedy as he rode in a motorcade while thousands cheered him.

This in no way is meant to compare the global impact of a world leader with that of a basketball player. But Bias, like President Kennedy, was youthful and vigorous and talented and charismatic.

Each was glowing in the national spotlight. Each had attained great heights in his respective world, each envisioned reaching even greater heights.

The first news reports said that doctors had not yet determined the cause of Bias's death. Was it, some wondered, a congenital malfunction, like Marfan syndrome? Later, there were unconfirmed reports of cocaine use Wednesday night, as Bias stayed up late celebrating his good fortune with friends in a dormitory room at the University of Maryland. Some cardiologists have said that cocaine can cause cardiac arrest.

If Bias had indeed been indulging in drug use, then he was not the kind of victim that Kennedy was, but had played with fire and got burned in extremis. He may have believed he could safely use a dangerous drug, that he could handle it. Look how much more he had handled on the basketball court. Others, not even basketball stars, had believed the same, and come to the same end. But now, in Bias's case, that was still a rumor.

Len Bias was born in Hyattsville, Md., just a few miles from where, in 1962, I was stationed with the 150th Armored Cavalry, at Fort Meade, Md., and about 50 miles from 1600 Pennsylavania Avenue, where Kennedy was then in residence. It was at Fort Meade that I first learned of something President Kennedy said that I would never forget. I was part of a call-up of the National Guard during the Berlin Crisis. Many reservists were unprepared when they were uprooted from family and business and school. I was in the last semester of undergraduate school at Miami University in Oxford, Ohio.

Thousands of letters of protest were sent by reservists to their congressmen, to their senators, to the president, asking for just a little more time to get their houses in order before they picked up their rifles, or shovels, or pencils, depending on their Military Occupational Specialty. I remember that the great young forward for the Lakers, Elgin Baylor, was also recalled.

To the many who complained that the speedy call-up was unfair, President Kennedy made his famous reply: "Life is unfair."

How ironic, how enraging, how tragic that within the space of about a year, life would be so unfair to John Kennedy.

This came to mind when a story, clicking on a wire-service machine in the office of *The New York Times* Thursday, reported the reaction on the death of Len Bias from the Celtics' star, Larry Bird. "It's horrible, I'm too shocked to respond," said Bird. "It's the cruelest thing I ever heard." In it were echoes of John Kennedy's words. "Len would've been a star," Red Auerbach, the president and general manager of the Celtics, said Thursday. "He was highly competitive. He could shoot and rebound and run."

The last time I heard Auerbach's voice over the phone, a few weeks ago, he was returning a call. For some reason, I didn't recognize the voice at first. He asked if this was me, I said it was, and he said, "Big deal." Then he laughed heartily, laughing, it was easy to imagine, through a cloud of cigar smoke. Now, the laughter was gone. His voice sounded weary and grave.

"What kind of player was he?" said Auerbach, about the 6-foot-8-inch, 210-pound Bias. "I'll tell ya. He had a little Michael Jordan in him, not quite as acrobatic as Michael but a better shooter. And he had a little Dr. J. in him, too."

Auerbach had known Bias for several years, since the young man had been a counselor in his summer camp. Auerbach had met with Bias's family several times, and affection had developed all around.

Bias dreamed of being a Celtic, and had said to Auerbach, "Please draft me."

On Tuesday in a Manhattan hotel, Auerbach did. According to one observer, Auerbach "looked like he had just drafted his nephew."

Bird had also urged Auerbach to draft Bias. "Larry told me," said Auerbach, "that that was all we needed. He said, 'If you get him, I'm coming to rookie camp to play with him.'"

Auerbach told Bias last summer that if he played for the Celtics, he would, of course, have to play behind Kevin McHale, the power forward, and Bird, the everything forward.

"Len said fine," recalled Auerbach. "He said, 'Those guys can help me learn.' He was humble. He was well-mannered. That's the kind of kid he was."

After two days in New York and Boston, Bias returned Wednesday night to College Park, Md., somewhat irritated, a friend recalled, by the heavy media attention he received. But he still was so joyous at the prospects of playing for the Celtics, of the huge amount of money that was certain for this son of working-class parents — he would sign for millions of dollars over the next few years — that he had sprinted to his car at 2 o'clock Thursday morning.

About 6:30 A.M., Bias was in convulsions, struggling to breathe, and was rushed in an ambulance to Leland Memorial Hospital in nearby Riverdale. He was pronounced dead at 8:50 in the morning.

As this is being typed, a press kit from the N.B.A. draft is on the desk. On the page about Bias, it tells of his "soft jumper" and his being "an explosive leaper." It relates that he finished his career as the Terrapins' leading career scorer, and was named first team All-American by The Associated Press and United Press International.

Lower, there is a quote: "'Every day I do things I didn't know I could do,' Bias says. 'I'm nowhere near my potential.'"

Road for Richardson
Leads Back Home

BY HARVEY ARATON

DENVER — The task of raising a most unpleasant issue was undertaken outside a home on Denver's east side, where a determined woman named Luddie Hicks raised seven children, all on her own. Micheal Ray Richardson was asked about the man who exited that house and his young life, beginning a pattern of paternal abandonment often hypothesized to be the sad social dynamic that sentenced him to a punishing drug hell.

A few years ago, the cable network TNT produced a documentary on Richardson's sensational fall from pro basketball grace in the 1980s and called it *Whatever Happened to Micheal Ray?* Now, sitting in the passenger seat of a friend's sport utility vehicle, steps from the brick-face house at 1625 Martin Luther King Boulevard, Richardson was asked: Whatever happened to the man who might have steered him to an alternative life path?

Whatever happened to his biological father, who went by the given name of Billy Jack?

Richardson turned to face his questioner and said: "My father was living in Texas until his mother died. My brother went and brought him back here, to Denver. I see him now, once or twice a week. To tell you the truth, it feels kind of strange. My father, he wasn't there, but he's still my dad."

He shrugged and added, "It is what it is."

Life can be what it is or what you make of it. Kicked out of the N.B.A. in 1986, Richardson was forced to become a citizen of the world and says he doesn't regret a minute of it. "I felt freer being away than I ever felt here," he said. "It was a great experience, but I stopped playing in 2001. I thought it might be time to come home."

Fifteen years after he left to salvage his career in Europe and rebuild his life, Richardson has returned to Denver, to an N.B.A. payroll. He has reunited with his father and his family, and benefited from a new surrogate daddy, the man who banished him from the N.B.A. house on Feb. 25, 1986.

"I had only been commissioner a short time, and it was not an easy thing to do," David Stern said by telephone from his office in New York, explaining why he helped Richardson land a job last spring as the community ambassador for the Denver Nuggets. "Here we were ending his career."

There were others who succumbed to the cocaine scourge, who violated the league's three-strikes drug policy and were sent away by Stern. Roy Tarpley. Chris Washburn. John Drew. None of them are on the commissioner's callback list the way Richardson has been since 1997, when he tapped Stern on the shoulder in Paris at a McDonald's Open game and thanked him for saving his life.

"I was quite taken when he said that," Stern said.

Outlasting most of the players who dribbled on without him, Richardson played ball in Europe, away from N.B.A. excesses, until he was 46. Then, in concert with Stern, he began working N.B.A. clinics abroad. Back in Denver for his sister's wedding last May, he contacted Stern to say he might be interested in a job. Stern called Kiki Vandeweghe, who runs the Nuggets.

"Kiki stepped up," Stern said, though he didn't want to specify the financial arrangement, and he worried how national attention might affect what he called "a fragile situation." Papa Stern has enough problems in Colorado, with training camps now open and Kobe Bryant due back next week for a preliminary hearing on the sexual assault charge against him.

Contrary to the allegations in the Bryant case and others that have recently plagued the N.B.A., Richardson never hurt anyone in the way he flagellated himself. Those of us who knew him as "Sugar" during his meteoric flash across the New York/New Jersey sky remembered him in his absence as wildly talented, often endearing, sadly troubled — searching for the grace of someone's good will.

Men who recruited Richardson in college and the pros were always promising to look after him but always had a way of falling out of his life, like Billy Jack. "A boy needs a father to teach him to be a man, but I take responsibility for what I did," Richardson said. "I did it to myself."

After all he's been through, Richardson looks and sounds remarkably the way he did when he was an All-Star point guard, a kinetic force of nature, with a mischievous twinkle in his eye. Except for a slight midriff expansion, his body is still lean, his face unlined. His sharply opinionated and often heartfelt or funny words, hindered by a painful speech impediment, still come in staccato bursts. But beyond appearance, his life is nothing like anyone could have imagined it would be when he went away, many fearing to a place from which he would not return.

The picture of American linear success he isn't, but, as Richardson asked, why dwell on alternative paths, on what might have been? "I could also have wound up like Len Bias and not be here," he said of the Boston Celtics' No. 1 draft pick who died of cocaine use. "I think I'm better off than he is. I'll tell you, I can wake up every day and look at myself in the mirror and say: 'I am happy. I am blessed.'"

He has lived to be a grandfather but is also the father of two young children, who are temporarily still in France with his Moroccan wife of five years, Ilham. He is the holder of an Italian passport, and the owner of a home in France between Cannes and Nice. He speaks fluent Italian and he understands French. His experiences include a year in Israel and having to flee the Croatian port city of Split by speedboat during a bombing raid.

He might have been a Hall of Fame player instead of the curiosity he was Monday afternoon at the small charter high school in his old east Denver neighborhood, where he went on behalf of the Nuggets. The kids had never heard of him and, frankly, the young teachers hadn't either. Seventeen years in sports may as well be 70. The kids know about Kobe's problems, not those that Richardson wasn't about to bring up, sticking to the scripted message of stay-in-school.

Better his long, complicated story be told in the book he said was in the works, or from the memorabilia and the memories spread around his mother's home, which Richardson and his friend and former Manuel High School teammate Sam Combs visited after leaving the school. Years ago, Richardson moved his mother out of 1625 Martin Luther King Boulevard, but the new house was repossessed when the drugs took over his life. Now, her new townhouse in the suburb of Aurora contains all the old trophies and photos, including those he is most eager to show off: him with his children, those grown and still growing, and the one grandchild who, at 6, is older than Richardson's young son.

Like Billy Jack, he hasn't always been the best father. But it is what it is, and he has a second chance. When Luddie Hicks mentioned that her 72nd birthday was tomorrow, Richardson told her, sorry, he was leaving today for France.

"I love you, Mom, but I got to go home, see my wife and kids," he said. "I'll be back."

He leaned over to kiss her, and she smiled, knowing from experience that her Micheal Ray, for all his failures, all his foibles, does come back.

10

Stars Come Out

In a classic example of bicoastal conceit, the nation's largest media markets in Los Angeles and New York long perpetuated the myth that the entertainment industry's enchantment with pro basketball began exclusively courtside at the Great Western Forum and at Madison Square Garden. In fact, the celebrity parade probably occurred before hitting those marquee buildings at frumpy old Cobo Arena in downtown Detroit.

After the Pistons announced they were returning to the city in late 2016, a jubilant Dave Bing, who launched feathery jumpers at Cobo in the late '60s to mid-'70s before becoming a local businessman and ultimately Detroit's mayor, reminded me that Pistons games had once been a magnet for Motown's most illustrious musicians.

"I already knew Marvin Gaye because we grew up in the same neighborhood in D.C.," he said. "But the Four Tops were at the games, the Temptations, Diana Ross. It was a fashion show every night."

Lakers and Knicks home games became showcases for a more diverse cast of celebrities. The marriage of sports and entertainment was in the works, but it wasn't until Nike cast Mars Blackmon (a.k.a. Spike Lee) and Michael Jordan in a black-and-white shoe commercial together that it was consummated.

In unlocking a vault of shoe company riches, Jordan set in motion the development of characters cuddly and edgy, from Lil Penny (Anfernee

Hardaway) to Charles ("I'm Not a Role Model") Barkley. Thus came a whole new creative realm of exposure for N.B.A. stars, along with the cultural phenomenon of the overpriced but status-driven sneaker.

Some N.B.A. players at least practiced what their leading men preached, as Scott Cacciola reported in a January 2014 story that began with the compulsive storage habits of P.J. Tucker:

"He keeps some at his home in Phoenix, where about 200 pairs are piled in boxes next to his bed," Cacciola wrote. "He stacks others in the locker room at US Airways Center, where he occupies two stalls. His mother has been gracious enough to stow several dozen at her home… and then there is the climate-controlled warehouse in North Carolina, not far from where he grew up, where Tucker stashes the bulk of his 2,000-pair collection."

He Loved This Game

by Paul Gilbert

Rule No. 1: Spartacus calls his own plays.

"Don't direct me, kid," Kirk Douglas growled. "I'm a Method actor."

Back in the 1980s, I had one of the most exciting jobs in professional sports, producing the promotional television campaigns for the National Basketball Association. My responsibilities included going to numerous games, working closely with the players and scouring video highlights for great plays, bloopers and fan cutaways to be used in our commercials.

In 1986, we hit on the idea of asking the galaxy of celebrities who attended games to do on-camera endorsements with our slogan, "N.B.A. Action... It's Fan-tastic!" My assignment was to go to games in New York and Los Angeles, scout for top-name personalities, recruit them on the spot, film impromptu performances and, later, edit them into the promos. All this for scenes lasting five seconds or less.

These people covered the entertainment spectrum — actors, musicians, comedians, athletes, power couples — the main criteria being that they had to be so famous that viewers would recognize them immediately without on-screen identification. For example, we filmed the hard-core hoops fan Spike Lee, but it was before he got game in the film industry, and he did not get the part.

As mentioned in *Variety*, appearances in these commercials soon gained a certain cachet in Hollywood and became a measure of a celebrity's star power.

My quasi–show business experiences ranged from exhilarating to exasperating. Directing larger-than-life personalities in front of thousands of people (and like the players, having to produce under pressure) was a huge adrenaline rush.

The flip side included Debra Winger's frosty look when I suggested a different reading; Jay Leno's agent screaming at me over the phone about ruining his career; and my wondering if Mike Tyson was going to lose it when I told his wife at the time, the actress Robin Givens, to please project a little more.

Most celebrities were extremely gracious about taking orders from a young sports executive, including megastars like Michael Douglas (yes, we got them both, and Kirk was only kidding), Elton John and Oprah Winfrey.

Others were a challenge, like Bill Cosby, the biggest name in TV at the time. Rather than repeating the lines as requested, he insisted on doing them his way. Like a coach, I wanted to yell, "Just run it like it's diagrammed!" but his ad-libs turned out better than the script.

Through five years of filming, my strange encounters of a sports kind ranged from a bickering couple, John McEnroe and Tatum O'Neal; a B-list actor named O. J. Simpson; the original Laker Girl, Dyan Cannon; and a smorgasbord of comedians, from Don Rickles to Garry Shandling. We even snagged Nancy Reagan, the first lady at the time, who was appearing at an antidrug rally at a Pacers game in Indiana.

But not all of our attempts were slam-dunks. My biggest disappointments were the best-known N.B.A. devotees on their respective coasts.

Woody Allen turned me down at a Knicks game, even after I repeated one of his gags about getting celebrities to do endorsements. Unimpressed, he replied, "Yes, but that was a joke." And the Big Kahuna himself, Jack Nicholson, responded to a request at a Lakers game with, "Sorry, I don't do TV."

Not so easily deterred, I answered, "But the campaign won't be complete without you."

"I know," he replied, with a rather smug grin.

The 1980s transformed professional basketball as Larry, Magic and Michael brought new energy and charisma to the game. It also marked a seminal change in marketing and promotion, with the N.B.A. positioning itself as part of the mainstream entertainment world.

With the biggest stars in the business joining in, the league and its players began working on this new crossover move, and we were just scrambling to get it all on tape.

Looking back on an era when I helped put the fans in Fan-tastic, nobody summed up those wild and crazy times better than the *Saturday Night Live* alumnus Chevy Chase.

"N.B.A. action," he said. "It's not bad."

FEB. 20, 1989

Nike Pairs Michael Jordan With a Down-to-Earth Guy

BY *THE NEW YORK TIMES*

As a comedy duo, Mike and Spike are no Laurel and Hardy. For starters, Spike Lee does all the talking, while Michael Jordan restricts his efforts to 360-degree reverse slam-dunks and other forms of basketball artistry.

But the 31-year-old filmmaker and 26-year-old athlete have formed an unorthodox and apparently successful team in an advertising campaign for Nike's $110-a-pair Air Jordan athletic shoes. The latest ads were introduced in Chicago on Friday.

Nike spent $40 million on advertising in 1988, says *Sporting Goods Business*, a trade magazine. During the year the company's market share jumped 20 percentage points, gaining ground on Reebok, the perennial market leader, according to NPD/Smart, a market research company. Nike, based in Beaverton, Ore., had sales of $1.2 billion last year while Reebok's sales were $1.79 billion.

Basketball shoes alone accounted for $213 million, largely on the popularity of the Air Jordan line. The company said Friday that it had signed the Chicago Bulls star to a contract to promote Air Jordan shoes for the rest of his professional career. A spokesman for Nike would not say how much the contract is worth, but said it is a multimillion-dollar agreement.

The Air Jordan ads are part of a campaign stressing high performance. In addition to Mr. Jordan, Nike uses Charles Barkley of the Philadelphia 76ers to promote another line of basketball shoes. The company has hired well-known directors like Mr. Lee and Leslie Dektor to direct ads in recent years.

Mr. Lee became a celebrity three years ago when his first movie, a low-budget comedy entitled *She's Gotta Have It*, was a surprise hit.

Mr. Jordan and Mr. Lee first got together in late 1987 to film two spots that were first aired during last year's National Basketball Association All-

Star Game. Following an enthusiastic response, Nike decided to bring them together again.

Filmed by the cinematographer who shot the movie, the three new ads have the same grainy black-and-white picture, choppy editing and roving camera work.

Ads for Nike's basketball shoes all have that gritty texture. "Our ads have a controversial edge," said Liz Dolan, a spokeswoman for Nike. "We're not afraid of scaring off people."

In the new ads, Mr. Lee plays his cinematic alter ego, Mars Blackmon, the star of *She's Gotta Have It*. Mars touts Air Jordans to the viewer; Mr. Jordan is seen in the background executing a sequence of preternaturally graceful moves on the court.

In one spot, titled "Can, Can't," Mr. Lee reassures the public that everyone can own a pair of Air Jordans, even if nobody can tear up the basketball court like Mr. Jordan.

In another, he complains that Nola, the beautiful heroine in *She's Gotta Have It*, is attracted to the suave Mr. Jordan rather than the nervous nonstop talker Mars. Tracy Camila John reprises her role as Nola in the film.

The ads were conceived by Wieden & Kennedy, a small agency based in Portland, Ore., that has a reputation for innovative advertising. Jim Riswold, an associate creative director at Wieden & Kennedy who wrote the ads, said he and a colleague were inspired to cast Mr. Lee and Mr. Jordan after seeing *She's Gotta Have It*.

"We saw this as a way to have fun with Michael," Mr. Riswold said. "We wanted to present the human side of him, not just the magnificent dunking machine."

For Mr. Lee, who financed his first film independently after struggling unsuccessfully for the support of a studio, the ads affirm his status as a major black artist.

Mr. Lee said he regarded Mr. Jordan's willingness to collaborate with him as a courageous move. He said successful blacks are sometimes hesistant to promote other blacks, particularly those with opinions that might be perceived as controversial.

11

Jordan Rules

I learned very early in Michael Jordan's N.B.A. career to ignore him at my own vocational risk.

On the morning of Sunday, April 20, 1986, then a reporter for the *Daily News* and with no local game to cover, I awoke with a playoff-game choice of 76ers-Washington Bullets in Philadelphia or Bulls-Celtics in Boston. Both were scheduled for 1:00 P.M. Both were Games 2 in best-of-five series. I could drive 90 minutes to Philly or take an hour's flight to Boston.

The top-seeded Celtics had won Game 1 handily and appeared to be in no danger against a Bulls team that had won 30 games while playing all but 18 games without an injured Jordan, in his second season. The 76ers, 15 regular-season games superior to the Bullets, had dropped Game 1 at home.

An upset was brewing, I figured. I chose Philly and blew it big-time.

While the 76ers won fairly routinely to even their series, I stood in the auxiliary press box of the old Spectrum, with one eye on a television, sadly watching Jordan torch the Celtics for a playoff-record 63 points. Led by Larry Bird's overshadowed 36 points, 12 rebounds and 8 assists, the Celtics eked out a double-overtime victory. No matter. This was clearly the day Jordan — hitting 22 of 41 shots and 19 of 21 free throws, while doing what he damn well pleased — announced himself as the sport's ascendant messiah.

Bird knew it too. "He is the most exciting, awesome player in the game today. I think it's just God disguised as Michael Jordan," he said afterward.

Even Pat Williams, the quick-witted 76ers' general manager who preferred watching games while pacing in the elevated press box, couldn't take his eye off the TV. When I sadly told him about my decision that morning and wondered how I would explain it to my editor, he offered no consolation.

"You effed up," he said.

OCT. 21, 1984

Jordan Makes People Wonder:
Is He the New Dr. J?

BY JANE GROSS

As the Chicago Bulls' preseason tour moved through provincial arenas in Peoria, Ill., and Glens Falls, N.Y., and metropolitan showcases like Madison Square Garden, Coach Kevin Loughery watched and waited, his gaze fixed on Michael Jordan, his enthusiasm barely contained.

During boisterous workouts, inconsequential exhibition games, hectic interview sessions and bus rides between one-night stands, the Bulls' coach studied his 21-year-old rookie, a sensation for three years at the University of North Carolina, the leader of America's gold medal Olympic basketball team and a 6-foot-6-inch aerial artist who has already pumped life into a moribund franchise.

"I don't think any player in a long time came into the league with this kind of hype," Loughery said of Jordan, who is playing three positions — lead, or point, guard, second guard and small forward. "He's got to produce immediately. It can't be down the road. The question is: Can this player do it?"

"It's generally more of a let's-wait-and-see attitude," said Rod Thorn, the Bulls' general manager. "He's been able to do it so far, but the demands will increase. I'm excited to see how he's going to evolve."

"I knew everybody's eyes would be on me," Jordan said, grinning with pride at his early success, which included an electrifying 23-point performance against the Knicks at the Garden last Thursday. "I'd been compared to Julius Erving and Jerry West, and people wanted to see for themselves. That's the way society is, but I have to draw a line between the expectations of me and what I expect for myself. I'm trying to play my natural game and I think I'm establishing myself, gaining the respect of the players. "

What Jordan has produced so far has been extraordinary and has drawn a chorus of praise from opponents and teammates. In his first six exhibition games, averaging 29.6 minutes of play, Jordan led to Bulls to a 5–1 record with 22.3 points and 5.4 rebounds per game and a total of 14 assists, 9 steals and 6 blocked shots.

Hubie Brown, the Knick coach, noted after his team's second exhibition loss to the Bulls that even against a perfect defense, Jordan's elevation and unselfish play create either a shot or a last-second pass. Bernard King, Trent Tucker and Rory Sparrow — all of whom have been matched against Jordan — agree that no single player could guard him.

The Bulls' coach and general manager are in a unique position to judge, guide and appreciate Jordan, who signed a seven-year, $6 million contract after Chicago selected him last spring with the third pick in the National Basketball Association draft. Loughery and Thorn coached the Nets in the waning days of the American Basketball Association, when Erving blossomed as a player and a personality and transformed a ragtag team into a champion.

Loughery and Thorn agree it is "heresy" and a "burden" to compare an untested rookie to a 15-year veteran like Erving, who has never played against or even met Jordan.

"It's hard in this day and age of athletics to compare anyone to Julius, on or off the court," Loughery said. "He was unbelievable for an athlete of his stature, the way he handled people and situations. No one else is even close. But Michael plays with an awful lot of charisma, and if he develops he has a chance to be one of the top-five draws in pro basketball."

Loughery, who never doubted Jordan's scoring or passing ability, compared the rookie's defense to West's in his ability to "use the angles and play guys from behind." The coach added that "Michael's honestly a better player than we thought because his ballhandling wasn't exposed in college or the Olympics. Nobody thought he was capable of playing the lead guard spot, but he is."

The Bulls' only tentative reservation is a result of the American domination in the Olympics, when a 32-point margin of victory made it unneccesary for Jordan to take charge of a game in its final seconds — the way he did as a freshman in 1982 with a 16-foot jump shot that secured North Carolina's national collegiate championship.

"A guy like Julius thrived on added pressure," said Thorn. "The more publicity he got, and the tighter the situation, the better he played. I can't say to you at this point that Michael Jordan will react to that like Julius Erving."

Jordan seems eager to try, describing his reaction to pressure with a mixture of modesty and cockiness. "I don't have the attitude of going to look for a situation to take over a game," Jordan said. "It's like a coincidence, maybe a knack I have, to always be in the right place at the right time. But I don't go hunting for it. I like it to come to me."

Jordan's high-wire act — the floating dunks and stuffs rarely seen on Bobby Knight's disciplined Olympic team — drew howls at Madison Square Garden and has drawn crowds at practice sessions. It also has had a modest effect on the advance sale of tickets in Chicago, where the rookie is the centerpiece of a newspaper and television advertising campaign.

Thorn said the Bulls would exceed last season's total of 2,500 season tickets. "He's as visible as any player in America because of the Olympics," Thorn said. "Everybody knows him, even people who don't follow pro basketball. We're trying to take advantage of that, in the best sense of the word."

While Thorn charts ticket sales, Loughery concentrates on the chemistry of his young team. "The best time for me to get a feeling for that," the coach said, "is traveling on the buses in the exhibition season and on the first West Coast swing, when you're living together for 12 days."

So far, Loughery sees several signs that Jordan will fit in. Perhaps he will even shape the Bulls in his image.

First was the challenge of impressing skeptical teammates. "That he's overcome with ability," the coach said. Second was seeing if Jordan held himself aloof from lesser players. "That he's handled with personality," Loughery added. Third was watching whether Jordan labored in practice or relied on superior skills. "He's all you could ask for," Loughery noted.

"I don't want to overshadow anyone," Jordan said.

It is that attitude, honed by Dean Smith in three years at North Carolina and Knight in one summer at the Olympics, that the Bulls hope Jordan will translate into leadership comparable to Erving's or West's. "If you know a person's background and his established patterns of behavior," Thorn said, "chances are that's the way they will be, but not always. When guys get into pro ball, with the huge money and the idle time, sometimes they change. They have to have character and they have to have their priorities in order."

Coaches like Smith and Knight, in varying degrees, suppress the natural bravado of players like Jordan, but in the pros, with an easygoing coach like Loughery, Jordan's personality is flowering. Asked to compare himself physically to Erving, Jordan deadpanned: "Dr. J has lived his time."

Asked how he would play defense against himself on a fast break, he boasted: "If I had a full head of steam, I'd get out of my way."

Asked if he were giving his teammates dunking lessons, he singled out Orlando Woolridge and replied: "Orlando's the king on this team, but he wants to pay me to teach him".

Jordan's controversial basketball shoes are a more visible sign that he is no introvert: black leather ones with red trim, three-quarters high, that were designed for him by Nike. So far, the Bulls insist he must wear standard white shoes, but Jordan aims to change their mind. "Hopefully little kids will pick up on them," said Jordan, who has an unusual royalty clause in his six-figure contract with Nike.

Jordan's gentler side emerges when he is asked if he sees himself in Erving's mold as a man of grace and poise. "Sometimes I wonder," he said softly. "I'd love to be what he is. Those are the same goals I have — I never want to forget where I came from — and I think I do have the same personality in that sense."

Such unassuming sincerity provokes secret smiles from Loughery, who has watched from a distance in recent weeks as Jordan conducted repetitious interviews. The coach noted that it would have been easy for Jordan to treat reporters shabbily in places like Peoria and Glens Falls, knowing that he probably would never encounter them again.

"I wanted to watch him for a month before I sat down to explain it to him," the coach said, "but I don't think it will be necessary. I think he understands it; I really do."

When Loughery's words were repeated to Jordan, he ducked his head shyly. "They've experienced it more than I have," he said, drawing Thorn into the conversation. "Anything they say or do is a big asset for me. In return, I'll do the best I can every time I take the court and try to be the basketball player and person they expect me to be."

MAY 27, 1993

Jordan's Atlantic City Caper

BY DAVE ANDERSON

Michael Jordan turned the Knicks' home-court advantage into the Knicks' home-casino advantage.

Monday evening and early Tuesday morning, in the hours when Jordan's time might have been better spent resting for the second game of the Eastern Conference final between the Bulls and the Knicks, he was sighted by hotel guests in the baccarat pit in Bally's Grand casino in Atlantic City.

After practice on Monday, he checked into Bally's Grand at 5:07 that afternoon according to a hotel employee, checked out at 11:05 P.M., was seen in the casino as late as 2:30 A.M., returned to New York and was on the Garden court for a midmorning shootaround, 10 hours before Tuesday night's game.

"You weren't taking golf lessons in Atlantic City, Michael," one Knick rooter yelled as the Knicks took a 2–0 lead.

"How's the wrist after the slots, Michael?" another shouted, referring to the brace on Jordan's damaged right wrist.

Jordan reportedly lost $5,000 playing blackjack in a private area in the baccarat pit, but that's not the issue. If he had won $5,000, it still wouldn't justify his being a two-hour limo ride from the Bulls' Midtown New York hotel at 2:30 the morning of a big game.

The issue is that arguably the best player in basketball history owes his teammates and coaches more dedication to what Jordan has called his "driving force" — the Bulls' opportunity for their third consecutive National Basketball Association championship.

If the Bulls are to win that third title, Michael Jordan must be what he is: basketball's Superman, larger than life and lighter than air.

In the box score Tuesday night Jordan justified his reputation, scoring 36 points in the Bulls' 96–91 loss.

But with more rest, might he have scored 46 points? With more rest, might he have scored more than 11 points in the second half, especially in the final minutes when the Bulls needed every basket? His teammates and his coaches will always wonder.

Jordan's shot also appeared tired in the final minutes of the Bulls' 98–90 loss Sunday afternoon, when he scored "only" 25 points, missing 17 of his 27 field-goal attempts.

Jordan is now 30 years old, and his shot should be tired.

Over the last 20 months he has been playing basketball virtually nonstop: the 1991–92 season and playoffs, the Olympic Dream Team campaign, a few weeks off, then the recent 82-game season and the current playoffs.

Jordan also has been bothered by a sprained ankle and a sprained wrist suffered during the earlier playoff rounds.

All the more reason not to wander down to Atlantic City the night before a game that, had the Bulls won it, would have snatched the home-court advantage from the Knicks in the four-of-seven-game series that resumes in Chicago on Saturday afternoon and Monday afternoon.

Apologists for the N.B.A. lifestyle argue that players are accustomed to staying up until the early hours, then sleeping late or taking a nap after the shootaround. Some N.B.A. players enjoy frequenting the Atlantic City casinos when their teams visit Philadelphia for a game.

But that doesn't prevent fans from wondering about Jordan's devotion to duty when he's sighted in a casino two hours away from his hotel at 2:30 in the morning of a playoff game.

Gambling attracts Jordan, often seen in the Monte Carlo casino in Monaco when the Dream Team was practicing there last summer before the Olympics in Barcelona, Spain.

Last year the N.B.A. called Jordan on the carpet after checks totaling $108,000 and another check for $57,000 were either signed by him or drawn on an account used by his ProServ management firm to pay high-stakes golf and poker debts in North Carolina. Commissioner David Stern found no cause for disciplinary action.

Jordan's visit to Atlantic City doesn't call for N.B.A. discipline. He's free to gamble in a legal casino, as he did in Monte Carlo. But his timing, usually so exquisite on a basketball court, was his mistake.

With the series in Chicago over the weekend, there are no nearby casinos to tempt Jordan, although there's always the chance of a back-room poker game somewhere. But unless the Knicks sweep both games in Chicago Stadium, the series will return to the Garden for next Wedneday's fifth game.

When the Bulls arrive at their Midtown hotel Tuesday, the Knicks should have a limo waiting for Michael Jordan at curbside.

There's nothing like the home-casino advantage.

— POSTSCRIPT —

DAVE ANDERSON, 2018: "Sometimes a story develops right out of thin air. I was covering the Knicks-Bulls game at the Garden, sitting behind the baseline, hearing a couple of fans yelling at Jordan — 'How's the wrist after the slots?' — about being out late the previous night in Atlantic City. It probably wouldn't have been a big deal if the Bulls had won the game, but they didn't. Jordan looked tired by the end, didn't shoot well either. Having covered a lot of boxing in Atlantic City, I called around the next day and found out that he had been at Bally's casino until after 2:00 in the morning. I heard some other details, how much he'd lost playing blackjack, and thought it was fair to question his priorities in a column. He boycotted the media for the rest of the series, the Bulls came back to win four straight, and there were people in New York who blamed me and *The Times* for ruining what they thought was the Knicks' best chance to beat Jordan in the playoffs."

A Legacy as Jordan Departs: Stars Are Corporate Heroes

BY HARVEY ARATON

Magic Johnson once told of how he tried, early in his career, to persuade the sneaker company he had a contract with to market a basketball shoe in his very famous name. He said he was told by a company official, with all due respect, that "no basketball player could ever sell a shoe."

"And then," said Johnson, "along came Michael."

Along came Michael Jordan, soaring to uncharted levels, on the court and off.

Enduring Images

At the news conference yesterday to announce what will one day be remembered either as Jordan's stunning retirement or an indefinite sabbatical from the Chicago Bulls, he was asked what he wanted his legacy to be. Although he offered a polite cliché about having always played the game "110 percent," it was a truly pointless question because Jordan, while usually articulate, has never been about words.

His career has been measured in powerful visuals, from a 17-foot jump shot that was worth a collegiate championship to an impossible contortion of his body in midair on the way to his first of three pro titles. From tongue wag to slam-dunk, from a comfortable pair of baggy shorts to his likeness appearing on T-shirts worldwide, Michael Jordan set professional standards and social trends. Though there is no one close to being as good as he is, he leaves the National Basketball Association, at least for now, with many who are nearly as leveraged.

He leaves behind a new breed of American team-sports athlete, the one-man corporate powerhouse. He leaves behind ballplayers from the boardroom, players like Alonzo Mourning, who worked first for Nike and then for the

Charlotte Hornets, and Shaquille O'Neal, who belongs to Pepsi at least as much as he does to the N.B.A. This all began the day Jordan sat down to negotiate an endorsement deal for one rather ugly, overpriced shoe.

There was almost a corporate-speak approach to yesterday's news conference at the Bulls' practice facility outside Chicago, as if Jordan was announcing that recent sales trends left him no choice but to shut the home office down. Few tears, if any, were cried — by Jordan or anyone. Naturally, David Stern, the N.B.A.'s empire-building commissioner, assured the paying public that "the season will still open on Nov. 5."

That's not to say basketball won't terribly miss this American and world icon. It is just going to be different than it was with the departures of Magic Johnson and Larry Bird. The basketball world was deeply in love with Johnson and Bird, and when they retired one year apart, it was as if they were dearly departing family members. For Jordan, there is more absolute awe than there is unbridled affection. The Bulls without him will feel as if they've suddenly lost a miracle invention, the computer chip, something they're not certain they can do without.

A Troubling Element

Jordan preferred it this way. He is nothing like Magic, who is attracted to attention like a moth to light. Jordan reiterated yesterday that he never wanted to be N.B.A. "ambassador." He was his own business entity, his personal interests vigorously pursued by influential lobbyists like Nike and his entrenched superagent, David Falk.

In forcing greedy owners to share the enormous profits derived from the burgeoning business of merchandising, it was a noble cause for team-sports labor that, unfortunately, was carried to selfish and self-righteous extremes. For even as Jordan was saying goodbye, his bitterness over his name being dragged through gambling headlines was obvious. He kept referring to the news media as "you guys," you problem makers, as if the news media had dug up Slim Bouler and Richard Esquinas and every other controversy that dogged Jordan the last two years.

That's the troubling part of the Jordan legacy, his lack of public acknowledgement that the persona he marketed so brilliantly, so lucratively, did not come with responsibility, with accountability. If the boardroom ballplayers he is leaving behind think all they must do to reap consumer millions is to be on time for the commercial shoot, then Jordan's legacy is partly sour.

There was yesterday a martyr quality to him that will leave many people thinking so-called intrusions into his personal life drove him out. That's silly, and unfair, and, besides, he insisted he just had nothing left to prove. Right now, that makes all the sense in the world. The thought of training camp followed by six grueling months of jockeying for playoff post position had to seem overwhelmingly trite two months after his father was murdered, and three months after he claimed the third straight championship that the dominant 1980s teams failed to win.

A fourth would be just another number in the record book. What might motivate Michael Jordan to return? Perhaps history noting that he not only controlled his opponents and his likeness but his career clock as well. A championship following a year or two of R & R will eventually seem like a challenge worth the effort.

Magic Johnson, remember, wanted to try it first.

12
Sweet Dreams

David Stern will go to his grave insisting that it wasn't his idea — or anyone else in the league's hierarchy — to have N.B.A. players invade the 1992 Olympics. The scheme, he claimed, was posited by Boris Stankovic, his international governing body counterpart.

"It was never about winning the gold medal; it was about Boris Stankovic and FIBA wanting to grow the game on an international level and believing that the best way to do it was to have us involved on the Olympic and world championship level," Stern told me for a column I was writing on the explosion of foreign journalists covering the 2012 finals.

Running contrary to Stern's claim is that by the time of the Barcelona Summer Games, the N.B.A. was five years into its global outreach via the annual McDonald's Open preseason tournament, matching one of its teams with several from Europe.

Whoever's brainstorm it was, the one (and only) Dream Team has been immortalized in memory, book and film, though its debut was not the glitch-free festival of shoe company pitchmen it is typically remembered as.

For starters, Isiah Thomas was outrageously left off the roster, owing to the fraternal squabbling that traced to his feud with Michael Jordan. The United States Olympic Committee winced at the team's luxury hotel accommodations, among other allowances ("jealous of the attention," Stankovic said of all critics). It didn't help that Charles Barkley dug an elbow into the chest of a skinny forward from war-torn Angola — whose favorite player happened to Barkley — in the Olympic opener and explained, "It's a ghetto thing."

In the final analysis, the Olympics had long made a sham of its amateur mandate, the Dream Team was a concept whose time had come and the poundings it inflicted on opponents were taken as badges of honor, learning experiences.

A grand time was had by all, especially the Croatian and Lithuanian teams, whose silver and bronze medal showings were authentic and heartwarming celebrations of national pride after gaining independence from the unraveling Yugoslavia and Soviet Union, reflective of a changing world eager to embrace a truly American game.

JULY 1, 1992

Ex-Soviet Coach
Saw Sport's Future in 1956

BY HARVEY ARATON

PORTLAND, Ore. — "Let me show you how we beat John Thompson's press," said the old Russian coach, who now makes his home in San Diego. He reached across the table in the hotel lounge for a reporter's notebook and pen.

Four years after achieving his lifelong dream, a gold medal in Olympic basketball, after being tossed triumphantly into the air like a beach ball by his players, 64-year-old Aleksandr Gomelski happily diagrammed the intricate series of screens and options he devised for Sarunas Marciulionis, Arvidas Sabonis, Titt Sokk, Sasha Volkov and the rest of the players he still endearingly calls "my boys."

Early in those Summer Olympics in Seoul, South Korea, Gomelski and his players watched the Thompson-coached United States collegians press some third-world basketball team right out of the gymnasium.

"The boys not believe they can win against this press," Gomelski's assistant told him.

"I say, 'Boys, we win against the Atlanta Hawks in Moscow,'" Gomelski said. "'We win against some of the great American colleges. I believe you win against the press.'"

Every practice session in Seoul, what would be the last Olympic basketball team from the Soviet Union worked on nothing else. By the semifinals, when the teams finally met, the Soviets had thoroughly incorporated this strategy, the result being a barrage of uncontested shots and a defeat so embarrassing to the American basketball establishment that it finally called out to its soldiers of fortune from the National Basketball Association.

Here, at the Tournament of the Americas, the United States has begun the mission to reassert its pre-eminence, and, if Karl Malone and Charles

Barkley have their way, reform all remaining socialist nations. Winning the gold medal in Barcelona, Spain, will not be enough for the U.S. of N.B.A. The job this summer is to crush all means of opposition, hoist the flag, lift the television ratings and carry on the global expansion of the N.B.A.

It is a demonstration of United States imperialism and crass commercialism that is likely to have Marx and Lenin doing 360s in their graves. But, let's face it, the Olympics as amateur competition is just as dead, and the bottom line is that the rest of the world seems as happy about it as the most passionate collector of official Dream Team trading cards.

Or as Marcel de Souza said after his jump shot gave Brazil a narrow victory over Mexico on the very day he had purchased a pair of Air Jordans from the local Nike outlet: "Maybe it was the shoes."

Everyone here seems to have a reason to appreciate the presence of the N.B.A., and Gomelski is no different.

"It is," he said, "the best thing for basketball all over the world."

The lesson to be learned is the lesson Gomelski learned in 1956, his first year as the Olympic head coach of the Soviet Union, the year he looked into the future of the game.

The world had never seen anything like Bill Russell, who, with K. C. Jones, led the United States to a succession of dreadful blowouts, including the most lopsided United States Olympic victory ever, 101–29 over Thailand. By the time Russell and Company got around to Gomelski's team, the Soviets were in awe and grateful to merely be beaten by 35 points.

"They press, and Russell stand in the back," said Gomelski. "We cannot compete. But we start to learn."

Sixteen years later in Munich, the Soviets won the gold medal in a disputed 1-point victory over the United States. To Gomelski, the decision being tainted by the infamous replaying of the final three seconds was not the point as much as it was the fact that the Soviets could at last compete. To Gomelski, it did not even matter much that he was not in attendance; his visa and his job had been revoked for losing a competition to Yugoslavia the previous year.

"Our old system," he sighed. "Not good."

Actually, he found a beautiful symmetry to his winning the gold and calling it a career as the Soviet coach by dismantling John Thompson's press, 32 years after Russell. Eight months ago, Gomelski joined one of his three sons, who lived in Chicago, before relocating to San Diego, where he is assembling a team of Russians and Americans to tour.

He is an unabashed fan of the N.B.A., calling it "the best business in America," and now the rest of the world can see, up close and personal, how it works. Someday, in Russia, he hopes professional basketball will flourish.

For now, he is prepared to watch his old players get walloped. His gold-medal team from 1988, he believes, was good enough to compete with the United States team he has come here this week to behold. "But they are four teams now," he said, alluding to their dispersal among the three Baltic states and the Commonwealth of Independent States.

There's a new basketball world order, Gomelski acknowledged, and no turning back.

"The president of my federation calls last week," said Gomelski. "He says, 'We have problems, come back and coach team.'

"I say, 'How much you pay?'

"He say, 'No money. You are a patriot.'

"I say, 'No thanks.'"

AUG. 9, 1992

Dream Team Justified More Dreams

BY GEORGE VECSEY

BADALONA, Spain — There were many dreams in the arena. There was Magic Johnson's dream to play again, to slip a pass to a teammate, to hear the crowd roar. There was the dream of Croatia and Lithuania to compete in the Summer Games, to show the world they exist.

Even cranks like me, who have brooded about bringing hard-bitten millionaire professionals into the formerly amateur Olympics, should be able to see that the Dream Team justified the dreams. There was, however, no dream of Croatia beating the United States in basketball, certainly not in the 20th century, and who knows about the 21st?

As Scottie Pippen put it: "I don't think they could ever beat us. When they get better, we'll get better. We are totally stacked."

Even when Croatia went ahead, 25–23, on a thundering dunk and a foul shot by the intimidator, Franjo Arapovic himself, the Croats knew they were playing the Dream Team.

"Up by 25–23, I was hoping we could get close, stay within 6, 8, 10 at halftime," said the ultimate realist, Drazen Petrovic, after Croatia had lost respectably, 117–85, to the 12 best players we may ever see on one team at one time.

The professionals on Lithuania, with their tie-dyed Grateful Dead outfits and their bronze medal, and the professionals on Croatia, with their silver medal, were proud to be on the same medal stand with the Dream Team.

I used to say there was such a thing called The Magic Line, that some of my favorite athletes like Boris Becker and Steffi Graf and Magic Johnson just did not belong with the canoeists and the kayakers.

Philosophically, I still believe that, but there are worse things about the Summer Games than a photo opportunity with Magic Johnson. The whole Olympic movement has been bought up by multinational corporations, with ugly yellow candy stands and gaudy soda umbrellas all over this otherwise distinguished city. The American players schemed to hide the trademarks of rival manufacturers.

But I have heard of little children in the United States and a hundred other countries who want Dream Team T-shirts, who instinctively understand the meaning of dreams coming true.

It takes childlike awe to appreciate Magic passing to Michael Jordan, with Larry Bird open in the corner, and Charles Barkley menacing from the wing, and David Robinson lurking near the basket. What if the frog turned into a prince?

Who am I to tell proud European professionals like Sarunas Marciulionis of Lithuania and Drazen Petrovic of Croatia, who have lived through shifting borders, oppression, revolt, bloodshed in the streets, that they should feel cheapened by the presence of 12 great colleagues? Three of the Lithuanian players had been stars of the 1988 gold medal team of the Soviet Union, when it was convenient to forget they spoke a different language, considered themselves a captive nation. The Lithuanians' 51-point margin of defeat to the United States on Thursday was an honor, like a fencing scar in the old university days at Heidelberg.

Arturas Karnishovas, a bubbly 21-year-old from Lithuania and Seton Hall University, plays in the Big East Conference, where they knock you down, step on your face, slander your name all over the place, and then call a foul on you for cluttering up the floor with your broken body.

"Karl Malone pushed me across the court like I wasn't there," Karnishovas said with a laugh on Thursday. "My coach said, 'You look like a girl.' I said, 'There's a lot of guys he pushes around like that.'"

They were all pushed around. Petrovic, a pretty good guard in the National Basketball Association, said it would take "maybe 15 to 20 years for European basketball to improve." But he saw his teammates come out "ready to play tonight" after the Croats had seemed in awe on the first meeting. And they cut the losing margin from 33 all the way to 32.

The wisest professionals were still in awe. Rimas Kurtinaitis, one of the Lithuanian stars, said: "We could play them 10 more games and have no chance to win. But we have more chance to cut 40 points difference to 20 points."

How does Kurtinaitis know there is not a young player back home in Lithuania who may be dreaming of being the next Michael Jordan?

"We don't have players like Michael Jordan," Kurtinaitis said. "He is fantastic player."

They are all fantastic players. That was the dream. For a few weeks, this team existed. We saw how it could totally dominate European stars without embarrassing them. It was a noble experiment, and it worked. It worked.

13

Goodbye to the Greats

Those of us who covered the Dream Team pretty much knew that Larry Bird couldn't play anymore. His degenerative back couldn't withstand the rigors of an N.B.A. season and it had taken Magic Johnson, his partner in primacy, to talk him into extending what turned out to be his final season into the Barcelona Olympics.

"I've been retired four years, only nobody knows it yet," a typically deadpan Bird cracked at the outset of the Games. His retirement announcement came about a week after the gold-medal ceremony and there would be no talking him out of it.

Magic had played only in the All-Star Game and the Olympics after testing positive for H.I.V., the virus that causes AIDS, in November 1991. His announcement shook the world, reduced tough hombres like Bird and Pat Riley, then coaching the Knicks, to tears. But as Magic's joy of sharing the ball in Barcelona abounded, people close to him began whispering that he was plotting a way back to the Lakers, perhaps with a reduced regular-season schedule of 60 games.

"They never had dealt with a big, strong athlete like me before," Magic said of the doctors who had advised him to quit as a precautionary measure but were rethinking their advice.

Unbeknown to him, his comeback announcement troubled many players, whose understanding of the risks of AIDS transmission was less than enlightened. Magic aborted the plan when he learned of the brewing tensions that erupted in my *Times* story, starring Karl Malone.

Magic did return for only a 32-game cameo in January 1996, leaving me with one sweet memory.

In his first game back against the Warriors, Magic missed one of his trademark shot-put jumpers but got the ball back when a long rebound was tapped to him by Vlade Divac. With his path to the basket impeded by a young Latrell Sprewell, Magic faked a shovel pass right. When Sprewell nearly lunged out of his sneakers toward a vacant baseline, Magic proceeded to the basket for a layup, eschewing a dunk and the video-game theatrics that would enhance or afflict the game, depending on one's point of view.

For Magic — and Bird as well — it was a reminder of their generational genius, a fundamental simplicity, the essential foundation of their showmanship.

Nov. 1, 1992

Johnson's Return to the League Isn't Welcomed by Some

BY HARVEY ARATON

Karl Malone, known around the National Basketball Association as the Mailman, delivered a strong message last week, challenging the accepted belief that Magic Johnson has been universally welcomed back to the league even though he has the virus that causes AIDS.

"Look at this, scabs and cuts all over me," Malone, the Utah Jazz All-Star forward, said last Tuesday night in the visitors' locker room at Madison Square Garden before a preseason game against the Knicks.

He pressed a finger to a small, pinkish hole on his thigh that was developing into a scab. "I get these every night, every game," he said. "They can't tell you that you're not at risk, and you can't tell me there's one guy in the N.B.A. who hasn't thought about it."

Gerald Wilkins, the former Knick who is now with the Cleveland Cavaliers, said: "Everybody's talking about it. Some people are scared. This could be dangerous to us all, but you're dealing with Magic Johnson, so people are handling it with white gloves. They're not going to say how they really feel."

But the outspoken Malone, who was one of Johnson's teammates on the United States Olympic team last summer, said Johnson's standing as one of basketball's great players should not prevent other players from voicing objections or concern.

"Just because he came back doesn't mean nothing to me," said Malone. "I'm no fan, no cheerleader. It may be good for basketball, but you have to look far beyond that. You have a lot of young men who have a long life ahead of them. The Dream Team was a concept everybody loved. But now we're back to reality."

Perhaps a majority of players and officials, including most of Johnson's Olympic teammates and his teammates with the Los Angeles Lakers, have publicly supported the enormously popular and respected Johnson. "I was with him all summer and never once thought about it," said the Phoenix Suns' Charles Barkley. "Never. Never. Never."

But others, some of whom requested anonymity, expressed emotions ranging from concern to fear of playing against Johnson in the physical and occasionally brutal N.B.A. regular season, which begins Friday night.

"I hear people saying, 'You got to guard him,'" said Malone's Utah teammate Jeff Malone, to whom Karl is not related. "There's concern, no doubt."

One prominent Western Conference guard said he could imagine himself "backing off" defending Johnson, which raises the question of the game's legitimacy, no doubt a serious problem for the league.

And one general manager, who asked that his name not be used, suggested that Johnson step aside, as the league and players would have to enter uncharted legal waters if they ever came to forcing the issue.

Tate George, the reserve Nets guard who has the same agent as Johnson, Lon Rosen, argued that the N.B.A. and its players ought to seek a higher plane than what he considers mostly baseless fear.

"This is historic what he's doing and we're all part of it," said George. "People ought to be proud for the opportunity to play against him."

The 33-year-old Johnson has said that he is returning to the Lakers as a player to make a statement for all people infected with H.I.V., the virus that causes AIDS. "The doctors have said there is no chance of me giving it to anyone," he said. "So there is no risk."

Other than a statement welcoming Johnson's return, the N.B.A. commissioner, David Stern, has avoided public comment on this issue. Efforts to reach him were fruitless.

The league, under advice by Dr. David Rogers of Cornell University, has implemented several precautionary measures on AIDS since Johnson's shocking announcement Nov. 7, 1991, that he had tested positive for H.I.V. He retired immediately from the Lakers, but played in the N.B.A. All-Star Game last February and the Olympics last summer in Barcelona, Spain, before rejoining the Lakers for their preseason training camp in October.

Among the precautionary measures is the rule that players who get cut during a game must immediately leave the court. Trainers have been instructed to wear latex gloves while treating players, and they must separately handle players' sanitary towels and other items.

In addition, the N.B.A. Players Association has developed its own health-education program in conjunction with Dr. Michael P. Johnson at Johns Hopkins University. A brochure circulated to every N.B.A. player states that H.I.V. "is not spread through contact during sports activities."

In a telephone interview, Dr. Johnson added: "The questions come up, 'What about playing with Magic? What if I'm cut and he's cut?' There is a theoretical possibility of that happening, but if there is a risk, it's incredibly low. But when it gets into the concept of zero risk, there is no such thing — for anything."

Most players understand that. As several said, "It may be a million to 1." But there is a palpable fear of being that unlucky one which, for some, obfuscates the medical world's statistical and logical assurances. The emotional perception of a player and his family members creates a distorted sense of risk and fear.

Chris Dudley, the Nets' reserve center, said that when Johnson announced his comeback, Dudley's father called from California.

"He said, 'I don't know if I want you playing against him,'" said Dudley. "He said, 'What if you get cut?'"

"Risk is risk," said Phoenix Suns General Manager Jerry Colangelo, who added that while he has special feelings for Johnson, he is troubled by the unanswered questions about the comeback. "I have a son-in-law who does surgery every day, and he wears gloves, goggles, masks and lives in mortal fear."

A second general manager who requested anonymity said: "A lot of guys won't say it, but their wives and girlfriends are concerned. Guys get teeth marks on their heads and arms all the time. They bleed. Doctors say there is no risk, but they don't really know."

Knicks Given as Example

"Look at how physical the Knicks play," Karl Malone added, referring to New York's reputation for intimidating defense. "Ask them what they think. If they're honest, they've got to say they're concerned."

But Doc Rivers, one of about 30 pro players who scrimmaged with Johnson in Los Angeles throughout September, insisted there was no problem last summer and there will be none, as far as he's concerned, this season.

"If I thought there was a threat, I wouldn't be out there," said Rivers, who was recently traded to the Knicks from the Clippers. "And we're going to play the same. If Magic comes down the lane and needs to be knocked down, then he'll be knocked down. If Magic thought that anyone had to alter their game to play against him, then he wouldn't play."

Karl Malone said that he could envision, in the final seconds of a 1-point game, Magic coming down the lane and himself stepping up to defend. But how aggressively?

"I can say, speaking for myself, that my competitive instincts will take over and I'll worry about the possible consequences later," Malone said. "But I can't speak for everyone in this room. That concerns me because I'm only here to win."

There is a belief among some that any other player, with the exception of Michael Jordan, would not have been welcomed back at all. "No way," said Detroit Pistons player representative, Darrell Walker.

In Colangelo's opinion, it is the dissenting players and no one else who might influence where this issue goes, if anywhere. "The only people who might have impact on Magic are the players," he said.

The players who object to Johnson playing, or are merely concerned, don't see it that way. When Magic Johnson comes rushing downcourt on the fast break at them, they see the tide of worldwide popularity. They see a player, as Wilkins put it, who is "holding all the cards."

— POSTSCRIPT —

HARVEY ARATON, 2018: "I walked into the visitors' locker room at Madison Square Garden early one evening in late October 1992 before a Knicks-Jazz preseason game, and found Karl Malone there by himself. He greeted me warmly, apparently recognizing me from my many weeks around the Dream Team that summer. I explained that I was preparing a story on Magic's return — like every other national N.B.A. reporter. I thought the interview would be routine, positive, until Malone steered it far off its intended course by saying, 'Look at this, scabs and cuts all over me.' The reporting took off from there and my story ran in *The Times* the following Sunday, one day after Magic was captured by a photographer being treated for a small cut during a preseason game by a gloveless Lakers trainer, Gary Vitti. Bolts of lightning burst through the clouds hovering over the sport. Magic aborted his comeback the day after the story ran, leaving me with some sadness for a player I truly admired. Not long after that, I had a chance to speak with him about it. 'You were just doing your job,' he told me. Class."

FEB. 5, 1993

A Worthy Bird Has an Unlikely Night

BY HARVEY ARATON

BOSTON — Rather than a laser show, Larry Bird surely would've preferred to have manufactured a few lightning bolts of his own from behind the 3-point line. He would've wanted high-fives from sweaty men in shorts, not handshakes from well-groomed gents in Celtic warmup suits. He would've liked to have dressed down a defender or two, not address thousands in the stands who wouldn't dare talk trash.

His choice would have been to go out with a spontaneous performance on the parquet floor, not in a planned extravaganza on a stage about six feet above it. But his back still hurts, and Larry Bird Night was an inevitability, one way or another.

About the only parts of tonight's celebration at Boston Garden that anyone could be sure Bird enjoyed were seeing old teammates like Cedric Maxwell and Rick Robey, sharing the stage in rousing moments with Magic Johnson and the rising to the rafters of his Celtics jersey, No. 33.

Motivation from History

Throughout his remarkable 13-year Celtics career, Bird had this habit of focusing during national anthems on retired jerseys, especially the No. 4 of the Bruins' hockey legend, Bobby Orr. Bird drew motivation from the building's history. It was as if, right from the start in 1979, he understood that even the great ones were hopelessly transient, but up in those rafters was where his star would forever shine.

Boston being provincial Boston, the Celtics being the 16-championship-banner Celtics, and Bird being one of the best to ever play the game, naturally the whole production was destined to get not only out of hand but completely out of character.

What made Bird in Boston the perfect fit was that he was the sharpshooting country hick in baggy jeans and flannel shirt headlining an arena known for dressing down, from quaint to ratty. No mascots here, no cheerleaders, no clattering infoboards with video screens commanding the fans to make some noise. Yet tonight, Boston, the Celtics and the National Basketball Association celebrated Bird's career for two solid, high-tech hours, NBC's Bob Costas signing on as host at 7:37 P.M. and Bird bidding the fans farewell at 10:02.

Time of show: 2 hours 25 minutes, or about what it once took Bird to get, oh, 38 points, 16 rebounds and 12 assists on an exhausting Garden playoff night.

"Small Town"

Only for Bird would Boston Garden be darkened, as if for a concert, as the fans strolled in, John Mellencamp's rock version of "Small Town" crashing off the yellow painted posts. Kevin McHale, noting that things might be different when the time comes for him and the venerable Robert Parish to say goodbye, quipped, "I told Robert that we'll probably get a 20-second timeout."

Not one but four video screens showed highlights of Bird's career, while the ubiquitous sports artist LeRoy Neiman contributed a still life. Bird's family members took a bow, including his mother, Georgia. Best wishes on video from stars around the N.B.A. were shown, from Michael Jordan to Patrick Ewing to Charles Barkley, who had the good sense to tell Bird, "Thank you for all the money."

Celtics past and present climbed the stage, including most of the three championship teams from 1981, 1984 and 1986. Maxwell, who had not been here to visit since a bitter departure in 1985 and has all but been written out of Celtics history by the team's general and grudgeholder, Red Auerbach, was back in town.

"I've never been one to fight city hall, and Larry is city hall," Maxwell said, adding that he, more than anyone, got a sneak preview of how good Bird was going to be that first training camp in 1979. Said Maxwell, "All I remember are those 20-footers raining down on me, and saying, 'Oh, this white guy really can play.'"

A Voice of Reason

Though Bird continues to live in town and collect a Celtics paycheck as a junior member of the team's front office, he had no comment on his night in the days leading in. Once upon a time, he was a silent Indiana State Sycamore. Over the years, as he and Magic and later Jordan drove the N.B.A. to unimagined heights, Bird became a wry voice of reason, with a knack for quickly making his point.

Tonight, Costas set him up for a slam-dunk by saying this was a perfect night even though Bill Laimbeer couldn't attend.

Bird shot back: "We'd probably hang him up there with my jersey."

Larry Bird was made into a lot of things by people who saw him as the torch carrier for his race in a sport dominated by blacks, but he was always his own independent man. A year ago this month, he ignored team orders to rest his back and not attend the retiring of Magic's No. 32 in Los Angeles. Tonight, Bird and Magic hugged tight, with eyes misty all around.

Larry asked Magic: "You're not coming back, are you?"

Magic: "Noooo."

Larry: "Then will you get the hell out of my dreams?"

That said, they exchanged Olympic diamond commemorative rings and vowed they would be forever linked, that theirs had been a great ride, and what a way to have gone out, with the Dream Team last summer in Barcelona, Spain.

David Stern, the N.B.A. commissioner, reminded them they could share another stage, when they go together to the Basketball Hall of Fame. "Five years from Monday," said Stern.

Now that was something for Bird to look forward to, so he said, "Tonight, I leave basketball forever." There were boos. "Sorry," he said, emotionless, "I'm gone."

14

Second Coming

With a two-word declaration — "I'm Back" — that was devised for social media that did not yet exist, Michael Jordan returned from a season-and-a-half sabbatical to a so-called Bulls supporting cast that hadn't quite collapsed without him.

Sans Michael, the 1993–94 Bulls won a robust 55 games while executing Phil Jackson's (or Tex Winter's) triangle to near perfection. It took an at-best questionable call by Hue Hollins on Scottie Pippen in Game 5 of the Eastern Conference semifinals to swing the series in the Knicks' favor and keep the Bulls out of the conference finals against an Indiana team they'd beaten four of five times in the regular season.

I always wondered how Jordan's legacy might have been altered had the Bulls even made the finals against a dominant Hakeem Olajuwon and the Rockets — an intriguing but ultimately irrelevant question. As great a disrupter as Pippen was, he wasn't a closer, and when Horace Grant defected to Orlando that summer, Jordan returned as much the savior he'd left, no matter the rust-shedding 7-for-28 shooting in an overtime defeat at Indiana.

He debuted at United Center, which had opened upon his departure, on a Friday night, March 24, against Grant and the Magic. The Bulls lost a 106–99 decision, previewing their playoff fate against Shaquille O'Neal and Penny Hardaway, a second-round series in which Jordan struggled and shed the jersey he'd worn upon his return, No. 45, while calculatingly setting off a buying frenzy.

Not everywhere, thankfully.

As I wrote after visiting a Michigan Avenue sportswear store while in Chicago for a Knicks game about three weeks into Jordan's second coming: "My poor 5-year-old at home still has No. 23 stitched onto his jersey, front and back. There has been no rush to the mall, no unconditional surrender to that marketing autocracy, the Republic of Jordan. We are holdouts, a traditionalist, skeptical and 45-less household."

No. 45 did become something of a collector's item, like a can of New Coke.

MARCH 29, 1995

Jordan Hits Garden at Cruising Speed: 55

BY IRA BERKOW

People were scouring the record books to find out when anyone had done in Madison Square Garden what Michael Jordan had done last night against the Knicks. Like most points in a half, or most points in a game, or most points in…. They were looking in the wrong place.

You don't find what Jordan did in the game in the record books. You check memories, like the time in the Garden that Ol' Blue Eyes had the joint swinging, or the Stones had it rocking, or Gunther Gebel-Williams tamed his lions and mesmerized the crowd, or the first Ali-Frazier fight.

The hype for this game was similar to that for the previous four Jordan had played in since he returned 10 days ago from his prodigal stint as a minor league fly chaser in the White Sox organization. That is, Michael Miracle is back. Over all, though, he had been simply a miracle waiting to happen.

Last night, it happened.

The World's Greatest Hoopster scored 55 points, including a jump shot to put the Bulls ahead by 2 with 25 seconds left in the fourth quarter. And then, with the game tied, and with 3.1 seconds left, he went up for the shot that everyone knew he'd take and, with Knicks lunging after him, he passed to Bill Wennington under the basket for the stuff that won it for the Bulls, 113–111.

The game opened about as spectacularly as it ended. Jordan hit a jump shot from the left to start the scoring. The next time down he hit a jump shot from the top of the key. He missed his next shot and then flew down the baseline and laid in the ball. He hit six of his first seven shots before Phil Jackson, the Bulls' coach, removed his shooting star, presumably for a rest. But perhaps he was taking pity on John Starks and Anthony Bonner and Derek Harper and Greg Anthony who, individually and en masse, were taking futile turns trying to guard Jordan.

Jordan returned and wound up with 20 points in the first quarter. At this rate, he would score 80 for the game. Inevitably, he cooled down. He only scored 15 in the next period — including one delicious double-pump shot off Patrick Ewing — dropping the pro rata to 70 points for the game.

And thus he wound up one of the most preposterous first halves in the history of the Garden. Jordan hit on 14 of 19 shots, including your occasional 3-pointer.

It was reminiscent of the first Ali-Frazier fight in which Muhammad Ali, so charismatic, with his red tassel white shoes and his dancing skills, dominated the spectators' attention. In the excitement, however, Joe Frazier was winning the fight. Similarly, at the half, the Bulls were losing, 56–50.

But it was everything and more than the capacity crowd of 19,763 could have hoped for.

In Jordan's four previous games since his return to basketball, he had fairly lackluster games, for him, other than the last one, against Atlanta, in which he hit a jumper at the final buzzer for a 99–98 victory. He seemed not quite his old self, even somewhat nervous, since he hadn't played a National Basketball Association game since June 1993, when the Bulls beat Phoenix for their third straight N.B.A. title.

His opener 10 days ago in Indianapolis saw him miss 21 of 28 shots. He appeared nervous, as he did last Friday night in his home opener in the new United Center in Chicago. When he was introduced to the crowd of 20,000, there followed a crashing, blinding, sound-and-light show that one might have expected for something else, like Moses receiving the Ten Commandments.

Both teams sought to make statements last night, the Knicks that they could whip the Bulls with Jordan, the Bulls that they were monsters once again.

And Jordan was eager to return as the great scorer he was when he left the game — he had averaged 32 points a game, the highest in history. But if there was a fault to his game last night, it was that he was looking for only one open man — Mr. Miracle. His first assist came with 50 seconds left in the game. He didn't get his second until — well, until it was time to win the game.

"When I was playing baseball, I still felt I could play this game," Jordan said with a smile in the interview room afterward. "I'm starting to get a little hang of it again."

In fact, for fans who came to see something memorable, a performance for the ages, they wound up in the right place. They hardly noticed that he had chilled from his hot start, and finished with only 55 points. For those scouring the record book, if they must, it was the most ever scored by an opponent in the new Garden. The previous mark was 50, by — who else? — Michael Jordan.

June 18, 1996
Genuine Jordan Puts Family First
by Harvey Araton

SEATTLE — He couldn't hit a jump shot, and he cried like a baby. Michael Jordan was almost an ordinary man here Sunday night, physically exhausted and emotionally spent. More human, more appealing, more like the Mike we could all very well be.

He misses his murdered father, and he was not ashamed to weep for him on worldwide television, on Father's Day. He said, of the Chicago Bulls' fourth championship, "This is for Daddy." Even the kids who were watching had to know that deep within Jordan is an emptiness that all the sneaker-generating revenue in the world can't fill.

There are societal criticisms of Jordan — some fair, some not — but one thing we should hope for is that he continues, in his advancing basketball age, to be a man who misses "Daddy," as well as one who looked up in the stands the other night at the signs his three young children were holding for him.

Jordan the champion. Jordan the gambler. Jordan the icon. Jordan the corporate front man. What makes up his global image creates in many minds a rather ambiguous portrait for someone as visible as him. But on the public issues of family and team, Jordan has been consistent and sure, at his best. He ought to get credit for that.

"Maybe I didn't feel as secure or as confident as I've been in the past," Jordan said after the Bulls closed out the Seattle SuperSonics and the long National Basketball Association season. "But what made the difference was my family's support, my wife and my kids. My wife pushed me every day. When I didn't feel like getting up and working with my trainer, she set the alarm and made sure I got up."

He gave Juanita Jordan as much praise as he gave his father, James. And he applauded Scottie Pippen, his Tonto-like "little brother," and then read a roll call of role players, from Jud Buechler to Steve Kerr to Randy Brown. He said he was thrilled for these basketball transients to have won their rings. His record says that he meant it, too.

When Trent Tucker and Darrell Walker were veteran spares on Jordan's 1993 title team, the two former Knicks were amazed how often Jordan talked about them having the chance to join him on the finals stage, how much he wanted that for them.

"Almost like a father wants to provide for his kids," is the way Tucker once put it.

It's not easy for any of them to play with Jordan, as demanding, as cruelly competitive as he can be. All season long, as the Bulls rolled on, Jordan claimed that his own artless struggles dealing with the culture of the curveball made him more tolerant of players less talented and driven. But as the Bulls temporarily lost their focus in the finals, Jordan could be seen barking at teammates, jumping at referees, seething in Seattle.

Hypocrite? Hardly. There are no parallels between Jordan's bullying and what has been decried, to the point of cliché now, as the trademark conduct of Generation X. If the Bulls were to win, someone had to steady the fragile Pippen, push the timid Toni Kukoc, restrain the rogue in Dennis Rodman. It can't be coincidence that with the Bulls, Rodman performed magnificently when he had to. It was partly Jordan, doing what the genteel David Robinson could not do last season in San Antonio. Get his house in order, no matter what it took.

Much as he loves teeing off, Jordan is no blithe country club aristocrat, and never will be. Graying baby boom sportswriters hold professional golfers up as America's true sportsmen now, as if there are any rational comparisons to be made between the sunny, exclusionary province of the rich and a grueling sport that finds much of its talent among the urban poor.

Jordan's world is somewhere between that, a working-class kid who has earned extraordinary wealth only to be viciously robbed of the father who was his most trusted friend. Ultimately, he is a man who brings to his work the entitlement of the chosen, but the edge and anger of the wretched. And those bottled-up emotions are unleashed in bursts of brilliance, or in heaves of sorrow on the locker room floor.

On the stage, at least, there is no argument about its being honest and real. Jordan shot woefully Sunday night, but was genuinely pleased to have had his teammates bail him out. It meant that he had done his job in other ways. He had provided leadership for his team, for his basketball brood. For Father's Day, he got a title instead of a tie.

JUNE 15, 1997

For Jordan, Four Mates, Five Rings

BY MIKE WISE

The play was designed for him, which was elementary to everyone. But in their haste to not let Michael Jordan end their season, John Stockton and the Utah Jazz discounted one vitally important quality in his arsenal: trust and belief in his teammates.

Throughout a decade of championship parades and trophy presentations, Jordan had never been afraid to let someone else take the deciding shot. And with perhaps the most timely assist of his career, his faith and his legend continued to grow.

The drive for five was completed in a grueling six games. Steve Kerr stepped up with five seconds left and dropped in a 17-foot jump shot in back of the free-throw line. For the fifth time in seven seasons, the National Basketball Association title belonged to the Bulls.

Their 90–86 victory before a wild mob at the United Center on Friday night not only featured several players holding aloft the five league championship trophies won by the franchise since 1991, but it also was the end of a long and rewarding struggle for the best player — and role players — in the game.

"It's been a fight," Jordan said after finishing with 39 points, 11 rebounds and 4 assists.

Averaging 31.1 points for the playoffs, he won his fifth championship-series most valuable player award, battling the flu the last three days and a plethora of expectations all season.

"It's all guts, deep down," Jordan said. "Determination. What your motives are, what your ambitions were from the beginning. It's easy to sit back and say: 'I've given my best. I'm tired. Somebody else has to got to do it,' whatever. I didn't take that approach."

Kerr's shot, along with Toni Kukoc's tipped inbounds pass and dunk that killed the Jazz's last hope, ended a classic, one that featured crucial shots, defensive stands and, finally, a very unselfish superstar.

"I saw him thinking for a long time," Kerr said of Jordan in the timeout huddle with 28 seconds left. "He finally turned to me and said: 'You be ready. Stockton is going to come off of you.' I said: 'I'll be ready. I'll knock it down.' And I was like, 'Will I?'"

Kerr entered the game shooting 6 for 20 in the series and only 3 for 14 beyond the 3-point line. Included in his misses was a 3-pointer at the end of Game 4 that could have helped end matters in Salt Lake City.

"Steve's been fighting himself since Game 4," Jordan said. "He missed a 3-pointer and he went back to his room. He doesn't know this, but his wife told me he buried his head in his pillow for hours because he felt he let us down. He said, 'Give me the ball,' in the timeout.

"That's typical of John Paxson," Jordan said of the guard who hit a title-clinching 3-pointer in 1993, and the player Kerr replaced. "He used to say the same thing."

The Jazz were beaten but unbowed. Stockton, asked after the game what impressed him most about Chicago once he stepped on the floor in the finals, was not enthralled with the question.

"The way you phrased it, it's difficult to answer because I think it implies awe," he said.

Each team had one blowout in the series, and four of the six games were decided by 5 points or less.

The Jazz had three opportunities to come away with victory rather than defeat — in Games 1, 5 and 6.

It may not have been as memorable a series as some of the Lakers-Celtics duels, but surely the pick-and-rolls, the passing and the teamwork beat the ruffian, one-on-one style of play that has enveloped the league. The Bulls won this series not only because their two superstars are still a plateau above Stockton and Karl Malone, who missed 8 of 15 free throws in Game 6, but also because they play team defense like no other unit of the past decade.

With Scottie Pippen's elongated reach, Jordan's tenacity and the strength and footwork of Dennis Rodman inside, they held the league's most accurate team to 40 percent shooting from the field in the final game. What's more, Chicago grew stronger as the series went on. In Games 4, 5 and 6, the Bulls thwarted the Jazz's offense in the final five minutes of the games — leaving Stockton and his teammates discombobulated and unable to run their offense. One of the league's most poised and mature teams was no match for that kind of pressure.

And credit must be given to Jerry Krause, the general manager who spent a pittance on Brian Williams at the end of the season for playoff insurance. Williams had a better series than Rodman and compensated for Luc Longley's bad stretches by taking the ball to the basket with force.

With speckled confetti raining down on the floor as if it were New Year's Day, and Jordan and his teammates climbing atop the scorer's table to be saluted by their following, the world's most impressive collection of basketball players had staved off another contender, their fifth in the decade.

There are many questions still surrounding the future of the Bulls, but another championship ring — one for the thumb — seemed to quell any real concern about whether Jordan or Coach Phil Jackson, both free agents, and probably even Pippen, whom trade rumors continue to circle around, will return.

Rodman is most likely gone, unless the Bulls deem their frontcourt too depleted. Without the Tattooed One and Williams, whom they cannot afford to pay under the salary cap, Jason Caffey becomes their primary power forward.

Still, Krause's ability to scour the world's gyms for a kid or a sage wanting to play for peanuts with Jordan cannot be discounted.

JUNE 15, 1998

A Steal, a Shot and One More Crown

BY MIKE WISE

SALT LAKE CITY — At some point, his skills will have to recede. He will not hit the last-second shot or drive the lane with fire and flair. He will be more than good, but less than great. He will not be able to put all the magic together in one unreal sequence — the way he did tonight, seizing another world title in 37.1 scintillating seconds at the age of 35.

In an encore that is not likely to be repeated — but who can tell anymore? — Michael Jordan stole the Utah Jazz's soul while adding the most incredible flourish yet to his legend.

He made an 18-foot jump shot from the top of the key with 5.2 seconds left, sending the Chicago Bulls to their sixth National Basketball Association title in eight seasons with a pulsating 87–86 victory in Game 6 of the finals. The shot came after he had stolen the ball from Karl Malone along the baseline with 18.9 seconds remaining and Utah ahead by 1 point.

He had already made a driving layup with his team trailing by 3 points with 37.1 seconds left. He scored the Bulls' last 8 points as they won the N.B.A. championship by four games to two.

After Jordan's final basket, John Stockton's 3-pointer just before the buzzer was off target, ending this wild game.

"When I got the ball, I looked up and saw 18.5 seconds left," Jordan said, describing the play that led to his last shot. "And I felt like we couldn't call a timeout; it gives the defense an opportunity to set up. It was a do-or-die situation. I let the time tick to where I had the court right where I wanted it.

"Great look. And it went in."

Stockton had made a 3-pointer to send the fanatical crowd into a frenzy with 41.9 seconds remaining, seemingly all but sealing a Game 7 here on Wednesday.

Never had Jordan's throne seemed so shaky, his dynasty so vulnerable.

And then he went to work. He could have been starring in a video game, or in a Hollywood fantasy — or both — when he drove the lane and scored almost uncontested. He had missed five straight shots from the perimeter before then, and had been lucky to get to the free-throw line on two out-of-control drives.

He stole the game from Utah. He stole the season. He tamed the rowdiest crowd in the league. And if he walked out of the dead-quiet Delta Center tonight and never came back to basketball, he could retire for the second time knowing he went out with unmatched brilliance. To go with his sixth championship trophy, he also won his sixth award as most valuable player of the finals.

"I think it's the best performance ever by Michael Jordan at a critical moment in a critical series," Bulls Coach Phil Jackson said as he puffed on a cigar after the game. "No one has ever done it better."

Jordan scored 45 points in 44 minutes, taking 35 shots because he had to. His teammate Scottie Pippen was suffering from back spasms.

Toni Kukoc finished with 15 points, and Pippen played as well as he could in 26 minutes. Malone finished with 31 points and 11 rebounds, working hard for every shot and trying his best to force a decisive seventh game.

Jeff Hornacek added 17 points for Utah, and Stockton was all over the floor, contributing 10 points and 5 assists.

But the night, as usual at this time of year, belonged to Jordan. With the Bulls trailing by 49–45 at halftime and by 66–61 after three quarters, he began to pace himself, almost as if he knew how the ending would play out.

The sequence that truly shifted the momentum involved Jordan's sneaking along the baseline like a blitzing linebacker about to blindside a quarterback. Malone had just received the ball in the post with less than 20 seconds remaining and the Jazz ahead. Suddenly, Jordan swooped in, and the ball was no longer Utah's.

"Karl never saw me coming, and I was able to knock the ball away," he said.

Pippen cried as he began embracing Jordan along with other Bulls teammates at midcourt, after Stockton's shot had been tipped out to the perimeter and the clock had sounded. It may have been the thought of this

Bulls team possibly not returning that got to him — along with Jordan, Pippen and Dennis Rodman, the Bulls have four other free agents — or it may just have been watching the greatest player ever performing another on-court miracle.

But as they raised their sixth championship trophy high into the air, the Bulls may have been celebrating their perseverance as much as their dominance. Less than 48 hours after losing their home-court advantage with a Game 5 loss at the United Center, they came out and proved their merit by winning a third straight championship for the second time in the decade.

"I saw the moment, and I took advantage of the moment," Jordan said. "I never doubted myself. I knew we had an opportunity to win this game."

Eight years ago, a sky-walking shooting guard emerged from the shadows of Larry Bird and Magic Johnson, grabbed the N.B.A.'s torch and gracefully elevated toward the rim. Eight years later, he refuses to come down.

The Bulls' two-year title gap in 1994 and 1995 covered Jordan's year-and-a-half experiment with baseball. Tonight, he looked as strong and agile as he did the night in 1991 when he performed a wondrous act of in-air artistry and produced an indelible N.B.A. finals image, rising for a dunk with his right hand before switching to his left for a layup at the last possible moment. He hit the same kind of shot in Game 1 a year ago against the Jazz in Chicago, putting the defender Bryon Russell on his heels until he had enough room to release the ball — just as he did tonight.

"He made a couple of big plays right down the stretch," Stockton said. "Mark another one in the books for him."

Added Jackson, "I don't know if anybody could quite write a dramatic scenario like that one."

After the champagne had been sprayed and the cigars lit, Jordan was asked more about his future than the game.

"Hopefully I've put enough memories out there for everybody to at least have some thoughts about what Michael Jordan did in his 13 or 14 years or whatever it takes, and put some comparisons up there for kids to follow and compare themselves to," he said. "I have another life and I know I have to get to it at some place and time."

Watching the televised replays of his astonishing finish, the general feeling among observers after tonight was: What's the rush?

— POSTSCRIPT —

MIKE WISE, 2018: "The deadlines were so tight that I had to prepare leads for the Bulls' winning and losing. I was sitting next to Michael Wilbon, a Chicago guy who had a personal relationship with Jordan. With a couple minutes left, Jordan kept missing and looked spent and Scottie [Pippen] was almost useless with a bad back. Wilbon looked depressed. 'Michael's done,' he told me. 'They'll have nothing left in Game 7 and he's going to finish up a loser.' Then Wilbon left the press area to watch the end downstairs. I got down there after the shot, after Jordan proved again that he lived to do exactly what he did. I ran right into Wilbon and said, 'He's done, huh?' We laughed. It's been cool all these years to look back and be able to say, 'I was there.'"

15

Moses to N.C.A.A.: "Stop Jivin' Me"

If the continuous '90s Jordan news wasn't all-consuming enough, a predominant narrative for the 21st century was authored at a Chicago pizza joint called the Home Inn on May 15, 1995, a day after the Bulls evened their playoff series with the Orlando Magic on the way to losing in six games.

Straight out of Farragut High School on the city's west side, Kevin Garnett, with a 6-foot-11 frame that weighed in under 200 pounds, declared himself ready to do battle with Charles Oakley and Karl Malone.

Having stayed over a day to cover the news conference, it was hard not to laugh — O.K., snicker — when the 18-year-old Garnett did a little shimmy after being asked if he was ready for the millionaire bachelorhood life of a likely high first-round pick.

"Come on, ladies, come on," he said.

In the back of the room, Arleen Daag, Farragut's assistant principal, rolled her eyes and prophetically sized up the reopening of the preps-to-pros jump first made decades earlier by Moses Malone, Darryl Dawkins and Bill Willoughby.

"The problem as I see it is that the N.B.A. doesn't have anything in place, a support system, to help these kids once they get there," she said. "Maybe the N.B.A. should use Kevin as a test case — there's a lot of talent at the high school level and a lot of these kids are going to be looking to see how Kevin does."

What high schoolers saw was Garnett's selection with the fifth pick by Minnesota, $5.3 million paid to him over the first three years of his career, by which he was good enough — at 21 — to command a six-year, $126 million deal that was bigger than Shaquille O'Neal's seven-year, $121 million free-agent haul from the Lakers in 1996.

Garnett's deal resulted in veteran resentment and the owners' demanding and getting a rookie salary scale. Didn't matter. The best and brightest of scholastic talent — 39 within a decade — quickly soured on the idea of being serenaded during March Madness by Dick Vitale. Some didn't make it in the league. Others became legends. Arleen Daag's take was always the smartest — whatever age limit the N.B.A. would have, it was bound to get younger and was going to need a support system. A developmental vehicle. An alternative to the hypocrisies of the N.C.A.A.

Nov. 10, 1993

Bradley's Eloquent Teacher

BY HARVEY ARATON

It may be surprising to learn that Moses Malone is only 38 years old, not even the elder statesman of the National Basketball Association. He seems to have been around, if not since the beginning of time, then at least before the creation of the 24-second clock.

Actually, he broke into pro ball in 1974, a year after Wilt Chamberlain quit. In the mid-1970s, Malone battled Dave Cowens and Kareem Abdul-Jabbar. In the mid-1980s, he tutored a college kid from Africa named Hakeem Olajuwon in sweltering Houston summer leagues and took a Georgetown rookie named Patrick Ewing to school in his first game for the Knicks.

Now he's back with the Philadelphia 76ers, 95–86 losers to the Knicks in last night's Madison Square Garden opener. Though he said, "I'm here to win games," Malone was really signed to become the hands-on instructor for the frail 7-foot-6-inch rookie, Shawn Bradley. It's a job he shares with the 76ers' assistant coach and former pivot brawler, Jeff Ruland.

Did we mention that Malone was traded for Ruland seven years ago?

Malone has made more than 9,300 field goals, 8,400 free throws, millions of dollars and hundreds of friends. The men who have coached and played with Malone always understood him better than others, recognized him to be a tower of strength, one of the great warriors of the game, its most accomplished offensive rebounder.

From the moment he became the first player to go directly from high school to the pros, it was easy to misconstrue what Malone was about, especially if you went by what you thought he said.

This was classically illustrated in the 1981 book, *The Breaks of the Game*, by David Halberstam, who told of how the young Malone, scrimmaging with the Portland Trail Blazers, motioned to the team's trainer, Ron Culp, who thought he heard Malone say, "Rest."

"Moses wants to come out," Culp yelled at the coach, Jack Ramsay.

"No," said Malone, holding up a wounded hand. "Not rest, wrist!"

His monosyllabic mumbling has, with good reason, become nearly mythologized, but Bucky Buckwalter, the Blazers' senior scout, claims there is a wonderful clarity to Malone that was as detectable 20 years ago as it was in 1983, when Malone predicted a 76ers championship in "Fo', fo' and fo'." (He was off by one game.)

As personnel director for the Utah Stars of the American Basketball Association, Buckwalter boldly got into a contest to lure Malone into the pros after he had signed a letter of intent with Maryland's recruiting charmer, Lefty Driesell.

"We had lost some good players from the year before," Buckwalter said yesterday from Portland. "We had no centers. I scouted Moses in high school, and he was such a dominant athlete, I thought he could help us right away."

Once Driesell realized that this renegade pro league was attempting to steal his ticket to the Final Four, he began making a daily pilgrimage to the Malone family home in Petersburg, Va. It was so modest, Buckwalter said, that the living room coffee table was an old milk crate, on which Malone placed his trophies when the basketball recruiters would come.

Young Moses, he recalled, always sat by the window and stared outside. Occasionally, he mumbled a few words to the older white men who talked about how much they could do for him, but never what he could do for them.

"Given the environment, and how little he said, you could understand how people would have got the wrong idea," said Buckwalter. "But every once in a while, he'd shoot something out, and if you listened to what he was saying, you realized that this guy was a lot smarter than people were giving him credit for, and that you should give it to him straight."

Whatever moral doubts Buckwalter had about thrusting an 18-year-old into the Darwinian society of professional sports dissipated with each Driesell pitch to compete with the money Malone's family desperately needed.

When, for instance, he sensed that he was losing the war, Driesell called on a higher authority. He told Malone that "the Good Lord won't mind you waiting a year or two" before he turned pro.

To which Malone is said to have snapped, "Stop jiving me, Coach!"

With those four words, a Hall of Fame career was born, and Malone proved that he saw through the hypocrisy of big-time college sports. It is that intuitive wisdom, plus 20 years of offensive skills and tricks, that Malone offers Bradley, the 21-year-old Mormon who played only one more year of college ball than his mentor.

"All the kid has to do is watch," said Buckwalter.

Moses, he knows, will be ready to show, if not tell.

FEB. 5, 1998

Heeere's Kobe:
It's Showtime Again in L.A.

BY MIKE WISE

LOS ANGELES — He emerges from a cramped room, loping along slowly like a college sophomore between classes. Moving through the Great Western Forum corridors and out the arena's side entrance, he squints at the sunlight beaming down on Los Angeles.

"Kobe! Over here!" someone yells. He signs a few autographs before gunning his jet-black BMW 740iL through the parking lot. The voice of the rapper Jay-Z booms through the speakers.

Suddenly, he slows down and lowers the volume.

"I just did an interview with Bob Costas," said Kobe Bryant, the 19-year-old wunderkind guard of the Lakers. "That's crazy, man. It's like I was just watching him on TV the other day, interviewing Magic and Michael. I mean, Bob Costas!"

His left hand is on the steering wheel and his right hand is palming Los Angeles. Like Magic Johnson's early years, Bryant's midair improvisation and open-court wonder are stirring the city's imagination.

"You can kind of sense that, that he's somehow pulling everyone together like a magnet," said Kurt Rambis, a Lakers assistant coach and Johnson's former teammate. "He brings back hope again. Initially, it came from Shaq. But Kobe has taken it to another level."

Bryant's abilities are not reflected in the box scores alone. The 6-foot-6-inch Bryant is averaging almost 18 points a game, third in scoring on the team behind Shaquille O'Neal and Eddie Jones.

He hasn't even started a game for the Lakers. But when he gets off the bench, a buzz circles the arena. Everyone sits up. Depending on whom you ask, it's either the Second Coming of Jordan or the Second Act of Showtime.

On Sunday at Madison Square Garden, Bryant will become the youngest player ever to start an All-Star Game. Since leapfrogging college and going straight to the National Basketball Association from high school last season, he has easily become the league's most breathtaking talent.

"Michael Jordan didn't come into the league as a high school player, but when he did come into the league he was one of those guys that really dominated from all standpoints," said Scottie Pippen, the perennial All-Star and Jordan's teammate on the Chicago Bulls. "I think this is the mentality that this kid is taking right now."

"Young fella," they call him. "My little brother," O'Neal says.

Bryant is the son of the former N.B.A. journeyman Joe (Jelly Bean) Bryant, who played overseas and for eight seasons in the league before retiring in 1983. The son claims he first beat his father in a game of one-on-one when he was only 14.

"Yeah, right," Joe Bryant said. "How can you beat somebody who is the official and the scorekeeper? I'm always up one. He scores five buckets in a row, I'm still up one."

Joe and his wife, Pam, and their 20-year-old daughter, Sharia, went with their son from Philadelphia to Los Angeles after he had been drafted by Charlotte 13th over all in 1996 and immediately traded to the Lakers. On Friday, the family will travel to Philadelphia to attend the graduation of Shaya, Kobe's 21-year-old sister, who will receive a degree in international business from Temple University. Then it's the All-Star Weekend in Manhattan.

The Bryants live in a posh Pacific Palisades home. Mom cooks. Dad, also a former coach, critiques. The kid has one side of the house to himself.

"We're just normal parents, no secrets," Joe Bryant said. "We look at it like Kobe has a good job. Some other kid might have a dream to play in the Boston Symphony. But what Kobe does is no more or less gratifying. If he had a paper route, he'd still be a young person trying to better himself."

Del Harris, the Lakers' 60-year-old coach, has seen two generations of Bryants. He coached Joe in Houston at the end of his N.B.A. career.

"He had as good a passing skill as anybody that played at that time, other than Magic," Harris said. "But Joe Bryant was big and bulky, with not the same kind of athletic ability Kobe has.

"He was more of a fun-loving guy. Kobe is just focused and all business. He smiles and has a good sense of humor, but I don't think it's necessarily like father, like son.

"Sometimes a father will teach his son to do the things he could have done better and didn't maybe."

If there is one quality Kobe Bryant's peers are praising besides his explosiveness to the basket, it is his ability to tune out all frivolous activity and concentrate on making himself a better basketball player.

During scrimmages in which his team is losing, he pouts on the sideline. If practice is scheduled for noon, Bryant is in the gym at 11:00 A.M. working to perfect his crossover dribble. He is often the last to leave.

"I was telling him that some of the things he was doing reminded me of what Pete Maravich was doing 20 years ago," said Jon Barry, the son of the Hall of Famer Rick Barry, and Bryant's teammate. "So he tells me he wants the Maravich video so he can perfect some of those moves. Kobe said, 'He might have more tricks than me now, but in time, I'll have more.' And I believe him."

Said Jones, "Every day Kobe comes to practice is a highlight film."

As he turns onto the 405 North freeway toward Santa Monica, the brilliant hues of the city illuminate his soft coffee complexion. Bryant has a koala bear smile and a goatee-in-training that will only get him carded at a nightclub. Not that he is interested in the L.A. scene. Amid the adulation over his ability to hang in the air for several seconds, he has remained grounded.

"People always talk about adjusting and who I'm going to let into my inner circle," he said. "I don't really need an inner circle or a bunch of friends. I have my teammates, a few friends and my family. That's enough."

Joe Bryant said: "People forget the influence of his mother sometimes. She was an N.B.A. wife and now she's an N.B.A. mother. He's been given both perspectives."

Lisa Leslie, the 25-year-old star in the Women's N.B.A., befriended Sharia and has become one of Bryant's key influences. The three often go out together and speak Italian (he is fluent as a result of his father's playing days there) when they do not want people eavesdropping on their conversation.

"I basically told him there are people who are going to try to entice him to drink, smoke, all that stuff," Leslie said. "I told him to maintain, to be himself off the court.

"I'm glad he doesn't act like a lot of these other guys. Maybe he'll get buck wild one of these days. But knowing Kobe, I don't think so. After all the adult stuff, we get to be kids."

After Jack Nicholson won a Golden Globe award last month, Bryant congratulated the actor and longtime Lakers fan at courtside. Asked what Nicholson said, Bryant replied with his best impersonation:

"Thank you very much, young fella. Now go out there and have a good game."

"You got to hear Jack," he said as he busts up laughing.

Just as when Paula Abdul was a Laker Girl and Pat Riley outdressed the Hollywood faithful, the team has Los Angeles' attention again. The Lakers will go into the All-Star Game break with the second-best record in the Western Conference.

"This city has definitely taken some hits," Bryant said. "We win a couple championships and turn things around a little bit, that would be nice. I don't know if I'm going to save L.A., but it would be nice to help. I don't mind the responsibility."

A rapper of some renown, Bryant is going to be coming out with his own compact disc soon. Jay-Z's gangsta lyrics are a little too harsh for his bubble-gum tastes. But he enjoys the beat.

"You like the Spice Girls?" he asks. "I don't really have a problem with them. I mean, they're doing their thing. They send out a positive message, and they appeal to kids."

He is asked if he ever speaks to 22-year-old Tiger Woods about incredible fame at such a young age. "Bunch of times," Bryant said.

"I love Tiger, man. All those young athletes doing their thing — Tiger Woods, Venus Williams, Martina Hingis — I respect them so much. The motivation they have is something we have in common. They don't let other people's expectations for them shatter their dreams. They went out there and got the job done, and they still manage to be young people.

"Martina Hingis is, like, 17 years old. When she's out there on the tennis court, it's about business. She's doing her thing. She's loving the game and she's winning. Off the court, she's a 17-year-old having fun. I really respect her for that."

There are moments when Bryant allows himself to contemplate how fast and how far he has come. They usually come in 10-second intervals and are always interrupted by the reality of the day.

On this day, it is Stephon Marbury and the league's other hot, young team, the Timberwolves. The Lakers would win by 7 points. Two days later, it would be Jordan and the Bulls. Remarkably, the Lakers would win that one, too, by 25. In both games, Bryant makes moves that make everyone — including Jordan — shake his head in amazement.

"Sometimes it just hits me," he said. "Most of the kids I went to school with are at Penn State now. I take a few seconds to think about things like that and realize I'm a 19-year-old kid who likes to play basketball and loves his family very, very much."

JULY 9, 2001

Hitting the Lottery as a Junior?

BY IRA BERKOW

TEANECK, N.J. — A stellar array of basketball cognoscenti that included scouts from almost every N.B.A. team and college coaches — pads and pencils at the ready, projected mental insights awhirl — flocked yesterday to see some 220 of the best high school players in the world showcased at Fairleigh Dickinson's Rothman Athletic Center. One player in particular, however, caught much of their attention.

He is a 16-year-old from St. Vincent-St. Mary High School in Akron, Ohio, who will be a junior in the fall. Many of the gathered connoisseurs believed that the lad, LeBron James, a 6-foot-7, 210-pound point guard, shooting guard and small forward — sometimes he plays as if he is all three in one, a kind of hoops Swiss Army knife — would have been taken in the first round of the most recent N.B.A. draft, possibly a lottery pick.

Hey, it was one thing for three of the first four picks in the draft to be high school seniors, for the first time ever, and four of the first eight — but a high school sophomore potentially going pro? "And next year," said Sonny Vaccaro, founder and director of the Adidas ABCD four-day camp, which began yesterday, "LeBron could surely go in the lottery. He'll be bigger, stronger and smarter."

O.K., still, a high school junior making the jump? Got to be kidding? No?

Tom Konchalski, who evaluates high school players for his respected *HSBI Report*, said: "LeBron isn't an extraterrestrial athlete, but he has a tremendous feel for the game. He sees situations two passes ahead of the play. He's been compared to Vince Carter and Tracy McGrady. But I think he has a better feel for the game than they do."

He meant than they did when they were James's age, right? "No, I mean right now," Konchalski said. "I doubt seriously if he's going to college."

So LeBron James, in a yellow uniform and wearing No. 155, his hair tufted out and his pants baggy, began one of the four games going on at once, after the first round of four games had been completed. There were marvelous players on the courts, including 6-6 Lenny Cooke of Old Tappan, N.J., and 6-8 Carmelo Anthony of Baltimore, but none except James made first team All-America last season as chosen by *USA Today*, the first underclassman named to the first team in the 18 years that such authoritative selections have been made.

He tried his first shot, a 3-pointer from the top of the key, and it swished. His next shot was a 3-pointer from the corner. Swish. There was a fast-break dunk, a clever pass for a basket, a missed jump shot, then he snared a rebound and stuffed it with both hands behind his head.

"Wow," one of the other players in the stands said. "Wow," said nearly everyone else.

James's mother, Gloria, watched her only child play. She is an enthusiastic fan of LeBron.

"What I want for LeBron is his happiness," said Gloria, who has worked in accounting and sales but is now unemployed. "He loves basketball. But I would like to see him graduate with his class from high school, at least. But we'll make a decision when the time comes. He's a level-headed boy. He's never given me a lick of problems. He's mannerable and respectful."

LeBron James, a solid B student, said that he wasn't sure what he planned to do. "College is important," he said. "You can't play basketball all your life. You should prepare for something else, too." To be safe, his mother said she was taking out an insurance policy on him.

Kwame Brown, the No. 1 pick by the Washington Wizards last month, received a $12 million contract for three years. "That's a lot of money," James said. "But we've struggled this long, a couple more years won't make that much difference."

Billy Donovan, head coach at Florida, had signed Brown to attend his university. "And he wanted to go to college," Donovan said. "But he made a decision that he thought was best for him, and his family. I can't fault him for that. "

Ernie Grunfeld, general manager of the Milwaukee Bucks, was in attendance, primarily, he said, because his 6-6 son, Danny, who will be a senior, was playing — he's a good player but not a pro prospect, yet. "I wish all the kids would go to college first," Grunfeld said. "But I also don't think you should prevent someone from trying to earn a living. I just hope the kids who do skip college have the emotional and physical maturity to succeed."

Among the players, 6-7 Demetris Nichols from Barrington, R.I., who will be a junior, dreams about an N.B.A. future, like many of his peers, but is also realistic. "We talk more about college than the pros," he said. He also thought there was substance in the talk that Kobe Bryant gave to the group Saturday night. Bryant, the Lakers' star, jumped from high school to the pros. "Kobe said: 'Go to college. You have something to fall back on. If you break a leg, then where are you?'" Nichols said.

But Kobe — who, like Brown, is an alumnus of this camp — didn't go to college. "He's good," Nichols said, with emphasis. He added that he has to be careful: "Everybody wants a piece of you. If somebody tells me I should go pro, I'm going to make sure he knows basketball."

From appearances, that could be somebody like LeBron James, counsel also to himself.

16

The *Space Jam* Launch

In favorably reviewing Spike Lee's *He Got Game* for *The Times* in May 1998, Janet Maslin had this to say about Ray Allen's portrayal of the hot college recruit, Jesus Shuttlesworth: "In terms of acting, Mr. Allen plays comfortably in the same court with Mr. Washington, giving a likable, unaffected performance that would be fine even if he weren't an N.B.A. star."

The "Mr. Washington" whom Maslin contended Allen didn't shrink in the regal presence of? That would be Denzel, akin to suggesting that some unheralded N.B.A. rookie met the standard of Magic, Larry or Michael in his debut.

If there was an Oscar (unrelated to The Big O) for the best screen performance by an N.B.A. player, it would have to go to Allen, who in January 2014 actually carried J. Shuttlesworth on the back of his Miami jersey when the N.B.A. authorized the occasional use of nicknames. Unlike most N.B.A. Hollywood adventures of questionable slapstick, Allen not only was a veritable co-star but also tackled a subject both serious and significant.

Shaquille O'Neal and Penny Hardaway weren't bad as BMOCs on the take in *Blue Chips*, but that was predominantly a Nick Nolte vehicle. LeBron James was "a surprisingly limber comic presence" in 2015's *Trainwreck*, alongside Amy Schumer and Bill Hader, according to *The Times*'s Manohla Dargis.

But for sheer impact, a measure of how culturally ubiquitous an N.B.A. star could become, it was Jordan's painfully wooden performance in *Space Jam* that commercially soared, released in 1996 at the height of Michael Madness. The film rocketed to No. 1 in the United States, grossed $230 million worldwide and introduced a generation of digitally savvy kids to the cartoon Dream Team of Bugs, Daffy, Tweety and Porky.

As for Shawn Bradley's being cast as one of the players whose basketball powers were stolen by the conniving Monstars — what could be loonier than that?

Nov. 15, 1996

Icons Meet: Bugs, Daffy and Jordan

BY JANET MASLIN

Space Jam may well be the only film in which Looney Tunes characters openly discuss merchandising tie-ins. As Daffy Duck asks Bugs Bunny when the subject of mugs and T-shirts comes up, "You ever see any money from that stuff?"

Maybe Bugs doesn't, but somebody will. *Space Jam* is all about salesmanship, though it also turns out to be a reasonably good big-screen babysitter for small children with savvy commercial tastes. It's both a frantic, innovative mixture of animation technologies and a fan magazine full of adulation for Michael Jordan. He handles this tribute with regal bearing and good grace.

As a sports star so celebrated that even the backs of his ears are famous, Mr. Jordan need do little more here than show off his sportsmanship and play ball. (Typical line: "Let's just go out and have fun.") It's baseball at first, which gives the one enterprising twist to an otherwise near-plotless spectacle. Mr. Jordan is first seen giving up basketball to try baseball, and the film makes knowing jokes about this switch. After all, it saves Mr. Jordan from being nabbed by animated space aliens who bewitch the film's other basketball stars.

(Parents who know they won't resist the juggernaut of *Space Jam* should take a popcorn break at this point. Skip the next two paragraphs. Also feel free to ignore this information when you see it on screen.)

Somewhere in animated outer space, a bunch of brightly colored bugs called Nerdlucks need a new attraction for Moron Mountain, their amusement park. They decide to kidnap all the Looney Tunes characters. Then Bugs challenges the Nerdlucks to a basketball game. The Nerdlucks, being wily (and with Danny DeVito supplying the voice of their ringleader), morph themselves into big, mean basketball aces by sapping the talents of Patrick Ewing, Charles Barkley, Muggsy Bogues and others.

But the Nerdlucks don't catch Michael Jordan. Since they're from another planet, they are able to mistake him for a baseball player, which no real earthling would do. Still, Mr. Jordan does not stay out of the fray. He's out playing golf with Bill Murray and Larry Bird when he gets sucked down a hole and dragged into Looneyland for the big game.

Back? Anyway, to make *Space Jam*, Mr. Jordan shot and dribbled among figures in special green suits, who were later replaced by animated versions of everyone from Tweety Bird to Foghorn Leghorn to Yosemite Sam. The juxtaposition of human and animated figures is very skillful, thanks to direction by Joe Pytka, a star director of television commercials. Mr. Pytka never need have a visual idea that lasts longer than 30 seconds here, thanks to the film's scriptless state and giddy, cacophonous style. This film was made very quickly by animation standards, and the haste shows.

"Space Jam" is also the brainchild of Ivan Reitman, who is one of the producers and whose own films (*Ghostbusters*, *Stripes*, *Kindergarten Cop*) also value high-concept thinking and loose, wisecracking style. In the energetic, mishmash manner of a *Mad* magazine parody, the film simply throws in every gag and non sequitur it can think of. ("I didn't know Dan Aykroyd was in this picture," says someone or something, misidentifying Mr. Murray.) Crammed with pop and sports references, the film also kids about its own crassness. One character succeeds in plugging Hanes, Wheaties, Gatorade and a Big Mac in a single sentence.

Wayne Knight, as Mr. Jordan's devoted gofer, is around to provide comic relief, which means being squashed flat by the film's animation tricks. Also on hand, in all their collective glory, are the celebrities of the Looney Tunes world. *Space Jam* is as much a fond tribute to their past as it is a product-plugging, high-tech, hip-hopping thing of the future.

"Space Jam" is rated PG (Parental guidance suggested). It's mildly rude but fine for young children.

SPACE JAM

Directed by Joe Pytka; written by Leo Benvenuti, Steve Rudnick, Timothy Harris and Herschel Weingrod; director of photography, Michael Chapman; edited by Sheldon Kahn; music by James Newton Howard; production designer, Geoffrey Kirkland; animation producer, Ron Tippe; produced by Ivan Reitman, Joe Medjuck and Daniel Goldberg; released by Warner Brothers. Running time: 99 minutes. This film is rated PG.

WITH: Michael Jordan, Charles Barkley, Patrick Ewing, Muggsy Bogues, Bill Murray and Larry Bird (as themselves); Wayne Knight (Stan Podolak) and Theresa Randle (Juanita).

WITH THE VOICES OF: Danny DeVito (Swackhammer), Billy West (Bugs Bunny and Elmer Fudd), Bradley Baker (Daffy Duck, the Tazmanian Devil and Bull), Bob Bergen (Bertie, Hubie, Marvin the Martian, Porky Pig, Speedy Gonzales and Tweety), Bill Farmer (Sylvester, Yosemite Sam and Foghorn Leghorn) and Kath Soucie (Lola Bunny)

FEB. 20, 2018

With *Dear Basketball,* Kobe Bryant Could Add an Oscar To His Victories

BY CHARLES SOLOMON

When the Laker superstar Kobe Bryant decided to make a film of *Dear Basketball,* his farewell poem to the sport he loved, he chose two collaborators who knew nothing about the game: the former Disney artist Glen Keane, who had animated *Aladdin, Beast,* and *Tarzan,* and the Oscar-winning composer John Williams. They were good choices. Their film won the Annie Award, the animation industry's most prestigious prize, for best short film of 2017, and is considered a likely favorite for the Academy Award for animated short.

"Even though, in his own words, I 'couldn't have picked a worse animator for basketball,' I felt Glen and I shared an emotional connection that enabled him to relate to the piece at a deeper level," Mr. Bryant, who retired in 2016, said in a recent phone interview. "He was at a time in his career that was parallel to my own — leaving Disney after so many years and starting something new."

"It was pretty surreal to see myself animated," he added with a laugh. "I once dreamed of having a signature Nike shoe, but I never thought I'd be animated by Glen Keane — that pretty much tops everything!"

Mr. Keane said it "was the most difficult thing I've ever animated," adding: "I was trying to draw a moving sculpture in space that had to look exactly like Kobe. I could draw Beast any way I wanted: Nobody knows what Beast really looks like. Everybody knows Kobe."

The film has generated considerable excitement in the animation industry for its celebration of traditional drawing. *Lou,* from Pixar, which has won the category four times, *Revolting Rhymes* and *Garden Party* are computer-animated; the fifth nominee, *Negative Space,* was done in stop-motion.

There is also some controversy surrounding the nomination: #MeToo activists say that a 2003 sexual-assault case against Mr. Bryant is reason not to reward the movie. (The case was dismissed.) An online petition is seeking to rescind the nod, and the argument has been taken up on social media.

Meredith B. Kile
@em_bee_kay

Follow

Crazy to me that, in the era of #MeToo and #TimesUp, we're still cool with Kobe Bryant being called on as the elder statesman of the NBA and sitting front and center in the Oscar nominee class portrait.

11:48 AM - 12 Feb 2018

Mr. Bryant deliberately chose an artist who didn't know basketball: "Someone who's been watching basketball their whole lives — and playing it — tends to miss the small moves, the details. When you come at it with fresh eyes, you look at every single thing because it's all new."

Mr. Keane said, "I've always believed animation can help an audience understand an action in deeper ways than live action."

"You can edit the movement, leaving out extraneous details and emphasizing the important points," he added. "There's something deeper and more emotional that art can communicate, even though you can take a photo of the same thing."

Mr. Bryant's poem begins with recollections of himself as a boy, practicing dribbling with a basketball made of his father's tube socks. He attains his dream of playing professionally, then realizes his career must eventually end: His aging body can no longer endure the demands of the sport. Mr. Keane's drawings juxtapose the boy and the adult.

Mr. Bryant, who spent two decades with the Los Angeles Lakers in a run that included five N.B.A. titles, said he wanted a younger generation of athletes to see the film and learn "about the emotional journey of having a dream, believing it'll come true; it comes true, then the realization that you have to wake up from that dream and move on to another."

Mr. Keane added, "The film doesn't have to be *Dear Basketball*, it's *Dear Animation*, it's *Dear Medicine*, it's *Dear Whatever-You-Dreamed-of-When-You-Were-a-Child*."

At Disney, Mr. Keane was known for loose, powerful drawings. Some of their strength was inevitably lost when they were traced, inked and painted for the films. Although this practice is standard throughout the animation industry, Mr. Bryant wanted the spontaneity and roughness of Mr. Keane's original drawings — which appear on screen.

"My career — like other things in life — was never perfect. There's beauty in those imperfections, and the last thing I wanted to do was create a film where all the lines were perfect and the coloring was perfect," he explained. "That would have taken away from the humanity of the piece, which is about creating and enjoying that journey of imperfection. It was really important for the animation to be 2-D and feel almost sketchy."

Three years earlier, Mr. Bryant had reached out to John Williams, but not about film. He thought understanding the composer's writing and conducting process might help him on the court: "How did he lead a large orchestra to create such beautiful music? I was trying to relate the art of conducting to leading a basketball team to a championship."

The composer was surprised when the athlete contacted him. "I couldn't imagine why Kobe wanted to meet me," Mr. Williams recalled. "I told him I had never been to a basketball game — high school, college or professional."

Nevertheless, they quickly became friends, and when he was asked to compose the score, Mr. Williams agreed immediately: "I thought *Dear Basketball* was a very reassuring and contributive little piece."

Although they're excited about the Oscar nomination and enjoyed working together, Mr. Keane and Mr. Bryant will not be collaborating in the immediate future. Mr. Keane is slated to direct the feature *Over the Moon* for Pearl Studio in China. "This has been an amazing moment in my artistic life, pushing me into a field where I felt I had no business," he said. "Then I realized, animation can go anywhere, can't it?

Mr. Bryant is developing other ideas for films. "Aging can be very difficult for athletes," he said. "We train our whole lives, we dedicate ourselves to a craft we have to leave early because our bodies will not allow us to go on."

"What you've done for so long becomes who you are, and it's very, very difficult to walk away from it and do something else," he continued. "So to be two years into retirement and have an Oscar nomination means so much."

17
N.B.A. on NBC

Minutes after the 1996 All-Star Game in the cavernous Alamodome, David Stern anxiously rushed through a courtside interview, on his way to San Antonio's University Hospital to check in on his good friend and partner-in-revenue-flow, Dick Ebersol, who was laid up after undergoing emergency angioplasty to free a blocked artery.

"It's been a tough weekend," Stern told me. "I've had to act normal at several functions while I knew what Dick was going through."

No partnership — not Jordan/Pippen, not Stockton/Malone — was more vital to the league's 1990s precipitous growth than Stern and Ebersol's. It wasn't until Ebersol and NBC pried the N.B.A. contract away from CBS in 1989 that a network put its collective might behind a sport that was already on the rise. The relationship between Ebersol and Stern became symbiotic.

NBC was riding high at the time with the hit comedy series *Friends*, *Mad About You*, *3rd Rock From the Sun* and *Seinfeld*. With Stern's urging, Ebersol went to his boss, Don Ohlmeyer, and said, with trepidation, "Do you think we could get the biggest stars to sit down and do promos?" Within a week, they were all on board, at no expense, happily hyping the N.B.A. on their own sets.

Flush with leverage thanks largely to Jordan, Stern imperiously dictated terms of the arrangement, especially which stories NBC could cover in its league-related programming. Ebersol said the arrangement "violated everything I believe in journalistically." But he knew the competition —

specifically ESPN — was circling, waiting for an opening in contract negotiations.

Meanwhile, the pot of television gold kept getting bigger, ticket prices grew steeper and the battles lines were drawn between owners and players over which side deserved to keep more of the riches.

JUNE 12, 2002

Final Buzzer for NBC and N.B.A.

BY RICHARD SANDOMIR AND MIKE WISE

The sun was setting in Marina del Rey, Calif., last Thursday, the night before Game 2 of the National Basketball Association finals. Guests walked into the open-air hotel restaurant, where four TV sets would soon blare NBC's N.B.A. theme music.

The annual NBC-N.B.A. finals party had taken on a wistful tone: The 12-year partnership, which coincided with Michael Jordan's magical run, could end as early as tonight if the Lakers sweep the Nets.

David Stern, the N.B.A. commissioner, had decided to leave NBC for a more lucrative six-year deal with ESPN, ABC and AOL Time Warner that will place many more games on cable, including the All-Star Game and the conference finals, longtime staples of NBC.

Dick Ebersol, the chairman of NBC Sports, handed Stern two gifts that underscored the path the commissioner is taking: one, a boxed set of *Friends* DVDs, a reminder of Stern's closeness to Ebersol but also of where the N.B.A. will no longer be promoted on the network's Thursday night schedule.

"David," Ebersol said, as he gave Stern a second gag gift, "you'll need this when you're trying to get the conference finals in the Town Car on the way home from the office."

From the bulky box, Stern pulled out 100 feet of coaxial cable — the better to get cable from a car that can receive only broadcast TV. "And it's good quality, too," Ebersol said, as about 100 N.B.A. and NBC employees roared with laughter.

"Nothing has meant more than our friendship and partnership," Ebersol told Stern after they swapped serious gifts. "Nothing."

Their relationship began in the spring of 1989 during their first meeting, at the Omni Berkshire hotel in Manhattan. Ebersol had just been hired to run NBC Sports and revive the spirits of a division sagging from losing the rights to carry Major League Baseball. On the day NBC got the deal, N.B.A. caps were placed on the doorknobs of every person's office at the sports division.

NBC's first four-year contract was worth $600 million and wrested the league from CBS. The second, worth $750 million, and the final one, for $1.6 billion, were negotiated without Stern opening the bidding to any other networks. Their business goals were for so long in sync.

"During our partnership, NBC became the most profitable and successful network, and each of us accounted for some of that," Stern said. "That's a good relationship."

The Stern-Ebersol relationship was so close that they would speak several times a day about business and personal matters. They shared the explosive growth of the N.B.A., the ascension of Jordan to global basketball deity, the Chicago Bulls' six titles and the first Dream Team of N.B.A. superstars at the 1992 Summer Olympics in Barcelona, Spain. They often sit together at games, discussing matters "from the profound to the adolescent," Stern said.

"David is the best adult friend I've made in the second half of my life," Ebersol said Sunday before Game 3 of the finals, at NBC's compound outside Continental Arena.

The NBC-N.B.A. relationship was nearly ideal. NBC made money and the league got a devoted partner. But last year, as the advertising market slumped, Ebersol saw his hopes of continued profits, and keeping the N.B.A., evaporating.

"I think it excited Dick and David that they were growing the enterprise, but it began to level off at the end," said Bob Costas, who has been a host for NBC's N.B.A. studio show and has called games over the past dozen years.

A year ago last week, Ebersol and Stern took a lengthy walk along the beach from Marina del Rey, strolling six miles to Venice Beach and Santa Monica and back.

"Let me point out to you how much money we lost last year, and how much money we'll lose this coming year," Ebersol told Stern. He would not only not pay more, he was looking to pay less than the current $400 million annual average.

Ebersol made no offer at the time, but Stern said he knew the chances of keeping NBC were no better than 50-50. "We knew that given the changing marketplace, and given the limitations NBC found itself under, we'd likely have to go to market on the bidding," Stern said.

The conclusion became obvious. NBC Sports has lost $300 million in the past two seasons. In recent years, it shed baseball and National Football League rights to cut losses.

"We're expected to grow our business," Ebersol said. "And we can grow it by giving things up."

Ebersol bid $1.3 billion for four years — but Stern signed six-year deals with ESPN, ABC and AOL Time Warner's TNT channel worth $4.6 billion. The N.B.A. and AOL are also creating a new sports channel.

That Stern pulled off such a deal is remarkable; since the mid-1990s, regular-season ratings have tumbled 42 percent. And since hitting a peak in 1998, finals ratings are down 46 percent to a 10.0 so far this year.

Although Stern believes the deal will redefine cable TV, where networks finance sports-rights payments with subscriber fees, Ebersol sees risk caused by broadcast television's reduced role.

"The casual fan will have a lot fewer opportunities to get involved in the games during the playoffs," he said, specifically those without cable during the cable-only conference finals. "You can watch regular TV if you're in the back seat of David's car. So far, no one has been able to pick up ESPN or CNN or CNBC in a car."

Losing a major property is a blow to any division. It took reacquiring N.F.L. rights in 1998 for CBS to recover from losing them in 1994.

Andy Rosenberg, NBC's longtime lead N.B.A. director, said he told his production crew before the playoffs: "When you get old and look back, say: 'You know what? That was the best part of my career.'"

When the N.B.A. and NBC said goodbye last week in Marina del Rey, guests watched a nine-minute retrospective of their partnership.

It highlighted Marv Albert's "Yes!" calls and Costas's play-by-play of Jordan's finals-winning shot in 1998. Rod Thorn, the Nets' president, jokingly reminisced about the many great games of the past — all of them carried by CBS.

But the biggest laugh came when Costas recalled his favorite moment during a Bulls-Knicks playoff game. "Coming back from commercial, the Madison Square Garden marquee outside the arena was panned," he said. "In the foreground, you noticed this man with a dog. The dog had a suit on, a blue blazer. It was wearing a beret and had a cigarette dangling from its mouth. There was this long pause when we came back, where no one really knew what to say. Finally, Marv looked at Mike Fratello and said, 'Mike, always troubling when a dog smokes.'"

The room erupted in laughter.

JAN. 18, 1998

How About a Show
About Life's Minutiae in Chicago?

BY HARVEY ARATON

The cast of *Seinfeld* was leaving Don Ohlmeyer's office at NBC Studios in Hollywood recently when the door to the waiting room opened and in walked the ensemble from the runaway hit *Michael*.

"Oh my God," Jerry said, turning around, jerking his thumb and making eye contact with George. "You're not going to believe...."

"It's him, it's him," whispered George, stepping behind Jerry and nudging him in the back. "Go on, get over there and introduce us."

Jerry held back. "He doesn't know who I am," he said. "And even if he does, what's the protocol here? Do I make the first move? Play a little hard to get?"

"Jerry, this isn't Keith Hernandez, for God's sake, it's Michael," said Kramer. He rushed past George and Jerry and threw himself to the floor, at Michael's feet. "Your Airness," he said.

The ice broken, George walked over and put a hand on Michael's shoulder.

"Listen, Mike — you don't mind if I call you Mike? I've been meaning to call and tell you this but my secretary back at Vandalay, very big firm, lost the number. I just had to tell you that you were the absolute best thing in *Space Jam*. Hands downs, no one else even close."

"Thank you," Michael said.

"The Academy, they should be shot, those misers," George said. "They robbed you blind."

George edged closer. With a wink and a head twitch, he said, "Mike, just between us, did Bugs and Lola, you know, ever...?"

Michael smiled sheepishly. "I was kind of wondering about that myself," he said.

Jerry and George began to argue about whether Bugs Bunny and Lola Bunny could possibly have had carnal relations, so Elaine stepped up and curtseyed.

"Pleasure to meet you," Michael said. "And this is my supporting cast: Phil, Scottie and of course you know Dennis."

"Dennis, of course," Elaine said, as Dennis bent over, licked her hand and said, "I dig your dress."

"Get out," said Elaine. She said to herself, "Does he mean he likes it on me or does he want it for himself?"

Jerry asked Michael, "So what are you guys doing out here?"

"My agent thinks they want to talk to us about a show," Michael said.

"Oh, a show," Jerry said. "You hear that, George? Ohlmeyer wants to see Michael about a show."

"A *show*," said George.

"So," said Jerry. "What is this show supposed to be about?"

"Beats me," said Michael. "Maybe about a basketball team. Maybe nothing."

"Nothing," Jerry said, thoughtfully. "Nothing might work."

"What about your show?" Michael said. "I heard you guys were breaking up next season, just like us."

"Yeah, well, we just thought it was the right time," Jerry said. "Get out on top."

"Ohlmeyer's in there crying his eyes out right now," Kramer said. "Offered us big bucks to stay. Huge bucks. Unbelievable bucks. But, nah."

"The Fat Lady has eaten," George declared.

"I know," Scottie said, nodding. "Sometimes, you just have to say, 'I'm out of here.'"

"What do you guys have planned for next season?" said Phil. "I'm thinking of a sabbatical myself."

"Oh, George and I here are already working on a new script," Jerry said. "It's about, well, you know…"

"Pez," said George. "A documentary on Pez abuse in Eastern Europe."

Michael said, "I see." He looked at his watch and said they were running late. The casts wished each other luck. But when the door to Ohlmeyer's office closed, Jerry fumed: "We're not even done shooting this season and he's got another cast coming in. The nerve."

Elaine came charging out of the bathroom with a glass. She gave it to Jerry, who handed it to George, who passed it to Kramer, who placed it against the glass door and put his ear to it.

"Guys, I won't waste time making small talk," Kramer heard Ohlmeyer say. "We lost football. *Seinfeld* is history. We can't lose you, Michael. I've talked this over with Ebersol, Stern, Reinsdorf and Falk. And here's the offer: You stick together, play two more years, and we'll give you the 9 o'clock slot on Thursday night."

"What would we do?" Michael said.

"Whatever you want," Ohlmeyer said. "Sit around your restaurant and talk, beat the Knicks, make fun of someone. You have someone you can rank on, like Newman?"

"Jerry Krause," Scottie volunteered.

"Perfect," Ohlmeyer said.

Michael and Scottie looked at each other. "If we make more than what *E.R.* is getting, and Dennis here gets a new wardrobe, it's a deal," Michael said.

"Whoa," said Phil. "I don't think so. I said I needed a break until the Knicks call me. I'm out."

Ohlmeyer threw his hands up. "Well, what do we do for a coach?"

Suddenly, Kramer came crashing through the glass door, landing again at Michael's feet.

Michael looked at Ohlmeyer. "Could work," Ohlmeyer said.

"He's very Zen," Phil said, caressing his beard.

Kramer got up, stumbled over the glass shards and fell into Michael's lap. "Giddyap," he told the network's prize Bull, and one of its few remaining cash cows.

18

Laborious Lifestyle

If ever there was a propitious time for N.B.A. owners to pick a fight with their players — lock them out and risk blowing up a season — it was in the summer of 1998, with the growing belief that Michael Jordan had played his last game for the Bulls and that the six-time champions were scattering in all directions.

On top of that, the players union by this stage was greatly influenced — or in effect run — by David Falk, Jordan's longtime agent, whose client list just happened to include the union's top two officers, Patrick Ewing and Alonzo Mourning.

Historically, probably not coincidentally, the most effective players in the N.B.A. labor movement had been canny guards — Bob Cousy, who founded the union in his friend's basement in Worcester, Mass.; Oscar Robertson, who spearheaded legal challenges resulting in free agency; and Isiah Thomas, who fought off the power agents to redirect salary cap money for improved pension plans.

Ewing and Mourning, both centers, came up with a particularly clumsy idea to raise money for some cash-strapped players who hadn't prepared for a long work stoppage: a game in Atlantic City with courtside seats priced at $1,000.

"They make a lot of money, but they also spend a lot of money," Ewing said of the spendthrift players in a December story in *The Times* by Selena Roberts.

Context notwithstanding, many fans couldn't believe what they were hearing. Buddy, can you spare a grand?

Professional athletes, of course, are always at a disadvantage in labor showdowns. Fans want their games and will typically hold players earning millions accountable when deprived of them. That doesn't put the much-richer owners, who typically feed at the taxpayer trough, on the right side of history. In the 1998 lockout, which resulted in a 50-game regular season, there were many victims, including David Stern, whose reputation as the Everyman Commissioner took a hit.

And then there was Kenny Anderson, who more than anyone drove the players' plight into a figurative ditch.

Oct. 26, 1998

When Millionaires Are Laid Off

by Mike Wise

Two months after the National Basketball Association's lockout came and his paycheck went, Kenny Anderson began contemplating the unthinkable. It had nothing to do with asking his mother in Queens for his old room back or taking a part-time security job; he figured there were only so many indignities young millionaires should have to face.

But with his penchant for buying what he wanted and his accountant having to borrow against his stocks to keep investing, Anderson realized it might be time to do without. Sort of.

"I was thinking about selling one of my cars," he said recently, laughing. "I don't need all of them. You know, just get rid of the Mercedes."

After all, he can always fall back on the Porsche Carrera, the customized Range Rover or the Lexus sedan. When you have eight vehicles registered in your name or your wife's, there are choices.

Insurance and maintenance on the cars and sport utility vehicles have been costing Anderson about $75,000 a year. Throw in a mortgage in New York, rent in Los Angeles, four daughters, one marketing company, an agent's cut and legal fees, and a rough portfolio of the veteran N.B.A. player begins to emerge.

He is often fabulously wealthy, but sometimes the opulent lifestyle collides with a monstrous tax bracket. Tremendous financial obligations mount quickly, which can sometimes lead to economic insecurity for even some of the game's highest-paid players.

"A lot of people can't understand why the owners and players are fighting over money and how it might hurt the season," said Anderson, referring to the league's growing labor chasm. "I'd be upset too if I was a fan, paying our salaries. But it's like they say: The more you make, the more you spend. And right now, without my check, I have to start getting tight."

Anderson, the 28-year-old point guard of the Boston Celtics, was due his entire $5.8 million salary for the 1998–99 season on July 1 — the day N.B.A. owners declared a lockout after the collective bargaining agreement expired.

He is one of more than 20 players who were supposed to get paid during the summer but did not, and one of 226 players with guaranteed contracts who will not be paid for the first two weeks of the season, which were canceled on Oct. 13.

More cancellations may follow, and if more than 30 games are cut from the 82-game schedule, the league will strongly consider not playing the season. The N.B.A. hopes that the financial pressure this will place on the players will eventually divide them and prompt the union to sign an agreement that slows the growth of salaries and puts a ceiling on how much one player can earn.

As a measure of how severely the players' resolve will be tested, Anderson is losing $76,000 a game.

"I wouldn't want to miss the season, not just for financial reasons but losing a year of my playing career," said Anderson, a seven-year veteran. "But if I had to, I can. I've been without before.

"The guy I feel bad for is the one with the two- or three-year deal and now their contract is up. In that case, I think people will have their own agendas. It's going to be sticky. There might be some guys branching off, saying, 'I can't do this.' Not being in their situation, I can't blame them. When that happens, everyone will go, 'Oh, he's selling out.' But, hey, you got to live."

Scott Bercu, Anderson's Manhattan-based accountant, said, "These guys have got to concede for a very simple reason: They're losing money every time they don't play a game."

In addition to players like Anderson, who at least are under contract even if they are not being paid, there are nearly 200 registered free agents who have some of the same bills that Anderson has. Having signed a seven-year deal worth $49 million with the Portland Trail Blazers two years ago, Anderson is in a much better position than many of his peers. His contract average of $7 million a year does not compare with Michael Jordan's $33 million deal, but his annual income dwarfs the league's average salary of $2.6 million. But for now, the cash-flow problem is the same.

"I've had to sell some mutual funds and borrow against stocks to keep investing," Anderson said. "I've got enough to hold me over. And I definitely don't want anyone feeling sorry for me. I mean, when you make money like we do, it's pretty hard to get public sympathy. But it's all relative to your lifestyle and obligations."

In his Midtown Manhattan office, Bercu punches up Anderson's finances on a computer screen. In a blink, you learn that playing basketball for a living does not only guarantee you celebrity and wealth; there are mounds of checks to sign, too.

Anderson; his wife, Tami Akbar; and their two daughters, Lyric, 4, and Kenni, 2, live in a five-bedroom home in Beverly Hills. The pastel peach house has large pillars, a four-car garage and a gazebo in the backyard. Two stories below are a pool and tennis and basketball courts. The monthly rent is $12,500.

Anderson pays $7,200 in monthly child support for Danielle, 8, and Kristinise, 5, who were born to different women. He has been involved in each child's life as much as he can be during the season.

"They can burn a hole in your pocket real quick," he said. "I'm not saying it in a funny way, but you've got your schooling, day care, nanny. It just goes on and on."

Anderson also pays $3,000 a month on mortgage, property taxes and maintenance for his mother's home on Long Island. Of the $5.8 million he is supposed to receive this year, the agent David Falk, who negotiated the contract, is entitled to 4 percent — $232,000. Bercu said Anderson's legal and accounting fees run about $175,000 annually.

And then there is Kenny the Kid Enterprises, Anderson's fledgling marketing company, based in Century City, Calif., which at this point does not bring in as much money as it spends. Run by his longtime friend Rodney Henry, the company exists essentially to handle all of Anderson's day-to-day operations and appearances. A clothing line is in its infant stages. The company also books musical talent for outlets like BET (Black Entertainment Television) and helps further the acting career of Anderson's wife, who has done commercials and was once a regular on MTV's *Real World*.

With teams unable to provide daily public-relations assistance to every player, and with agents like Falk too burdened with other prominent clients to concentrate on promotion, many players are hiring or developing their own marketing firms. The cost for five employees, office space, supplies and telephone for Kenny the Kid runs $250,000 a year.

"Kenny doesn't live a life of Riley; he doesn't have unlimited money," Bercu said. "Without many shelters and at such a high tax rate, he's literally a partner with the government. Of the $5.8 million, I'd say he probably sees about $3 million."

Anderson said he used to give family members and friends loans of $3,000 to $5,000, but he has stopped doing that since the lockout began.

"I've got to get tight," he said. "I've cut back on certain things I usually do. You got to watch your money when it comes to family. I have to say no now even though I don't want to say no."

Bercu said: "He calls them loans, but I call them gifts. He's too generous and sweet sometimes for his own good. Especially when it's family. But then, when you come from where he came from…."

A New York schoolboy legend at Archbishop Molloy High School in Queens, Anderson has played for four teams the last three seasons. Once regarded as an heir apparent to the N.B.A. career assist leader John Stockton, Anderson has weathered injury and expectation while settling into a role of a solid playmaker the last several seasons. If his career lasts more than 10 years, he will be among the fortunate players.

"His life is really a short-lived life from a financial point of view," Bercu said. "One of the things I do for Kenny is invest for him, so I rely on money coming in to set aside long-term savings. Before the lockout began, we started borrowing against his stocks. We're talking a substantial loan. And then with the losses in the market. You know they're going to rebound. Still, for a lot of these guys without their salary checks, it's a bit of a nightmare situation."

Anderson is not clipping coupons yet. A rough estimate of his total financial obligations, not including personal expenses, runs $1 million annually, leaving him with $2 million in reserve. Anderson is allotted $10,000 a month by Bercu, "hanging-out money," as he likes to call it. Tami gets $3,500 from a special household account.

His favorite car is his 1995 Mercedes SL500 metallic red sedan — one of eight vehicles in a price range from $50,000 to $120,000.

"Those cars are extremely hard to insure," Bercu said. "Because of a couple of speeding tickets, we've had lots of difficulties. But what can you do? Ballplayers are into cars and jewelry. It's what they like. You can't help it."

Extravagant and expensive tastes have been a hallmark of young millionaire athletes. But without games and paychecks, N.B.A. players are about to learn the frugal side of living large. How long many of them can cope without a biweekly salary may mean the difference in their economic game of chicken with the owners.

"I just look at it as when this thing finally gets done, I get my money," Anderson said.

— POSTSCRIPT —

MIKE WISE, 2018: "The assignment was to find a player with real-life financial issues due to the lockout. Kenny was someone I knew well, a sweet guy who was usually an open book. He agreed to let me talk to his accountant to go over his finances, all of it. That's when he talked about — though I did note that he was laughing when he said it — having to sell one of his eight cars, the Mercedes. Not long after that story, I did a follow-up column on Kenny helping people in Lefrak City, the Queens housing development where he grew up, around Thanksgiving — you know, the *real* Kenny Anderson. But the column didn't get good play, no one paid it any mind and I always felt some regret about the first story because it had unintended consequences. It helped tilt public sentiment to the owners, enhanced the wrongheaded perception that there was no real lockout, just greedy players wanting more."

19

The Jordan Heirs

During the 2001 N.B.A. finals, Richard Sandomir of *The Times* delivered a story about the marketing residuals of Allen Iverson's breakout season with the 76ers as they battled (and lost) to the Lakers.

He wrote: "On Sunday, Reebok offered a new Iverson commercial during Game 3 of the N.B.A. finals, a frenetic visual recap of this season, in which he was the league scoring champion, led the Sixers to the Eastern Conference title and was voted the most valuable player of the regular season and the All-Star Game. The spot ends by asking, 'Any more questions?'"

Todd Krinsky, Reebok's general manager for its sports division, had one. In Sandomir's story, he said, "We're asking the public, 'What else does he have to do for America to embrace him?'"

Iverson was nicknamed The Answer, but there was no satisfying one for Krinsky's question. Rare was the player who sacrificed and got more out of his body than Iverson, the explosive flyweight for whom there was no unshakable defender off the dribble. But however fierce and fearless, Iverson broke rules, flouted defiance, and that limited his appeal in post-Jordan America to a rebellious youth culture, urban and suburban.

That made him a force in selling jerseys and sneakers, but as the league grew younger, with more of a hip-hop motif, older fans were more inclined to mourn the passing of the Jordan/Bulls era, and tune the sport out.

Bill Carter, *The Times*'s television critic, had addressed the problem, reporting in March 2000 that NBC's N.B.A. ratings had gone into a tailspin, down 20 percent from its 1998 peak. "After spending $1.75 billion on rights for four N.B.A. seasons starting last season — more than double the previous amount — NBC is now suffering through a terrible N.B.A. year," he wrote.

What happened? Jordan's departure was obvious, but David Stern began to believe that the influx of high school players — no longer products of the March Madness hype machine — was deeply problematic. So was the shoe company agenda, churning out youth-targeted spots that were edgier, angrier. Even the three-title teaming of Shaq and Kobe in the L.A. megamarket, coached by Phil Jackson, couldn't match the standard set by Jordan.

They all had their own shoes now, but filling Michael's was out of the question.

MAY 27, 2001

He Just Wins, and Wins

BY MIKE WISE

LOS ANGELES — In September 1999, Phil Jackson closed up his home in Montana for the winter, packed up some clothes and embarked on the long drive to Los Angeles, where the Lakers and his new life awaited.

Beyond the professional challenge of trying to harmoniously converge two of the game's brightest young stars — the team led by Shaquille O'Neal and Kobe Bryant had months earlier been swept by the San Antonio Spurs in the second round of the playoffs — Jackson had other things on his mind.

He and his wife, June, were going through a painful separation that Jackson feared would cost him his family. The man who had won a championship as a player in New York, won six titles as a coach in Chicago, was on his way to L.A. to complete a coastal transformation.

In the middle of the Sierra Nevadas, Jackson pulled over to the side of the road and wept.

"My daughters had made this tape," he said. "It was about going out and living life again, going out and finding love again. They were trying to tell me, 'You've got to find this passion again about moving on.' I felt so fortunate that they were so supportive, I just crossed a little two-lane highway and went to this space. I just felt like, 'Man, I've been given this unbelievable opportunity.'"

On Sunday afternoon at the Staples Center, Jackson and the Lakers will try to complete an astonishing four-game sweep of the Spurs, a team regarded as the most formidable challenge to the defending National Basketball Association champions.

Dismantling San Antonio by 39 points in Game 3 of the Western Conference finals on Friday night, the Lakers have not lost in 56 days, winning 18 straight and 10 in a row during the playoffs. They are playing so dominantly that the thought of the first unbeaten postseason in league history is being seriously bandied about.

What's more, as a coach, Jackson is on the verge of winning a record 19 straight playoff series, dating from the 1995–96 Chicago Bulls team he coached, a mark that would surpass the legendary Red Auerbach, whose Boston Celtics won 18 straight series in the 1960s.

"I didn't realize there was a record for that," he said on Friday afternoon at the Lakers' practice facility. "I'm not familiar with it.

"It's really hard to be a gracious winner. I've tried to be a gracious winner in the past, but it doesn't matter what you do. Whether it's confidence or your own accomplishments that stay with you, then it somehow is read as an arrogance. I always try to work against that.

"One of the things that I remember on my father's desk when he was superintendent of the churches in the state — there was a caricature of a guy with a balloon head, string attached to the shoulders, little teeny feet. The caption on it read, 'The bigger your head gets, the easier your shoes are to fill.' That, to me, personified my father, who was a very humble, very approachable man. That's who I tried to emulate growing up."

Many of his peers and his staunchest critics watched him almost fall on his face less than three months ago, as the tumult of the regular season reduced the defending champions to a dysfunctional group with no title aspirations. A more willful Bryant wanted more freedom, a stubborn O'Neal wanted the ball. Their petulant public feud, combined with mounting losses and injuries, had Jackson suddenly facing a genuine challenge to his glistening-trophy image.

How could this have happened to the Zenmaster, the counterculture coach? The players' agents, the fans and the news media kept telling him to do something, anything.

The 55-year-old graying man had to reach out to a 22-year-old All-Star guard.

"What I said to Kobe was, 'If you're really unhappy, then I'll help in this situation,'" Jackson said of a February meeting between him and Bryant that he now considers the turning point of the season. "'I'll find a way to trade you to a situation where you'll be really happy.' That was a question I didn't want him to answer, but I wanted him to think about. I just talked to him about finding a happiness playing basketball. I wanted him to be settled."

Jackson said the meeting lasted half an hour on a Saturday before a Sunday game. "Kobe was playing really well, but there still wasn't that fulfillment in the game for him. In the process, I told him, 'You see how Iverson has to play, you see the abuse that he's giving his body?'" Jackson said, referring to Allen Iverson of Philadelphia. "'This is what's going to happen if you force that kind of activity. This tears up a guy's body. We run an offensive system where you can do a minimal amount of wear and tear to get the maximum out of your physical effort. We want to save you for the real dramatic effort, which is the playoffs."

"What I've wanted him to do, and what he's doing now, is to develop that trust between his teammates. When you're a coach and see that a player has a great game like he had earlier this season, and the players on the bench aren't rooting for him, and players on the floor are upset about it, and guys on the bench are making comments — 'Pass the ball!' — well, the coach has to take control of the situation."

In hindsight, Jackson views the O'Neal-Bryant feud as an evolving relationship between two superstar teammates symbolic of any N.B.A. era.

"Back in my playing days, there was a situation where we were playing the Baltimore Bullets in the sixth game of the playoffs, and Willis didn't get the basketball and Clyde shot a bunch of shots," he said. "Wesley Unseld had about 35 points and 35 rebounds, or something incredible. Willis had to just say: 'Hey, Walt, get me the ball. I need the ball more in the post.'

"This has been going on ever since I've been playing. This is what goes on in basketball."

Jackson added: "It's like a marriage. Marriage can go along blissfully and then someone can make a mistake and be in a very awkward position. And it upsets the whole apple cart. I'm not talking about infidelity, it could be something very minor, like you forget a gift for an anniversary. Relationships are something you have to keep mending all the time, and this is what basketball really is about, too."

The most striking images seen on national television today are of O'Neal and Bryant embracing. The pouting and the petulance — like the losses — have long disappeared.

Jackson's coaching, however, has taken its toll. He filed for divorce from June two years ago. They still share the cabin they have in Montana, taking turns so their children can visit each parent during the summer. Jackson said he had made a concerted effort "to see that a loss of a life partner was not going to destroy my family or my attachment to my family."

"It's something that a lot of men go through," he said. "Having come out of a career, having raised a family, having that be the focus. How do you keep your relationship with your kids intact? That's been my challenge."

Jackson said he returned to therapy for two years "to become more developed as a person" but is no longer seeking counseling. Since December 1999, he has been dating Jeanie Buss, the daughter of Jerry Buss, the Laker owner. Jackson said he was often ribbed for "dating the boss's daughter."

Jackson still gives his players personalized books, and he occasionally dims the lights at practice to lead yoga sessions. Not that his players are buying into all his methods. "Those books look great on my shelf," Ron Harper said.

Steve Kerr, the San Antonio guard, played on three of Jackson's championship teams in Chicago. "That whole counterculture thing was kind of a crock in Chicago, too," Kerr said. "He loves to play it up.

"I think it was the truth in New York when he was playing. He was legitimately — and maybe somewhat embarrassingly to him now — the hippie, the counterculture guy, the foreign substances or whatever. But in Chicago, he was a family man, a guy who sort of enjoyed the limelight, enjoyed sort of manipulating and tweaking the press and the fans a little bit. He enjoyed the whole process. I see the same thing here."

Jackson said: "That's accurate. It's obvious that I like to do some things that are eclectic and different. But I haven't smoked weed in 30 years. As part of my past, it will always be there, because I've admitted to it. But the reality is, I meditate. I'm a meditator. I sit in the mornings. I have a quiet life, a peaceful life, and that's the way I try and run my personal life."

Jackson and his longtime friend Charley Rosen released a book in the spring, *More Than a Game*. In it is a scene in which he watches the Lakers lose Game 4 to the Spurs at a motel in Laramie, Wyo. — he remembers the analyst Doug Collins going on about the Lakers' being "chronic underachievers." The book also details his trip from Montana to Los Angeles, how his professional journey became a personal one.

"I was overwhelmed with all these feelings and then I realized this is a wonderful opportunity to explore," he said. "I'm going out to a whole new place, with no support structure. I have to build a new home on my own, and I've got to find a comfort zone to work with these players.

"I knew I could adapt. I could change."

JUNE 13, 2002

Renting Space in Shaq and Kobe's World

BY MIKE WISE

EAST RUTHERFORD, N.J. — The big man was in the lane, turning this way, feinting that way, before releasing a soft, eight-foot floater in the face of a front line that never had a chance. One minute 24 seconds remained in another championship season for Shaquille O'Neal and his Los Angeles Lakers, and all he could do was turn toward the stands and begin shouting defiantly.

"He's playing for everything anybody ever said about him," Magic Johnson said a few minutes later, amid the celebration on the Continental Arena court.

Kobe Bryant, O'Neal's partner in time, had jackknifed through two defenders earlier, scoring on one of those degree-of-difficulty layups that pushed the lead to 9. They combined for 59 points in Game 4 of the N.B.A. finals, and the Lawrence O'Brien trophy was again theirs, picking up where all their Lakers ancestors left off.

"When you mix those two together and you have a superb, super coach in Phil Jackson, who never lets things get too complacent, oh, man," Johnson said, shaking his head, "that's a bad combination."

Barely audible chants of "Three-peat! Three-peat!" began to seep out of the building, and the Lakers were suddenly no longer two-time defending champions. They were an official dynasty again, alongside Magic and Kareem, George Mikan and all the rest. Not counting Minneapolis or Jerry West and Wilt Chamberlain, that is eight titles in 22 years.

"They talk about the Yankees," Johnson said, beaming as if he had played instead of watched as a Lakers vice president. "Well, we're the Yankees of our sport."

This was the classic Lakers playoff victory, laced with equal parts grit and grace. They weathered Jason Kidd's binge of points and Kenyon

Martin's tenacity, and Robert Horry, Derek Fisher and Rick Fox played as magnificently as they have all postseason in the 113–107 victory.

Rick Fox smiled the other day when asked about winning four championships in a row, something only Bill Russell's Boston Celtics — who won eight straight — have done in N.B.A. history.

"Kobe's in the locker room talking about putting in double time this summer," Fox said. "I've already committed to the strength coach to get back on my program of two years ago. Shaq has even said he's going to do his body right this summer.

"If anything came from that series with the Sacramento Kings, they gave us enough of a battle to have us think about some of the greater things we can do as a unit."

Fox went on, elaborating the point: "You don't want to get beyond the moment of Wednesday, and this opportunity of winning another championship. But the thoughts and talk have turned to making this more than just this year, more than just a three-peat."

The Nets had fight last night. Martin and O'Neal tugged on a loose ball like siblings tug on wishbones with about six minutes left, and Martin was giving no quarter to the 7-foot-1 Goliath.

Kidd was pumping in shots in the third quarter, trying everything he could offensively to bring the Nets back. But it was never a fair scrap. The Nets were just in the way, is all, like everyone else in the league.

This is the harsh reality for the next few years. It's Shaq and Kobe's world, and the rest of the N.B.A. is just renting space in it.

Oh, there will be a Sacramento now and then to rock the boat, and who knows, maybe a real center will migrate to this side of the Mississippi before Kobe is endorsing the Skywalker land speeder. But it does not look good today.

Think about it. O'Neal missed a bunch of games this season because of toe surgery, battled balky knees and sutures in his hand and still won his third straight title. Bryant was fed intravenously for three days while he battled food poisoning, and the Lakers still managed to fend off the Kings in the Western Conference finals.

"The first one is a novelty and it feels good," Bryant said. "The first one will always be the best one. The second one, the adversity that we went through throughout the course of the year made that one special. We proved that we belonged.

"And this one, it's kind of making a step as one of the great teams. It feels great. Having a seven-game series against Sacramento, being down 3–2, it challenged us. We responded to it. It makes this one that much more special."

For the second straight season, the Lakers did not have the best record or home-court advantage in their own conference — and still won. Players actually acknowledged they did not get incredibly motivated for the regular season, saying that the emphasis was on getting their bodies and minds right for the playoffs.

When the marquee team can take nights off and win, what's to stop more teams from coasting and still finding a way into the playoffs? The competition is just not as keen as it was when it was important for Michael Jordan's Bulls to win 72 games in 1996.

There will be blockbusters and draft unknowns coming to the fore. But for now, only two tantalizing N.B.A. personnel stories are out there until next summer:

Whether San Antonio can convince Jason Kidd that the Spurs are for him when Kidd becomes a free agent next summer, and whether Orlando can convince Tim Duncan that playing alongside Tracy McGrady will be more rewarding long-term than sticking it out in San Antonio when Duncan can exercise his option in the summer of 2003.

As for the knocking off the Lakers in the next five years, get in line.

O'Neal was asked the other day what he thought about Mikan, the gargantuan star of his time, too big and talented for anyone to stop him. Mikan was the last Laker center to lead the franchise to three straight titles, something Kareem Abdul-Jabbar and Chamberlain never accomplished.

"I've never seen him play," O'Neal said of Mikan. "When you look at the records, though, he's up there."

O'Neal said he speaks often to Mikan, now retired and battling health problems in Arizona. "He tells me how I'm a great player, how I'm a joy to watch," he said. "Coming from a guy like that, it's a boost."

Of comparing eras, he added: "You can't compare a 1960 Benz to a 2002 Benz. We're just made different. Same level. Same greatness."

Same old story. From Mikan to Magic, to Shaq and Kobe, passing titles like batons through time. The Lakers. Again.

Dec. 17, 2004

The Collapse of Kobe

by Howard Beck

LOS ANGELES — Kobe Bryant got everything he wanted. Isn't that what everyone said last summer? Wasn't that the premise when the Los Angeles Lakers gave Bryant, their star guard, a $136 million contract and banished his two greatest tormentors, Shaquille O'Neal and Phil Jackson?

Hollywood was supposed to become an all-Kobe, all-the-time paradise, with Bryant the dominant figure, on and off the court. After eight years of sharing the stage with O'Neal, the superstar center, and five bumpy seasons of playing under Jackson, the superstar coach, Bryant was, finally, indisputably, the center of the Lakers' universe.

Somehow, paradise turned to paradise lost.

And on Wednesday night, Bryant was squirming uncomfortably in his chair, hooked up via satellite, as the ESPN anchor John Saunders confronted him, bluntly, about his "fall from grace." The choice of words by Saunders was a harsh but accurate summation of Bryant's past 17 months.

He has been accused of sexual assault. He has publicly admitted to adultery. He has lost millions of dollars in endorsements. His personal life has been dissected publicly. His popularity has plummeted. And he has been blamed, some say unfairly, for the breakup of the Lakers, the league's reigning dynasty, with three championships since 2000. So there was Bryant, on national television, fiddling with an earpiece and trying for the first time to make amends to a disenchanted public.

"I can't sit up here and say I'm not at fault at all for anything that took place," Bryant said, in a rare mea culpa. "I mean, if I could go back and do some things differently, I would. The Shaq thing, the Phil thing, and all of that. But there's nothing I can do about it now. I can only learn from what took place in the past and just try to move on and just try to do the best job I can and just try and help us win ballgames."

"I've seen," Bryant said, his voice growing tight, "a lot of dark days."

The Lakers, the N.B.A.'s most venerated franchise, and Bryant, formerly its most glorified icon, remain the league's most compelling drama. It's just that in the past few months, the soap opera subplots are no longer offset by spectacular basketball.

The Lakers were 12–9 going into last night's game with Sacramento, third in the Pacific Division and eighth in the Western Conference, just barely in the playoff picture. Bryant, the league's pre-eminent shooting guard, is struggling to prop up a team constructed largely of role players. He is averaging 27.1 points a game and on pace for career highs in assists (6.8 a game) and rebounds (7.6), but is shooting a career-low 39.7 percent from the field.

Worse, Bryant is again at the center of controversy.

Bryant recently accused Karl Malone, a future Hall of Famer, and a former teammate and friend, of flirting with Bryant's wife, Vanessa. The rift between Bryant and Malone sprang into view over the last week, dragging Bryant and the franchise down another notch.

"This thing is out of control here," a longtime Lakers official bemoaned. "It's a disaster."

Critics and supporters of Bryant believe that his wife, Vanessa, is the source of many of his troubles.

By Bryant's admission, it was his marriage to Vanessa that caused the estrangement from his parents, Joe and Pamela Bryant.

Over time, Bryant's inner circle collapsed. He also became cut off from his two sisters and dumped his agent, Arn Tellem, who had represented Bryant since he came out of high school in 1996.

Now, Bryant's inner circle is a two-person committee: Vanessa Bryant and his agent, Rob Pelinka. As Bryant's relationships with others, including Jackson, eroded, there was no voice of reason to guide him, longtime Lakers staff members said.

The team's troubles had been brewing for years, with Bryant alternately feuding with O'Neal and Jackson, even as the triumvirate combined to make the Lakers perennial championship contenders.

It all melted down last spring, when the Lakers lost to the Detroit Pistons, four games to one, in the N.B.A. finals. The Lakers had five presumed Hall of Famers — Bryant, O'Neal, Malone and point guard Gary Payton, all guided by Jackson — but they were no match for the more unified Pistons.

A month later, the dynasty was smashed into bits. O'Neal, believing correctly that the Lakers' owner, Jerry Buss, was determined to rebuild around Bryant, demanded a trade. The Lakers sent O'Neal to the Miami Heat.

Jackson, who at the midway point last season told Lakers officials that he could no longer coach Bryant, was not offered a new contract. Payton was traded to Boston, and Malone underwent knee surgery that put his career in doubt, and the Lakers had suddenly been stripped of their vaunted star power. They also lost two valued leaders when Rick Fox was traded (he later retired) and Derek Fisher signed with the Golden State Warriors. The only one left was Bryant.

For several months last season, he boasted to teammates and coaches that he would leave as a free agent, putting everyone in the front office on edge.

When free agency came, Bryant spoke to five other teams and entered into a serious courtship with the Los Angeles Clippers.

Though tempted by the Clippers, Bryant finally re-signed with the Lakers on July 15, a day after O'Neal was traded to Miami. Every day since, Bryant has tried to live down the notion that he was responsible for the team's breakup.

"I didn't chase anybody out," Bryant told ESPN.

That is a decidedly gray area, however, and few people seem to believe Bryant.

"My sense is that it's tough to be owner, coach, G.M. and player," one Western Conference general manager said, referring to Bryant. "He obviously is a great player. It's not a healthy situation." Clearly, Buss chose to rebuild around his younger star, the one with the dazzling moves and the otherworldly dunks, the one who, at 26, was entering his prime and was renowned for his dedication.

The only problem is, this Kobe Bryant was no longer the media darling who graced magazine covers starting at age 18 and made corporate sponsors swoon with his smile and charm.

The battles with Jackson and especially O'Neal, who is wildly popular among N.B.A. players, left Bryant with a bad reputation in the league. The rape charge in the summer of 2003, though dropped this September, left Bryant tarnished everywhere else.

His decline in popularity is starkly reflected in jersey sales, according to data provided by SportScan INFO, which compiles sales information from sporting good retailers across the United States.

In 2002, three versions of Bryant's jersey placed among the top 20 in sales, a combined total of 312,665 jerseys, according to SportScan. In 2003, that figure plummeted to 89,831 before rebounding to 136,964 for the current year.

For the four-week holiday shopping period, Bryant had no jerseys in the top 20.

"The fact that he doesn't have any jerseys right now in the top 10 or even the top 20 is a real fall for Kobe Bryant, a genuine fall," said Neil Schwartz, director of marketing for SportScan, which is based in West Palm Beach, Fla.

O'Neal and Jackson have criticized Bryant in recent months. The Seattle SuperSonics star Ray Allen described him as a selfish player. In a new song titled "These Are Our Heroes," the rapper Nas mocks Bryant's sexual liaison with a 19-year-old hotel concierge, the woman who later accused him of rape.

"You can't do better than that? The hotel clerk who adjusts the bathroom mat? Now you lose sponsorships that you thought had your back," Nas raps, referring to the abandonment of Bryant by McDonald's and Nutella, among others.

The Lakers' sole concern is Bryant's ability to lift his new teammates. Bryant has been hard on teammates in practice, at times profanely calling out players for a lack of effort or precision.

"I don't think anyone likes him," an agent with a client on the Lakers' roster said. "He's a means to an end."

Long perceived as arrogant and aloof, and known to be intensely stubborn, Bryant is trying too hard to become a leader, a longtime Lakers official said.

"His heart is in the right place," the official said. Team officials say Bryant has been a tireless cheerleader on the court, and sometimes selfless to a fault.

"I don't know what else honestly we could ask from him or what else he could do," another longtime staff member said.

Yet the ill perceptions remain, that Bryant is a bad teammate and a difficult personality. Some believe it will hurt the franchise's ability to attract free agents. But the general manager, Mitch Kupchak, said the team would weather the storms.

"Time has a way of minimizing the media hype surrounding an event," he said. "It just does. It may take six months, it may take a year, but Kobe's going to do the right thing.

"We do the right things as an organization, and it will outlast any quote-unquote hit we've taken the last couple days."

Dec. 13, 2006

The Synthetic Jordan Era Has Lost Its Air

by Harvey Araton

The anticipated trading of Allen Iverson by the Philadelphia 76ers will mark an unofficial end to a dubious period of professional basketball. Call it the Synthetic Jordan Era, when young, emerging stars had a sole shoe company-driven agenda to be like Mike.

Except it was less about the core values on which six Bulls championships were built across the 1990s and more about the trappings of personal transcendence, that existential place where a team, above all, is a platform for its premier celebrity pitchman.

It turns out that a penthouse in Philadelphia is an unfulfilling perk, a lonely palace, and after 10-plus years, 16,253 shots and 19,583 points, playoffs excluded, Iverson has apparently decided he can't take it anymore.

With his 76ers locker already cleaned out of do-rags and flat-brim caps, he will be happy to hook up with, among others, Kevin Garnett in Minnesota or Paul Pierce in Boston. Times have changed. LeBron James aims to share and Dwyane Wade's championship love-in with Shaquille O'Neal last season was 1960s old school. While dodging trade specifics before coaching the Celtics to a 97–90 victory over the Knicks on Monday night at Madison Square Garden, Doc Rivers said he understood why Iverson, the so-called Answer, would suddenly demand to go someplace where he would have to shoulder only half the questions.

"The pressure of carrying your team is unbearable," Rivers said. "And no single player has done it successfully."

No single one? Here we run smack into that double-edged Jordan legacy on which the young swashbucklers of the mid-to-late 1990s couldn't help but impale themselves.

They were unwitting byproducts of the most prolific promotional campaign the sports industry had seen, a blitz so consuming that we didn't think twice about shrinking Jordan's teammates into his supporting cast, his elfish Jordanaires.

Forgotten was the fact that Jordan barely scratched the postseason surface before Scottie Pippen and Horace Grant came along. Ignored was the startling sum of 55 victories accumulated by the Bulls when Jordan first took leave of the sport on the eve of the 1993–94 season, an achievement unmatched by any N.B.A. team in its post-franchise-player incarnation.

What am I saying? Certainly not that Pippen was Jordan's equal, but that his contributions and Hall of Fame credentials and those of others were often minimized by the Nike-inspired and league-abetted sell. Players who earned what has come to be known as max money under the salary cap became more warlord than leader in the post-Jordan years. Skewed were the standards of stardom. The concept of multiple great players or even two sharing the ball and the attention, coexisting in pursuit of a common cause, was largely lost on the new breed.

"I think every player grows up wanting to be the star," Rivers said. "But at the end of the day, you hope that winning shines brighter in their minds."

That, unfortunately, wasn't the case when Alonzo Mourning divorced Larry Johnson in Charlotte; when Stephon Marbury set out on a search for the inner Starbury because he couldn't stomach being second in salary to Garnett in Minnesota; when Philadelphia wasn't big enough for Iverson and the young Jerry Stackhouse; when Tracy McGrady refused to play Pippen to Vince Carter's Jordan in Toronto and subsequently suffered through nightmarish losing seasons while playing part of that time for Rivers in Orlando.

On and on it went, into the 21st century when Kobe Bryant had to prove his manhood sans Shaq in Los Angeles, the high-end talent spreading thinner and the basketball public turning increasingly contemptuous of players it perceived as overhyped and underachieving. They were far from faultless, but as always in this sport, the players were the most convenient targets, as opposed to industry forces that produced them. How would Larry Bird and

Magic Johnson have been perceived if they'd come along 15 years later and wound up on desultory teams in Toronto and Orlando?

"People get mad at me in Boston when I talk about Larry, but great as he was, and Larry was great, how would he have done if he didn't have Hall of Fame players around him — not one, when he won his first championship, not two, but three," Cedric Maxwell, the former Celtic, now analyzing games on Boston-area radio, said Monday night.

In no particular order, he meant Robert Parish, Kevin McHale and Tiny Archibald, the Iverson of his day until Achilles surgery and the Celtics' selfless system forced him to adapt his explosive small-guard skills.

In Maxwell's typically direct opinion, the ghost of Red Auerbach will not haunt the Celtics if they land the shot-happy Iverson, as long as they don't surrender too much of their future. As a synthetic Jordan, at least Iverson has been uniquely talented, a gritty little crowd-pleaser who carried the 76ers past a weak Eastern Conference into the 2001 league finals.

It's one thing to be a Jordan wannabe, another to be an Iverson knockoff. The Knicks have managed to wind up with two, Marbury and Steve Francis (who laughably answers to the nickname Franchise), both struggling now to fit in as playmakers after years of bullheaded rushes to the rim or passes from compromised airborne positions.

Tattoos, warts and all, Iverson can make a strong case that he has been the Philadelphia franchise for a decade, no insignificant contribution to that city, but, upon further review, not exactly a ringing endorsement for the sport at large.

20

Slam Bang

There was a moment in a playoff game in mid-May of 1999 that symbolized where the N.B.A. product was headed in the post-Jordan era, when a game once celebrated for its balletic beauty and uncommon dexterity was turning into a macho demolition of brute force.

It was another of those annual Knicks-Heat scrums of attrition always flirting with near atrocity, Game 4 of a first-round series in which Pat Riley's Heat exploded for 87 points while the Knicks were erupting for 10 fourth-quarter points on the way to finishing with an unsightly 72.

I was sitting at a baseline press table near the Miami bench as the Heat's Terry Porter sped the other way on the break. Latrell Sprewell — his team down 11, pretty much conceding the night — chased Porter down and hammered him to the floor, just for the hell of it.

Stan Van Gundy, Riley's lead assistant, bolted out of his seat and walked vigorously down the aroused Miami bench, planting seeds for a decisive Game 5. "Remember all that," he screamed. "Remember what they do!"

They, of course, being the team coached by Van Gundy's kid brother, Jeff.

Why, exactly, had too much of the N.B.A. devolved into feuding gangs that couldn't shoot straight? The rules, allowing for hand-checking, among other defensive advantages, were a major reason. But so were the meet-force-with-force mentalities, principally espoused by Riley during his early '90s

Knicks days, and coinciding with the rise of Shaq, whose impressive skill set was initially less celebrated than his ability to bring down a backboard.

The more physical the game grew, the more combative the sides were and the more foul-mouthed and fiery many courtside fans became. The lines were blurring between the N.B.A. and WWE and finally, on one disastrous night in November 2004, those lines disappeared completely. As if timed for maximum promotion, the riot that became known as Malice at the Palace (of Auburn Hills) ended just in time for the 11 o'clock news.

There was one bit of positivity from the Pacers-Pistons fiasco that spilled into the stands, thanks to a reprobate fan and the player-pugilist later known as Metta World Peace: The rematch of the teams just happened to be scheduled for Christmas night on national TV. In the long run, selling car wrecks was not what David Stern had in mind.

JAN. 5, 1994
Shattering Shaquille's Slamfest
BY HARVEY ARATON

A new television commercial for a long-distance telephone service concludes with Shaquille O'Neal's father hanging up the line in a phone booth. In a parody of his son's signature dunk, Phillip Harrison slams the receiver down. The glass enclosure shatters. "And you wonder," says Daddy Shaq, "where he gets it from."

Actually, we don't have to wonder why Shaquille O'Neal doesn't quite get it.

He's only 21 years old, this 7-foot-1-inch, 300-pound spectacle and marketing sensation, so it's unfair to expect that he grasp the enormous influence of his visuals being beamed into living rooms worldwide. What is sad is that his father would not only let his son be packaged as basketball's robo cop in search of an auto wreck, but would participate in this socially repugnant campaign.

Going into last night's 100–95 loss to Patrick Ewing and the Knicks at Madison Square Garden, O'Neal happened to be the leading scorer in the National Basketball Association, second in field goal percentage, third in rebounds and fifth in blocked shots. Yet the geniuses who represent O'Neal and the sponsors whose products he endorses are peddling O'Neal as a player who devastates backboards, not opposing defenses.

"It's not as if he hasn't lived up to expectations, that he needs this kind of sales pitch," said Russell Granik, the N.B.A.'s deputy commissioner. He said the league's take on the O'Neal ad campaign is that it is doing no one any good, that it wishes it could help make it disappear. For starters, the N.B.A. could cease putting its licensing stamp on video games like Acclaim's "N.B.A. Jam," stylistically complete with "backboard-breaking jams."

In his soft drink commercial, O'Neal bends a rim. In a basketball shoe spot incessantly shown, he confounds the backboard architects by smashing their supposedly unbreakable product to smithereens.

As O'Neal did twice as a rookie last season, Darryl Dawkins shattered backboards a dozen or so years ago. Compared with the game's emerging passing wizards Magic Johnson and Larry Bird, Dawkins developed the reputation of a one-trick dunce. He made up cute rhymes celebrating his worthless feats of strength that sent glass flying everywhere and delayed the game for up to an hour.

In America's celebrity mart, yesterday's rhyme is today's rap. In one of the songs on his album released last summer, O'Neal brags, "I jam it, I slam it, I make sure it's broke."

What's wrong with these pictures and lyrics? O'Neal's commercial persona represents an insidious glorification of needless destruction. It is the exponential advancement of showboating and trash talking, all for effect. With youth violence a national scourge, here we have basketball's most visible star telling kids that the coolest thing they can do on a basketball court is to disable it.

O'Neal's agent, Leonard Armato, says that's missing the point. He compares O'Neal's backboard busting to psychologists who advise clients to beat up their pillow. "A new-age thinking," said Armato. "It says, 'Don't blow up a building; take it out on a rim.'"

Altogether missing the subtlety, the 4-year-old in my home occasionally wants to hang on the rim of his Nerf ball set until the backboard dislodges and the stickers peel the paint off the wall.

The *New York Post* columnist Phil Mushnick wrote recently of an outbreak in New York City schoolyards of rimless backboards and the efforts of an organization called the Gabe Velez Foundation to raise money to fix them. According to John Murray, the head of the Department of Human Development and Family Studies at Kansas State University in Manhattan, Kan., this may be an exercise in futility, thanks to O'Neal.

"Shaquille sends a message about how the game is played now, about force and power," said Murray, who has done extensive research on TV violence and its effect on children. "It's another example of how violence has permeated all sports, how it's become the primary sports marketing outtake."

"Watching the games over the holidays, it seemed to me that it's worse than ever," Murray said. "Of course, it affects kids' behavior. Ripping down the rim isn't supposed to be part of basketball, but kids see Shaquille doing it, so it becomes incorporated into their culture."

He knows this firsthand. The father of two boys, 12 and 8, Murray came home from the office recently to find the family's fiberglass backboard crashed to the driveway cement.

"One of the neighbor's kids was hanging from the rim," he sighed. "The whole thing collapsed."

May 3, 1998

In Aftermath of Fight, Van Gundy Became the Little Big Coach

By Mike Wise

Kim Van Gundy tuned in to talk radio on Friday, just to see what Greater New York was saying about her husband. Between suggestions that Alonzo Mourning might need a tetanus shot and someone wondering if Madison Square Garden had stooped to midget wrestling, callers to WFAN were merciless.

"I don't know why I listened, because he got beat up pretty bad," Kim Van Gundy said. "They kept saying it was not a good idea for him to come off the bench. Was it stupid because he's 5-9? I don't know, but his size hasn't hurt him yet."

Exactly what was the itty-bitty Jeff Van Gundy thinking when he sprinted onto the basketball court Thursday night, jumped into a fight between the brawny 6-foot-10-inch Mourning and the 6-7 Larry Johnson and ended up polishing the floor with his jacket?

"I look at the tape and I look like I'm overmatched," Van Gundy said. "Obviously, I was. But I don't regret what I did. People were trying to make it like I was attacking him. I was just trying to make sure it didn't escalate. Guess I was a nonfactor, huh?"

Indeed, the replays show Van Gundy clinging to Mourning's leg like a 2-year-old who does not want to be left with the babysitter or, as Chris Mills put it, "like a jockey who fell off his horse and held on for dear life."

Back on his feet, Van Gundy went off on a tirade as a grinning Charles Oakley held his fiery coach back.

This was not the basketball insomniac who spent hours dissecting game film in his paper-strewn office, the Little Coach Who Could. Nor was it the dour-looking, pasty-faced figure whom one Chicago columnist said needs to go a little lighter on the formaldehyde. "The national poster boy for nerds" was how the columnist Greg Cote put it in yesterday's *Miami Herald*.

"Man, Jeff has unbelievable heart and courage," Allan Houston said. "You guys just never see it."

With the decisive game in this impossibly insane series to be played today at Miami Arena, you no longer know if the Knicks coach is diagramming plays or waiting for Pat Riley and the Heat after school, behind the cafeteria. Either way, the brutal humorists who make fun of his physical appearance have new material.

"That's O.K., we've heard them all," Kim Van Gundy said. "From 'he looks like a funeral home director' to the comments about the dark circles under his eyes. One of the papers ran a fashion comparison between Pat and Jeff, making fun of Jeff's suits because they're bought off the rack. I mean, this is the guy I've gone out with since I was 15 years old. It hurts for a lot of reasons, but mostly because, well, I buy his suits."

In fact, the bags under Van Gundy's eyes still seem too cumbersome for the overhead compartment. The receding hairline has taken its hits. And if short people have no reason to live, as Randy Newman once sang, the argument also goes that they certainly don't have a reason to coach.

Here is America's uninformed perception of Jeff Van Gundy: He is the sarcastic drone who pokes fun at Michael Jordan and Phil Jackson; a career assistant who just happened to be in the right place at the right time when Don Nelson was fired in 1996, a 5-9, 160-pound Division III point guard who could not possibly know the dynamics of the National Basketball Association game unless Riley held his hand.

Here is the truth: He is one of the few genuine people left in the league, a person who spends more time preparing his team than any other coach (Riley included), a patient listener who expects his players to work as hard as he does. And, yes, he is 5-9, 160.

"Only once did someone talking about my appearance bother me," he said, recounting the time in 1988 when the Providence College coaching staff was fired and Van Gundy had his boss, the current Boston Celtics president and coach Rick Pitino, call a college coach to recommend him for a job.

"That guy told him that he thought I was very good, but he thought I was too short," Van Gundy said. "I was shocked by that. It raised my awareness that some people are shortsighted enough to think that you get respect based on how you look.

"I think I have a feeling for what maybe a Mike Fratello had to go through," he said of the Cleveland coach who stands barely 5-7.

Such criticism tiptoes around the real accusation: that Van Gundy is too small in stature to possibly hold the respect of 6-10, physically superior athletes.

"That has about as much to do with his job as Tiger Woods has to do with this series," Houston said. "The reason we respect Jeff is because he works hard. Believe me, he's tougher than he looks."

"You want to find Jeff Van Gundy at 7:00 A.M. in July?" Jeff Nix, a Knick assistant coach, said. "Check the office. He is a workaholic. Nobody gave him this job; he earned this job. He's the most prepared, organized coach I've ever been around. Very few head coaches, let alone assistant coaches, would answer their phone at 2:00 in the morning and have John Starks say, 'Hey, let's go shoot some baskets,' and then get in the car and meet him at the gym. But that's the type of guy Jeff Van Gundy is."

Nix's take of Van Gundy's actions in Game 4 was this: "It's not a defining moment, but it's a situation where he was trying to break up a fight and people will remember it. I'm sure it defied a lot of stereotypes about him."

Game 4 was not the first occasion when Van Gundy has lost his cool. During the 1995–96 season, when a reporter covering the team telephoned Starks's grandmother to ask her how the Knick guard felt about playing for Nelson, Van Gundy lashed out at the reporter, accusing him of lacking ethics.

When Starks wanted to physically confront the reporter, Van Gundy held his player back. "He's not worth it, John," Van Gundy told Starks.

Nearly a week later, a high-level club official was asked if the incident might tarnish Van Gundy's career.

"I think it might actually help him," the official said. "No one had seen that kind of fire from Jeff before. At least I hadn't."

He added, "If he plays his cards right, I think he'll eventually wind up with a head coaching job at a small college."

You wonder why he would risk life and limb to break up a brawl with such huge men? When you're constantly fighting perceptions, sometimes it is better to be the aggressor.

When Rob Ades, a Washington-based lawyer, was negotiating an extension for Van Gundy after last season — a three-year deal worth more than $2 million a season and an option year — he kept referring to the lack of marquee respect his client was receiving.

Beginning each sentence with "This is not some run-of-the-mill kid who got lucky, this is Jeff Van Gundy we're talking about here," Ades proceeded to try to bolster Van Gundy's image. The inference being, of course, that Van Gundy, in the eyes of the Knicks, would always be viewed as the intern who started in the mailroom, not the candidate with the exotic résumé from abroad.

"Somebody made a comment that Phil Jackson looks like Theodore Kaczynski," Nix said. "Well, he does, but what is a coach supposed to look like? Does George Karl look like a coach? Does Rick Majerus look like a coach? There is no blueprint.

"I think what has happened here and in college is that everyone is so into individual marketing. What's the image of your coach, your players?"

And when it's discovered that Van Gundy drives a Honda Civic and lives for McDonald's drive-through, he is taken off the cutting-edge list.

"He's been going through that all his life, trying to break the walls down and show people he belongs where he is," Kim Van Gundy said. "Being compared to Pat Riley, I mean, what a wonderful comparison. But the whole notion of, 'He's doing everything Pat did,' it gets old and it's not fair."

She was asked if her husband's performance on Thursday night will change perceptions about him.

"Maybe," she said. "I mean, if the most people ever make fun of is his appearance, I guess we should be so happy. But after what happened with Mourning, I'm thinking about calling him the short assassin. Does that sound good? Maybe I should call that into the FAN."

Nov. 21, 2004

There Are No Innocents in a Meltdown by Artest, His Mates and Their Hecklers

BY WILLIAM C. RHODEN

At the Summer Games in Athens in August, everyone walked a tightrope of tension.

The N.B.A. players, the symbol of American strength and arrogance, were potential targets of violence. The team was housed on a ship and protected like no other athletes in the history of the Olympics. No chances were taken, no expense spared: Navy SEALs were in the water, helicopters in the skies. When the Games finally ended without episode, we all breathed a sigh of relief.

So where did violence break out? Where were N.B.A. players attacked? In Title Town, U.S.A. In the Detroit Pistons' suburban arena, the Palace of Auburn Hills.

Pistons fans set a new standard for boorish behavior when they turned the Palace into a combat zone in the final minute of Friday night's game against the Indiana Pacers. In the most horrific episode of violence in recent N.B.A history, fans threw drinks, tossed chairs and exchanged blows with players.

The violence was the worst I've ever seen, and Pistons Coach Larry Brown said he had never seen anything like it.

This was a rainbow riot. Black fans, white fans and brown fans, spurred by alcohol and the more intoxicating prospect of turning an N.B.A. game into reality TV, fought with players on the court and in the stands. Let's be very clear about this: The melee was caused by fans, drunken fans, riotous fans.

But the villain of this drama is Indiana's Ron Artest. His foul on Detroit's Ben Wallace, when the game was all but decided in the Pacers' favor, was a dirty little push, but a far cry from his most flagrant fouls. It was the sort of irritating needle he is famous for.

An enraged Wallace pushed Artest in the face. The benches emptied. For effect, Artest stretched out his 6-foot-7 frame on the scorers' table, drawing more attention to himself. When Artest was struck by a cup thrown by a fan, he leaped off the table and jumped into the stands, throwing wild punches as he climbed over the seats.

Several of Artest's teammates followed him into the unruly crowd. Security guards, ushers and Rick Mahorn, a former Piston who is now an analyst on the team's radio broadcasts, tried to break up the fighting.

The officials stopped the game with 45.9 seconds left, giving the Pacers a 97–82 victory. As the Pacers left the court, fans rained debris on them.

If Artest had wanted to remove himself from the action, he should have stood in the middle of the floor or taken a seat on the bench. To lie down in full view of hostile fans while tension swirled about was inflammatory. Maybe, just maybe, Friday's brawl will prompt Artest to begin to see a glimmer of light. His behavior finally came back to bite him and jeopardized the safety of his teammates and his opponents. Yet, he was innocent by his standards.

The N.B.A. is huddling and shuddering behind closed doors in an attempt to find out how this will affect its carefully manicured image. Yesterday it suspended Wallace, Artest and two of Artest's teammates, Stephen Jackson and Jermaine O'Neal, pending further review of the incident.

But Commissioner David Stern's larger problem is that the N.B.A. image is changing before his eyes. A league once defined by nonthreatening figures like Michael Jordan, and Magic Johnson and Larry Bird before him, is becoming younger and more aggressive and more concerned about being real than making fans, sponsors, coaches and even the commissioner comfortable.

Artest's decision to go after a fan who had disrespected him is not an aberration but a signature of the new N.B.A. generation.

This riot was provoked by fans and executed by fans, and if I had my way when these teams meet again in December and March, I would place a net cage around the court to separate fans from players.

An athletic event is an unscripted live drama in which emotions between audience and entertainer can boil over. We saw it happen in major league baseball in September, when Frank Francisco of the Texas Rangers hurled a chair into the seats in Oakland, Calif., and when the Dodgers' Milton Bradley menaced fans in Los Angeles with a plastic bottle. We saw it the N.B.A. in 1995 when Houston's Vernon Maxwell went after fans in Portland, Ore.

At every N.B.A. game, fans who feel the price of their ticket gives them license to shout obscenities at players set the tone for a potential riot. The presence of security guards and the restraint of players are all that stand between war and peace.

No one is without blame for the incident: the city of Auburn Hills, N.B.A. security, Pistons security, the players, the fans.

A riot isn't triggered by one event but is the accumulation of events. Artest's conduct has been building since his freshman year at St. John's. He has always operated on the edge, grabbing teammates and intimidating coaches.

Reporters tended to overlook all this because he was a quotable, honest player and essentially a good person, with issues.

The signature of Artest's game is tough defense, flagrant fouls punctuated by pokes and slaps. His career has also been distinguished by bizarre, not criminal, off-court antics. As a rookie, he wanted to work at an electronics store to get a discount. Two weeks ago, he was benched for two games after asking Coach Rick Carlisle for time off because he was tired, he later said, from promoting a rap album. The N.B.A. should not be caught up in the details of thee brawl. This was the league's wake-up call. It had better ratchet up security, put everyone on high alert and treat every season as if it were the Summer Games.

The N.B.A. can no longer assume that violence is a foreign affair.

Dec. 25, 2004

Pacers-Pistons:
A Tense Holiday Meeting

BY LEE JENKINS

INDIANAPOLIS — As Monica Foster prepared her stuffed beef tenderloin on Friday and wrapped her remaining presents, she debated what would be the most suitable outfit to wear with her family around the dinner table this Christmas.

The black T-shirt with large block letters reading "Suspend Stern" or the gold T-shirt with the message, "Indiana Subs vs. Detroit Thugs Christmas Day 2004."

"I know the gold one is probably better for this occasion," said Foster, a Pacers season-ticket holder and a public defender who represents prison inmates on death row. "But with the way I feel right now, I think I'll be more comfortable in the black one."

So much for Christmas sweaters Saturday at Conseco Fieldhouse, where the Detroit Pistons will play the Indiana Pacers for the first time since Nov. 19, when they participated in one of the nastiest brawls in sports history. The fight consumed the court and spilled into the stands, resulting in eight suspensions covering 132 games, and 12 criminal charges handed out against five Pacers players and five Pistons fans.

Now, these two teams are expected to co-star in the N.B.A.'s *A Christmas Story*. A sellout crowd and a national television audience will be watching, not necessarily because the Pacers and the Pistons were Eastern Conference finalists last season, and certainly not because they are both 12–12 this year. Rather, the biggest draw will probably be the lingering threat of violence.

Even though the temperature dropped below 5 degrees in Indianapolis on Friday, a foot of snow had covered the area and many local churches had canceled services, the Pacers still expected a packed house. They have issued 50 extra media credentials for the game and recently installed a tarpaulin over each entrance onto the court to protect players from fans.

"This is an unpredictable situation in a lot of ways," Indiana Coach Rick Carlisle said Friday. "The most important thing about this game is that it just needs to happen. It needs to happen because what went on Nov. 19 can never happen again. I think it's all going to come off and there aren't going to be any problems. It is important for everyone in our sport that this game happens in a way that shows integrity."

As Carlisle spoke, Jermaine O'Neal shot jumpers on the Pacers' practice court. The last time O'Neal was an active member of the team, he was punching a fan at the Palace of Auburn Hills. But since a judge on Thursday upheld an arbitrator's decision to reduce O'Neal's suspension to 15 games from 25, his return becomes all the more dramatic. He is back early, he is back for Christmas and he is back for the Pistons.

O'Neal is trying to bring a message of warmth and peace, apologizing to the states of Michigan and Indiana for the events that started when Ron Artest fouled Ben Wallace on Nov. 19, and still have not ended.

"Everybody wants to give their opinion on who we are as people and who we are as a league," O'Neal said. "They're saying the N.B.A. is too hip-hoppish. Come on now. A lot of good things happen in this league and there are a lot of good people. Like any other incident in any other sport, you have to eventually let it go. Let this go."

For at least one more day, public fascination will be fixed on the Pacers and the Pistons, and even afterward, the fight will likely remain more significant than the Kobe Bryant-Shaquille O'Neal feud or the Red Sox-Yankees rivalry. When ESPN began planning coverage of the game, there was an immediate understanding that it could not be billed as a potential battle royal, but should be handled with heightened sensitivity.

"You look at Kobe-Shaq, the bench brawl in the Yankees-Red Sox, a hockey fight, those are human dramas," said Len DeLuca, ESPN's senior vice president for programming. "What happened on Nov. 19 was out of hand. This story doesn't need hype. There is no reason to sensationalize it. There is a need to treat this responsibly and really play it straight."

The players and the broadcast teams acknowledged some anxiety, but Indiana fans seemed eager to vent more than a month's worth of frustration. Foster has designed and sold souvenirs along with her colleague, Rhonda

Long-Sharp, to promote this game and their dissatisfaction with the suspensions levied by Commissioner David Stern.

"The city is jacked up," Foster said. "But I really don't think there will be any funny business."

Pistons guard Chauncey Billups told The Associated Press on Thursday: "I don't know what to expect from the fans. It will be a hard-fought game, I'm sure, but their fans are always a little rowdy when we come to town, and I'm sure it will be even more so this time after the incident."

Pacers guard Anthony Johnson, who was suspended five games for hitting a fan in the brawl, said: "They will let Detroit know what kind of class people we have here. It will be a loud building, a playoff environment. There will definitely be extra tension in the arena, but it will be directed toward the Pistons and their players."

Neither team seems capable of absorbing any more blows. They have each staggered through the past month, enduring constant questions about the fight at every stop on every road trip. Detroit Coach Larry Brown said in a television interview this week that his team had not fully recuperated, that his young son was still afraid to go to games, and that he had serious doubts about wanting to coach anymore.

Brown campaigned against having the game on national television and said the thought of people tuning in to see what would happen "makes me sick." Others believe the rematch is an integral part of the healing process, and that the Pacers and Pistons must demonstrate that they can coexist on Christmas Day in order to move on.

Some of the principals are still absent — Indiana's Stephen Jackson has to serve another 15 games of his suspension and Artest will not be back this season — but several will be clashing elbow to elbow. There is a strong chance that, at some point, O'Neal will go hard to the hoop and Wallace will be in his way and an entire arena, an entire league, will cover its mouth and hold its breath.

What happens next could determine whether the Pacers and the Pistons can finally exhale.

21
Game of Thrones

Jerry West won one championship during his 14-year career with the Lakers, reaching the finals nine times and losing in every one of them except in 1972, when the Knicks were without their injured center, Willis Reed. Yet West — whose silhouetted image famously became the league logo — is considered one of the greatest guards in N.B.A. history.

Half of the most awe-inspiring assemblage of talent in American team-sports history — the 1992 Olympic Dream Team — finished their careers ring-less, although Christian Laettner, whose inclusion was a bone thrown to the college game, would be on no one's list of N.B.A. elites.

Is the ranking of players by rings won a media invention that is fundamentally unfair to those who lacked the co-stars or complementary talent or whose timing — West's Lakers against Russell's Celtics; Utah's Stockton and Malone against Jordan's Bulls — practically ordained them as second best?

In most evaluative ways, yes. Not all. While the definition of greatness must inevitably be subjective, there is a fair case to be made that basketball, of all the team sports, allows for or even demands that its superstars exert an uncommon influence on the outcomes given the ability to affect each and every possession, on both sides of the floor.

In every star-laden career, there are watershed moments that provide for some debate clarity. Take the case of Patrick Ewing, whose best chance for a ring was in 1994, when his Knicks lost a tight game in Houston to Hakeem Olajuwon's Rockets.

Having covered all of Ewing's career, I sat a few feet from the Knicks bench as Olajuwon statistically outplayed Ewing — no disgrace there. But where Ewing fell short was in allowing John Starks to continue firing up blanks on the way to a ghastly 2-for-18 night. This was Ewing's team and his time, but not once did he grab Starks by the jersey and order him to cease, desist and get him the ball.

By and large, those with on-court charisma, communication and certitude — all essential to leadership — have been the sport's greatest winners.

June 13, 1993

Sunshine Loyalists Perturb Sir Charles

by Tom Friend

PHOENIX — Charles Barkley is not guilt-ridden. In one season, he christened Phoenix's new arena with a conference title, gave Madonna a reason to visit town and inspired local junior high school students to shave their heads.

Cross him once, though, and he will knock a city on the seat of its pants (see Philadelphia).

Friday night, when Suns fans saw their team lose once again to the Chicago Bulls, 111–108, and noticed that Kevin Johnson had contributed just 4 points, they booed their beloved point guard. An offended Barkley, abruptly ending his honeymoon with Phoenix, looked squarely into a camera and told the community: "If you're not going to be with us through the good times and bad times, we don't want you here. And I'm not concerned if they don't like it. They know where to find me."

No Civic Booster

The Suns' fan base is finally finding that Barkley is unpredictable. The team trails the National Basketball Association finals by 2–0 with no home games in sight; its best defender, Dan Majerle, is hardly getting a hand in Michael Jordan's face; and Barkley will not complain about the defeats. Clearly, many people in this city overrated a team that now has an 11–9 postseason record and has lost five playoff games at home, although Barkley refuses to symphathize with their disappointment.

"Just because basketball is not the most important thing in my life, I apologize to the world," Barkley said. "I said I won't slice my wrists if we lost, but they're mad at me, though. Listen, I just make sure my wife and daughter have everything they want. If we lose, I'm disappointed, but, like I said, I won't slice my wrists."

This four-of-seven-game championship series, as brief as it may turn out to be, has mostly been about friends, or the lack of them. Barkley saw Richard Esquinas, the noted San Diego golfer, betray Jordan by writing a book about his gambling losses, and Barkley saw Phoenix fans betray Johnson.

In Defense of Johnson

"Hey, K. J.'s our point guard," Barkley said. "We'll win with him and we'll lose with him. We're not going to say anything bad about him. He's our man. We couldn't have gotten here without him. Those people booing him, that's why you can't get close to anybody. Those people are not your friends unless you're doing well. That goes for the media, for the fans. Because if you're playing well, everybody's swinging on your uniform. But when things go bad, everybody turns against you. That's why I'll be my own man and why I ain't close to anybody.

"See, it's up to me keep it in perspective. No one can keep it in perspective except players. These people don't care about us. If he wasn't Michael Jordan and capable of making a lot of money, he'd just be another black guy walking around. People don't care about you. They love me when I'm winning, but, if I lose, they'll all be over me like a cheap suit."

The prospect of losing has definitely set in here, like a rare fog. Barkley fell on his right elbow in Friday night's loss, could not flex it fully later in the evening and has a limited amount of fuel left in his body. He did more than his duty in Game 2, scoring 42 points and squeezing 13 rebounds, but the Suns are a freelance team that currently has only one player freelancing: Barkley.

No Room to Improvise

"Sometimes we're not sure what we're trying to accomplish," veteran Suns guard Danny Ainge said after the game, and the reason is the Suns generally make things up as they go along. The offense consists of Johnson's and Barkley's creativity, but improvisation is difficult against a helping defense like Chicago's. Johnson has sometimes evaded his opponent, B. J. Armstrong, only to find Horace Grant and Scottie Pippen waiting with their long arms. Against other, softer opponents, Johnson penetrates at will and kicks out passes to a free Majerle. Against the Bulls, Johnson has nine turnovers in two games, a team high, and was benched in Friday's fourth quarter at the crux of the game and the season.

What is more, the Bulls are forcing the Suns into a snail-paced, halfcourt style that is foreign to them. Fast-break points were their regular meal during their 62-victory regular season, but Johnson is not an accomplished decision-maker when standing still.

"We need more movement of the ball to take the pressure off of K. J.," Ainge said.

A Canyon Looms

Two more losses, and Barkley will not retire. He had previously said, with a straight face, that he would consider quitting this summer if the Suns took the title, but all signs are he will need a 1993–94 parking space.

"We're in a hole right now, and we're in the right state for big holes," Barkley said. "We'd fit right in to the Grand Canyon."

Looking back, he has had a season fit for royalty.

Barkley just happens to be playing in the wrong era: Jordan's.

June 14, 2004

A Teammate Winces as Malone Hits the Wall

by Harvey Araton

AUBURN HILLS, Mich. — From a seat on the Lakers' bench he was itching to get off, Bryon Russell at least had the best view, the most focused perspective, on the painful saga of Karl Malone.

As Malone's former teammate with the Utah Jazz, Russell saw Mount Malone miss the grand total of five regular-season games over nine years. He knew the Jazz could count on Malone for about 38 grueling minutes, for perfect harmony with John Stockton on the screen-and-roll, for filling the lane on the fast break.

Now Malone still looks like a masterpiece of athletic sculpture, but he runs like one, too.

"I know this hurts him, especially after the way he played against Tim Duncan, against Kevin Garnett," Russell said of the injury to Malone's right knee. "That's why I wish I could give Karl my knees, to see him go out there and play 100 percent."

There would be no ligament transplant, no medical miracle, in time to save the Lakers from losing Game 4 of the N.B.A. finals to the Pistons, 88–80, last night and falling into a 3–1 hole at the Palace of Auburn Hills. On a night when no other Laker besides Shaquille O'Neal and Kobe Bryant scored in double figures, all Malone could do was strap on the loathsome brace, drag 260 pounds around, contribute 21 labored minutes, score 2 points and wonder what if?

Malone, almost 41, is hobbling to the finish line of a marathon season and probably a remarkable 19-year career. His deterioration is different from what makes the Lakers seem so collectively worn, from the petty feuding between O'Neal and Bryant to Coach Phil Jackson's whining about discrepancies in fouls.

Given the number of Lakers complaining less about calls and more about Coach, Jackson's time in Los Angeles is probably concluding. After Game 3, even his ally, O'Neal, wondered why Russell, reunited with Malone this season, was being ignored.

"Great shooter, pretty good defensive player, has been to the finals twice," O'Neal said. "I don't have an understanding of why he's not in the game."

Who would have more incentive to help Malone along on his career-sunset quest for a championship ring than the man Michael Jordan made part of the poster punctuating his sixth and final title with Chicago?

Russell said that he and Malone never rehashed the play in which Jordan used his left arm to nudge Russell off balance, clearing space for the jumper that gave the Bulls a 1-point victory over the Jazz and the title in Game 6 of the 1998 finals in Salt Lake City.

"I've had referees come up to me and say they would've made that call, but who was going to call a push-off at that time on the greatest player to ever play the game?" Russell said. "But that night, it just felt like they weren't going to let us win."

He wasn't crying fix, only asserting that sentimentality played a role in the Hollywood ending. Jackson probably believes the Lakers deserve the same treatment his Bulls received because they actually are Hollywood. But three titles notwithstanding, they have not come close to matching Chicago's demographic appeal. There has always been something prefabricated about these Lakers, from O'Neal's defection to Los Angeles from Orlando to Bryant's orchestrating his way there in a trade and his uncanny Jordan impressions (though other than Game 2, in this series, he hasn't looked much like a clone or an heir).

It's as if the league needed a ratings blockbuster to succeed *Friends*, and the Bulls maestro and Zen master Jackson was hired to direct. Only now, with the Lakers facing elimination and the harsh facts of championship shelf life, the plotlines seem flat and the stars sound sick of each other and the only pathos is for Malone.

He doesn't need the ring to be remembered as one of the all-time greats, and stand-up guys. I'll personally attest to the latter, after printing Malone's

1992 concerns regarding Magic's return to the game while carrying the virus that causes AIDS.

There was no recording of the quotes and I wondered if he would cry journalism foul, as many athletes might. Malone did not; he stayed as true to himself as he has to his Louisiana roots.

In Utah, Russell quickly came to know why they called him the Mailman. Malone delivered, with rare exceptions, one being a 1997 finals game, when he missed two late-game free throws and the Jazz lost on a Jordan buzzer jumper, after which Scottie Pippen quipped, "The Mailman doesn't deliver on Sunday."

Only the cruelest of critics accused him of that last night, another Sunday, when Malone came to sacrifice on one good leg. "Karl couldn't come back in the second half and play with any quickness or reactivity," Jackson said. "We had to pull the plug."

Malone went to the bench by the middle of the third quarter and watched Luke Walton, a rookie, and Slava Medvedenko, a journeyman, try vainly to slow Rasheed Wallace from erupting for 17 of his 26 points in the second half.

With Jackson searching for shooters, grasping at straws, even Russell checked in for one late-game possession. There was no stopping the Pistons, though, no Jazz left in the Lakers. The heavy odds are that their championship run will end, for Malone, with another hollow ring.

APRIL 4, 2008

The Not Michael Jordan Club: It's Growing

BY WILL LEITCH

For a league that seems to be reinventing itself every three years or so, the N.B.A. sports a fan base and chattering class that are awfully concerned with its players' legacies. It is an old maxim that an athlete's career is never quite complete unless he wins a championship. But there's a difference between the way Ernie Banks and Barry Sanders are remembered, and the way, say, Charles Barkley, Patrick Ewing and Karl Malone are remembered.

Part of this, of course, is because of the structure of the individual sports: Great as he was, Sanders was only one man among several dozen — and in Detroit, it was a pretty motley few dozen. His legacy will be his jaw-dropping moves, untarnished by the fact that his miserable franchise never came close to winning a title. Banks happened to be a Cub. Enough said. There was only so much these players could do. So they are mostly forgiven, seen as almost tragic figures, superstars trapped in their respective circumstances.

Not so in the N.B.A. There, if you can't win a title, it is a failure not of your team but of you, personally. And winning just one isn't enough. The whole Title Envy thing has a machismo aspect to it that slots superstars into one of several tiers under the general heading of "Cómo Macho Es Usted?" And this barroom stratification can be traced — as can everything with today's N.B.A. — to Michael Jordan. Here are the principal tiers:

Sorry for Overhyping You: Would-be superstars who once showed some dominance but were expected to be so much more than they were. (This excludes Stephon Marbury and Steve Francis.) Historic examples: Chris Webber, Kenyon Martin, Vince Carter. Current playoff example: Dirk Nowitzki.

Warrior: Guys who never had a legitimate chance at a title but won credits just for getting close and not dying while making the attempt. Historic and current example: Allen Iverson. (Iverson is in a category of his own in so many ways. In a way, his failures enoble him — because of his size, his heart, his upbringing.)

Your Fault: Players who had all the talent to lead their teams to a title, but fell short because of their own perceived shortcomings. Historic examples: Karl Malone, Charles Barkley, Patrick Ewing. Current examples: Steve Nash, Kevin Garnett, Tracy McGrady, Jason Kidd.

You Made It, but One Is Just One: Guys who broke through and won a title or two, but aren't considered Legends. Historic example: Hakeem Olajuwon. Current examples: Dwyane Wade, Rasheed Wallace.

You're Not Jordan: Amazing, twice-in-a-generation players who win multiple titles but are not, in fact, named Michael Jordan. Historic and current examples: Tim Duncan, Shaquille O'Neal, Kobe Bryant.

Jordan: Michael Jordan. Requires six titles and psychological mastery over all who meet your gaze. Duncan and Shaq have two to go, Kobe needs three.

LeBron James is a grand example of a player whose greatness will be judged not by whether he wins a title but by whether he joins the Jordan Tier. But this madness has now extended to even the first round. Tracy McGrady, despite his obvious brilliance, has never made it out of the first round, and seems unlikely to do so again this year. The mind shudders to imagine how little macho cred he will have now. The man might as well play baseball.

SEPT. 5, 2008

Asking 'What If?' as Ewing Is Inducted

BY HARVEY ARATON

SPRINGFIELD, Mass. — The man sitting between Patrick Ewing and Pat Riley happened to be the one who flicked away their best shot at a championship, denied their four-year union and the Knicks' longer Ewing era its ultimate definition.

As Hakeem Olajuwon remembered it, he momentarily stumbled while switching off Ewing and onto John Starks after a high screen set by Ewing, but chased Starks into the left corner and deflected "with my fingertips" a 3-point shot in a 2-point game.

Only a center with the gracefulness of a guard could have recovered quickly enough to keep that conclusive attempt in Game 6 of the 1994 N.B.A. finals from reaching the rim.

"Patrick was a turnaround jump shooter, an incredible worker, a classic power center," Riley said. "Hakeem was the first real transcendent center who was so athletically different."

They were heralded stars, positional rivals, at the highest levels of the college game, where Ewing's team got the better of Olajuwon's for the 1984 title. But by the more common measure of N.B.A. rings, the difference between Olajuwon and Ewing was that the former won two while the latter claimed none.

And while the consensus opinion is that Ewing's greatness and value to his title-starved franchise are unassailable, Olajuwon's induction into the Basketball Hall of Fame here Friday night, along with Ewing's and Riley's, was an unmistakable quirk of fate and a reminder of how unsympathetic it was to Ewing, No. 33 in your retired Knicks jersey program.

Headlining a class that included Adrian Dantley, the women's coach Cathy Rush and the broadcaster Dick (Can You Hear Me Now?) Vitale, the Ewing-Riley-Olajuwon troika presented an intriguing juxtaposition of possibilities. What if, for instance, that 1994 series had ended with the Knicks as champions, with a Broadway parade in the Canyon of Heroes?

Would the life of Riley have taken a fateful turn one year later, when he faxed in his resignation for more power and money in Miami? Would Ewing have been haunted by the collective inability to manufacture one additional victory against Olajuwon and an otherwise unimposing Rockets team in Houston?

With a title in tow, it can be assumed that Ewing's standing in New York would have been elevated beyond petty or legitimate reproach. There would have been nothing to prove as the championshipless years dragged on, as his overtaxed body wore down, cruelly sidelining him when the Knicks returned to the finals in 1999.

There would have been no reason for him to put pride before pragmatism, to demand a trade that sent him to fade away in strange uniforms and set the Knicks on a course of disastrous salary-cap mismanagement.

"Sometimes you get tired of hearing the same thing over and over, that the team is better off without you," Ewing said during a morning news conference. "But, yeah, there is some regret. In hindsight, I should have stayed and finished my career in New York."

He talked about coming to the United States from Jamaica as a boy, stepping onto a playground in Cambridge, Mass., gangly and uncoordinated and thoroughly unfamiliar with the game that would earn him unimaginable fame and wealth. Olajuwon was older when he touched down in Texas, recruited out of Lagos, Nigeria, to play for the University of Houston. Both were welcome harbingers of what was to come, an invasion of N.B.A. talent from abroad.

Ewing had the greater profile, the grander stage, first at Georgetown under John Thompson, college coach, mentor for life and Hall of Fame presenter Friday. In New York, Ewing became a fascinating study of a tall man on a tightrope between fame and failure, and perhaps most admired for never falling off.

"He played in one of the toughest markets and cities and took it all for all those years," Riley said.

Much worse than the volatility of the environment was the instability of the Knicks franchise until Riley came along with the aura of four Lakers titles won with Magic Johnson (his presenter Friday along with Jerry West). But it can also be argued, sadly for Ewing, that Riley was the most accomplished co-star he ever had.

Contrary to his stature, it always seemed that Ewing needed a leading man to shoulder the fourth-quarter burden. Based on personality, not ability, he was probably closer to a Pippen than a Jordan, which best explains why Starks had the ball at the end of Game 6 and continued shooting it, a historically awful 2 for 18, the next night.

Riley has often talked of being haunted by Game 7 decisions, but rather than dwell on who lost, better to credit Olajuwon for winning. This soft-spoken devout Muslim, who spends half the year now in Amman, Jordan, was better than Ewing in that series. He obliterated the young Shaquille O'Neal in the finals a year later.

"The great ones will lift you above and beyond," Riley said of the still stunningly fit man who came between him and Ewing, affecting their careers forever.

Ewing was many estimable things, above all a deserving Hall of Famer, but he was not that.

22

Changing the Game

Television ratings are the lifeblood of a sports league. When they measurably decline, and when a valued network partner cries no mas, as NBC did in 2002, it is time to tinker. To say the least.

It wasn't as if the N.B.A.'s appeal and hype machine had dried up, not when megastars like Shaquille O'Neal and Kobe Bryant were fashioning a three-peat in Los Angeles, even while behaving like antagonistic schoolchildren, living large on a fault line. Michael Jordan's two-season comeback in Washington was also good for nostalgic reverence.

But the league did get the message, even with ABC/ESPN upping the rights fees ante, that its game overall had reached the stultifying stage. It needed to address the dominance of defenses, loosen up the court, appeal to adult fans whose basketball sensibilities were under assault with all focus on dunking, preening and, on occasion, brawling.

By mid-decade, the Spurs, fortified and electrified by an infusion of foreign-born talent in Manu Ginobili and Tony Parker, were the under-the-radar team for mature audiences. In Phoenix, Coach Mike D'Antoni handed the ball to the ultracreative Steve Nash and allowed him — conceptually, at least — to manufacture a shot in seven seconds or less.

Scores turned upward and the game was seemingly trending in a more artful direction — though for one longtime, expert fan, not quite fast enough.

His name was Jimmy Goldstein, a wealthy businessman out of Los Angeles, who was unmistakable at most league events with frizzy, flowing hair under his python-skin hats and in his skintight leather pants.

I ran into Goldstein in an airport during the 2007 playoffs — a week or two after D'Antoni's Suns were victimized by the league office with the questionable suspensions of Amar'e Stoudemire and Boris Diaw for a crucial Game 5 at home against the Spurs in the Western Conference semis.

The suspensions for leaving the bench area after Robert Horry set a vicious screen on Nash wound up costing Phoenix the series. Goldstein contended that the events in the long run would be damaging to the N.B.A.

"It's a copycat league and if the Suns had gone on to win the title — and I think they would have — then more teams would play like they do," he said. "Now it may never happen."

Not to worry. Never is a long time. As it turned out, Goldstein wouldn't have to wait too many more years for a golden state of affairs.

APRIL 22, 2005

High-Flying Suns
Look to Keep Running

BY LIZ ROBBINS

The first 82 games and 9,054 points were a warm-up for the Phoenix Suns, whose high-speed chase left opponents wondering what had hit them.

On the heels of their N.B.A.-best 62 victories — 33 more than last season — the Suns are surging into the playoffs, but how long can they outrun their critics or their history? Conventional wisdom says the playoffs grind to a halfcourt scrum, a clutch-and-grab clinic in which defense decides championships. The formula worked for the Detroit Pistons last year and the San Antonio Spurs the year before.

Where does that leave the unconventional Suns? Their free-flowing offense (110.4 points a game) is a showstopper, but their matador defense (allowing 103.3 points) is an also-ran.

While Coach Mike D'Antoni admitted the obvious in a telephone interview this week — "we have to play better defensively" — he quickly added: "I don't think we have to play as well defensively as a nonoffensive team. It gives us a lot of chances to mess up, and we will."

The Suns lead a leaguewide offensive charge that is more lethal than it has been in eight years. New rules were introduced this season to curtail hand-checking, clarify blocking fouls and call defensive three seconds to open up the game. Suddenly, six teams averaged more than 100 points, as Phoenix, Washington, Boston and Miami joined the usual suspects, Dallas and Sacramento. And in the 40 games since George Karl took over in Denver (and installed Doug Moe as an assistant), the Nuggets have averaged 104.4 points.

The Suns, who meet the Memphis Grizzles in the first round, starting Sunday in Phoenix, average a league-high 98.7 possessions a game, and their 110.4 scoring average is the highest since the Magic (110.9) in the 1994–95 season. With Steve Nash at point guard, the Suns are the next incarnation of the Lakers' Showtime, whose run-and-gun roots trace back to Moe's Nuggets in the 1980s and were born in Bob Cousy's Celtics, the 11-time champions of the '50s and '60s.

But those Celtics had Bill Russell and Pat Riley's Lakers had Kareem Abdul-Jabbar as defensive stoppers to clog the middle and grab rebounds to ignite a fast break.

"Once we got Russell, end of story," Cousy said yesterday from his home in Worcester, Mass. "To ultimately win, I doubt whether you can win with only offense. But if the Suns rebound effectively, then, hopefully, their offense will carry the day. I would love nothing better. Talk about the impact that would have on schoolyards of the world."

Cousy is a traditionalist — but only because he wants to return to a time when teams played like the Suns.

"That's the only way to go," Cousy said. "That's what Naismith was thinking about. It's a game of free flow, that's the beauty of it. If basketball is an art form, it's in the movement of these 10 huge but graceful bodies moving up and down, making these constant, instantaneous decisions."

Watching teams struggle in halfcourt sets, he said, is "like watching grass grow for me," adding, "all you're doing is inhibiting superior talent."

Enter Phoenix, a team that is looking to rewrite the adage: Offense sells tickets, defense wins championships.

Amar'e Stoudemire stars at center, out of position and undersized at 6-foot-10, but not underestimated at age 22. With Nash, Shawn Marion, Quentin Richardson and Joe Johnson on the wings, the Suns have five players who sprint into the frontcourt looking for the quick score.

"Don't say it can't be done," said Don Nelson, the former Mavericks coach whose teams, with Nash until this season, went to four straight playoffs but never to the finals. "It depends on the personnel you have," Nelson said. "I think there's a sentiment out there that a run-and-gun team won't do well in the playoffs.

"There hasn't been as much talent on the floor as Phoenix has had in the modern era," Nelson added in a telephone interview last week. "They have the best chance of doing it. No one else has had Stoudemire as their big man. He's unplayable, he's unguardable at this point. You can't guard him with a small, you can't guard him with a big."

More than the other offense-oriented teams, the Suns are an anomaly in their speed, decision-making and five-man commitment to the fast break. They can go from 0 to 94 feet in under five seconds, closer to three.

The Suns' coaching staff recorded the team's fastest score after taking the ball out of bounds. In one game, Nash got the inbounds pass, threw a bomb to a sprinting Marion, who took two steps and dunked. Elapsed time: 1¾ seconds. "I think Phoenix can win a title, and I am the biggest proponent of the fast-break game," said Bill Walton, an ESPN analyst. "You have to have great players, regardless of style."

What makes the Suns so difficult to defend is their improvisational skills. They have trailers on the fast break working the pick-and-roll. Other times, they stop, pop and shoot. They set an N.B.A. record this season with 796 3-pointers (a league-high 39.3 percent). "It's very hard to prepare for us other than having guys getting back — they have to do it on the fly," D'Antoni said.

The Suns average the most rebounds a game — 44.13 per game. But they also allow opponents to grab a league-high 46.13 rebounds.

One number showed situational defense; the Suns were ranked 14th in the league in field-goal defense. Marion, a 6-7 power forward, is the team's best defender, averaging 11.3 rebounds a game, 2 steals and 1.5 blocks.

"Phoenix has the players and a style that can be successful," Pistons General Manager Joe Dumars said in a telephone interview. "I'm not ready to hand them the trophy, but it's wrong for people to write them off as not being a serious threat in the playoffs."

The last team to take the up-tempo style into the finals was the Nets, led by Jason Kidd. Los Angeles and Shaquille O'Neal slowed down the Nets' fast break in 2002, and Tim Duncan and a lack of disciplined shooting ruined the Nets' chances in 2003.

"People say when we first got to New Jersey and put in the offense, that offense is not going to be good in the playoffs — too many people touch the ball," Wizards Coach Eddie Jordan, who was an assistant coach on those Nets teams, said last week.

"I think we just ran into a better team," Jordan said. "I thought we were competitive at both ends of the floor and we had great defensive players."

Those players, like Kidd and Kenyon Martin in 2003, determine a defensive-minded team. "They're not your beat-'em-up, highly experienced defensive-type players," Jordan said. "We use what we have. We use our length, our athleticism, not our bulk."

Unlike the Suns, who score 7.5 more points than they allow, the Wizards averaged 100.4 points in the regular season while allowing 100.7.

In Dallas, the trend has started to change under the new coach, Avery Johnson. The Mavericks are 16–2 since he took over, holding opponents to 6.1 fewer points a game than they did under Nelson.

Nash cited the defensive deficiencies of his Mavericks teams (and his own struggles) to motivate his Suns teammates to be more active and disruptive. "I continue to harp on it," Nash said. "In the middle of the season, we got a little complacent, a little tired, the schedule was tough in January. But the last few months, we slowly picked it up."

Not that the Suns do anything slowly. In place of size and bulk and ferocity, the Suns have fast feet and boundless energy.

"We have a great quickness and athleticism on our team," Nash said. "We're going to have our tough nights. We're such a good team offensively, we'll be fine."

If the Suns' fast break is not operating at warp speed, their inside-out game generates plenty of points underneath and their halfcourt offense thrives on movement to cause disarray. One thing the Suns cannot control, however, is how much the referees let physical play rule the game.

"During the playoffs, certainly, teams are more focused defensively, have a day in between games, and our coaches are terrific in terms of their preparation, and we are going to have some games that are stifling," Stu Jackson, the N.B.A.'s senior vice president for basketball operations, said in a conference call Wednesday. "But over all, I don't see teams that have played wide open changing their style."

D'Antoni does not want to change now that the playoffs are here. "We're best this way," he said. "Although we don't have a lot of experience, we have five guys that want to take the big shot in the end. Because of that, we're going to be dangerous."

If the Suns were to win a title playing this way, wouldn't that validate the view that offense can win championships? D'Antoni just laughed and said, "Nah, if that happens, at the end of the day, people will just say, 'They really picked their defense up.'"

MAY 13, 2005

Four Years Later, N.B.A. Sees the Points

BY HOWARD BECK

There is change and then there is evolution, and the difference between the two explains the curious and sudden appearance of a points explosion in the N.B.A.

Scoring this season spiked from coast to coast. The jump-shot jubilee was led by the rollicking Phoenix Suns, who literally sprinted to the league's best record, then claimed trophies for the most valuable player (Steve Nash) and the coach of the year (Mike D'Antoni).

Like a contagion, the higher scores spread from city to city until even the supposed slowpokes of the league, San Antonio and Detroit, hit the century mark with some regularity.

If the story ended there, it would be just another hiccup in league history, a strange uptick on the statistical charts, and the Suns would be just another one-year wonder.

But what happened this season, with six teams averaging at least 100 points a game, was neither sudden nor transitory.

It was deliberate and it was planned, through a series of often unwelcome rules changes and rules emphases, aided by an influx of new talent on the court and, finally, abetted by coaches who saw no choice but to adapt.

This is the game the N.B.A. wanted when it overhauled its defensive rules four years ago. It just needed several more tweaks and some fine-tuning to get it here.

"As far as the way the game looks and the way it's being played, it's really in a good place," said Stu Jackson, the N.B.A.'s senior vice president for basketball operations.

The Suns are the model, an entertaining throwback to the 1980s, a modern-day reflection of the Los Angeles Lakers' "Showtime" era. But five other teams joined them in averaging at least 100 points this season, and the league average of 194.4 combined points a game was the highest in five years. Even the N.B.A.'s deeply ingrained conventional wisdom has not stopped the trend.

Scoring has historically declined in the playoffs, but not this year. Through Wednesday's games, the average combined points a game was 197.5, a 3-point increase over the regular-season average, and an incredible 21-point increase over the 2004 playoffs.

The trend is not limited to the Suns and other run-and-gun practitioners like the Dallas Mavericks and Seattle SuperSonics.

The Detroit Pistons, who muscled their way to the 2004 championship with bruising defense, are averaging 96.1 points in these playoffs, a 9-point increase over their 2004 postseason average. The San Antonio Spurs, long known as a halfcourt team with a defensive bent, are averaging 101.9 points, a 12-point increase over their 2004 average.

"Teams are playing faster," Sonics Coach Nate McMillan said. "They've changed their style. You don't see as many teams playing a primary halfcourt game."

The statistics give the appearance of an overnight transformation. But the revolution has been emerging in subtle steps for four years.

In 2001, the N.B.A. scrapped its illegal-defense rule, which generally dictated that each defender be attached to a specific offensive player (with or without the ball). So the game was often reduced to eight players standing still on one side of the court while a skilled ballhandler went one-on-one with his defender on the other side.

These "clear-outs" were deemed unsightly and bad for the game.

"It was boring, and it wasn't the intent of how the game should be played," said Jerry Colangelo, the Suns' chairman and chief executive officer. Colangelo recalled telling Commissioner David Stern, "If I get turned off, it's a serious problem."

Colangelo headed a committee that called for elimination of the illegal-defense rule and the introduction, for the first time, of zone defense to the

N.B.A. The committee also cut the time allotted to advance the ball from the backcourt, from 10 seconds to 8.

"We were going to try to dictate a faster game," Colangelo said.

At the time, many coaches and players assailed the changes. Pat Riley, the Miami coach at the time, called them "a huge mistake," saying zone defenses would clog driving lanes and destroy the league's most entertaining feature — flashy drives to the hoop. (Colangelo's committee instituted a three-second rule for defenders in the lane to address that concern.)

Rather than impede the game, zone defense arguably has helped foster the offensive renaissance by giving teams more incentive to score on fast breaks.

"Coaches like the idea of running the ball and getting into an early offense before the defense is set," said Washington Wizards Coach Eddie Jordan. "Because they can get set in a zone and slow you up. So it's all about fast break, early offense, fast break, early offense."

The new defensive rules went into effect for the 2001–02 season. Two years later, the league's offense bottomed out, with a .421 field-goal percentage in the playoffs and an average combined score of 176.1 points a game. That was not the result anyone wanted, but in the N.B.A., evolution is slow.

Coaches needed time to teach zone defense, and players needed time to learn how to play it. They also needed to learn how to attack zones, through better ball and player movement.

"I think since the major rule changes of three and a half, four years ago, stylewise, we've become a better ball movement league," said the Indiana Pacers' coach, Rick Carlisle. "We've become a higher basketball I.Q. league."

Dwane Casey, a Sonics assistant, agreed.

"The new rules have given players more freedom of movement," he said. "The fact that there are no illegal defenses has increased ball movement and increased man movement that make it hard to defend. And more coaches are relinquishing control. You look at Phoenix, the coaches give up control of the offensive set. That's no disrespect to the coaches, but a lot of plays you just can't really design a defense for. That makes for more points. I think players today are better offense players. Shooting has improved. Ballhandling has improved."

Yet it took one more sweeping dictum from the commissioner's office to produce the point-a-palooza.

Last fall, the league highlighted two areas for enforcement by referees. The league put more onus on defenders to establish position before drawing a charging foul, which led to more blocking calls and more incentive for players to drive to the rim. And the league instructed referees to tighten enforcement of forearm-checking by perimeter defenders.

In past years, the league had cracked down on hand-checking, but players adapted.

"Defenders then started to use their forearm in the shoulder area and hip area of offensive players in an effort to reroute the offensive player or to slow them," Jackson said. "Forearms started to creep into the game."

Again, there was howling in some quarters. "Rules Changes Could Hurt Pistons," declared a headline in *The Detroit News*. The Pistons won the championship in part by setting a league record for fewest points allowed (83.4 per game).

"I don't understand," Pistons guard Chauncey Billups said then. "I think you should reward hard work, not try to make it softer."

But the Pistons, who are battling the Pacers in the Eastern Conference semifinals, adapted along with everyone else. A league once dominated by the defensive preachings of Riley and Chuck Daly is now being personified by the fast-and-loose approach of D'Antoni.

"The coaches are letting their players play," Stern said. "It's all about the coaches."

No one is more pleased than Colangelo, who said he always believed it would take several seasons for his committee's rules changes to make their full impact.

"Now we're starting to see the benefit," Colangelo said. "The game looks better."

So are the higher scores and fast-paced offense here to stay? Jackson said he was "cautiously optimistic."

"I really feel it's an evolution and a journey," he said. "Our players and our coaches, they're the best in the world. And they find ways, new ways, different ways, to skin the defensive cat. And if there's another defensive scheme or another technique to be used, they'll find it. It's really incumbent upon us at the league level to monitor it and be nimble, to adjust if we need to."

23

Crashing the Borders

Ten years after the Dream Team's colorful and thorough demonstration of United States basketball invincibility, Mike Wise filed the following lead for *The Times* one wild September night in 2002 from what was then called Conseco Fieldhouse in Indianapolis:

"Down by 20 points before halftime, dumbfounded by a former Temple University point guard in need of work, 12 N.B.A. players and their tortured coach were shockingly outplayed by a team from another continent tonight."

The coach was George Karl. His team — led by Reggie Miller and Paul Pierce — was an unprepared, unsuspecting United States entry into the world basketball championships. The opponent was Argentina, led by the Temple alum Pepe Sanchez and a player described by Wise as "Emanuel Ginobili, a 6-foot-6 shooting guard drafted by the San Antonio Spurs, whom most of the world has yet to hear about."

I actually had heard of Ginobili, who was nowhere close to being known simply as Manu. On a trip that summer to Tbilisi in the Republic of Georgia for a story on 19-year-old Nikoloz Tskitishvili, who had come literally from nowhere in a basketball sense to being the fifth pick of the 2002 draft by Denver, I stopped off in Treviso, Italy, where Tskitishvili had played half a season in the Italian league for Mike D'Antoni.

Ettore Messina, the new Treviso coach who had had Ginobili in Bologna the previous season, told me that Ginobili was a can't-miss dynamo who would "change the culture" in San Antonio. I sarcastically thought, yeah, of course he will. And then, sitting alongside Wise that night at Conseco, I watched Ginobili absolutely abuse the United States guards and confound Jermaine O'Neal and Ben Wallace at the rim, while Argentina cut and passed the fundamentally lacking Americans to death.

A new day had arrived, and more international talent was coming. I realized why in Tbilisi when I visited the small apartment Tskitishvili had lived in with his mother and younger brother in a run-down old Soviet Bloc building, with a satellite dish primarily used for N.B.A. games.

On the wall in one corridor I noticed a poster of Michael Jordan soaring for one of his patented dunks, ball palmed high in his right hand. Looking closer, I realized the photo had been taken at Madison Square Garden and, even closer, that one of the courtside reporters looking up in awe was clearly me.

I called over my hosts — which included Tskitishvili's youth coach and his Georgian agent — and pointed to myself. They hugged me, pounded my back. "Friend of Jordan!" they cried.

Dirk Nowitzki was already a rising N.B.A. star in Dallas, stretching the floor, changing the game. "Next Nowitzki" was what Kiki Vandeweghe, the Nuggets' general manager, was thinking when he drafted Tskitishvili, who never made it in the N.B.A. As with many American draft projections that backfired, he wasn't the only international flop. But that's not the point, which was that the N.B.A. by the turn of the century was truly a global phenomenon.

All around the world, Nike-wearing, Gatorade-drinking boys were growing up, dreaming of the league of opportunity and opulence, wanting to Be Like Mike.

FEB. 7, 2001

The Americanization
of Dirk Nowitzki

BY MIKE WISE

DALLAS — On one of his first road trips with the Dallas Mavericks in 1998, the young, shy German Dirk Nowitzki had to ask somebody to explain the term shoot-around, the routine game-day preparation for all N.B.A. teams.

"Shoot-around is like a rehearsal," Gary Trent, a teammate, told him.

The rookie nodded his head knowingly before looking back at Trent, somewhat puzzled.

"What's a rehearsal?"

Becoming fluent in English and fluid in the National Basketball Association has taken time. Language barriers, quicker and bigger players and unrealistic expectations had to be overcome.

But in less than three years, Nowitzki, a 22-year-old, 7-foot forward, has done more than merely win the transition game. Shooting 3-pointers with aplomb and depositing baseline dunks on the foreheads of future Hall of Famers, Nowitzki is becoming one of the more entertaining draws in pro basketball.

His teammates used to call him Irk, because, they say, "when he first got here, there was no D in Dirk." While defense remains a weakness, Nowitzki is among the main reasons the rejuvenated Mavericks (31–18) are on track to make the playoffs for the first time since 1990. They will meet the Knicks tonight at Madison Square Garden.

"We now call him Work," Trent said. "Dirk the Work. When he's got his rhythm, he can't be stopped."

Nowitzki, who will participate in the AT&T long-distance shootout on Saturday in Washington, one of the events during All-Star Weekend, has a decent shot at eclipsing the highest single-season N.B.A. scoring average by a

European. At 21.3 points a game, Nowitzki and the Yugoslav Peja Stojakovic of the Sacramento Kings are chasing the mark of the Croat Drazen Petrovic, who averaged 22.3 points for the Nets during the 1992–93 season.

Nowitzki was also close to becoming the third European to play in the All-Star Game, after Detlef Schrempf, his countryman and three-time All-Star, and the Dutchman Rik Smits. With Lakers center Shaquille O'Neal ailing, Nowitzki may yet be named as a reserve. In his last 18 games, he has averaged 23.1 points and 10.4 rebounds in almost 40 minutes a game. Against Orlando on Jan. 18, he had a career-high 38 points and 17 rebounds.

Ambidextrous and a multiposition player, he shoots 46.3 percent from the field and 84.2 percent from the free-throw line. Despite being 7 feet, he has made 83 3-pointers this season. "If you can't guard them one on one, the young man in the corner may have the best stroke I've seen since Bird," Rick Pitino said in his final days as the Boston Celtics' coach. "He's a terrific basketball player."

After a loss to Dallas this season, Coach Byron Scott of the Nets said his players were shocked at Nowitzki's agility and skill, adding, "We didn't know how to guard him."

Al Harrington and Rashard Lewis were in the same predicament almost three years ago in San Antonio, when a wispy 18-year-old walked onto the court of the Alamodome for the Nike Hoop Summit during college basketball's Final Four weekend. Harrington and Lewis were among the stars on a heavily favored USA juniors team about to play the international juniors, which included Nowitzki.

"I don't think any of them thought we had much talent," Nowitzki said.

Almost nobody in this country had heard of the German youngster when his coach, Holger Geschwindner, encouraged Nowitzki to leave the national team during the European playoffs to play in the event.

"We come from a soccer country," Geschwindner, who still works with Nowitzki, said. "If he was ever going to be an N.B.A. player, he had to be discovered. The Hoop Summit was his only chance to play against that kind of competition. I felt we had to go."

Lithe, active and dominant, Nowitzki collected 33 points, 14 rebounds and 3 steals as the international team stunned the Americans.

"Everyone at that game said, 'Who is this kid?'" recalled Kim Bohuny, the N.B.A.'s vice president for international basketball operations, who has worked with Nowitzki during his adjustment. "The general feeling was, where did he come from?"

Donn Nelson attended that game as a Mavericks scout. He is now the team's interim coach while his father, Don, recovers from prostate surgery. "I couldn't believe what I was seeing," Donn Nelson said. "A versatile 7-footer who could shoot from out there and run the floor? I was looking around to see who else was watching."

In June 1998, the Mavericks pulled off a draft-day deal with Milwaukee, which had the No. 9 pick, to acquire Nowitzki.

"Western Europe is pretty well combed over as far as N.B.A., college and even international scouting," Donn Nelson said. "He was a true sleeper. Normally that happens in Eastern Europe and third world countries. But to have it happen in the heart of Western Europe — in one of the most Americanized countries — is a huge oddity. A kid from Würzburg, Germany? Amazing."

His Statistics Jump, Too

Nowitzki's mother, Helga, who stands about 5-10, played for the German national team. His father, Joerg, is 6-1 and was an elite handball player. But other than good genes, there is little from Nowitzki's background to explain his emergence.

Würzburg is a picturesque Bavarian town in south-central Germany, a community of 128,000 surrounded by forests and vineyards. A three-hour drive north from Munich, the town straddles the muddy Main River and is known for its art, architecture and white wines.

"The competition wasn't that bad," said Nowitzki, who played for an upper-echelon professional team in Würzburg, the equivalent of a Division II or III college team in the United States.

Dallas point guard Steve Nash, who visited Nowitzki in Würzburg last summer, said: "They've got a nice gym that Nike built, and some players that work very hard. Still, you look around and you think to yourself, it's pretty inexplicable.'"

Nash, a Canadian, took Nowitzki under his wing in his first season and the two became the best of friends. They were trying to make it in the N.B.A. and, at times, they both struggled.

In his first N.B.A. game, Nowitzki matched up against Schrempf, the German-born forward who was then playing for the Seattle SuperSonics. The German press hyped the game as the changing of the guard. When Don Nelson boasted of Nowitzki's making a run for rookie of the year before he played his first game, the pressure mounted.

"They kind of set him up to where all he could do was fail," Nash said. "It was a tough situation, but the adversity helped him."

Donn Nelson said: "It was his first experience away from home. We made the mistake of getting overly excited about Dirk early. Expectations went up. We learned a hard lesson there."

Nowitzki said: "It's a little dramatic to say I was ready to go home, but I got pretty down. It was just a big adjustment, coming from Germany and never playing against American college guys, to the N.B.A."

Physically handled by his opponent in many games, he averaged 8.2 points on 40 percent shooting his first season. But last season he started all but one of 82 games and averaged 17.5 points. This season his numbers have jumped dramatically, to 21.3 points and 9.4 rebounds a game.

He returned to Seattle last December, and in one breathtaking sequence, drove the baseline and dunked over Patrick Ewing and Vin Baker, drawing a foul in the process.

"His eyes were really opened the first year, like, 'Whoa, what's this?'" Nash recalled. "Now he's taken a step in toughness, in physicality and confidence. He thinks he belongs physically instead of just saying he's going to get by."

Nelson said the team took a lot of flak for drafting the German.

"I don't feel vindicated, I feel relieved," said Donn Nelson, whose team passed up a chance to acquire Boston's Paul Pierce. "That was a major, major gamble for us. He was a high lottery pick that you don't often get a chance at. We never lost complete faith, but when he got off to a slow start, there was a feeling of, 'Is this guy going to pan out or not?'

"Internally, we knew it was a matter of time."

A Coach's Five-Year Plan

When asked how a foreign-born player managed to adjust and to thrive in the N.B.A., Nowitzki simply says: "Holger. I was lucky to meet the right coach."

Geschwindner, a member of West Germany's 1972 Olympic team, saw the Russians capture their controversial gold medal over the American team in Munich. He learned the game from United States soldiers stationed in Germany after World War II. "They had children and their children had children," he said. "Pretty soon, you have some good players."

In 1995, he was playing on a third-division team outside of Würzburg, waiting for the youngsters to finish, "when I saw this tall, skinny dude running around," Geschwindner said. "He was about 16, but he had no technical skills. I asked who he was working with. He said no one."

Beginning with shooting drills, Geschwindner mapped out a plan for Nowitzki to maximize his talent in five years. Post moves. Confidence building. Strength classes. Developing his left hand.

"Every aspect," Geschwindner said, acknowledging that Nowitzki still needs help defensively. "I still have two more steps to go. Sometimes I think about how much more you can add to his toolbox. Imagine what will happen then."

Nowitzki's Americanization is almost complete. His sister, Silke, 26, was recently hired by the international television division of N.B.A. Entertainment. She has seen the transition firsthand, how her tall, gangly brother went from brush-stroking ceilings for the family's Würzburg house-painting business to an emerging N.B.A. star.

"Some of the people I work with come up to me and tell me Dirk is on their fantasy team and to congratulate him on his game last night," Silke said. "I think he's more of a star here than he is back home. He can walk around Würzburg with no problem. But when I go to Dallas, he can barely get through the grocery store without signing many autographs."

Nowitzki's blond locks resemble some teenage idol from another decade, maybe Duran Duran's Simon Le Bon in high-tops. "Him and Steve Nash are going with the surfer look," Trent said. "So we let them surf."

Though growing up he loved Scottie Pippen's game, the fact that he is white and can shoot with either hand makes people gravitate toward the easiest comparison, Larry Bird.

"I think it's terrible," Nowitzki said. "It's unfair to him. He's one of the greatest players ever. I'm just getting started."

He has made the adjustments on the court, and he has blended in socially. He was once called every imaginable German stereotypical nickname. "Colonel Klink this, Wiener schnitzel that," Donn Nelson said. "It went on and on."

Today Nowitzki joins in the ribbing process. After a Dallas victory in which Nowitzki scored 14 of his 28 points in eight minutes, he made fun of Christian Laettner.

Hearing the commotion, Laettner entered the training room and half-heartedly confronted Nowitzki, who cowered on the training table.

"Just joking, Late," he said. "Just joking."

Nash said: "His first year he was a little scaredy-cat, but now he busts on guys more than anyone. Part of it is tongue-in-cheek, but his whole vernacular is comical. He'll say, 'What's up, yo?' or 'I'm just chillin',' like he's from the Bronx or something. It's classic. He gets snippets from rap songs and uses them in his everyday speech. One of his favorites is, 'Holler at a player, yo.' Dirk is ridiculous.

"From his game to everything else, it's scary how quickly he became Americanized."

SEPT. 26, 2000

A Mediocre Victory Punctuated by Carter

BY MIKE WISE

SYDNEY, Australia — Sometime between last May and tonight, Vince Carter developed a serrated edge on the court. Gone is the cuddly Toronto Raptors acrobat with the postgame disposition of a koala and the "Inside Stuff" smile.

At the Olympic Games, of all places, he has decided to share with the world an unmerciful, take-no-prisoners side of himself. Carter's performance here has come with preening after a score, altercations with inferior players, jeering from Australian fans.

Who knew that the guy whose mother put encouraging notes on his hotel pillow after a playoff loss had any outlaw in him?

But Carter has also provided splendid athletic moments, too, breathtaking plays to make everyone forgive and forget. And tonight, no transgression could stop the crowd at the Dome in Olympic Park from rising and cheering the most spectacular dunk anyone could recall in international competition.

With 16 minutes left in the second half of Team USA's 106–94 victory over France, Carter intercepted a lazy behind-the-back pass a few feet in front of the midcourt line. All that stood between his 6-foot-6 frame and the rim was Frédéric Weis, a gawky, 7-2 Frenchman trying to draw an offensive foul some four feet from the basket on the left side.

Carter took one power dribble and rose. And rose. And rose. "I felt like I took off a long way out and wasn't sure if I was going to make it," he said.

He did. Carter somehow leaped over Weis, using the Frenchman's head for balance as he slammed the ball with his body splayed in spread-eagle fashion. He resembled a boy leapfrogging a parking meter. The rim and the building shook.

"Le facial," a member of French news media said.

"He joked with me at the end, 'Did you see that dunk I put in your face?'" said Weis, taking the harsh postgame humor in stride. "I didn't see. Was too quick. I was not moving, trying to take a charge. But he jumped over me. It's unbelievable."

"I said, 'Why on me?' I'm going to be the poster dunk and I don't like this. He started laughing."

The Americans were impressed as well. "The only time I've ever seen a play like that is when I jumped over my 4-year-old son on one of those Nerf-ball baskets," United States Coach Rudy Tomjanovich said.

Jason Kidd, the Team USA point guard, said: "I think everybody was in awe, and nobody thought he was going to attempt that. To me, that was probably the greatest play in basketball I've ever seen."

Carter's liftoff and splashdown over Weis, the much-maligned Frenchman whom the Knicks shockingly took with the 15th pick in the 1999 National Basketball Association draft, obscured another mediocre outing from Team USA. France's 12-point margin of defeat was the second-lowest margin of victory by a team of American professional players since the international basketball federation began allowing N.B.A. players to compete in 1992. Last Thursday, Lithuania lost, 85–76, to the Americans and trailed by only 5 with 1 minute 9 seconds remaining.

Team USA, which finished 5–0 atop Group A, will meet Russia (3–2), the fourth-seeded team in Group B, in the quarterfinals on Wednesday. But in incremental ways, the Americans continue to show their fallibility against patient and physical teams. Tim Hardaway and Shareef Abdur-Rahim both got into altercations with French players, drawing technical fouls and the ire of the crowd.

It is not always the United States instigating the trouble. Grabbing, clutching and using their forearms, many international players clearly hold this collection of N.B.A. All-Stars in much less esteem than they did their Olympic predecessors.

"The international players are getting better because there are more players coming to the N.B.A. to play," Kidd said. "The fear of the Dream

Team is gone; '92 was the best team ever assembled. Now guys aren't as scared or afraid to play against us and you can see that in the first five games."

Canada (4–1) pulled off perhaps its greatest international upset tonight, knocking off the defending world champion, Yugoslavia (4–1), 83–75, to win Group B and avoid the Americans at least until the gold medal game. Steve Nash scored 26 points.

Australia (3–2) was also the beneficiary of good fortune after a 91–80 comeback victory over Spain (1–4). By taking third place in Group B, the host nation will meet Italy (3–2) in the quarterfinals. The Australians also set themselves up to avoid meeting the United States until the gold medal game.

Lithuania (3–2) meets Yugoslavia in the other quarterfinal, with the winner most likely meeting the Americans in the semifinals.

There are still indelible moments, however, when the game is more of a show than a contest. When Carter dunked over Weis, he said he felt as if he was literally flying.

"I went to track and field last night and I was telling my mom that I was itching to do it," he said. "I just wanted to try it, just to say I did it."

AUG. 10, 2008

Injured and Defeated, Yao Treasures the Moment

BY HARVEY ARATON

BEIJING — For this special night, Yao Ming dragged his giant's body back on a broken foot not fully healed. He risked the rest of his professional life for the opportunity to play a definitively competitive quarter and a half before losing to the United States, 101–70, in the most heralded game a Chinese basketball team has ever played.

But a 31-point differential was not the point, merely the exclamation point to a tsunami of American fast-break dunks. "This game was a treasure, and it will be for the rest of my life," Yao would say, without explaining why.

He didn't have to, because anyone with eyes half open Sunday night could see this was a celebration of Yao the ambassador, who, by making a large living in America, has done more for China as a burgeoning sports power than a thousand gymnasts and swimmers.

In a new arena with loud music, luxury boxes and lithe dancers that sounded and played like Oklahoma City, U.S.A., the flashbulbs popped for Yao and the Chinese national team making its entrance to the court as they did for Michael, Magic and the original Dream Team in 1992.

Yao was back, and proud, especially of his role in the coming-out party for his country of 1.3 billion. The Chinese fans responded by showering him with affection and showing an unyielding passion for the game. But their beloved national team needs to begin developing midsize athletes if it hopes to ever contest with the explosive American players.

Another Yao, if that is possible, would also be a fine idea. The original, with only so many basketball minutes left in his 7-foot-6 frame, deserves the rest of his days off from the arduous demands of the national team after the Beijing Games, for good behavior and common decency.

In a blowout midway through the fourth quarter, he was still grabbing rebounds, taking up space and taking the occasional charge. He absorbed the brunt of a Dwyane Wade drive, and got up hobbling. You worried for Yao at that moment, or at least the Houston Rockets surely did. But who couldn't admire his loyalty, his commitment, his readiness to play when a medical license wasn't required to know he couldn't fully be ready after his third broken foot, sustained in February?

"Yao is an unbelievable person," the American point guard Chris Paul said. "This wasn't just a basketball game for the people here, and Yao understood that."

Those of us who have closely watched the rapid development of the international game from the Dream Team in 1992 to the necessity for an American Redeem Team in 2008 will never forget our first Yao sighting halfway through that 16-year period, early in the 2000 Sydney Games.

At 20, he was one-third of a frontline predictably called the Great Wall of China. Yao was far and away its most intriguing member, and soon showed why by blocking Vince Carter's shot early in a game against the United States.

After watching Yao play that night, I wrote that if China got the 2008 Olympics, as it did the next year, he would be in the N.B.A. by 2002. It was a rare prognosticative triumph, although Yao was beaten to the league of opportunity and opulence by Wang Zhizhi, his 7-1 teammate, who signed with Dallas in 2001. Wang soon after took a liking to the no-strings capitalist lifestyle and was excommunicated from the Chinese national team for refusing to report for tournament play in the summer and fall of 2002.

In sharp contrast, Yao dutifully — and some would say foolishly — returned whenever summoned, unless injured. Wang was gone for four years, until his N.B.A. visa was revoked after five marginal seasons. In 2006, with the Olympics two years away, Wang publicly apologized to all of China, returned to its pro league and was reinstated by the national team.

He, too, said he could not imagine missing a game that would have blown the Nielsen computer had its viewership in China been measured by the American standard.

For about 15 minutes, long enough to make most people happy, it was actually a game. The latest version of David Stern's dunk-and-pony show still can't hit jumpers with reassuring regularity, and it doesn't defend the perimeter that well while scrambling to cause turnovers that can unleash its weapon of choice, the fast break.

These flaws could be a concern against the likes of Spain. Against most, as it was with China, it will be a matter of time before superior athleticism and full-court pressure brings an unmatchable tempo. The fans rocked when China tied the game at 29–29, but then came a series of turnovers and dunks that two Bush presidents enjoyed and even 18,000 Chinese fans could appreciate.

They know their basketball because, as Paul said: "Yao opened the door for everyone here. And he's not just big in China; he's a world icon."

He is an athlete who imperiled his health to please his heart and was removed after that fourth-quarter spill, leaving with his arm and fist raised high. The crowd roared as Yao walked off with his trove of treasured memories.

July 14, 2015
For Frédéric Weis, Knicks' Infamous Pick, Boos Began a Greater Struggle
BY SAM BORDEN

LIMOGES, France — On the morning when Frédéric Weis tried to kill himself, he dreamed about owning a beach house. A beach house had been Weis's dream for a long time. In France, in Spain, in Greece — wherever his career as a 7-foot-2 professional basketball player took him. He liked the sand, he liked the surf. A beach house was a good dream.

But on that day, in January 2008, the dream did not make him smile. Weis got into his car in Bilbao, Spain, around 10:00 A.M. and began the drive here, to this small city in west-central France best known for its production of fine china. He was on his way to see his wife and son. About 90 minutes into the drive, Weis suddenly pulled over at a rest area near Biarritz, a French town not far from the border.

He stopped the car, leaned back in his seat and, at 30 years old, considered all that had happened to him during his career. There were the early years playing in the French league. There was the night in 1999 when the Knicks made him a first-round draft pick. There was the disappointment of feeling as if the Knicks' coach, Jeff Van Gundy, did not actually want him. There was the vicious dunk from Vince Carter — just Google "le dunk de la mort" (Dunk of Death) if you have somehow missed it — that transformed him into an on-court victim.

And there was, of course, the cold recognition of his personal reality: that the label affixed to him as an N.B.A. bust/cautionary tale — at least if the memory of Weis in the public reaction to the Knicks' recent drafting of the Latvian Kristaps Porzingis is any indication — will, almost surely, last forever.

Weis thought about all this for a while. Then he thought about the beach house. Then he thought about his son, Enzo. Then he reached over, took out the box of sleeping pills he had brought with him and swallowed every single one.

Unlike Porzingis, who heard firsthand the boos and catcalls from angry Knicks fans at Barclays Center just seconds after his name was called during last month's draft, Weis had no idea that he was immediately hated in New York. He found out he was drafted when his agent, Didier Rose, called him at a Paris hotel room in the middle of the night on July 1, 1999. (Weis was with the French national team preparing for a game.)

Weis and his roommate had stayed up past curfew waiting for the phone to ring. When it did, Rose delivered the news by saying, "Fred, you got everything you wanted."

Weis called his father and howled into the phone. He just assumed everyone was as ecstatic as he was.

It was only weeks later, when Weis arrived in New York for a brief training camp with the Knicks' summer league team, that he learned most fans were angry the Knicks had drafted a mostly anonymous European big man as opposed to a more widely known American college player. (Many had wanted Ron Artest, who is from Queens.)

Knicks officials alerted Weis to the discontent in a short, somewhat awkward meeting. According to Weis's wife, Celia, Weis was told, "You're not really the guy we were supposed to draft," and he was informed that "some fans might not be so happy."

Nonetheless, Ed Tapscott, the team's interim general manager, who had drafted Weis, told him the Knicks were excited to have him and looked forward to seeing him play in the summer league.

Weis was excited, too. But his exuberance was quickly tempered after a few choppy interactions with Van Gundy, who did not seem pleased with Weis having been the team's draft choice. During phone calls with Celia, Weis described Van Gundy as having been "cold" to him and showing little interest in him. He told her a story about how Van Gundy had seen him wearing his watch just before practice — Weis was always a stickler for being on time — and berated him about whether he planned to wear it once workouts began.

Van Gundy, in an interview, said he had no particular recollections about his interactions with Weis — there were few, he said, and all took place more than 15 years ago — but added that he had "nothing bad to say about him."

"To be honest, what stands out to me is that I remember him being an incredibly nice and sweet guy," Van Gundy said.

With the Knicks' summer league team, Weis's play was limited and mostly unremarkable. The end of that summer league tournament, however, was the beginning of Weis's spiral. Weis could have signed the standard first-round draft pick contract with the Knicks — which would have required he stay with them — but he declined, choosing instead to play another year in France. That decision, which he later admitted regretting, was almost surely influenced by Rose, the agent, who also owned a piece of Weis's French team; Rose subsequently went to prison on charges related to financial impropriety and conflicts of interest.

Weis never played for the Knicks again, in the summer league or otherwise. Explanations of why vary, but Weis said top Knicks executives never directly contacted him about returning. That may be a matter of semantics — the Knicks, like most teams, had a European scout keeping an eye on Weis (and other players) — but, from Weis's perspective, he believed he was not wanted. So he continued playing in Europe. At the 2000 Olympics — despite being dunked on by Carter — he generally played well as France won the silver medal. From 1997 to 2000, Weis played in four consecutive French league All-Star games.

"I never heard from them," Weis said. "So what was I supposed to do?"

From the Knicks' side, the belief was always that Weis was not truly motivated to ever come and play in the United States. Scott Layden replaced Tapscott as general manager in August 1999, and while it was clear he was not especially enamored of Weis, he did express curiosity about Weis's potential. The Knicks, according to team officials, would have liked to see Weis at least play in the summer league again, and a bevy of news reports from the summers of 2000 and 2001 include quotations from representatives of Weis claiming that Weis, for various reasons, would not return to the Knicks' summer league team. Weis claims that he had only loose associations with those agents and that they never accurately conveyed to him the Knicks' desires.

Celia said that Weis was sad he never got to play with the Knicks — "It was something he very much wanted" — but was nonetheless pragmatic about it.

"He knew it was business," she said. She shrugged. "In a lot of ways, the truth is that all of that had nothing to do with what happened to him later."

Troubles After a Son's Birth

In 2002, three years after Weis was drafted, Enzo was born. Weis, always known as more of a gentle giant, was jubilant; being a father was something he had often said he felt he was born to do.

But something was not right with Enzo. Outwardly, the boy seemed O.K., making baby sounds and even saying some distinguishable words as he neared his first birthday. It soon became clear, however, that Enzo was only mimicking sounds he was hearing others say and not actually learning how to communicate. His ability to focus — on a person or a task — was nonexistent. If the family tried to eat at a restaurant, Enzo would shriek and shout and shake.

Weis was playing in Spain at the time, and a Spanish doctor ultimately declared that Enzo had a form of autism. Celia was devastated; Weis was despondent and, then, destructive.

He began staying out late. Never much of a drinker before, Weis routinely closed down bars in Bilbao, often drinking as late as 5:00 A.M. He went out on weekends. He went out on weeknights. He went out on nights before games, and he went out on nights after them. When he and Celia separated in 2004 — she moved back to France with Enzo — Weis's nocturnal habits worsened.

Off the court, he was erratic, moody and, as he admitted, "too interested in doing all the bad things." On the court, he was sluggish and ineffective; during the 2004–05 season, he averaged fewer than 3 points and 16 minutes per game, both career lows for any season in which he played at least 30 games.

Weis struggled to balance his emotions about Enzo with his need to continue playing basketball. He tried to visit Celia and Enzo as often as possible but could not hide his disappointment at not being able to do what other fathers did with their children. He could not take Enzo to the movies (films were too long for Enzo). He could not play board games. He could not do puzzles.

Enzo liked basketball — he would go to Weis's games sometimes and sit in the stands for short stretches — but he could not play. On the court, when it was just the two of them and Weis was hoping for anything, just a shot or a pass, Enzo only ran, around and around, while his father held the ball.

By January 2008, Weis hit bottom. Shortly after New Year's Day, he decided he wanted to "stop it all," as he said. And so he took the box of sleeping pills, drove to the rest stop in Biarritz and closed his eyes.

Recovery, Then Retirement

About 10 hours after he swallowed the pills, Weis woke up. For several minutes, he was confused and could not figure out where he was or what had happened. Then he saw the empty box and felt what he described as a "surprising" relief. He had failed, and for once, this made him happy.

"It was the luckiest I've been in my life," he said.

He picked up his phone and dialed Celia, who had been expecting him five hours earlier and had called, over and over, while he was unresponsive. When she answered, he told her what he had done and then waited — first as she wept and then, much longer, as she had a friend drive to Biarritz to pick Weis up.

"When he told me what had happened, I cannot say I was surprised," Celia said. "But I hoped that afterward would be different."

It is never quite that simple. Yes, Weis's failed suicide attempt was the catalyst for a change in his behavior (he quit drinking, he said), and yes, he and Celia did begin a reconciliation that ended up sticking (the couple have been together ever since). Weis went on to play a few more seasons in Spain before finishing his career in France and retiring in 2011.

But now, four years after retirement, 13 years after Enzo was born and 16 years after the Knicks drafted him, Weis still battles depression. Weis hides it well; he and Celia own a tobacco store and a bar in Limoges, and outwardly, Weis seems content.

Certainly his basketball career — even the parts that never fully developed — is not a source of stress. During a recent interview at a brasserie in the center of town, he laughed often and frequently poked fun at himself, chuckling as he told the story of when he visited New York a few years back and was recognized by the passport officer at the airport.

"Aren't you that guy the Knicks drafted?" the officer asked, and, startled, Weis quickly crouched a bit lower. "No, no — that's my cousin," he replied as the officer quizzically waved him through.

"I don't know if he was a fan or not," Weis said as he recalled the exchange. "But I didn't want to get in any trouble."

When it comes to Enzo, though, Weis still struggles. He speaks with obvious pride when he describes how Enzo, now 13, has improved his motor skills and his focus, but Celia said there are still so many mornings when she finds Weis lying in bed, grim-faced and morose. There are still so many times, too, when Weis has mood swings; one recent day at the store, Celia said, Weis lashed out at a customer who had come in and whistled since both Celia and Weis were in the back.

"What, am I your dog?" Weis yelled before Celia calmed him down.

"I have asked him about seeing a therapist," Celia said, "but he doesn't want to. He won't go. He says, 'Why do I need to talk about things to someone? I can talk about them to you.'"

Weis says he is fine. He has made peace with what his basketball career was and what it was not — "life is not perfect, sometimes" — and he is doing his best to deal with being a parent to an autistic child.

"I still dream about the beach house," he said in a wistful lilt, but it is different now. Now, he does not think about the beach house as a luxury item or a perk for a basketball superstar. Instead, he thinks of it as a haven — the only place, perhaps, where he can feel like a father giving something to his son.

"The tides make Enzo happy," Weis explained, "and so I want to take him there. I want to let him run out with the ocean because he loves it."

Weis smiled.

"He loves to feel like he is running on top of the water," he said.

— POSTSCRIPT —

SAM BORDEN, 2018: "I went to live in Paris as the paper's international sports reporter and Frédéric Weis was on an original list of stories I wanted to look into. I later found an interview that he had done where he mentioned that he owned a tobacco store in Limoges, about three hours away by train. I called the store, spoke to his wife and asked if I could come talk with Frédéric. She said, sure. I walked in, asked Frédéric if I could buy him lunch and we went next door and spoke for over two hours. His emotional availability was remarkable, revealing all that had led him to try to kill himself. I had worried about being from New York, a place in which he hadn't had the best experience — I acknowledged that when we sat down and made sure to explain I was there to tell his story. In retrospect, I think he wanted it told, completely, so those in New York and the States would know that there was much more to him than what happened with the Knicks and one monster dunk in the Olympics. He'd actually had a good career in Europe, the French people largely embraced him and he had survived."

24

Deep in the Heart

Between Games 1 and 2 of the 2007 N.B.A. finals — a Spurs' four-game demolition of a 22-year-old LeBron James and a random assortment of dudes named Boobie, Zydrunas and Sasha — Sam Smith and I followed Gregg Popovich out of his mass press conference and asked one of those leading questions that Popovich, typically too smart to play by reporters' rules, usually bats away with a smirk.

"How is it," I said, "that after three championships and the very good possibility of a fourth, and with a group that truly plays committed team basketball, the belief is still that the Spurs are not sexy enough to help the N.B.A. draw big ratings?"

Fortunately, Smith, then of the *Chicago Tribune*, and I had found Popovich in a playful but truthful mood. Here was the gem of a quote we recorded:

"That's their problem, not mine," he said. "I can't help them, poor souls. They've got to live in their ignorance. I can't make them keep watching us, but it's always dumbfounded me, since the arrival of Tony [Parker] and Manu [Ginobili]. If you can't enjoy watching those two guys play and you don't understand that they're as much fun to watch as a lot of other people in bigger markets, then I can't help, and it means you're not much of a fan and you don't understand the game, anyway, and you should probably tune in HBO."

I reminded Popovich that Game 2 of the finals would be going head-to-head with the final season's last episode of the HBO blockbuster series, *The Sopranos*. He didn't miss a beat.

"Fifty-fifty I'll get booted so I can watch it," he said.

I never tried to hide my fondness for Pop, Tim Duncan and the Spurs in my columns. Having grown up with the early 1970s Knicks of Red Holzman, Clyde Frazier and Willis Reed, I maintained that if the Spurs had been magically transplanted to New York, they would have the toast of the United Nations with their blend of international stars. Duncan would have been cast as the second coming of Willis, the always-in-motion Ginobili as the athletic enhancement of Bill Bradley and the unflappable Parker as a zippier, French version of Clyde.

It would take a quite a few more years before the Spurs got their due, thanks in part to LeBron.

May 2, 2004

The Spurs Are the Anti-Lakers

by Chris Broussard

SAN ANTONIO — The San Antonio Spurs do not have bickering superstars, rapping superstars or disgruntled superstars. They do not have a player who has declared disdain for his coach or a coach who is celebrated as a master of Eastern mysticism. They do not have anyone facing the prospect of life in prison and they do not have two future Hall of Famers who must rue the day they forsook millions of dollars for a season of dysfunction.

The San Antonio Spurs are a basketball team, not a soap opera.

The question is: In this day and age of trash talk, televised street ball, personality-driven marketing and preening and gloating after baskets, is solid basketball enough?

It's certainly enough to win the N.B.A. championship, as the Spurs proved by capturing their second title in five years last season. But is it enough to captivate the hearts of fans and viewers outside of San Antonio the way, say, the Los Angeles Lakers have?

"We're just vanilla," swingman Bruce Bowen said after San Antonio snapped the Lakers' 11-game winning streak last month. "Whereas the Lakers are Chunky Monkey or something like that."

The two flavors will collide today in San Antonio in Game 1 of their four-of-seven-game Western Conference semifinal series. Many analysts say the series will determine this season's champion. It will be the fifth playoff meeting in six years for the clubs, which have combined to win the past five N.B.A. titles.

San Antonio won last year's second-round series, four games to two, but one wonders if Commissioner David Stern is privately rooting for the Lakers, considering how the nation tuned out the Spurs's 4–2 victory over the Nets in last season's finals.

The series against the Nets, the most competitive finals since Chicago beat Utah in 1998, was the lowest-rated title series since the networks stopped showing the finals on tape delay in 1981.

"They play an efficient game that isn't pleasing to the eye in terms of having highfliers," Kenny Smith, the TNT analyst and former player, said of the Spurs. "They don't have guys who make spectacular plays on a regular basis. They're more of a grind-it-out team. They're very similar to those old Detroit Pistons teams, without the attitude. If you take away the attitude of the Detroit Pistons and take the Bad Boy name off of them, that's what you've got — the Spurs."

Like the Spurs, the Pistons' championship teams of 1989 and 1990 had one superstar and a terrific supporting cast. But their superstar, Isiah Thomas, was one of the game's most exciting players. The Spurs' Tim Duncan is one of the game's greatest players, but neither his game nor his laid-back personality can be described as electrifying.

Moreover, Duncan does not go out of his way to engage the news media. He is accommodating and polite, but he will never make comments as the sometime-rapper Shaquille O'Neal did after making the winning basket against Houston two weeks ago — "a hero ain't nothing but a sandwich, and I'm trying to give up carbohydrates."

The N.B.A. is telling itself that Duncan is beginning to come out of his shell. The belief is based on his entertaining commercial with Julius Erving in which a distraught Duncan lies on a couch confessing his love for the Larry O'Brien championship trophy. "I'm a pretty emotional guy, Doc," Duncan says in a play on his typically stoic demeanor.

The commercial, part of the league's campaign to promote the playoffs, has been so popular that a second one with Duncan and Erving is in the works.

There are other indications that fans may be embracing the Spurs. Duncan's jersey, the 15th-best seller last season, was No. 6 this season. And the Spurs ranked eighth in team merchandise sold at the N.B.A. Store as well as on NBA.com. Last season, they were not in the top 10.

Duncan seems not to care about his popularity, though, and his indifference toward hype and hoopla rubs off on his teammates.

"I know Tim doesn't give a darn about all that stuff," said Steve Kerr, a TNT analyst who won titles with the Spurs in 1999 and 2003. "He just wants to win, and for the most part that's the way it is with all those guys. That's one of the reasons they're so good — because they focus on what it takes to win and nothing else."

The Spurs have been nothing if not focused lately. Although the squabbling Lakers are far too talented to be counted out, there is no question that the Spurs are entering this series as the league's hottest team.

They have won 15 consecutive games, including their four-game sweep of Memphis in the first round. Their average margin of victory in those games was 14.5 points, and they have not lost a home game that Duncan has played in since Jan. 29.

"I picked the Lakers to win it all at the beginning of the season, but they've had too much turmoil and they're too inconsistent," Kerr said. "Now I think the Spurs are the better team and I think they're going to win. They're so much more solid than the Lakers night in and night out."

San Antonio Coach Gregg Popovich likes to say the Spurs are not the defending champions because they have had so much roster turnover. The starters David Robinson and Stephen Jackson, and the key reserves Speedy Claxton, Danny Ferry, Steve Smith and Kerr are gone, replaced by Rasho Nesterovic, Hedo Turkoglu, Robert Horry and Jason Hart.

The core of Duncan, Tony Parker, Manu Ginobili and Bowen remains, and after a sluggish 9–10 start, the Spurs have not missed a beat. This season's team is more athletic than San Antonio's two previous title winners, and Popovich has capitalized on that by incorporating more motion into the offense.

The Spurs won their first championship, and to a lesser degree their second, by mimicking the Rockets' game plan when Hakeem Olajuwon led them to titles in 1994 and 1995. With Duncan and Robinson inside, they passed the ball down low, waited for defenses to double-team, then buried them with 3-point shooting.

This season, there is more movement, and the pick-and-roll has become a staple. That pick-and-roll could be the Lakers' undoing because O'Neal has trouble guarding it and Parker has the quickness to get past Gary Payton, who joined the Lakers in the off-season along with another star veteran, Karl Malone. "I can't wait to play L.A.," Parker said.

Defensively, the Spurs are as stifling as always with two shot-blockers in Duncan and Nesterovic and the lock-down artist, Bowen, at small forward. Bowen was such a nuisance this season that several players accused him of playing dirty.

No one can be expected to shut down Kobe Bryant, the player openly disdainful of Coach Phil Jackson, but Bowen can contain him as well as anyone. As for excitement, well, the Spurs can at least offer Parker, one of the game's quickest players, and Ginobili, who comes off the bench behind Turkoglu and Bowen. Ginobili, a 6-foot-6 swingman from Argentina, is one of the league's more acrobatic players, capable of snatching away the ball on defense and slicing to the hoop on offense.

Whereas Bowen will make Bryant work on offense, Ginobili will make him hustle on defense.

Still, whether San Antonio beats the Lakers and whether viewers embrace the Spurs will depend on Duncan, who lifts the team with his ability and keeps it grounded with his personality.

"There's a disparity between guys who can sell product and guys who win games," Kenny Smith said. "Tim Duncan is the latter. He might not sell as many products, but he wins a lot of games."

The Lakers, with all their drama and charisma, are an easy sell. But can they win against Duncan and the Spurs?

APRIL 15, 2012

In San Antonio, a Coach's Player, a Player's Coach

BY HARVEY ARATON

SAN ANTONIO — Gregg Popovich has never worried that Tim Duncan will lobby management to get rid of him behind his back. They are as tethered to each other as this city is to the Alamo. For 15 of his 16 years as the Spurs' coach, Popovich has told assistants, "We have the easiest job in the N.B.A. because of Tim Duncan, because of who he is and the way he conducts himself."

But here in the land that N.B.A. time forgot — where there is no "I" in team, only in Tim — folks still face a universal chronological challenge. If growing apart is not a problem, growing old is. Duncan, the most minimalist superstar of the modern professional basketball era, will turn 36 on April 25. Popovich, the only N.B.A. coach Duncan has had and with whom he has won four championships, is 63.

Though reports of the Spurs' competitive death were greatly exaggerated after they lost in the first round of the playoffs to Memphis last spring after a 61-victory regular season, the question persists even as their quest for a fifth title continues: How much life do they really have left in them?

"As for us being dead, it's that way every year," Duncan said with a shrug. "For a while now, it's been, 'We're getting too old.' I guess it's going to happen eventually. Somebody's going to be right."

Duncan sat down to talk last week a few minutes after the doors to the Spurs' practice center opened on the morning of their first meeting with the Los Angeles Lakers this season. A handful of reporters strolled in and scattered to various players and coaches, leaving Duncan to a rare visitor from out of town at the far side of the court.

After the interview, Tom James, the Spurs' director of media services, said it had been the longest Duncan had done in a while. It had lasted 10 minutes.

Such is life with No Drama Duncan, who has become such a predictably understated fixture for this franchise that on some days he might as well be one of the basket stanchions. He has never sought attention or glory. When he considered leaving San Antonio as a free agent in 2001 — for Orlando — he did so without fanfare or folly.

Ultimately, Duncan stayed in San Antonio, where he lives year-round, and seems overwhelmingly likely to finish his career as that rarest of N.B.A. commodities: a leading man who never forced change on himself (to another city) or on the franchise (by demanding a new coach).

On both of these issues, why would he have had to? Since Duncan has been here, patrolling the paint, the Spurs have never won fewer than 50 games in a nonlockout season and have the best winning percentage — just short of .700 — among franchises in the four major North American team sports.

"Unlike some other guys, I've been lucky," he said. "With the teams we've had, with the focus of the people here wanting to put winning teams together, of having a system and sticking to it. There's no better way to do it. It's a special situation, obviously, and everybody can't have it.

"In other places, coaches come in and out, and there are guys who have four or five in the same amount of years, and that's a situation I can see why you'd want to get out of. But people changing for size of market? That I really don't understand."

When Duncan was asked if any of the young N.B.A. power brokers — for instance, Dwight Howard, who reportedly went backdoor in an attempt to oust Coach Stan Van Gundy in Orlando while refusing to commit to the franchise beyond next season — had ever sought his counsel on the benefits of laying deep roots, he shook his head and said, simply, "Nope."

Told of the exchange, R. C. Buford, the Spurs' general manager, laughed and said, "Very few people can have a conversation with Tim that would last long enough for them to get that much out of it."

A star player does not have to be a lifer to develop a strong relationship with a coach that positively affects his team. A new coach can draw the very best from a player, as Phil Jackson proved in Chicago and Los Angeles with Michael Jordan, Kobe Bryant and Shaquille O'Neal. Perhaps Carmelo

Anthony is on the way to establishing that brand of simpatico with Mike Woodson in New York.

But given the length of the Popovich-Duncan marriage, two competitive souls together for 15 years in so pressurized an environment, Buford called the dynamic almost too good to be true and virtually unheard-of in the N.B.A. John Stockton and Karl Malone come to mind, but they did not play for Jerry Sloan during their early years in Utah, and Bill Russell — not Red Auerbach — coached himself during his last three years with the Celtics.

"I think this term is often overused, but there are very few relationships where the relationship between player and coach can be described as a real soulmate," Buford said. "But we've been fortunate enough that Pop and Tim are connected that way. When things are tough, they've got that. That's their rock."

It is not because Popovich, an acerbic Air Force veteran, has not had his less amicable moments with Duncan.

"I probably get on him more than I get on, say, Gary Neal," Popovich said, referring to a Spurs reserve guard. "'Timmy, you getting a rebound tonight or are we just going to leave and go to dinner?' He'll look at me say, 'Hey, I'm trying,' but he can be criticized. He's not embarrassed to be called out in front of the team."

Over the years, Duncan has been granted some roster input, especially as the Spurs have overhauled a supporting cast for him, Manu Ginobili and Tony Parker that had become long in the tooth and heavy in the legs. The additions of young players like Kawhi Leonard, Danny Green and DeJuan Blair — all starters in a deep, minutes-sharing rotation stitched together by Buford — have allowed Popovich to limit the minutes of Duncan and Ginobili, 34, while not missing a regular-season beat.

But is it enough for the Spurs — with their lack of high-wire skills and reliance on an international blend of team-first players — to survive two playoff months?

After his team briefly supplanted Oklahoma City as the Western Conference leader, Popovich unapologetically left Duncan, Parker and Ginobili home for a road game in Utah, where the Spurs' 11-game winning streak ended. Three nights later, in what Popovich called "an embarrassing loss," the Bryant-less Lakers dominated the Spurs with Andrew Bynum and Pau Gasol making them appear small, earthbound and creaky.

The next night, Duncan put up vintage numbers (28 points and 12 rebounds) in a 107–97 victory over the Grizzlies, moving Popovich to gush, "He was a monster."

Duncan's contract is up after this season, and he dismisses talk of retirement.

"As long as I'm healthy, as long as I'm effective, I'm taking it as it comes," he said. "It's been a great year for me. Minutes are down. As a competitor, I want to play more, but honestly, I can't beat feeling as healthy as I do. That's why Pop regulates my time and being the bad guy at times when I want to be out there. In the long run, it helps me."

And there lies the basis for longevity: a fundamental trust that can be confounding and elusive to some, not all, of the young and the restless.

"He's got that kind of character, and a lot of people don't understand what that means life-wise," Popovich said. "You're taking on a personal challenge. You put it on yourself. 'No, I don't need to be with so-and-so, and I don't need to go someplace else. I'm going to do what I have to do, and I want to get it done here.'"

Here in south Texas, where Duncan has followed David Robinson's lead of staying put, where the public-address announcer simply says "Tim at the line" when he shoots free throws and where even Popovich becomes misty-eyed when he takes a moment to consider the eventual end of the era.

As to its lasting effect on him, Popovich said, "It's been an incredible opportunity, an incredible responsibility and an unbelievable gift to have somebody who is not just that good a basketball player, but is so respectful of the process that he trusts and allows us to coach."

To which the beleaguered fraternity of X-and-O N.B.A. lifers would say, amen.

July 23, 2018

For Gregg Popovich, a Second Job Comes at Just the Right Time

by Marc Stein

Had he stuck to his oft-cited timetable, Gregg Popovich could have dodged the whole Kawhi Leonard commotion. The escape path had been established long before this summer's trade saga that dragged the previously drama-proof San Antonio Spurs into the N.B.A.'s ever-spinning reality show blender at last.

How many times over the years did Popovich tell us he would be walking right out the exit door behind Tim Duncan when the greatest Spur of them all decided to stop playing?

"I kind of believed that," Popovich said the other day in a telephone interview, harkening back to what became one of his go-to proclamations.

"Or maybe I was trying to make myself believe it — that I was just going to go out on Timmy's coattails."

Duncan, of course, retired after the 2015–16 season. Popovich, the Spurs' coach since 1996, not only has one season remaining on a five-year contract extension he signed in 2014 after San Antonio won its last championship — he's about to start a second job.

On Thursday in Las Vegas, Popovich's tenure as the next coach of the United States men's basketball team — and the successor to the wildly successful Mike Krzyzewski — begins in earnest. Thirty-five American stars have been invited to two days of light practices and bonding meetings to launch the transition from Duke University's Coach K to San Antonio's Pop.

"This summer is more about camaraderie than coaching," Popovich said.

That certainly covers the national-team portion of Popovich's off-season, but the rest of it can't be so neatly summed up. On the court, and especially off it, Popovich has never faced a more challenging period.

Impervious to player insurrections for nearly two decades — thanks mostly to Duncan's unwavering devotion to the organization after his free-agent flirtation with the Orlando Magic in 2000 — Popovich's Spurs are reeling in the wake of Leonard's departure.

Leonard informed the Spurs in June that he wanted to be traded and would leave them without compensation in free agency in July 2019 if they didn't accommodate the request. Last Wednesday Popovich and R.C. Buford, the Spurs' president, reluctantly complied.

San Antonio dealt Leonard to the Toronto Raptors after conceding that Popovich, who said he had fielded a similar request for the first time as a coach from the All-Star forward LaMarcus Aldridge last summer, wouldn't be able to talk his way into a reconciliation as he did with Aldridge.

In addition to the unprecedented organizational turmoil, Popovich's return to the floor this week comes amid great personal loss. His wife, Erin, died in April at age 67 after dealing with a long-term illness, which led Popovich to step away from the Spurs' final three games in their first-round series with the Golden State Warriors.

Popovich's re-emergence into the public eye came Wednesday at a hastily called news conference after the Leonard trade. Asked how he had been coping with events both at and away from work, Popovich offered a brief acknowledgment that "it's been difficult."

Popovich's closest friends, then, are understandably hoping that stepping into the U.S. national team role — his dream job — can provide a sanctuary from everything else.

"He doesn't need any advice from me," said Don Nelson, whose bond with Popovich dates to Pop's time as an assistant under Nelson with Golden State in the early 1990s.

"It's a hard job, but he's been around this team before," said Nelson, who coached the second incarnation of the so-called Dream Team at the 1994 world championships. "He knows what to do. Hopefully it'll be good for him."

Popovich was indeed an assistant with the national team, first under George Karl and then Larry Brown, with squads that flopped at the 2002 world championships in Indianapolis (finishing sixth) and the 2004 Olympics in Greece (finishing third). The subsequent decision of U.S.A. Basketball's managing director, Jerry Colangelo, to name Krzyzewski as Brown's replacement, instead of Popovich, spurred a frostiness between Colangelo and Popovich that took a decade to thaw.

But Colangelo had only one name in mind when Krzyzewski decided he would step down after the 2016 Summer Games in Rio. So he courted Popovich hard in 2015 and convinced the former Air Force Academy cadet to add international basketball to his Spurs duties. Popovich, for the record, agreed to take the job only if Colangelo pledged to stay on through the 2020 Olympics in Tokyo.

"This will probably be good for Pop to be able to focus on something a little bit different than Spurs business, even if it's only for a few days," Colangelo said. "I recall with Coach K, people would always ask him, 'How are you going to handle two big jobs at once?' He always said that it's not only refreshing but, 'I need this.' It kept him re-energized."

Different adjectives may apply if Leonard attends the minicamp. All eyes at the open-to-the-media workouts are bound to laser in on every coach-player interaction should Popovich and his now-former franchise player wind up in the same gym — especially with DeMar DeRozan, San Antonio's prime acquisition in the trade with Toronto, also on the list of invitees.

But U.S.A. Basketball officials are bracing for Leonard to invoke his right to pass on the non-mandatory sessions, as LeBron James and Stephen Curry have done, as he continues his recovery from the mysterious quadriceps injury that led to the unraveling of his relationship with the Spurs. Leonard, after all, might dread the glare of the spotlight more than Popovich.

"He's a maybe," Colangelo said of Leonard's attending the camp.

Popovich, mind you, is not likely to reveal much about any interactions with Leonard even if the player does show, whether in front of the audience at U.N.L.V.'s Mendenhall Center or in private.

Those who know Popovich best have said he had long been curious about what it would be like to coach beyond Duncan, even as he frequently stated publicly that he would retire with him. Yet he remains as consistent as any coach the N.B.A. has ever seen — which means you needn't hold one breath waiting for Pop to expound on classified team business.

"I'm not too interested in talking about the past," Popovich said of the Leonard situation. "It doesn't do us any good whatsoever."

As fiercely patriotic as anyone in basketball, Popovich inevitably prefers to focus on the new gig. He turns 70 in January, and suddenly must replace perhaps the most imposing two-way force in the game at his day job, but there was only ever going to be one answer when Colangelo proposed doubling his workload.

"It's an absolutely humbling endeavor and an honor to be asked to do this," Popovich said. "It's bigger than any one game or any one season.

"I feel that already. I think about it every day to some extent."

25

Old Enough to Fight, Too Young to Play

To his credit, David Stern never patronized high school players, telling them they needed a year or two of academic refinement before setting out in the real world. When defenders of the college game — meaning those who fed at its generous trough — howled over the N.B.A.'s acceptance of Kevin Garnett and then Kobe Bryant, Stern in so many words told them to shut the hell up.

"Where was the outrage for Martina Hingis, for Chris Evert, for Jimmy Connors?" Stern told me in 1996. When white children of athletic privilege were involved, few, if any, worried about them missing out on freshman English, or, worse, attending high school on a Florida tennis academy hard court.

Stern was right when he cited a moral double standard regarding young African-American men. So what changed when the N.B.A. locked high school players out in 2005, legislating that they couldn't be drafted until they turned 19 or finished their freshman year in college?

Stern didn't patronize — but he did needlessly punish.

It was simply a better business practice, he rationalized. The league was becoming too young, which wasn't untrue, but also wasn't the real point of the one-and-done era. Keeping kids out for a year did nothing to ripen the N.B.A. product. And being begged for one season of service and a semester of class attendance did little for anyone's social development.

For years, the N.B.A. had enjoyed the indisputable marketing benefits of March Madness, its future stars parading across America's television screens before the ceremonial draft cap was placed on their heads. By 2005, the draft procession was consisting of too many little-known teenagers and foreign-born players. One-and-done was a compromise and concession to America's institutions of higher dribbling that was destined to create even greater exploitation and unseemliness.

It took more than a decade before the narrative imploded with the 2017 seizure of the player agent Andy Miller's computer by the F.B.I., unearthing a widespread recruiting scandal that cost Rick Pitino his job at Louisville while implicating other Division I programs.

The drumbeat of potential doom for college basketball's dark web of deceit promptly reignited the one-and-done debate. Rediscovering its conscience, the N.B.A began laying the groundwork for welcoming high school players again with much greater investment in its G League, or development vehicle. Which should have been its policy all along.

Nov. 13, 2005

The N.BA.'s New Age Rule Will Get Old In A Hurry

BY SELENA ROBERTS

They are certainly a breed of wildlife fitted in custom suits for their harrowing journey to March Madness in search of a perfect end, but this isn't the methodical *March of the Penguins.*

This is Coach K, his arms waving on the sideline with the desperation of a stranded motorist. This is John Calipari, his jaw comically dropping with a "Zoink!" sound effect on every foul call. This is college coaching.

And these obsessive souls of the business are enough of a whirling dust devil on the job without feeling pressured to try on Don King's dust-bunny wig.

And yet, in the leadup to last week's national signing day, some must have felt forced to all but sign one-year promotional deals with talented teenagers who might have been bound for the National Basketball Association if not for the new age-eligibility requirement.

It's 19, not 18 anymore. It's one year of college, not a prom-and-done proposition now. It is an ill-conceived piece of phony feel-good legislation on every level.

A year to mature, a season to grow, the N.B.A. caretakers will tell you. As if a freshman year is an introduction to adulthood and responsibility instead of beer bongs and campus gals who aspire to be Carolina Panthers cheerleaders.

As if it would have been better for good-citizen LeBron James to put on a freshman 15 rather than for Carmelo Anthony to put in a cameo at Syracuse before appearing in the underground *Snitch* DVD as an N.B.A. player.

The Pacers' Jermaine O'Neal eloquently described the age limit last year as an unconstitutional rule directed at black athletes. Together, with the recent Mister Rogers dress code, the N.B.A. is precariously close to being perceived as a league trying to brush itself with a whitening system.

While the National Hockey League promotes the wholesome Sidney Crosby, and the Ladies Professional Golf Association benefits from Michelle Wie's pro decision on her Sweet 16th, the N.B.A. is hoping its future stars of the baggy-jean age outgrow their hip-hop phase with a year in the hands of a college coach.

Let Bob Knight teach, mold and scold them into scouts. Let Mike Krzyzewski shower them with warm hugs as he transforms them into upstanding Dukies. Let college be the N.B.A.'s fly-by farm system.

As a reward, top college coaches will receive a teenage savior on their roster. But the N.B.A.'s added rule is not college basketball's gain.

Did Ohio State Coach Thad Matta receive a gift or a burden on signing day? He is the recruiting genius of the moment after Greg Oden, the 18-year-old 7-foot center from the Hoosier State, proclaimed his love for the Buckeyes.

Oden said he had planned on giving college a try, but, in truth, he didn't really have an option. He was forced to pass on millions as the N.B.A.'s projected top draft pick when the age rule went into place during the summer.

Legal to vote, Oden's freedom of choice was stripped away. He is the object of college expectation now. If the Ohio State faithful believe a national title is just a season away, so does Texas after the next-best high school prospect, Kevin Durant, hooked on.

Who will coach the next Carmelo Anthony? Who will coach the next Dajuan Wagner?

In his freshman year, and his only year, Anthony left Syracuse Coach Jim Boeheim with a life-affirming title. In Wagner's one and only season at Memphis, he left Calipari on a stopover to the N.B.A. How is a coach supposed to guide a player who is on a temp job?

"In terms of public perception, yes, there is pressure on the coach," said Jim Haney, the executive director of the National Association of Basketball Coaches. "People say, 'We're a lock to be successful; we should be the national champion.'

"They want this player to be to their school what Carmelo Anthony was to Syracuse. But in reality, that was an anomaly."

In reality, insta-saviors are problematic for a coach. The high school players know what their alternatives to college are — invisibility playing in Europe or risk of exposing weakness in the N.B.A.'s development league — and crave the N.C.A.A. limelight to improve their draft status.

"The big thing is if the player is thinking of a one-year stint in college as his way out," Haney said. "He may not be playing for the team, but for his rookie contract. That's a real issue."

The one-year delay strategy by the N.B.A. does not aid in development, it only complicates it for the starry-eyed player and the frenzied coach.

"If you're a player who has one foot in and one foot out of the relationship, it's destined not to go very far," Haney said. "A coach has to wonder: Is this someone who is going to be attentive? Is he going to put time into the weight room or be part of the team?"

All good questions. But who has time for perspective?

The N.B.A.'s new age requirement doesn't encourage a cozy connection between a college coach and a high school star. It only confuses the roles between diva player and diva coach.

June 28, 2007

The N.B.A.'s Dropouts

by Oscar Robertson

CINCINNATI — Tonight will be the first National Basketball Association draft in the era of "one and done." Draft eligibility now begins at age 19, so most high school graduates have to attend college for a year or sit out a year before turning pro. All the focus seems to be on the two most coveted former freshmen, Kevin Durant of the University of Texas and Greg Oden of Ohio State, and how the teams that draft them will fare as a result.

While Durant, Oden and several other draftees will become instant multimillionaires, rookies of any age who have both the athletic skills and the mental approach necessary to turn around a team immediately are rare. The N.B.A. wants new stars, so expectations often exceed reality. Meanwhile, other, less-heralded freshmen who have come out for the draft may not be selected by an N.B.A. team and will soon disappear from view.

"One and done" is a dramatic change from the system put in place in 1976, when the "Oscar Robertson rule" — a court settlement between the N.B.A. and its players association — removed all restrictions from the N.B.A. draft. I believe that policy should still be the case. If an 18-year-old can fight and die in the military, why can't he pursue an N.B.A. career if he's good enough and someone is willing to offer him a contract?

The larger issue is why anyone thought "one and done" was a good idea in the first place. It's counterproductive for the N.B.A., which wants more mature and better-behaved players (the N.B.A.'s commissioner, David Stern, first proposed making players wait until they were age 20 or two years out of high school before they could enter the draft). Nor is it in the interest of the National Collegiate Athletic Association, which wants to promote the idea of the "student athlete" and improve its graduation rates.

If the N.C.A.A. really wants bona fide student athletes, then it should allow athletes of any age to enter a professional draft without forfeiting their collegiate eligibility. Under the current policy, college players who declare themselves eligible for the N.B.A. draft can return to the N.C.A.A. only if they withdraw their names at least 10 days before the draft. In addition, college athletes can test the professional waters like this only once.

Remove the restrictions on entering the draft and two things will happen. First, a lot of teenage athletes will get a reality check as to their readiness for N.B.A. careers. Second, the N.C.A.A. and its member schools will benefit by having more players who realize that college is their better option. With luck, they will take their education more seriously. A revolving door of talented freshmen brings no growth or stability to a college's athletic program, nor does it reinforce the "student athlete" ideal, because these "one and done" players don't really even have to attend class in the second semester.

Under "one and done," a few college programs may get more television exposure, and their exceptional freshmen can increase their market value. But there is already buzz about the best youngsters while they're in high school. (Today, college coaches are seeking oral commitments to attend from potential stars who haven't finished the eighth grade.) Will freshmen fixated on an N.B.A. career be inspired to stay in college after the mandatory one year? Will they be more mature and better-behaved once they turn pro because of a single year in college? Not likely. In all walks of life, some people mature early, and some remain jerks no matter how much education they've had.

Unfortunately, we place far too little value on education. As a result, too many youngsters see professional sports as their only option, instead of preparing for real life — which comes for every player, either in lieu of sports or after retirement.

For every LeBron James or Kobe Bryant, there are hundreds of other teenage athletes who have been mistakenly led to believe they're ready for the N.B.A. Once they enter the draft and find out they're wrong, it's too late: they're not allowed to attend or return to college on an athletic scholarship.

In no other line of work is someone penalized for leaving or delaying school and returning later. Besides, college coaches — who can make millions of dollars — negotiate with other colleges, or with N.B.A. teams, all the time. They don't forfeit their employment if they decide to stay put.

Athletic scholarships should be guaranteed for four years, instead of renewable year to year by the college. College athletes should also receive a modest stipend and more realistic expense money. If athletes have to struggle to get by, of course they will want to turn pro as soon as possible. They're also more likely to accept money from agents who want to sign them, although agents aren't the only people who slip money to college athletes. (Signing with an agent makes players ineligible for the college game, whether or not money has changed hands — but coaches are allowed to collect fees for referring agents to players!)

The N.B.A. and the N.C.A.A. have brilliant people working in management. Certainly they can come up with a better system than "one and done" that is equitable for the colleges and the athletes, gives athletes an incentive to stay in school and reinforces the value of education.

If I were graduating from high school today, could I resist the big money and go to college instead? That's hard to say. But I do know that I wouldn't trade my college education for anything. It prepared me to become a better citizen and a more productive member of society. I grew as a person and made lifelong friends. I value my degree as much as any of my achievements on the basketball court.

26
Fashionistas

One summer day in 1996, a short item appeared in a people-oriented column in *The Times* called Chronicle, by Alan Flippen, about Dennis Rodman's visit to midtown Manhattan to promote his best-selling autobiography, *Bad As I Wanna Be.*

The former Bad Boy of Detroit was riding higher than ever as a robo-rebounder for Michael Jordan and the champion Bulls while establishing himself as the league's most flamboyant player, multihued head-to-toe.

As Flippen wrote, "He arrived in a police-escorted horse-drawn carriage at Barnes & Noble on Fifth Avenue yesterday in a lacy white wedding dress with long gloves and a veil over his neatly coiffed, bright orange hair. The bridegroom (or was he the bride?) was surrounded by a group of beautiful ushers (or were they bridesmaids?), all in black tie."

Rodman was clearly a man (or a man in drag) ahead of his time. Pro basketball stars had long been flashy dressers, but Rodman took it to a new promotional and profitable level of self-expression, setting his own rules of engagement.

A decade later, when new dress codes were established by the league, many players resented being dictated to by David Stern, who seemed in the aftermath of Jordan Mania and before the LeBron James era to be on a mission to make the league more presentable to Middle America.

In what became a testament to Stern's marketing acumen and serendipity but more so to the players' creative flexibility, dressing to the nines on game night eventually became part of the N.B.A. star's practiced routine, opening yet more potential endorsement revenue streams.

The last laugh was on the many reporters (myself included) who responded to the players' complaints about their individual rights being compromised, and with racial implications. Once the postgame locker room turned into a fashion runway, the waiting time for the generic franchise player to button himself up (or down) and for the postgame cameras to leave averaged about an hour.

Those of us in New York whose careers spanned Patrick Ewing and Carmelo Anthony were left to wish for the days when the Big Fella would be front and center, soaking his knees and feet in ice when the locker room door opened, and offer three minutes of humorless clichés before cutting us off.

At least we made deadline.

Dec. 7, 2005

N.B.A. Dress Code Confuses the Long and Short of It

by Selena Roberts

A twisted version of *Nanny 911* is unfolding in N.B.A. arenas, where league observers are paid to be virtual seamstresses as they eyeball the hemlines of players.

In Catholic schools, young ladies are scolded for wearing skirts that flirt upward to reveal too much thigh. In the David Stern Academy, grown men are rapped across the knuckles with a $10,000 fine when their shorts go south of a kneecap.

More skin, Commissioner Stern has demanded. Dare to bare, he is saying.

He isn't promoting sex appeal, but suburban appeal. By forcing N.B.A. players into resembling the Jerry West template for the league's ancient logo — short shorts, please — Stern has turned courts that used to be catwalks for shoe trends into places for perp walks for those players in violation of the "shorts code."

The rule calling for shorts to be one inch above the knee has been around for several years, but it has not been vigorously enforced until now. The league has fined twice as many players for uniform violations this year as it did during the 2004–05 season, as Stu Jackson, the N.B.A.'s official disciplinarian, said by telephone yesterday.

In recent weeks, union officials have tallied more than a dozen players who have been nabbed, including Philadelphia's Allen Iverson, Denver's Andre Miller, Indiana's Jermaine O'Neal and the Knicks' Stephon Marbury and Nate Robinson. (At 5 feet 9 inches, with the wind at his back, Robinson is apparently expected to wear shorts fitted for a shot glass.)

Players already have to arrive at arenas in the threads of a game-show host as part of the new off-the-floor dress code, but now they have to take their uniform cues from John Stockton.

"What's next, we can't wear our hair in cornrows?" O'Neal said. "You wonder where all this is going."

That is a good question. Why the hike in hemline sirens?

"The reason is this year we noticed more numbers of shorts that were long," Jackson said, adding that the league used in-arena observers, videotape and photographs as evidence to warn and fine players. "Our ability to scrutinize is more extensive than ever before."

The league is not simply hooked on the gizmos and gimmicky of *MacGyver* technology. In the context of the latest wardrobe rules, and with new age-eligibility measures to prevent high school seniors from becoming N.B.A. rookies, something else is driving the N.B.A.'s obsession with uniformity: a suburban outreach.

The league is determined to satisfy ticket-holders who are uncomfortable with a league they cannot relate to. Baggy jeans on the sideline, long shorts on the court, bejeweled teenagers on the floor, they're all code for hip-hop to red-state ears.

The league is asking players to be anything but individuals; in the process, Stern is spoiling the diversity he should be embracing.

"Do we have to change everything about ourselves?" said O'Neal, who tried to comply with the shorts bylaws by changing twice before being fined anyway. "The message to us is that we're too urban."

Demanding that the players act as Stepford Wives, nagging them into submission, does not improve the league.

What the league needs it cannot tailor. It is desperate for a superstar the public can love, for that rare player who is both likable and deadly at the buzzer.

Once, Kobe Bryant fit that ultimate mold as upstanding and bilingual, sophisticated and talented. But then the revelations of arrogance surfaced along with a rape accusation, all before a messy split with Shaquille O'Neal.

It's odd, but Bryant has always been known as a snappy dresser. So the length of a player's shorts does not define the measure of the man.

Stern knows this, but playing nanny is a way to assert his authority.

He is in control, just so you know. More than a year ago, his grip on his players was cast into doubt when Stern — and the rest of the world — witnessed replays of a Pistons-Pacers brawl that spilled into the stands.

Had his league spiraled out of control?

Stern has used the melee at the Palace as a cudgel over the players, getting what he wanted out of collective bargaining, putting in the dress code to soothe suburban ticket buyers, prosecuting hemlines to protect a bottom line.

O'Neal said: "Instead of sending out people to determine if a player's shorts are too long, the league should be trying to make the game better by improving officiating and the way the game is played. They say they want the best product on the floor, but it would help if guys felt comfortable."

It's troubling to see the league's effort to create a comfort level with fans leaving some players feeling as if they don't belong. Outcasts in long shorts. Misfits in baggy jeans.

"What's all this leading to," O'Neal said. "I just don't know."

It's leading backward. Stern created the N.B.A.'s star factory, but he doesn't seem to like the hip, young product now. He wants to go retro. He wants to go back to a time before players were outsized celebrities, back to a period even before Jordan, Bird and Magic.

In micromanaging his players' images, right down to their shorts, Stern is asking them to live up to the silhouetted image of a great player who retired in 1974.

Instead of using Jerry West as a template, Stern should update the logo — and his shortsighted thinking.

In the N.B.A.,
a Game of Clothes Horse

by Matthew Schneier

The Cleveland Cavaliers, with an assist from a New York-based designer, made their first big play on Friday night just by entering the arena. As they paraded into Bankers Life Fieldhouse in Indianapolis before Game 3 of their playoff series with the Indiana Pacers, the Cavaliers wore coordinated ensembles: made-to-measure suits, ties, shoes, bags and eyewear by Thom Browne.

The scheme was hatched a while ago by Dwyane Wade and Browne, then kept alive by LeBron James after Wade was traded back to the Miami Heat in February.

"All of us suiting up together was just a new idea and something we all wanted to try," James, a four-time winner of the league's Most Valuable Player Award, wrote in an email.

For players at the top of the professional basketball food chain, just showing up has become an opportunity to preen. No matter that the corridors may be lined with trash cans. The walk from the team bus to the locker room is a runway, with attendant paparazzi.

"It's become a way to one-up each other," said Calyann Barnett, a stylist who works with players like Wade and the Pelicans' Rajon Rondo. "It's become almost like high school. Who's going to have on the best outfit? Everyone's going for that Best Dressed. Now, what is Best Dressed? It's as many labels as you can throw on."

The Cavaliers intend to wear the suits for away games for the remainder of the postseason — however long that may last for the team.

"We have the same outfit on every night when we warm up," James wrote. "Dressing the same isn't special. Being in a designed suit by a master craftsman is truly special."

So is a sense of off-court unity.

"We haven't seen this before," said Brennan Rabb, a stylist who works with James. "There's a deeper message about unison."

That message is especially important to the Cavs, given their roster shake-up in February and rumors of James's possible departure in the off-season. For now, though, the team is focused on trying to reach the league finals for the fourth consecutive year.

Usually, the outfits and accessories worn by players off the court — versus the standard uniform on it — have emphasized the individual, rather than the team.

"There are a lot of basketball fans who root for players and not necessarily for teams," said Juliet Litman, the managing editor of The Ringer, a sports and pop culture website.

Fashion allows certain players — like Wade, Oklahoma City's Russell Westbrook and Golden State's Kevin Durant — to distinguish themselves. Westbrook, who translated his stylishness into a collection for Barneys New York, has put out a book of his collected outfits and inspirations.

"It's so much easier to feel like you know a basketball player than it is to feel like you know a baseball player," Litman said. "In concert with the league and through their own brute force, they have carved out a niche where they are legit celebrities and they are their own brand."

The modern era of the label-flexing player began with the institution of the N.B.A. dress code in 2005, widely seen as an attempt by David Stern, then the commissioner, to curb styles like baggy jeans and do-rags that were worn by players like the former Philadelphia 76er Allen Iverson. The code mandated "business casual."

But the rules are broadly interpreted, and the league has issued a few warnings to players who pushed the limit this season.

Today's superstars, multimillionaires enjoying their bounties, have cultivated a taste for the finer things: wine, cars, jewelry, luxury fashion. Once hobbies like these occupied the off-season. Now, the lines blur. Courtside at Fashion Week, front row at the arena — what's the difference, really?

"Expressing myself through fashion is such an important part of my N.B.A. experience," James said. "It's really another way to have fun and experience my love for the game. I love mixing it up with my shoes on the court, sometimes at the podium post game. And of course there is the walk into the game. Using the tunnel walk to express yourself, say what you're feeling — that is a very cool change my generation brought to the game."

Blogs and websites have chronicled every four-figure Amiri shredded jean, Saint Laurent jacket and Off-White sneaker — a de facto uniform if not a codified one. DM Fashion Book feverishly tracks every appearance; even ESPN occasionally joins the fray.

For his Cavaliers project, Browne said in an interview, he wanted to emphasize not the individual player but the collective unity of the team.

James and Wade already counted themselves among his fans and clients, and his tailoring, introduced in the early 2000s, helped redefine the silhouette of fashionable suits for a generation, not least by hiking up the pants to high-water, ankle-baring heights. In their matching gray suits, cardigans and high trousers, the players entering the arena Friday looked freshly imported from one of Browne's typically Kabuki Paris runway shows. (The headlines write themselves: "Cavs Debut Calves.")

James said he was grateful to Wade, whom he called one of the N.B.A.'s "most important fashion innovators," for passing along the project before he returned to the Heat.

"It represents all of it — camaraderie, solidarity, brotherhood," James wrote in his email. "It definitely creates a feeling like we are one and in this together."

Browne began a discussion with Wade last fall at the Fashion Group International Night of Stars awards, where Wade presented him with an award.

"Wouldn't it be interesting if they all wore tailoring, and tailoring in a very uniform way, to really show the strength in a uniform?" Browne said of the discussion.

Browne knows whereof he speaks. As a swimmer at Notre Dame, he was required to wear a navy jacket and gray trousers to meets and, as an adult, hews closely to his standard wardrobe of his own gray suits (with long pants in the winter, shorts in the summer).

"I wanted to represent the team as a strong unit," he said. "It's not a fashion thing for me — it's more of a cultural image." A company spokeswoman said Browne did not pay the team to wear the suits as a promotional agreement, though she declined to go into further specifics.

Browne, who follows the Heat and the Cavs and who grew up on the 76ers and Michael Jordan–era Bulls, said he would be watching — from Hong Kong, where he is traveling on business.

"These guys represent so much to so many people, especially young kids," he said. "They look up to these guys to see what they can aspire to. And they represent working hard to be really good at what they do. That's ultimately what everyone is going to see."

27

Bicoastal Conundrum

The N.B.A. has long proved that it can thrive without playing well in one or both of its two mega-markets. It also never hurt to have contenders in Los Angeles and New York. Each city contains two teams, but only one has been able to claim meaningful existential significance. L.A. has the Lakers. New York has the Knicks.

Any comparative analysis between those franchises pretty much ends there.

Since the Knicks won their second championship in franchise history in 1973, the Lakers have won 10. The Lakers' roster of marquee stars has included Kareem Abdul-Jabbar, Magic Johnson, James Worthy, Shaquille O'Neal, Kobe Bryant, Pau Gasol and now LeBron James. The Knicks have countered with Bernard King, Patrick Ewing, Carmelo Anthony and Kristaps Porzingis.

Jerry Buss ingeniously owned and operated the Lakers from 1979 until his death in 2013. The Knicks passed from one clumsy corporate daddy to another until James Dolan of the Cablevision Dolans became one of the most meddlesome and disliked executives in the history of New York sports.

Buss once invited Knicks beat reporters to leave the Great Western Forum after a game in his limousine to hit one of his favorite nightspots with a few of his leggiest lady friends. Dolan has for the better part of two decades treated reporters like recruits of ISIS and once told a fan who sent him a critical letter to go root for the Nets.

Buss hired the franchise greats Jerry West and Johnson to run his team. Dolan shunned Ewing after his playing career and had his security force carry out Charles Oakley — a beloved Knick enforcer during the '90s — in handcuffs during a game in February 2017.

Then Dolan, a recovering alcoholic, went on a radio show and implied that Oakley was an alcoholic.

Buss created employment for young women with the Laker Girls. Dolan hired Anucha Browne Sanders as a Knicks marketing executive, fired her for complaining about misogynistic harassment, refused to settle and dragged the entire organization through a civil trial that smeared reputations — including that of Isiah Thomas, his friend — and cost himself jury-awarded damages of $11.6 million.

Buss made the Lakers great and their games musical events of fancy. As the front man for his blues band, Dolan wrote a song called "Fix the Knicks," whining, "Everywhere I go, I hear everybody say, what you gonna do to make that team play?"

The obvious answer: not enough.

The Garden Needs a Warning Label

BY SELENA ROBERTS

As the legend goes, it was years ago, aboard a sleek family yacht, when Charles F. Dolan asked his executive crewmates an earnest question: What about Jim?

His son needed an occupation. Something to divert his rock-star ambitions. Something to focus him. So he decided to give James L. Dolan what amounted to a skate key to Madison Square Garden, a business irrelevant to the Cable Daddy's vast bottom line, a playground where his son could do no harm.

Except Jim turned his toy into a weapon. Inside the Garden, "Got Hurt?" has become the slogan for vulnerable staffers. For years, he has wounded careers and savaged dissenters while assembling a cult of personality where only his sycophants survive amid a game of Jim-nastics.

Bend around his outbursts — or you'll end up like the employee fired for serving flat cola. Maneuver past Jim's insecurity — or you'll be eviscerated like the security guard who didn't recognize the Garden owner's face.

There are so many hothead tales. But the tawdry, hostile dark side of the Garden remained largely a secret kept through confidentiality agreements and severance payoffs that functioned as hush money.

Reality had no voice until Anucha Browne Sanders took the stand. Truth had no visuals until she provided them in court. Against Dolan's circle of mercenary lawyers, and Isiah Thomas's courtroom charisma, she was the one jurors believed.

The jury not only found that Thomas sexually harassed Browne Sanders and that the Garden retaliated against her for complaining, but its three-week journey to a verdict also uncovered Dolan as a sort of Seventh Avenue madam behind the World's Most Infamous Arena.

Under Jim's reign, a perverse office lingo developed, filled with b-words and p-words — the alphabet soup of misogyny — that functioned as daily salutations.

Under Jim's ownership, a rise in superstar entitlement provided Stephon Marbury with a green light to rock his truck during some backseat boogie with a Garden intern after a strip-club escapade.

Under Jim's nose, Thomas added to the Garden's creepy vibe by dismissively treating Browne Sanders as if she were nothing more than a groupie he once charmed during his playing days.

All this, and with a case of *Kama Sutra* on the way. Soon, a former Rangers City Skater is expected to take the Garden to court for yet another sexual harassment claim in what is expected to be a lewd depiction of her workplace environment.

How low can the Garden go? There is only one man who can stop this race to the bottom. Papa, can you hear me? Only Charles Dolan has the power to take away the Garden club from his son before one more person gets hurt.

But will he? Commissioner David Stern has offered a public silence over yesterday's verdict in the civil case between Browne Sanders and the Garden, but N.B.A. team officials privately believe he will seek a discussion with Charles Dolan in an effort to diminish Jim's power at the top.

It would not be surprising if N.H.L. Commissioner Gary Bettman, no doubt bracing for the Rangers' trial fallout, followed Stern to the doorknocker at Daddy Dolan's office.

By all accounts, Charles is a gracious soul, a true gentleman. He would listen to Stern and Bettman like a reasonable man. Charles has always been loath to confront Jim on Garden matters, but this latest episode of *Animal House* isn't a scandal about firing a coach or buying out contracts or trading for a miscreant. This is about professional decorum, about fair treatment, about a family legacy.

Right now, the Garden has one rule: Whatever Jim wants. But there are signs his iron fist has fissures. Two people familiar with the workings at Madison Square Garden said a group of staff members felt uncomfortable with a plan by management to have employees come forward to express their workplace joy yesterday. They refused to take part in the public relations ploy, and the plan never materialized.

Maybe peaceful resistance is a start. But to restore civility, to reclaim team dignity, a restructuring of power is a must. Jim was at his best as a figurehead before 2001, before he pushed aside Dave Checketts as the chief decision maker, before some of the more talented minds in sports began an exodus.

If Jim remains as the Richie Rich in charge, you can count on the following: The Garden will bury Browne Sanders in appeals to drive up her legal fees as punishment for her courage.

This strategy doesn't mean Thomas is safe, though. Jim will turn on him at the slightest sign of Knick distress. Jim's loyalty is limited to his own self-preservation.

Everyone else is a fall guy for Jim. Everyone else gets hurt. The Garden is not a toy. In Jim's hands, it's a weapon.

— POSTSCRIPT —

SELENA ROBERTS, 2018: "At different times covering the Knicks, I'd hear a staffer say, 'I just want to get out of here clean.' The Garden was full of dirt under Jim Dolan, much of it spilling out in the seedy courtroom drama won by Anucha Browne Sanders (and avoided in the hockey sexual harassment case, settled out of court 16 days later). She took a stand. Others? Not so much. Despite all the tales of Dolan's insecurity, irrationality and incompetence — all trickling down to the Knicks on the floor — I was always amazed by the many employees who stuck by the Garden boss even as he bullied and demeaned them. Stockholm syndrome? Not hardly. For a time, I thought Dolan mistook money for intelligence. How else to explain the serial use of huge payouts for numerous personnel mistakes? But maybe he was smarter with his inheritance than I knew. Money didn't buy his staff happiness, but for years it purchased their complicity."

FEB. 18, 2013

The Owner Who Made the N.B.A. Cool Again

by Howard Beck

The enduring, clichéd myth of the Los Angeles Lakers — perpetuated mostly by envious fans in other cities — is that the franchise owes its aura to its surroundings. That Hollywood made the Lakers cool, and the sunshine made them desirable. That the city made the dynasty.

The premise is irresistible. Los Angeles is alluring in a way that few places are, a magnet for supreme talent, fame seekers of all types and anyone who loves palm trees. Glitz and glamour are the city's birthright. Stars come. Championships follow.

The premise is false. Los Angeles did not make the Lakers great. Jerry Buss did.

Buss, the Lakers' legendary owner, who died Monday at 80, was among the first to recognize that basketball is a production, that sports can be glamorous and that nothing sells like star power.

Buss created Showtime, the slogan that became synonymous with the charismatic running, gunning Lakers of the 1980s. He hired an in-house band. He created the Laker Girls, to make the experience at the Fabulous Forum a little more fabulous, to keep the fans entertained through every timeout.

Every franchise now has a dance team (or several), and every timeout at every N.B.A. game is now a nonstop whir of kiss-cams, halfcourt shooting contests and T-shirt cannons. The N.B.A.'s deft fusion of sports and entertainment is part of Buss's fantastic legacy, along with those 10 championship banners — the most by a single owner in any league. Like Commissioner David Stern, who is retiring next February, Buss was a visionary in the art of marketing the game.

It is, of course, the banners that ultimately set Buss apart, that qualify him as perhaps the greatest owner in North American sports history. Contrary to the mythology, the banners did not hang themselves.

The Lakers have the benefit of a large market and a temperate climate, but so do the Clippers, who have also called Los Angeles home for 29 years, with none of the presumed advantages of the 213 area code.

No one ever demanded a trade to the Clippers. In fact, many begged to be sent elsewhere.

What made the Lakers great was Buss, who in so many ways was the model owner, the sort that every fan wants: generous with his payroll, methodical in his decisions, competitive and engaged, but never a meddler.

Buss paid to acquire the best players, rarely thinking about his profit margin. He hired the best basketball minds — Jerry West, Pat Riley, Phil Jackson — and got out of their way, recognizing that riches do not equate to basketball expertise.

"His vision was second to none," West said in a statement. "He wanted an N.B.A. franchise brand that represented the very best and went to every extreme to accomplish his goals."

In West, Buss had a basketball savant running the show. And he gave him all the autonomy and resources he needed to build and rebuild the dynasty, from Magic and Kareem to Kobe and Shaq. After West stepped away, his protégé Mitch Kupchak refashioned the dynasty once more, acquiring Pau Gasol to help Kobe Bryant win two more titles.

It is sometimes forgotten amid the glow of all of those Larry O'Brien trophies, but the Lakers took a huge risk in the summer of 1996, tearing up their roster to make a (then unprecedented) $120 million offer to Shaquille O'Neal. In the process, they traded their star center, Vlade Divac, to acquire the draft rights to Bryant, an unproven teenager. It was West who maneuvered the Lakers to create one of the greatest tandems, but it was Buss — a devoted and skilled poker player — who trusted and empowered West to make this calculated gamble.

"He's meant everything to me," Bryant said of Buss last week. "I mean, he took a chance on a 17-year-old kid coming out of Philadelphia when nobody really saw that potential. And he believed in me the entire way."

When the time came to break up the Shaq-Kobe partnership, Buss wisely gambled on Bryant, trading away O'Neal.

Last summer, the Lakers struck again, acquiring Dwight Howard and Steve Nash, demonstrating once more Buss's commitment to winning at all costs. The Lakers' luxury-tax bill this season is a projected $30 million, and if the roster is kept intact, it could leap to as much as $78 million next season.

This has fueled another Lakers myth: that they simply spend their way to success. There is a sliver of truth here — no team can retain the best talent without spending generously — but the Lakers are not the league's biggest spenders over the past decade. (The Lakers trail the Knicks, the Dallas Mavericks and the Portland Trail Blazers in taxes paid, according to the salary-cap expert Larry Coon.) Nor did Buss, a millionaire in a league of billionaires and corporations, have the deepest pockets.

The competitor in Buss always valued skills over spending power. When the luxury tax was introduced, Buss vowed never to cross the tax threshold. Not because he wanted to save money, but because he wanted to beat everyone on a level playing field.

"What they're trying to do is say, 'Let's all have the same number of chips and we'll see who can build a team the best,'" Buss said in 2000.

Eventually, other teams sprinted past the threshold, forcing Buss to do the same, but he was always the poker player at heart, angling to beat you with his intellect and his foresight and his bravado.

"I like the concept of having the same number of weapons and just see who can run the ship the best," Buss said. "That's competition."

For the last 34 years, Buss was simply better at it than everyone else.

— POSTSCRIPT —

HOWARD BECK, 2018: "Jerry Buss rarely spoke to reporters during his later years as the Lakers' owner. But if you wanted a glimpse, you knew where to catch him. Minutes after every home game, Buss would amble through the corridor adjoining the locker rooms. Ambling with him, to his left and right and on various diagonals, were very attractive, very young women. Buss was usually smiling. And why wouldn't he be? He stewarded one of the premier franchises in professional sports — winning 10 titles in his three-plus decades — and clearly enjoyed every minute of it.

"Knicks owner Jim Dolan doesn't speak with reporters much, either. But you always know where to find him: Slouching in a baseline seat at Madison Square Garden. Arms folded. A scowl on his face. Scowling with him, to his left and right, are paid spokesmen and henchmen. And why wouldn't they be?

"Under Dolan's stewardship, the Knicks have been one of the most hapless franchises in professional sports — with more controversies than playoff appearances. In two decades of covering the N.B.A., including seven assigned to the Lakers and nine as a Knicks beat writer, I've never seen a starker contrast in leadership styles than Buss to Dolan."

What Were They Thinking?

A story in *The Times* under the dual byline of Steve Popper and Lee Jenkins in January 2003 more or less summed up the mostly sad, sorry existence of the New Jersey Nets and, in a larger sense, the league's behavioral contraventions that have been mostly whacky but on occasion ranged from bat-shit crazy to downright scary.

The one that occurred at a Nets practice was an example of clashing egos begetting the height of insensitivity, but it might have turned out much, much worse.

Alonzo Mourning, then struggling to keep his Hall of Fame career alive after undergoing a transplant in a battle with kidney disease, got into it with Kenyon Martin over the latter's practice habits.

"You can't be a leader in the trainer's room crying, 'My ankle, my ankle,'" Popper and Jenkins quoted Mourning, scolding Martin about a sprained ankle that had sidelined him for five games. To which a mocking, knuckleheaded Martin responded, "My kidney, my kidney." Who knows what would have transpired had Mourning not been restrained by several teammates — perhaps a reenactment of Latrell Sprewell's 1997 choking attack on his coach, P.J. Carlesimo?

Across the decades, what hasn't the N.B.A. experienced? Guns in the locker room? Check. A corrupt ref (Tom Donaghy) who bet on games he officiated and went to prison? Uh huh. Audio evidence of one white team owner (Donald Sterling) spewing contempt for black people, and revelations of widespread misogyny entrenched in the organization of another (Mark Cuban)? Oy. A popular star spitting at a fan and hitting a young girl instead? The one, the only and occasionally ugly Sir Charles.

I once asked Rod Thorn, who for 14 years served as the league's executive vice president for basketball operations — in effect its dean of discipline — what that job was like. "Entertaining," he said, laughing, "and with the potential for having to work overtime every night, including the off-season."

It was much easier, he added, as the chief basketball executive of the Bulls and the Nets. "Just worried about 12 or 13 guys doing something crazy, as opposed to 400."

Oct. 31, 1999

The Sprewell Weave of Love and Hate

BY SELENA ROBERTS

Juror No. 1 was struck by how Latrell Sprewell's fingers curled long and thin like water from a drinking fountain, how his array of eyeglasses and finely crafted braids made him look bookish but hip, how respectful and nonthreatening he appeared as the defendant in a civil trial almost four weeks ago.

During courtroom breaks, he paced in his tailored suits, stopped by a stroller to visit his newborn son and made eye contact with everyone he spoke to. It was easy for some of the jurors to be enamored of his presence — and for most of them to be won over.

"To me, he was cocky, but I have to say, when he's sitting there, he's a beautiful-looking guy," said juror No. 1, Nancy Hurwitz-Kors, who was against the California jury's favorable decision toward Sprewell when they ordered him to pay $105,000 to the two plaintiffs who were seeking close to $3 million after being injured in a March 1998 automobile accident.

"If he had come across differently," Hurwitz-Kors said, "if the jurors had been afraid of him, it might have been a different outcome, but they weren't afraid of him. He probably worked at that."

And yet, finding forgiveness seems to come so easily for Sprewell. Despite each transgression, he has not only gained acceptance from the Madison Square Garden fans who crave his frenetic playing style, he has accepted a five-year contract extension with the Knicks worth $61.8 million. In delicately handling their star, management is willing to look the other way on his behavior, cross its fingers on his troubled history and bet that a team with Sprewell can find its way to the National Basketball Association finals again.

Last year, their public relations risk paid off. Since the Knicks made the trade for Sprewell last January, he has parlayed his flaws into a fortune, turned his mistakes into a marketing strategy while creating a popularity that has crossed racial and economic boundaries.

"I'll have a businessman come up to me and say, 'My son wants his hair done like yours,'" Sprewell said after a recent workout. "I'm like, what have I started here? But I think it's great that people are open and not afraid to try a different idea, even if it's just a hairstyle.

"For me, I'm not trying to be different or make any kind of statement," Sprewell said. "I just don't want to be like everyone else."

He is distinct in style, original in substance. But in many ways, Sprewell stands before you like an inkblot, something different to everyone. To some, he's the menacing figure on the floor, the sinewy player in the No. 8 jersey who growls and flexes like a cartoon action figure. To others, he is the soft-spoken star who is refreshingly honest about his missteps. Yes, he missed training camp for an impromptu road trip. Yes, he should have called. But this is who he is, no apologies.

"I was pretty much the same way as a kid," Sprewell said. "I can remember there were things I wanted to do — things maybe my mother didn't want me to do — and even if they would get me in trouble at times, I would do them anyway."

This is not exactly the desired behavior trait consistent with the team concept Coach Jeff Van Gundy emphasizes at every practice, team meeting and film session. But Van Gundy — who caught the glaring stare of Sprewell as he stewed on the bench last year and who wasn't always pleased with his star's takeover mentality — doesn't see him as a disciplinary problem.

"I don't think he has ever shown a lack of respect for me in that gym," Van Gundy said. "He has tried to do what we wanted. When I talk about relationships with players, that's when I know I have a good one. He's willing to be coached and performs at a high level. Does that mean he's going to like everything? No."

When Sprewell doesn't agree, he vocalizes it. It was hardly a problem last year, when Sprewell, fresh off his league suspension, exhibited mostly model behavior. But there is a notion that the financial security of a contract extension will create an opening for Sprewell to act out, ignore authority and be disruptive. Before he was ever offered a deal a week ago, he skipped training camp.

"Like I said when he missed training camp, he was wrong," Van Gundy said. "But I don't know if you can draw from that incident that there is going to be a pattern of not respecting authority."

Perhaps to rationalize their lucrative contract offer to Sprewell, the Knicks have to ignore a pattern of misbehavior established by Sprewell. Instead, they have catered to his every need, first making him a starter and then allowing him to design his own contract extension. As one Knick player privately noted, the "special treatment" for Sprewell has left some teammates grumbling about a double standard.

"It's like there are two rules," the player said. "Is it a problem? Not if we win."

Success fed the Sprewell frenzy last year, at least in New York.

"On a local basis, he's very popular," said Bob Williams, president of Burns Sports, a Chicago-based marketing firm that matches athletes to advertisers. "If he does not perform on the court this year, I think you could be looking at an ugly situation. New Yorkers are quick to get down on a player, as they have in the past. By pushing the envelope on behavior as he does, it doesn't leave much margin for error."

In a television commercial for And1, Sprewell sits in a chair with his hair blown out into an Afro as a hairdresser begins the braiding process. In a haunting tone, he decries his image as a nightmare and declares himself the American Dream. The ad was unique and shocking, just the qualities some fans relate to Sprewell.

"A lot of people like the underdog," Sprewell said, trying to explain his rapport with the New York fans. "And I've been put in that situation basically ever since the P. J. incident."

P. J. Carlesimo was the Golden State coach who tried to rein in the star's free spirit two years ago and ended up prying Sprewell's fingers off his neck. Sprewell has explained the situation as "just a bad day." Take away the violent aspect of the infamous confrontation, and Sprewell all but sees himself as the symbol of every employee who has longed to stand up to the boss, but couldn't.

"I think a lot of people identify with that," Sprewell said. "A lot of people go to work and have a difficult time with their supervisors or bosses or whatever it is. Sometimes, you just want to tell them how you feel."

He says this in all earnestness, with his eyes focused on yours. Part of Sprewell's allure, he will tell you, is that he is articulate and intelligent, a side of himself he puts emphasis on when he wears clear-lens glasses that are more a fashion accessory than necessity. On the flip-side of the brazen emotion he shows on the court is a man who once majored in social work at the University of Alabama. Full of contradiction, Sprewell is able to pull out a personality trait to match any occasion.

It has worked to captivate New York fans, and served him well before a California jury. But a deputy sheriff who fingerprinted Sprewell upon his reckless driving charge that led to the civil trial had a different take on his appearance.

"He was cordial and cooperative," said Deputy Sheriff Rudy Bowers of Contra Costa County in California. "When I worked the jail, there was one officer for every 64 inmates, and they act as gentlemanly as a guy next door. What changes is when they don't get their way. As far as Latrell Sprewell, I look at him as any other of these guys. If pushed or if he doesn't feel like he's getting his way, he can snap at any moment. If you or I had wanted to ram another car because it was driving slow in front of us, you would hit the switch that says, Don't do it. People like Latrell Sprewell don't have that switch."

Sprewell admits that he acts on every impulse. And if there is a fine to pay, so be it. If there is a punishment that comes along, O.K. So far, all has been forgiven. So far, he has been granted New York's unconditional love.

"You know, that's just the way Americans are," Sprewell said. "They like to root for the underdog."

— POSTSCRIPT —

SELENA ROBERTS, 2018: "Sprewell arrived as a Knick wearing a dad sweater at his first press conference. In the early months, it seemed the Good Spree was part of an image rehab con. But soon it became obvious that the truth was in his complexity. He was fascinating — and Knicks fans embraced the paradox when the fierce star lit up the arena. But lots of players have different on-court, off-court personas. To cover Spree was to be aware of the third rail of his personality: zero impulse control. He was prone to road rage on any surface. You could see the Knicks tiptoe around his unpredictability at times. But what were his tripwires? That part is still a mystery to me. As smart and talented as he was, I'll always wonder how long Spree would have sustained his greatness if he had only owned a pause button."

JAN. 2, 2010

Arenas Cites Bad Judgment In Gun Case

BY ADAM HIMMELSBACH

WASHINGTON — Gilbert Arenas stood at his locker with his back to about 20 reporters and cameramen. He smiled as he dressed after the Washington Wizards' 97–86 loss to the San Antonio Spurs on Saturday, seemingly amused by the fuss.

"I wish it was like this every day," Arenas said.

Then Arenas, a three-time All-Star and self-proclaimed goofball, alternated between regret and humor as he talked for more than six minutes about the investigation regarding his placement of guns in his team locker.

"It was bad judgment, having the weapons here," Arenas said. "It was bad judgment, and I'll deal with that."

Arenas, who is in the second season of a six-year, $111 million contract, has admitted storing unloaded firearms in his locker. He said he took them there to keep them away from his newborn child, and that he then turned them over to team security. On Saturday night, he said keeping the firearms in his locker was better than throwing them into the trash.

The New York Post reported that Arenas and Wizards guard Javaris Crittenton drew guns on each other in the locker room during a Dec. 21 dispute over a gambling debt. Arenas said he could not speak specifically about the investigation, but said that he and Crittenton remained friends. He added that he gave away money, so if he had a debt, he would pay it.

Arenas said that he was scheduled to meet with law enforcement officials Monday, but that he was not nervous.

"I'm a goofball, that's what I am," Arenas said Saturday night. "Even doing something like this, I'm going to make fun of it. That's how I am. Some people say I'm not taking it serious, but why be depressed at home when I can just make myself laugh?"

In 1997, the team's owner, Abe Pollin, held a contest in which fans could choose a new name for his basketball team, which was then named the Bullets. Pollin, who died Nov. 24, did not want his franchise to be associated with gun violence. On Saturday, his family did not temper its criticism.

"The fact that guns were brought to the Verizon Center is dangerous and disappointing and showed extremely poor judgment," the statement said. "Guns have absolutely no place in a workplace environment, and we will take further steps to ensure this never happens again."

Arenas said he agreed with the sentiments of the Pollin family.

"Yeah, I could've chosen better judgment in bringing them here," he said. "But the only thing I could think of at the time was to get them out of the house, and the second place I come is here."

Arenas had 23 points and 8 assists against San Antonio, as Washington dropped to 10–21 and remained in last place in the Southeast Division.

Arenas received an indifferent reaction from the fans at the Verizon Center. They groaned when he shot an air ball on his first field-goal attempt and cheered when he made a halfcourt shot to end the first quarter.

The N.B.A.'s collective bargaining agreement prohibits guns at league facilities. Washington also has some of the strictest gun laws in the country.

Arenas was suspended for the first game of the 2004 season after failing to properly register a handgun in California in 2003, when he played for the Golden State Warriors.

He has missed most of the past two seasons because of knee injuries, and is averaging 22.7 points a game this season, his first as a team captain.

Arenas said he had stayed upbeat during the investigation by watching comedies on television. And, as is his way, he smiled and chuckled.

"I'm a jokester," he said. "Nothing in my life is actually serious."

JUNE 7, 2018

The Story of the Wife Who Defended Her Husband in a Way That Left Him Unemployed

BY SCOTT CACCIOLA AND VICTOR MATHER

A wife appeared to care so much about her husband and his reputation that she went on social media to defend him. She used confidential information to disparage his current and former employees. She even went after people who made fun of his shirt collars. And she did it all anonymously.

All of this happened — perhaps a slightly misguided expression of love? — and blew up in spectacularly inglorious fashion, in full public view. The husband was a prominent sports executive. His employees were famous athletes. And the story ended with his resignation.

Bryan Colangelo stepped down from his position as the president of basketball operations for the Philadelphia 76ers on Thursday in the wake of a soap opera that had gripped the N.B.A. in recent days, even as the Golden State Warriors and the Cleveland Cavaliers continue to vie for a championship.

It was a stunning fall for Mr. Colangelo, 53, a two-time winner of the N.B.A.'s Executive of the Year Award. After tenures with the Toronto Raptors and the Phoenix Suns, Mr. Colangelo was put in charge of the 76ers in 2016 following the resignation of Sam Hinkie, a statistics wonk who had navigated the team through one of the boldest experiments in pro sports history: the so-called Process, which entailed purposely losing a lot of games over several seasons to collect as many top draft picks as possible and build for the future.

The strategy irked league officials, though, and a sizable chunk of the team's long-suffering fans. After Mr. Hinkie was essentially forced out, Mr. Colangelo was hired to lead the front office.

This season, the 76ers finally began to reap the benefits of Mr. Hinkie's oft-maligned handiwork. The 76ers, with a core of young stars, finished with their best record since 2001 and advanced to the Eastern Conference semifinals before losing to the Boston Celtics. Ben Simmons, a 6-foot-9 point guard, is favored to win the league's Rookie of the Year Award. Joel Embiid, a gifted center, has all the skills to become a perennial All-Star. And Mr. Colangelo appeared set to guide the organization for years to come.

But then, in a matter of days, in a string of developments that were almost unfathomable, Mr. Colangelo saw his career come apart, an apparent casualty of spousal support gone wrong.

"While this was obviously a mistake," he said in a statement, "we are a family and we will work through this together."

It all started with an investigation by the sports website The Ringer, which said it had received an anonymous tip from someone who claimed to work in artificial intelligence. This person told the site that he had used a data analysis tool to link five Twitter accounts with names like Still Balling, HonestAbe and Enoughunknownsources. They were all anonymous accounts — "burner" accounts in the jargon of social media, meaning no real names were attached to them.

But the tipster suspected that one person was operating all of them, and that person was likely Mr. Colangelo.

Why? Because the accounts at times revealed proprietary information that would have been available to only a small number of people — namely high-ranking 76ers officials. The most obvious example was a post that disclosed that Jahlil Okafor, a former top draft pick, had supposedly failed a physical that nixed a trade. Another post panned Mr. Embiid's attitude.

"If I had a medium-size ladder, I would love to knock some sense in Joel's head right now," Enoughunknownsources wrote. "He is playing like a toddler having tantrums."

Another post questioned the contract extension of Masai Ujiri, an executive who had replaced Mr. Colangelo with the Raptors. And there was the now-notorious rebuttal to a fan who had critiqued Mr. Colangelo's sartorial flair: "That is a normal collar. Move on, find a new slant."

When The Ringer contacted the 76ers in the course of its reporting, the site told the organization that it knew of two suspicious accounts, but did not mention the other three. Mr. Colangelo acknowledged that one of them, @Phila1234567, belonged to him, but said that he had never posted any messages using the handle. He denied being behind the other account.

But shortly after that exchange, according to The Ringer, the other three accounts quickly — and curiously — switched from public to private. Who else but Mr. Colangelo, or someone close to him, would have known to do that? It could not have been a coincidence.

When The Ringer published its report late last month, it rippled across the league like a storm cloud.

"BRUH," Mr. Embiid wrote on his Twitter account.

The 76ers soon announced that they had hired the New York law firm Paul, Weiss to conduct an independent investigation. The firm collected multiple devices, including laptops and mobile phones, and pored through text messages and emails. Above all, the firm attempted to do what it described as a "forensic analysis" of the anonymous Twitter accounts to determine who was behind them. The investigation lasted seven days.

One of the phones that the firm collected belonged to Mr. Colangelo's wife, Barbara Bottini. But before turning it over, according to the firm, she apparently attempted to scrub it of data by resetting the device. It hindered the investigation, the firm said in a statement, but not enough to derail its findings — that Ms. Bottini had created and operated the accounts. She admitted as much to investigators, who said that they could not conclude whether Mr. Colangelo had been aware of them.

"Mr. Colangelo denies any such awareness and we have not observed any forensic evidence established that he had knowledge of the Twitter accounts," the firm said in its statement.

At the same time, the firm said there was "substantial evidence" that Mr. Colangelo had been the source of sensitive material posted by the accounts, and that he had been "reckless in failing to properly safeguard sensitive, nonpublic, club-related information in communications with individuals outside the 76ers organization."

Less than an hour after the team released these findings on Friday, Mr. Colangelo fired back with a statement of his own — even though he had already resigned.

"I vigorously dispute the allegation that my conduct was in any way reckless," he said in his statement. "At no point did I purposely or directly share any sensitive, nonpublic, club-related information with her." He went on to describe his wife's burner accounts as "a seriously misguided effort to publicly defend and support me."

But the damage was done.

"It has become clear Bryan's relationship with our team and his ability to lead the 76ers moving forward has been compromised," Josh Harris, one of the 76ers' managing partners, said in a statement. "Recognizing the detrimental impact this matter had on the organization, Colangelo offered his resignation."

There is one mystery that remains unsolved, however: Who was the tipster who went to The Ringer with his or her findings about the burner accounts? Theories abound. Was it really just a tech-savvy fan? Or could it have been a rival with an ax to grind? No one appears to know.

For now, Brett Brown, the team's coach, will oversee the organization as the 76ers search for a new general manager. The N.B.A. draft is later this month. The 76ers have more picks to make.

29

Drafted, Decided, Delivered

Reporting for *The Times* from the N.B.A. draft lottery on May 22, 2003, Chris Broussard presaged the rise of Cleveland's unaccomplished, unsexy market to the center of the N.B.A. universe for the better part of the next 15 years.

Broussard wrote: "James, from St. Vincent-St. Mary High School in Akron, will play 40 miles from home for the Cavaliers. Gordon Gund, the Cavaliers' owner, unveiled a No. 23 Cleveland jersey with JAMES on the back moments after winning the first pick. 'Thank God we got him,' said Gund, who called it the most exciting thing ever to happen to the Cavaliers' 33-year-old franchise. 'I'm tremendously excited for the fans in Cleveland and all of northeast Ohio. It's a big day in Cleveland sports.'"

Unfortunately for Gund and theoretically for James, it wasn't big enough for Gund to resist selling majority ownership of the Cavs to Dan Gilbert two years later. Gund cashed out and thus missed out as James delivered on his draft-day promise to have Cleveland "lit up like Vegas."

His four-year detour to Miami was above all a tribute to the impact that one infamously orchestrated decision could have on the culture, from the sports section to the op-ed pages. No one's scorn was more juvenile than Gilbert's, essentially calling James a traitor in a letter to the fans and hilariously promising his destitute Cavs would succeed before James, Dwyane Wade and Chris Bosh with the Heat.

Despite Gilbert, James returned to raise the Cavs' maiden championship trophy and the city's first major pro title in 52 years before again becoming an ex-Cavalier. Upon the second departure, Gilbert wisely kept mum as James's reputation was beyond reproach in northeast Ohio. He left after reaching four consecutive finals, including the 2016 takedown of the 73-win Warriors.

As an owner, Gilbert is destined to be remembered as the dude from Detroit who got rich on a company providing easy-access loans but who failed to provide enough supporting talent and thus lost the best player of the century twice, getting nothing in return. And while James was exiting in the summer of 2018, the city and the county were agreeing to fund a $140 million Quicken Loans Arena face-lift — "a perfectly legal shakedown of a not-so-economically-healthy city," as Michael Powell reported in his *Times* column.

James? His foundation provided millions of dollars to send kids to college and his parting gift to his native Akron was a public school for at-risk children. Home, as James has proved, is where the heart is, not necessarily where the paycheck is pulled down.

MAY 16, 2010

A Healthy Garnett Puts Another Title in the Celtics' Reach

BY HOWARD BECK

When the Boston Celtics were sent packing by the Orlando Magic last spring — extinguishing their title defense, stirring doubts about their future — Kevin Garnett was a bystander. A tall, ferocious, foul-mouthed, finely tailored bystander making odd gestures on the sideline.

The Celtics were clearly a different team, a diminished team, without Garnett and his unique brand of channeled fury on the court.

It was evident when Boston fell to the Magic in the Eastern Conference semifinals last May. It was even more pronounced last week, when the Celtics — powered by a healthy Garnett once more — shoved the heavily favored Cleveland Cavaliers out of the playoffs.

When LeBron James looked for gaps to penetrate, Garnett was there. When Antawn Jamison tried to break free for a shot, Garnett was in his space. Garnett bullied Jamison in the post, shot jumpers over Shaquille O'Neal and barked at anyone nearby, even if it was only himself.

"It's good to see him playing like that, so well and consistent, because we are going to need him," the Celtics' Paul Pierce said. "And there's no way we can win a championship without him."

A championship. Suddenly, the phrase does not sound ludicrous coming from the Celtics, despite every ill perception of a team that had seemingly become too old and stale to make another title run, as they did in 2008.

"I had never given up on the team," Celtics General Manager Danny Ainge said, but added in his next breath, "Sure, you have doubts."

By record and by reputation, the Celtics will be underdogs when the Eastern Conference finals begin Sunday at Orlando. But they are not the same team that wobbled in January, stumbled in early April and finished with a modest 50 victories.

Perhaps they should not be underdogs at all, not after ousting the Cavaliers, who won the most games in the regular season. Boston dominated the series, winning four games by an average of 17.3 points. The Celtics bottled up James for much of the series and neutralized a pricey supporting cast that included O'Neal, Jamison and Mo Williams.

Credit Garnett, the 6-foot-11 do-everything power forward. Garnett turns 34 on Wednesday and is just 12 months removed from surgery on his right knee. But he is playing with a youthful vigor and confidence once more. Garnett averaged 18.8 points, 8 rebounds and 2.2 assists and shot 52.1 percent against the Cavaliers, while holding Jamison to 11.8 points and 42.2 percent shooting. In 2008, Garnett was the linchpin in the Celtics' suffocating defense, using his mobility and length to crowd the paint and roam the perimeter, often on the same possession. Teammates and rivals are seeing that form again.

"He's back now," Magic Coach Stan Van Gundy said. "He had kind of a rough year on the leg, but I think if you've watched him in the playoffs, he's back."

They all are. The Celtics drifted through periods of the regular season because of nagging injuries, personnel changes and a general lack of urgency. It happens to veteran teams, especially those with 30-something stars and championship aspirations. The regular season becomes a grind. Individual games lose their luster.

Ainge said the Celtics looked as if they were pacing themselves.

"Sometimes, it almost seemed like an exhibition season, where we showed that we could play well but didn't have the resolve to fight through some of the adversity that we were facing at the time," he said.

The Celtics went 6–11 from Dec. 27 through Jan. 31. They went 5–8 over the final 13 games of the regular season, slipping from third in the East to fourth, behind the Atlanta Hawks.

Coach Doc Rivers said last week that the Celtics never lost their identity, "but we lost our way" during the season. Then the playoffs arrived. They crushed the Miami Heat in five games in the first round, and suddenly the 2008 Celtics seemed to re-emerge.

"I think the regular season was draining on Doc," Ainge said. "I think it was an emotional roller coaster for a coach who prepares the same every game, and to not see that resolve, when we know what the individuals of the team are made of."

In February, the Celtics were linked to trade discussions involving the Washington Wizards' Caron Butler. The trade would have cost them Ray Allen, a member of the Big Three that delivered the 2008 title.

Ainge said he was never ready to break up the core of the team, although it would have been understandable if he had. Instead, the Celtics picked up the veteran Michael Finley off the waiver wire and acquired the impulsive Nate Robinson from the Knicks in a deal for Eddie House. The guard shuffle was another disruption to the team's chemistry.

Now it all looks like a minor blip. Robinson, Finley and Marquis Daniels, a guard acquired last summer, are out of the rotation. The Celtics are defined still by the Big Three and the Emerging Two, Rajon Rondo and Kendrick Perkins. Since 2008, Rondo has blossomed into a certified star, making this Celtics team even more talented, if slightly older, than their title team.

When Ainge acquired Allen and Garnett in 2007, he figured on a three- to four-year window for winning titles. That window is nearly shut. But not quite. Garnett, healthy and feisty once more, is holding it open.

"We're a veteran team," Garnett said. "We understand when it's time to lock in as a group, as a unit. I think we did just that."

JULY 10, 2010

Miami's Hoops Cartel

BY MAUREEN DOWD

WASHINGTON — After the heady courting, the King changed courts.

And there were such loud howls about betrayal, disloyalty, selfishness, revenge and intrigue that it might have impressed even a Shakespearean court.

"I'm going to take my talents to South Beach," LeBron James told Jim Gray on ESPN's special — and specially obnoxious — show, *The Decision*, as though he were going on spring break.

It's always a bad sign when people begin talking about themselves in the third person. "I wanted to do what was best, you know, for LeBron James, what LeBron James was going to do to make him happy," LeBron James told Michael Wilbon on ESPN after the special.

ESPN's 28 minutes of contrived suspense over James's narcissistic announcement that he was going, aptly, to My-Am-Me played like *The Bachelor*, without the rose for the winner.

"Kobe Bryant has twice re-signed with the Lakers — no TV special," said David Israel, an L.A. TV writer who had a renowned sports column at *The Washington Star* when I had an obscure one about tennis. "Alex Rodriguez got more than twice as much money when he left his first team, Seattle — no TV special. Tom Brady, three Super Bowls in the nation's most popular sport, quietly re-signs with the Patriots when his contract expires."

The special was packaged by Gray and James's agents, with Gray asking lame questions. CNBC reported that Gray was paid by James, a claim the veteran sports broadcaster denies. It drew more than nine million viewers — more than baseball games, home run derbies and even some N.F.L. Monday night games.

The setting of the Boys and Girls Club of Greenwich, Conn. — with no interaction between the King and the kid-props — was weird.

"What was up with that?" wondered Israel. "He wanted to show how much he cares about the welfare of the children of hedge fund managers?"

Asked by Wilbon about Cleveland fans burning No. 23 jerseys in the street, James noted that if "you put the shoe on the other foot and the Cavs would have got rid of me at one point, would my family burn down the organization? Of course not. This is a business."

James said he did not want to make "an emotional decision." But it was a personal decision. The kid who grew up poor in Akron without a father — moving 12 times between 5 and 8 — regards his teams as family. So much so that he ruled out bidding teams, like Chicago, that ruled out putting any of his "LeBrontourage" on the payroll.

His decision came after he consulted with his mom and formed a hoops cartel with his pals Chris Bosh and Dwyane Wade. It's usually women who get accused of needing to go places (restaurant bathrooms) together.

James wanted to be wooed because he missed any courtship when he was drafted by the pros right out of high school. But the 25-year-old superstar, who tweets as King James and tattooed "Chosen 1" on his back, got lost in the stratosphere of sports marketing advice and wound up with too many people whispering in his ear. He seems to have no idea of the public relations damage he has inflicted on himself.

"Never has so much time, effort and money been expended by an individual to diminish himself," Israel told me.

A sports TV executive I know agreed: "I don't think he has any concept that people will be rooting against Miami harder than ever. These three players have attempted to hijack the league and said, 'We're all good buddies who are going to gang up and go to one team and dictate who wins championships.'"

After seven years as the local hero, James should have shown more class than to let the Cleveland owner, coach and fans hear about his defection on TV, broadcasting from cosseted Greenwich to struggling Cleveland.

It is true, as the *Washington Post*'s Mike Wise put it, that a message to fans from the Cavaliers owner Dan Gilbert, accusing James of a "cowardly betrayal," sounded like "the kind of psycho, ex-girlfriend letter that certifies LeBron made the right decision." But you feel the rabid pain of Gilbert, who was clearly played. He exacted further revenge by dropping the price of a life-size James decal from $99.99 to $17.41, the year Benedict Arnold was born.

In essence, James was acknowledging that he didn't think he could lead a team — or at least that team — to a championship on his own.

"The King abandoned the throne like Edward VIII, not for love of a latter-day Wallis Simpson, but for fear of failure," Israel said. "All the bravado has been a pose. He's not a leader, he's not an alpha, he's just a pack animal. In Miami, Dwyane Wade is the alpha dog."

Israel believes James would have had a better chance to win in Chicago: "These guys don't fit together on the Heat. It's kind of like asking Jackson Pollock to finish a painting Picasso started."

June 20, 2012

James Gives Riley the Spectator a Moment to Cherish

BY HARVEY ARATON

MIAMI — When the network camera found Pat Riley standing by his seat across the way from the Miami bench, his face suddenly had the gray pallor of his combed-back hair. LeBron James was being carried off the floor late in the fourth quarter, and Riley was as stunned as any Heat fan — and just as helpless to do anything about it.

"As far as me missing it, I don't really miss it," he had said earlier in the night about coaching, long before the Heat survived James's cramping to beat Oklahoma City, 104–98, and take firm control of the N.B.A. finals, three games to one. "I feel it in the gut right now, like anybody else, but we have a very, very good young coach, who's growing by leaps and bounds."

So it was Erik Spoelstra's challenge to confront the gathering storm, Thunder and dark late-night clouds inside American Airlines Arena, as James left the game and the young Oklahoma City team pushed back against the Heat and made a run for its life in the series's swing game, possibly with the fate of the Heat hanging in the balance.

Across two and a half decades, from Kareem and Magic to Shaq and Wade, Riley lived for such moments, with his twitching neck betraying his grand sartorial cool. More than anything else in what he acknowledged was a narrow world of interests, he relished the opportunities to coax the great young talents to push beyond the pain and pressure, to cross the border between misery and winning while wholly embracing the Riley maxim that there was really nothing in between.

Shedding the public cocoon he has developed as the Heat's president to accept an N.B.A. Coaches Association lifetime achievement award named for Chuck Daly, who died in 2009, Riley had talked earlier about how fortunate he had been to coach so many N.B.A. stars along the way to five championships. Conveniently forgetting Phil Jackson for the moment, he called himself "the most blessed coach of all of them."

But he had had enough; the answer to the obvious question of whether he would ever coach again was no.

"I'm jumping out of my skin in my mind sitting there calmly," he said, before adding, "I will not be jumping out of my skin trying to get back out on the floor."

You had to wonder about that as the Heat medical people worked feverishly on James, as play continued without him and as Kevin Durant pulled up from 19 feet and gave the Thunder their first lead of the fourth quarter, 94–92, with 4 minutes 21 seconds left in Game 4. You wondered if Riley wished he could get right to work on James's mind while the trainers addressed the barking muscles in his upper right leg.

The Thunder had struck quickly, galloping to a 17-point first-quarter lead behind the slashing, hot-shooting Russell Westbrook, who was telling the world what it could do with its preference for pass-first point guards. But the Heat had eventually taken control — James, actually, by drawing double teams, and picking the Thunder apart with assist after assist, with overpowering dashes to the rim, the Magic-and-Michael hybrid skills fully on display.

Riley recruited James during the Wild West summer of 2010; laid a cloth bag of championship rings on the table — he actually has gold and silver versions to match his outfits — and blew away the field. Riley knew that James could be the best of all those he had coached, the most complete package, if he could take that leap across expectation and fear and make that last championship push with a little help from his friends.

James failed badly in the finals last season with Miami in the same place, holding a 2–1 series lead. Strangely enough, it was Rick Carlisle — the Dallas coach whose defenses had befuddled James — who moderated the news conference to present Riley as the Daly Award winner.

If James had lost the mind game last spring, would it be his body that betrayed him this time? Would the Thunder even the series and begin Miami's march to misery all over again?

"He's a freak of nature, but he's still a human being," James's teammate Udonis Haslem said. That disquieting thought sobered the arena as Durant gave the Thunder the lead and Mario Chalmers, who played an otherwise brilliant game, threw the ball away at the other end. The game clock read 4:05. And here came James, rehydrated, if not necessarily ready.

Westbrook lost the ball out of bounds. Chris Bosh scored inside. Westbrook missed from 20 feet. Now James had the ball on the perimeter, Thabo Sefolosha in his defensive crouch.

Why Sefolosha would back off a cramping player was anyone's guess. Spoelstra said the series was coming down to "four or five plays," but the difference between 3 and 1 has been Oklahoma's penchant for ill-timed errors of omission and commission and youth. Given the air space, James rose on his balky leg and nailed a 3-pointer. The game was not over, not by a long shot, and James would have to watch it conclude with Westbrook blemishing a 43-point night with a horrible foul on Chalmers late in the shot clock and the Thunder still within 3.

But James was the hero, finishing with heart, making the old coach proud.

It was impossible not to marvel at Riley's news conference performance, a trademark display of passion and conviction that left you wishing for more. Riley said he was back "for a moment," but he seized it, even going to the trouble of distributing cards to reporters with the Irish blessing that begins: "May the road rise up to meet you. May the wind always be at your back."

He said it was in honor of Daly, but now the wind is with James and the Heat, one game from a title after James aced Riley's finals exam and moved to the threshold of championship authenticity. No doubt the cramping tale one day will get the full Riley treatment, in front of some corporate audience, or maybe a bunch of wide-eyed coaching aspirants. Riley will set the scene, recount every glorious detail and recall it as a night of sheer perfection.

Except for one thing: He was in the stands to watch it, and not on the bench to work it.

JUNE 19, 2013

Heat's Ray Allen Knows All About Hitting Big 3-Pointers

BY HARVEY ARATON

MIAMI — He ended the bromance of one so-called Big Three and might have saved the future for another. There was symmetry to Ray Allen's fateful and figurative moment in the South Florida sun, coming on a day when his former Celtics teammates and their popular coach produced the biggest off-finals N.B.A. news.

"They went in their direction and obviously I went in mine," Allen said in summary remembrance after a truly unforgettable Tuesday night at American Airlines Arena spilled exhaustively into Wednesday morning.

Kevin Garnett refused to acknowledge Allen when the Celtics opened the season here against the enemy Heat last fall. We better understood why when Allen hit a game-tying 3-pointer from the far right corner in regulation Tuesday night that sent Miami to a 103–100 overtime victory over the heartbroken San Antonio Spurs in Game 6 of the N.B.A. finals.

"I've been on the other end of seeing him get them feet down, putting them stupid two fingers after he makes the shot," LeBron James said after the Heat survived to force Game 7 on Thursday night. "Not so stupid anymore now that he's my teammate."

Allen spared the lightning rod we know as James a summer of torment for two last-minute turnovers that seemed to have sealed a fifth title for Tim Duncan and the Spurs. He pardoned Dwyane Wade for another dalliance with mediocrity on the game's grandest stage. He made a hero of the much-maligned Chris Bosh for merely grabbing the rebound of a missed James jumper and having the good sense to pass it to the N.B.A. career leader in 3-point shots.

In doing that and subsequently what he has always done best, Allen at least temporarily quelled the inevitable speculation that Miami's Big Three will by next summer become Balkanized, consigned to league archives.

The subject of legacies — primarily James's and Duncan's — was unavoidable and in James's case typically overstated before Allen's shot. The sequences that preceded it were instructive in reminding us just how many variables, luck included, go into the construction of a title.

In San Antonio and elsewhere, millions had to wonder why Spurs Coach Gregg Popovich sat Duncan (as he often does in such situations) for two late Heat possessions when Miami had to shoot 3s and wound up making two on second-shot chances. Or why Popovich did not foul (as he never does) when the Spurs, after an otherwise stalwart Kawhi Leonard left the door ajar by missing a free throw, were defending a 95–92 lead with 19.4 seconds remaining.

Of course James had the first look — after a 3-pointer off a fortunate rebound bounce landed in Mike Miller's hands — at keeping the Heat's title defense alive. He missed badly, but Bosh, unencumbered by Duncan's size in the lane, grabbed the rebound to the right of the rim.

It was the second time this spring that an opposing coach — Indiana's Frank Vogel was the first — curiously made his team smaller and not better at a crucial time. That was not Bosh's problem.

"I was just trying to win the play," he said. "To be honest, I couldn't tell you who was in the game, except Ray."

Allen instinctively moved closer to the basket when James's shot was launched but backpedaled quickly when he saw the ball in Bosh's hands. James, wanting another crack, was waving frantically for the ball up top, but Allen was in Bosh's line of vision.

Allen is a sprightly 37, but the sight of his jump shot never gets old. As smooth and effortless as it appears, as unpretentiously classy as Allen has been, he was compelled to say that the art of retreating, catching and getting his legs set under him most certainly was not as easy as it looked.

"It's tough, but believe it or not, I work on it quite often," he said. "I try to put my body in precarious situations coming from different parts of the floor, different angles to try to get my momentum going moving forward.

"I honestly can say I gave myself a great opportunity, a great chance to make that shot. And it wasn't unfamiliar to me positionally. When it went in, I was ecstatic. But at the same time, I was expecting to make it."

No doubt that Doc Rivers, Paul Pierce and Garnett — wherever they were — recognized the gravity of the situation for the Spurs when the ball left Allen's hands, with Tony Parker running at him. Those who have played with or guarded Allen know he has impeccable timing — including the sense of when to change uniforms.

With the Celtics on the verge of sliding precipitously in the East and now facing dissolution of their 2008 championship core, Allen made the smart career choice. He moved south with the mantra, jump shot for hire.

Pat Riley, the Heat's president, already had shooters surrounding James, but he and James knew Allen was one for the ages.

"I called him, texted him," James said after 50 minutes, 32 points, 10 rebounds, 11 assists. "I just knew what he could bring to our team. He's big time, big time!"

Allen acknowledged seeing James begging for the shot. But in the scramble of bodies, trusting his feel for the floor that he was behind the 3-point line, he had space. He had the season in his soft hands.

"If there's one guy you want to have the ball in that situation, it is Walter Ray Allen," said the Heat's Shane Battier, going all formal. Asked if he had time to process a thought when the ball went from Bosh to Allen, Battier went theological.

"Thank the Lord for Jesus," he said.

The man called Jesus Shuttlesworth in Spike Lee's *He Got Game* saved Miami's Big Three with a divine bolt from the corner. In the aftermath of Game 6, it looked like a mortal wound for the Spurs.

JUNE 20, 2016

A Long-Sought Title Belongs To LeBron James

BY MICHAEL POWELL

OAKLAND, Calif. — To try to pick the inflection point in this spectacular and deciding game of the N.B.A. finals, to lay a wager on which arcing shot, improbable steal or rebound would turn this game, was to ensure you'd go flat broke.

There were 20 lead changes and 11 ties, waves of emotion surging through the arena and the teams like electrical pulses.

With just under two minutes left in the game and the score tied at 89–89, the Cavaliers' Kyrie Irving missed a spinning drive, and the Warriors were off to the races. The sore-backed Andre Iguodala passed to Stephen Curry, who flipped it back to Iguodala, who went up for the layup.

Or not, as the case would be.

Sprinting five or six steps behind was that 6-foot-8 Erie Lackawanna freight train known as LeBron James. His strides got longer and faster, and now he was airborne, his eyes nearly even with the hoop. He blocked the shot, his hand pinning the ball to the backboard.

For a moment, players on both teams paused, as if not sure, in their game intensity, of what they had just seen.

In the next minute, Irving, a spinning top of a guard, hit a fall-back-baby 3-pointer in the face of Curry, and that was more or less that, aside from a free throw tacked on by James to make the score 93–89 with 10 seconds remaining.

After a futile Warriors possession, the horn sounded, and the reigning champions, who held the single-season record for wins, were dethroned. James fell to his knees and covered his eyes.

James's performance in this series was overwhelming. He was the first player to lead both teams in points, rebounds, assists, steals and blocks not only in the N.B.A. finals but in any postseason series of any length, according to the Elias Sports Bureau.

Two summers ago, he had returned to Cleveland, a wayward son grown sated on the humid languor of South Beach. He had also made that most dangerous of vows, promising to bring a championship to his hometown.

The self-imposed pressure became fathoms deep. The Warriors most often play with a loose-limbed intelligence and joy, channeling the jazz of America's beautiful game. James and his mates often play no less astutely but as if consumed, aware that no end suffices save victory. At game's end, James, J. R. Smith and their coach, Tyronn Lue, sobbed without shame.

"I never cry; I've always been tough and never cried," Lue said. "A lot of emotions just built up."

To watch the players before the game was to sense that cord of tension. The Warriors tried to keep their cool-cat vibe. Asked about his game day ritual, Coach Steve Kerr replied that he and his assistant coach Luke Walton had done hot yoga.

"I'm guessing Bill Belichick and his staff don't do that," Kerr said, smiling. "Just throwing that out there."

Curry, in his warm-up ritual, is usually bubbly. On Sunday, his face was stone impassive. When the time came for the national anthem, the Warriors restlessly swayed from foot to foot.

On the other side, LeBron James stood still as a statue. He is 31 years old, a long remove from the man-child who came into the league 13 years ago. He had reached six previous championship series and come away the winner twice. Last year's loss to the Warriors left him near broken. As the anthem played, he said, he thought of the task at hand, how great the Warriors were, how important it was for his team to keep its head.

Then he acknowledged another thought, as he peered intently about the darkened arena.

"Just living in the moment," he said. "I told my guys before the game: Listen, there is a game to be played, but there's not many guys, there's not many teams, that get an opportunity to be in the N.B.A. finals in a Game 7. There's just not.

"Don't take it for granted."

One of sport's fascinations is to watch as a young man or woman comes to full and introspective flower. James is the son of a single mother from a tough corner of a tough city. He is a star, an on-court coach, and he speaks about police and gun violence. In different circumstances, had he not been blessed with preternatural ability and drive, we very likely would not have known of talents that have nothing to do with hitting a fall-back 3-point shot.

What a shame that would have been.

Kyrie Irving is 24, with a valise full of ankle-breaking moves. He reportedly chafed at the intensity of playing with these Cavaliers. He had his moment of clarity Sunday. He spoke of his good luck to spend his formative N.B.A. years playing with an impresario.

"I watched Beethoven tonight," Irving said. "I watched LeBron James compose a game."

He shook his head, chuckling at the absurdity of it, amazed that James had a "triple-double in Game 7 of an N.B.A. final": 27 points, 11 rebounds and 11 assists.

Irving got at what so many miss when they complain that James does not commandeer games like a Michael Jordan or a Kobe Bryant. James has a point guard's temperament; he will spend quarters orchestrating, trying to get his team to play as one.

"I can't do it by myself, so that was my mind-set," James said. "Like Jay-Z said, you've got to stay low and keep firing."

So it was in the first two quarters as James pitched the ball to Kevin Love, the power forward who can seem uncomfortable in his playing skin. Love was wide open at the 3-point line, yet he missed each shot. By game's end, however, he had pulled down many rebounds. In the fourth quarter, Love spun into the lane and hit a sweet push shot.

He did so off a pass from James.

"He protects every single one of us," Love said.

The Warriors go into the books as having collapsed on the cusp of victory, up by three games to one. That narrative is flawed, not least because they played a fine last game. All season, they dispatched opponents in a hail of precision passing and 3-point shooting.

In the first quarter, Irving hounded Curry beyond the 3-point line. So Curry dipped beneath him and put up that most improbable of shots, a teardrop 3-pointer.

It slapped through the net.

Yet Curry and Klay Thompson struggled with their shooting. And Curry made some unaccountably sloppy plays, like a behind-the-back fourth-quarter pass that sailed out of bounds rather than into Thompson's hands. Afterward, he was in no mood, after nine months of playing, to cut himself a break.

"It is extremely hard to win a championship," he said. "That's why you pour Champagne on yourself."

Draymond Green played like a man possessed. He drained six 3s, and in the absence of the team's injured center, Andrew Bogut, he was often the center. He is just 6-7 and 230 pounds, but he was like a knight on the parapets, swinging his mace at all comers.

Yet he lives with the knowledge that his Game 5 suspension in the finals might have been the turning point, as his team lost a home game it expected to win.

James walked into the postgame news conference wearing a cut-down net like a necklace. His two boys took seats at either side of him; he carried his toddler daughter, Zhuri, in his arms and kissed her between each question and answer.

He spoke of the sorrowful history that is Cleveland's sports legacy, rattling off the lowlights like any fan, if a tiny bit inaccurately (John Elway's drive was 98 yards).

"You could look back to the Earnest Byner fumble, Elway going 99 yards, to Jose Mesa not being able to close out in the bottom of the ninth, to the Cavs went to the finals — I was on that team — in 2007, us getting swept," he said, adding, "For us to be able to end this, to end this drought — our fans deserve it."

James's sense of history extends to his sport. On the riser, he handed the championship trophy to a teammate and set off to find the great Boston

Celtics center Bill Russell, for whom the Most Valuable Player Award of the N.B.A. finals is named. James gave Russell, the snowy-haired old shot blocker, a long hug.

Later, as cleaning crews moved through Oracle Arena and the press emptied into the parking lot, James stood in the Cavaliers' locker room, a cigar in one hand, a bottle of Champagne in the other. He was loose and funny, and he looked younger than he had in years. He regaled teammates with tales of past championship games, and he chased his daughter, who darted like a rabbit about the boxes in the room.

He posed for a last photo. Then he put up that big hand that had made that flying block: Enough.

"I got to shower," he said. "We got to get back to Cleveland. We're going home."

30

Shoot the 3. Don't Stop.

Not to pick on Red Auerbach — he wasn't the only basketball purist who disdained the idea of a 3-point shot, considered it a gimmick of a desperado league, the A.B.A.

But in 1979, Auerbach, along with Jack Ramsay, were the leading opponents to the adoption of the rule as the N.B.A. confronted popularity declines. "We don't need it," the Celtics legend told Sam Goldaper of *The Times* at a league meeting in Washington. "I say leave our game alone. Putting in the 3-point play reminds me of a team that trades four, five and six players every year. Everybody starts panicking. TV panicked over the bad ratings."

Auerbach wasn't wrong when he argued that the league was soon to be infused with new, charismatic blood in Magic Johnson and his man, Larry Bird. But he was outvoted on the league's 11-man competition committee, drowned out by visionaries like Pat Williams, the 76ers general manager, whose opinion had been shaped by Billy Cunningham, his coach, who had played in the A.B.A.

It's one thing to make a rule; another thing for coaches to make it a staple of their offenses. Five years after the N.B.A.'s implementation of a 3-point shot, I covered Bernard King's 60-point explosion on Christmas night as the Knicks lost to the Nets, 120–114, at Madison Square Garden. King took 30 shots, made 19, and sank 22 free throws. In 41 minutes of play, he took not a single 3-pointer. The teams combined to take six for the game, making none.

Sports do evolve, like all forms of entertainment and business. The European invasion of players like Dirk Nowitzki and other perimeter-oriented bigs opened the paint for shifty point guards and the passing lanes to those spotting up. The notion of watching a Dwight Howard back his way in for a jump hook or two shots at the line he figured to clank became far less alluring to the news media, fans and kids knocking around schoolyards and gyms.

It's impossible to pinpoint the exact moment the analytic wisdom of the 3-point-shot mentality took root. For me, it was the 1995 playoffs, Reggie Miller's wiping out a 6-point Knicks lead with two treys in 3.1 seconds and nailing down a highway robbery of a road victory seconds later with two free throws.

"Realistically, I thought we had no chance," said Larry Brown, the Pacers' coach.

The 3 ball meant there were few deficits that couldn't be overcome in an N.B.A. game. That was the point of the extra point.

April 26, 2013

N.B.A. Landscape Altered by Barrage of 3-Point Shots

by John Branch

OAKLAND, Calif. — When Reggie Miller entered the N.B.A. in 1987 as a skinny rookie with a high-arcing jump shot, about 1 of every 18 field-goal attempts in the league was a 3-pointer. This season, 3-pointers represented almost 1 of every 4 shots taken.

Miller broke Larry Bird's rookie record for 3-pointers made, with 61. He laughs at that number now.

"Today, Steph Curry, he gets that in a month," Miller said in a phone interview.

Evidence of the steadily rising influence of the 3-pointer can be seen across the basketball landscape. Teams averaged a record 20 attempts a game this season, and the trend is pushing steadily upward, or outward, really, far from the basket and beyond the line painted 23 feet 9 inches away.

Golden State's Stephen Curry set a league record with 272 3-pointers this season. Two teams, the Knicks and the Houston Rockets, attempted more 3s than any other N.B.A. teams in history.

All are in the playoffs, where the 3-point shot, a novelty when it began in the N.B.A. in 1979, is the star attraction. Some see it as something like art.

"Did you see the Warriors and Denver the other night?" asked Chris Mullin, who, like Miller, began his career in the 1980s and is in the Hall of Fame. The Warriors tied their first-round series with the Nuggets on Tuesday, 1–1, while trying 25 3-pointers among 79 field-goal attempts. Golden State made 14 of them and cruised to a 131–117 win.

"That was beautiful," Mullin said. "It was even more beautiful because they were making them. But, still, you're playing, you're getting up and down, you're running and you're passing. That's the game, to me."

Other parts of the postseason have been similarly punctuated by the exclamation point of the drained 3-pointer — as crowd-provoking as a dunk, but worth 50 percent more on the scoreboard. On Wednesday, the Rockets and the Oklahoma City Thunder both tried 35 3-pointers — 40 percent of the total shots — in Game 2 of their series. The Thunder made 11, the Rockets made 10, and Oklahoma City won by 3 points to take a 2–0 series lead.

The Knicks, who took more than a third of their shots in the regular season from behind the 3-point line — they established league records for made 3-pointers (891) and attempts (2,371) — took a 2–0 lead on Boston as nine Knicks attempted at least one 3-pointer. That sort of across-the-roster barrage was unheard-of only a few years ago.

"That's pretty much what we do," Knicks Coach Mike Woodson said this month. "They're not bad shots. You've got guys who can make them. If I didn't have players who could make them, trust me, I wouldn't be shooting them. We've got a bunch of guys who can make the 3, and we've shot it with high percentages this year. When you've got them, you've got to take them."

The 3-point line was borrowed from the American Basketball Association, the footloose '70s-era rival to the staid N.B.A.

The league was an offense-happy one. In 1975–76, the last season before the two leagues merged, A.B.A. teams averaged 112.5 points per game. The N.B.A. average was 104.3.

The N.B.A. imported most of the A.B.A. stars and four of its franchises: the Denver Nuggets, the Indiana Pacers, the San Antonio Spurs and the New York (later New Jersey) Nets. Also hoping to import some of the A.B.A.'s attitude, it added the 3-point line for the 1979–80 season.

It was largely a gimmick. Even in the freewheeling A.B.A.'s final season, 3-pointers represented only about 1 of every 25 field-goal attempts. They were used in desperation, not as inspiration.

In the N.B.A.'s first season with a 3-point line, overall scoring actually dropped slightly. The average team attempted only 2.8 3-pointers per game, or about 1 of every 33 shots from the field.

When the Philadelphia 76ers won the 1982–83 N.B.A. championship, they shot a total of 109 3-pointers (they made 25) during the 82-game regular season.

It was not until the 1986–87 season that N.B.A. teams averaged more than one made 3-pointer per game.

"Probably my first 10 or 12 years, the whole thing for every team was that you had to pound it inside," said Miller, who played 18 with the Pacers. "You had to get it to your center. You had to establish the paint first. And the center position really is gone in the N.B.A., and in college, really. Gone are the days of a David Robinson, Patrick Ewing, Shaquille O'Neal, Hakeem Olajuwon, Rik Smits, Alonzo Mourning."

Teams, historically built around the center, began to turn themselves inside out behind the shooting touch of big men like Dirk Nowitzki of the Dallas Mavericks. Slowly, power forwards within a couple of inches of 7 feet began to hover near the 3-point line, pulling defenders with them.

The rise of the "stretch 4," as power forwards who play mostly far from the basket are called, may have propelled the proliferation of the 3-pointer more than anything. The defensive slogs of the 1990s gave way to persistent motion and more long jumpers. Defend too close, and the shooter has more room to drive past. Stay too far back, and he has room to shoot something that, in the case of Curry, he makes about 45 percent of the time.

"It's an exciting brand of basketball," said Mark Jackson, Golden State's coach, who played point guard for 17 years in the N.B.A. "Who wants to see a point guard back down for 20 seconds? It's a different game. It's much more enjoyable — talking as someone who did that."

It has helped raise scoring, which dropped to 91.6 points per game in 1998–99, to about 100 points per game — still 10 points shy of the averages in the 1980s.

A growing ratio of those points comes from 3-pointers. Making them was never the issue. While it took a few seasons to find the shooting form, success on 3-point attempts have been above 30 percent every season since 1986–87. For more than two decades, it has settled around 35 percent. This season, the field-goal percentage for 3-pointers was 35.9, typical of the past 10 years.

What has changed markedly is the number of attempts. They have risen steadily.

Coaches have found that the 3-pointer can be a more efficient way of scoring points — far more so than midrange 2-point jumpers. In the simplest terms, making one-third of your 3-point shots adds up the same as making half of your 2-point shots.

The Knicks made 37.6 percent of their 3-point shots, and 48.7 percent of their 2-point attempts. Their total output (minus free throws) would seem to rise when they shot more from behind the arc than within it.

But that can be a fickle way of scoring, undermined by streaky shooting — a potential downfall in a taut playoff series. But coaches worry about that less than ever, since rosters are filled with 3-point threats. The Rockets and the Knicks, for example, each had more than 10 players average more than one 3-point attempt a game in the regular season — and more than 10 who made more than 30 percent of them.

The two teams had a combined eight players with more 3-pointers made than what Miller had 25 years ago, when he broke the rookie record.

Miller retired in 2005 with an N.B.A.-record 2,560 3-pointers. Ray Allen, now with Miami, has since moved into the top spot. Miller laughed when considering whether he was simply ahead of his time, now that the N.B.A. seems to have fully adopted his long-range game.

"If I would have played in the last five years," Miller said, "Ray would never have passed me."

Nov. 24, 2015

The Artistry of Stephen Curry

BY SCOTT CACCIOLA

Taras Domitro was not a basketball fan when he joined the San Francisco Ballet as a principal dancer in 2008.

"But I became one," he said.

Domitro, who was born in Havana, happened to arrive in the Bay Area one year before the Golden State Warriors drafted Stephen Curry. That fortunate turn of events goes a long way toward explaining how Domitro grew to enjoy watching the game.

"What I see the most when I watch Steph is the incredible coordination he has with his arms, his legs and the way he handles the ball," Domitro, 29, said before drawing a comparison between their respective disciplines and referring to the way male dancers support women as they execute a lift or a jump. "We don't use a ball, you know. We use a woman. But the way he dribbles the ball is the way we handle a woman on stage."

The defending champion Warriors are at it again — scoring points, winning games and setting ridiculous standards. On Tuesday night, the Warriors (15–0) could break an N.B.A. record for the best start to a season by defeating the Los Angeles Lakers at Oracle Arena in Oakland, Calif. Curry, the N.B.A.'s leading scorer and last season's most valuable player, has been at the center of it all, having added a new title to his résumé: the N.B.A.'s unofficial artist-in-residence.

"It's beautiful to watch," said Graham Lustig, 61, the artistic director of the Oakland Ballet Company.

With each 3-pointer and every spinning layup, Curry somehow seems to transcend the sport, turning the game into theater. Domitro and Lustig said that much of Curry's aesthetic appeal was rooted in what ballet dancers seek most: to make their art look effortless.

"We don't want to see any pain when dancers are finishing their final variation of something," Lustig said. "You don't want to see them screwing up their faces and giving the impression they can hardly make it through to the end of a solo."

In a league full of behemoths who sweat and strain on every possession, the 6-foot-3 Curry has been operating on a different plane — one that has struck Lustig as deeply familiar.

"Steph doesn't really look like he's putting in a lot effort, does he?" Lustig said. "I'm not suggesting at all that he doesn't use effort. It's just that he doesn't display it, and I think that's probably at the core of what this is about."

Lustig said he was particularly impressed by Curry's body control, citing a move that Curry made against the Detroit Pistons this month. After dribbling past his primary defender, Curry launched himself at the rim before he managed to rotate his torso away from a second defender. He proceeded to flip the ball off the glass and through the hoop.

"He's like a magician, juggling the basketball while he's four feet off the ground," Lustig said.

When dancers jump and twist and glide across the stage, they rely on centripetal force — essentially the energy that pulls toward a center — for balance, Lustig said. But they must also possess remarkable core strength to be able to spin and soar at such dizzying heights.

Lustig sees that type of strength whenever Curry leaves his feet, and especially when he lands, as strange as that might sound.

"It's a lot easier to throw yourself up in the air and try to do something than it is to come down with control," Lustig said. "And he's not even trying to do something beautiful. His coach isn't telling him how to land, but he does. It's innate. His whole body knows what to do both in the air and in the return."

Every movement in ballet involves a great deal of skill, but the aerial theatrics are always rooted in the same foundation: bending at the knees, a movement known as plié. Dancers bend their legs before they leap, and they bend their legs before they land — all of it designed to ensure balance and to make their bodies more elastic.

"That is the baseline that everyone is working from," Lustig said.

It seems safe to suggest, then, that few players in the N.B.A. have a more graceful plié than Curry, whose long and lean physique also lends itself to a certain elegance.

"The thing about ballet is that you don't want to look bulky on stage," Domitro said. "Steph is not a bulky guy."

Any extraordinary moment in a performance — athletic or artistic — is the product of years of training and preparation, Lustig said. The act itself might look spontaneous, but little happens by accident. Domitro often trains from six to seven hours a day. Lustig danced professionally for 19 years before he succumbed to the effects of age and effort.

Like dancers, basketball players use their bodies as their instruments. The behind-the-scenes work is painstaking.

"That knee, that foot, that shoulder, that wrist joint — that's what they have," Lustig said. "So they have to take care of their bodies because they're going to push it to the limits."

With that in mind, Lustig noted one element of Curry's pregame routine, which involves sprinting from halfcourt to one of the baselines immediately before the opening tip. That simple act provides a small window into the physical maintenance that Curry must do on a daily basis.

"That's something dancers do all the time," Lustig said. "They're in the wings about to come on stage, and they're jumping around, they're stretching and they're going over their moves — some of the stuff that challenges them the most. That happens quite a bit. And then I see Steph preparing: Zoom!"

But while Domitro and Curry both rehearse (Curry would call it practice), Domitro and Lustig marvel at Curry's ability to improvise — the quick wit to lull a defender into a state of paralysis by dribbling the ball between his legs, over and over, before dashing past him. Curry must create something new nearly every time he touches the ball.

"There's a certain sense of musicality to the way his body works," Lustig said. "It looks like he's moving in a slightly different dimension as everyone else, and I think that ties into his sheer speed and power and control — incredible, unbelievable control. And that's what you want in a dancer."

Domitro explained how it takes an entire community to make a production work — the dancers, the orchestra, the stagehands, the audience. Much like a basketball game, he said, everyone involved plays a role in creating a theatrical experience.

"We principals are nothing without the corps," Domitro said. "We wouldn't be able to do what we do."

The same is true of Curry, whose dance partner is often his defender. There are moments when he seems acutely aware that he is performing before a crowd.

Lustig observed how, after the Warriors' Harrison Barnes raced in for a dunk in that same game against the Pistons, Curry stood in the backcourt and celebrated by flapping his arms like a bird — three, four, five times.

"I'm flying!" Lustig said. "Even the way he does that is graceful."

The Oakland Ballet Company has been at work on a seasonal production of *The Nutcracker*, set to debut next month at the Paramount Theatre. Lustig said he had no doubt that with the proper training from an early age, Curry would have been a fine dancer. Lustig was asked how he would have cast him.

"Oh, he'd have to be the cavalier, right?" Lustig said. "He has to be the leading man."

31
Dribble Handoff

In 2005, I published a book about the fallout of the Pistons-Pacers Malice at the Palace debacle and the residual challenges facing the league in its aftermath. The broadcaster Michael Kay had me on his ESPN-New York radio show to discuss the project and cleverly timed the interview to begin near the end of another one he was conducting with David Stern.

"So, Commissioner," Kay said, forgetting or not knowing that Stern was always just good old informal David to those of us covering the league. "In his new book, Harvey Araton says...."

Stern calmly waited for Kay to finish the book's summary argument about how the league was in a serious image crisis before saying, without raising his voice, "He's been wrong before." And hanging up.

Classic Stern. To be on the wrong side of a commissioner whose run lasted 30 years (and 48 overall, counting legal association) was to be the target of his straightforward ire. Many times my telephone would ring on the morning a column that he did not like appeared. Upon answering, I would hear, without introduction, "Complete bullshit!"

And yet Stern almost never cut off access because he typically differentiated the intentions and tenor of his critics — ultimately pardoning or even favoring those who had committed a solid portion of their working lives to covering a sport they loved, even as they dissected its flaws.

Adam Silver was Stern's protégé despite differences in appearance and approach — Silver tall and slender to Stern's short and stocky; a practitioner of subtlety to Stern's sledgehammer. But Silver, too, was adept at getting his point across.

During the 2015 finals, the issue of players breaking down over the long season arose when Kyrie Irving and Kevin Love were forced out of the Cavs' lineup. Writing after Silver addressed questions on the subject at his pre-finals news conference, I noted in my column that, "like a zealous education reformer, Silver is enamored of that four-letter crutch word — data — and applied it to several questions."

A couple of weeks later, I emailed him on an unrelated story. He wrote back: "No problem. Let me pull the data."

Touché, I thought. Like his predecessor, Silver doesn't miss a beat, even as he avoids the verbal beat-down.

Jan. 25, 2014

In a Transition Game, David Stern Is Passing N.B.A. Commissioner's Hat to Adam Silver

BY HARVEY ARATON

David Stern stepped into a conference room through a side door from his office. He carried a can of soda and a small plate of tortilla chips.

"My lunch," he said on a recent weekday afternoon as he settled in to be interviewed jointly with Adam Silver, who will succeed him Saturday as N.B.A. commissioner.

Silver was late for the appointment. "Where's Adam?" Stern said to Tim Frank, his senior vice president for basketball communications, after several minutes.

Frank went to check and returned. "On a call," he said.

Coincidence or not, the new order, at least symbolically, was upon us. After 30 years on the job, 48 over all in association with the league, Stern was all but officially done shepherding a growth enterprise with which he had become synonymous, or practically symbiotic. The transition of power seemed to have already occurred when Silver eased his tall, slender frame into a seat at the table perpendicular from Stern's.

Asked how he preferred to be addressed, he said, "Adam, please."

Not Commissioner Silver or Mr. Commissioner, as it has been with the leaders of the competing major sports, especially football and baseball.

"I'll be Adam because David set the tone," Silver said. "I think he enjoyed that sports fan relationship with other sports fans and I think they understood, even if they criticized him for certain decisions, that he was trying to do what he thought was in the best interests of the league, if not for an individual team."

Silver added: "His dad owned a deli. He went to public school. He was a regular guy who was not born into this."

In other words, Stern was not like at least some of the owners he has served — men who began life with a 15-point lead and less than two minutes to play — and once was not unlike many of the upwardly mobile players he governed. And even as the stakes changed along with the increasingly digitally connected world, and as the number of critics gained on his admirers, Commissioner Stern remained David to the news media, the unabashed point man for a once-withering product now awash in $5.5 billion in annual revenue.

As Silver finished his thought, Stern chimed in, "I used to say to people, commissioner is my job description, not my title."

Yet one's station in life, regardless of when it is achieved, opens doors to the proverbial next level. Stern, 71, was, in the 1970s, a rising star at the New York law firm Proskauer Rose, which provided legal counsel to the N.B.A. and created a way inside the sport he followed growing up across the Hudson River from Manhattan in Teaneck, N.J.

Silver, 51, spent much of his youth in Rye, north of New York City, the son of a Proskauer partner.

"My parents were divorced when I was young, and my father lived in the city," he said. "One of the activities I would do with my father was going to Knicks games. Following the Knicks was part of my family DNA."

He cheered for the 1970 championship team and wore Walt Frazier's signature Puma Clyde sneakers. He went on to Duke, where he watched the likes of Mike Gminski and Eugene Banks. He was at Cameron Indoor Stadium for the debut season of the now-institutional Mike Krzyzewski.

After graduating from the University of Chicago Law School, Silver seemed to be following in the legal footsteps of his father. "I loved basketball, but I never dreamed about playing in the N.B.A. or certainly working for the N.B.A.," he said.

The credentials and connections couldn't have hurt after he wrote a letter to Stern seeking career advice. Silver joined the league in 1992 as Stern's special assistant and subsequently became chief of staff, the senior vice president of N.B.A. Entertainment, and the deputy commissioner when Russ Granik left that position in 2006.

"We've been working intensely close for 22 years," Stern said. "I've been giving him advice and he's been giving me advice for over two decades. It depended upon the owners ultimately, but I thought he was the logical successor."

Such is the rebuttal to the social media chatter about the commissioner's office being too New York-centric, or even too Jewish. Support for Silver, according to league insiders, was widespread. His understanding of the business is unquestioned and his relaxed demeanor has long been cited as a perfect complement and now replacement for Stern's more contentious nature.

But when Stern said, "We think alike about a lot of things — not just about basketball, but about life," he was stressing a more essential point that N.B.A. owners seemed to grasp.

Straddling a Line

Whether one views Stern as a great commissioner or an unrelenting capitalist, it is hard to argue that he was not what the noted black sports sociologist Harry Edwards once called him — "an honest broker" — for a largely African-American player pool as it ascended to the pantheon of mainstream American and international entertainment.

That was apparent when HBO's Bryant Gumbel compared Stern to "some kind of modern plantation overseer" during a player lockout in 2011. The comment, called "an occupational hazard" by Stern, gained no traction.

Not surprisingly, Stern cited the Knicks of his early days as the league's outside counsel for forming a sense of what its social contribution could ultimately be on a much grander stage.

"Bill Bradley from Princeton and Willis Reed from Grambling being part of a championship team has something to teach the rest of society," he said. "I think the N.B.A., just by its very being and its march, has been very important."

But even as his league rode the talent and charisma of Magic Johnson, Larry Bird, Michael Jordan and now LeBron James to once-unimagined popularity, Stern had to straddle the line between advocacy for his players and the greater culture they sometimes offended, justifiably or not.

Silver was a dozen years into his N.B.A. tenure when Ron Artest charged into the stands at the Palace of Auburn Hills, Mich., setting off the notorious Pistons-Pacers brawl in November 2004. Along with video of the episode rewound over and over came harsh denunciations of the league's players that often veered into racial stereotyping.

When told that the N.B.A., because of its players' high-recognition factor, has been the home office for the kind of firestorm that recently enveloped Richard Sherman and the N.F.L., Silver nodded.

"Behind closed doors, we happen to bemoan the fact that we are held to a very different standard than some of the other leagues because of who our players are," he said, citing as example the reactions to fighting in the N.B.A. compared with the N.H.L.

In this realm, Silver sounded much like his mentor, Stern, though he added, "I agree we're far from a postracial society, but I don't think it's nearly the same challenge that David faced."

Be it with draconian punishments for violent transgressions — as in the cases of Artest and Latrell Sprewell — or a dress code for players in 2005, Stern was an obvious and sometimes too easy target, as a white authority figure setting limits on what was considered black expression.

But as Silver said in defending the dress code, "There was some resistance initially, but I think the players understood why we collectively thought it was necessary and they bought into it and have had fun with it by letting their unique personalities come out through their wardrobes."

In fact, most star players now prefer to dress to the nines before they are interviewed after games in an effort to enhance their brands. For Stern, that outcome may be the marketing equivalent to slam dunking the game-winner at the buzzer.

But he let Silver explain: "The fact that we happen to have an African-American president now, who happens to be a huge N.B.A. fan, it's just a very different time. We have said that if a player makes a mistake, that individual player would be held accountable, as opposed to a player making a mistake and the public saying, 'Yeah, all those N.B.A. players are thugs.'"

There was a time, Silver contended, when the objectionable behavior of even a former player — Dennis Rodman's journey to North Korea, for instance — might have set off another round of collective head-shaking.

"Nobody was condemning the N.B.A. based upon the foolish performance by Dennis," Stern said. "The outliers are there, but, in a positive way, we may be past that."

A Sports Marketing Genius

For all its progress in the form of heightened global interest, glittering new arenas and ever-increasing television revenue, the N.B.A. still grapples with a product that has exceeded the affordability of many fans and has several teams that barely qualify as an attraction in indifferent markets.

Over all, the league seems to occupy a glass house in one significant way that football and baseball — however troubled by their own institutional problems — do not.

N.B.A. outcomes, especially in the playoffs, have long drawn skepticism in the form of conspiracy theories about preferred teams and players receiving help from the officials in conjunction with the league office. The 2007 scandal involving Tim Donaghy, the former referee who admitted to betting on games, did not help.

From the New York perspective, one could needle Stern and Silver on the way they failed to arrange a championship for their once-beloved Knicks for 41 years and counting.

"Sorry," Stern said, smirking, before dismissing, as always, the conspiracy charges, but with a more reflective tone.

"I blame this on myself," he said. "Because of my respect for the people in this game, I didn't blow my top as commissioner when a Phil Jackson or a Pat Riley — because they were fighting with each other to win a game here and there — would say, 'Oh, the network wanted another game.' That was part of the gamesmanship that went into thinking they were working the officials, motivating their players. If you weren't already crazy, being in the N.B.A. playoffs made you crazy, and I may have underreacted."

Noting that franchises typically prefer their cable announcers to favor the home team in a game that is so hard to officiate, Stern suggested that fans tend to be led to suspicion much in the way Fox News and MSNBC fire up the political masses in their respective camps.

"I'd add it is frustrating," Silver said. "There seems to be a higher level of chatter in this league than in other leagues. I have no solution to offer, but we have to take a fresh look at it because it is corrosive to the sport."

With the passing of the torch days away, Silver said he remained committed to a favorite Stern project, the W.N.B.A., whose original business plan he helped write. He will continue to push the N.B.A. Players' Association — especially after it chooses a replacement for Billy Hunter — to increase the age limit for incoming players to 20.

"There are plenty of things we will change over time, but I'd like to believe David would have made those decisions had he remained commissioner," he said, with a nod to his boss.

He called Stern "one of the founders of modern sports marketing," pointing out: "When I arrived at the league in the early '90s, leagues weren't considered brands the way they are now. Everyone talks about the N.F.L. shield now, but back then, there was the N.F.L. People never even said M.L.B. about Major League Baseball. But I think David was one of the first — there was Phil Knight and certainly others — to take modern state-of-the-art marketing practices, whatever the technology happened to be at the time, and apply them to sports leagues."

He looked at Stern and said, "Do you disagree?"

"No," said Stern, content to let Silver define his legacy. His self-evaluation was limited to one summary sentence.

"Look at the body of work, where we were and where we are," he said.

He once explained the sport's hold on him by recalling the title of a book written by his predecessor, Larry O'Brien, about O'Brien's time as a strategist for the Democratic Party: *No Final Victories*.

But could we say that the 2011 labor peace — with the owners gaining a 50-50 split of the revenue — represented his final victory?

Silver, who will be empowered with increasing revenue, with potential European expansion and developing interest in India, Africa and elsewhere, answered first.

"Not a fair question," he said. "He already said there are no final victories."

All right, then. Most cherished on-court memories?

Stern leaned back and pointed to a photograph propped against the wall of him presenting Magic Johnson with the most valuable player trophy at the 1992 All-Star Game, months after Johnson retired from the Los Angeles Lakers upon disclosing he had contracted the virus that causes AIDS.

That was one, Stern said. The other, he said, was "was what the Dream Team represented, this much-maligned group of players and sport, on the march to the gold medal stand, being feted like a combination of the Bolshoi, the Philharmonic and the Beatles."

Stern paused and offered one final plug that made the long voyage sound like the continuing mission of the U.S.S. Enterprise.

"And therein launched the globalization of the game," he said. "Again, no final victories."

32

Culture Warriors

Twenty years after Magic Johnson stunned the world by announcing he had tested positive for the virus that causes AIDS, he was alive, well and still raising the productivity bar for athletes in their post-playing lives.

He was no total cultural game-changer like Jackie Robinson, or antiwar icon in the mold of Muhammad Ali. But in a May 2012 column, I argued that it was "fair to say that Johnson has earned a place on the mythical Mount Rushmore of his generation's athletes, whose social contributions have significantly built on competitive triumphs."

The sports ethicist Richard Lapchick agreed, contending that Johnson, by refusing to hide his H.I.V. diagnosis in 1991, as did other celebrities, had humanized the challenge of living while infected with the virus in the face of ignorance and fear.

"I have always talked about Nelson Mandela and Muhammad Ali being the two men who could bring people together on a global level," Lapchick told me. "But Magic could be in that category as well. When he goes somewhere, he's going to draw people of any race, any age. He has that charisma, and magnetism."

The N.B.A. had across the years earned mostly top grades in Lapchick's annual reports on the hiring practices of major professional and college sports, be it of minorities or women. The league was also steeped in historic milestones, such as Oscar Robertson's becoming the first black president of a major pro sport's players union in 1965 and Michele Roberts's appointment in 2014 as its executive director.

In a reprise to some extent of the 1960s, an era of players' and coaches' outspokenness on a host of polarizing issues was unfolding. But it was important to note that players did not necessarily have to be controversial or defiant to be impactful. They had climbed to a different financial platform, and with money came opportunity.

Long before LeBron James earned glowing praise for launching his I Promise public school in Akron in 2018, David Robinson had contributed millions to fund a faith-based school in San Antonio for underprivileged children.

"Players should feel free to speak their minds if it works for them," Kevin Johnson, the 1990s All-Star turned Sacramento mayor, told me in 2014, weeks before he was to resurface in the N.B.A. as a pivotal point man in the Donald Sterling case. "But I don't think everything has to stay along party lines. David Robinson was speaking out when he started a school in San Antonio. Dikembe Mutombo was speaking out with the charity work he did in his African homeland."

Magic had the access and acumen to bring corporate businesses and jobs into parts of urban America that had been traditionally ignored. And while Michael Jordan had long cemented — and in many ways earned — a reputation as a socially indifferent tool of corporate America, he did pave a path for athletes to leverage their commercial appeal.

Thanks to Jordan, they could dream far beyond the bench or the broadcast booth. They could even sit in the owner's chair and wield all the power that came with it.

APRIL 14, 2008

Jordan Steps to the Line In Charlotte

BY JONATHAN ABRAMS

CHARLOTTE, N.C. — Whenever cigar smoke wafts through the door and floats over the cubicles where various Charlotte Bobcats employees work, it means the boss is in. Michael Jordan's office sits close to an exit, and from there he can easily step outside to a balcony and gaze down to where the Charlotte Bobcats, the team he recently purchased for $275 million, practice on the floor of the Time Warner Cable Arena.

In some ways, the smoke was a perfect metaphor for Jordan, who, until recently, had not been all that visible in the four years he has been a member of the Bobcats' hierarchy. Take, for instance, the team photos that hang on the corridor walls outside Jordan's office. From year to year, the cast of faces changes, with one constant: Jordan's is nowhere to be seen.

Although he is the most iconic and marketable player in N.B.A. history, Jordan, 47, essentially stayed away from the spotlight since arriving in Charlotte in 2006 as a minority owner and the managing member of basketball operations. He was not asked to be in the forefront, and he did not want to be.

But he did field phone calls at all hours from his chosen general manager, Rod Higgins. Sometimes, Jordan made judgments about team personnel but left it to others to publicly explain them. He was here for Bobcats games more than most people realized, but he often pinned himself to the back of his suite, out of sight of the cameras and the fans.

Gradually, there was a shift. Jordan moved from his suite to the seats, paying $1,500 a game for two courtside chairs. Then, last month, his visibility soared when he became the first former N.B.A. player to buy a majority interest in an N.B.A. franchise.

Jordan's money is now on the table, backing a belief that he can increasingly fill the arena with fans and victories. There is reason for guarded optimism on both fronts. The Bobcats are playoff-bound for the first time in their six-year history, and Jordan has pledged his involvement in the form of $275 million.

"It makes the statement about how serious my commitment is," he said in a recent telephone interview, referring to his outlay. "I've always been an ambitious person, and this is something I envision seeing my children being a part of."

Jordan's decision to buy the Bobcats comes at a time of movement in N.B.A. ownership. The Russian billionaire Mikhail D. Prokhorov is set to acquire the Nets. Chris Cohan recently stated his intentions to sell the Golden State Warriors. George Shinn may soon sell the New Orleans Hornets. The deaths of Abe Pollin, the owner of the Washington Wizards, and Bill Davidson, the Detroit Pistons' owner, will cause shifts within those franchises.

But it is Jordan who will attract a good deal of the attention.

"There are a lot of people watching him, and it's going to be an interesting situation, both for himself and the league," N.B.A. Commissioner David Stern said. "I believe that Mr. Jordan will ultimately be viewed as a very astute buyer."

Jordan appears confident and hardly concerned that he is again putting his post-playing legacy on the line. His first job as an N.B.A. executive ended acrimoniously in 2003, when Pollin dismissed him as the Wizards' director of basketball operations. The decision stunned Jordan, although the team was a cumulative 110–179 while he was there and there was evidence of team dissension.

One columnist in *The Washington Post* wrote: "After this performance, Jordan doesn't need to be the president of anything. He needs a junior executive training seminar." But another wrote, "He was the only reason people started to care about the Wizards again, the only credibility and legitimacy the whole operation had."

Pollin cited a fracture between players on the team and Jordan after he came out of retirement to play for the Wizards for two seasons, 2001–02 and 2002–03, while still making personnel decisions. In some ways, his tenure is best remembered for his using the first overall selection in the 2001 draft on the high schooler Kwame Brown, who turned out to be a bust.

"You can have an idea on how things should go and people can disagree and they can go in another direction," Jordan said. "It happened to me in Washington."

Fred Whitfield, a longtime friend of Jordan's who was the Wizards' director of player personnel and is now the Bobcats' chief executive, argued that only one of the first nine picks in that 2001 draft, Pau Gasol, developed into an All-Star. Few remember, he said, that Jordan cleared the Wizards' payroll of the bloated salaries of Juwan Howard, Mitch Richmond and Rod Strickland.

"That's what we were really challenged to do," Whitfield said. He described Jordan as "intense in Washington" while learning the business side of basketball and said that it was then that Jordan started thinking about becoming a majority owner.

Before he joined the Wizards, Jordan had tried to buy a substantial interest in the Charlotte Hornets, but talks fell apart when Shinn would not relinquish control over basketball decisions. As a member of the Wizards, he was a minority owner until he had to relinquish his share when he came out of retirement. After leaving the Wizards, Jordan headed a group that nearly acquired the Milwaukee Bucks before United States Senator Herb Kohl decided to keep them.

In 2006, the Bobcats' owner, Robert L. Johnson, coaxed Jordan into coming aboard as a minority owner and top executive. They first met through the actor Denzel Washington, a mutual friend, while Jordan was playing in Chicago.

"Michael got a little bit frustrated," Johnson said of Jordan's failed talks with Kohl to buy the Bucks. "It led to his hiatus of wanting to be separate from the N.B.A. until I kept convincing him to come to Charlotte. Basketball is in his blood. You can only play so much golf."

Jordan quickly placed longtime associates in significant roles in Charlotte's front office: Whitfield; Higgins, who was his assistant general manager in Washington; and Buzz Peterson, a college roommate who is director of player personnel.

In conducting his first draft for the Bobcats, Jordan selected Adam Morrison with the third pick. But Morrison never made an impact before the Bobcats traded him to the Los Angeles Lakers last year.

Brown. Morrison. Two bad lottery picks is not the way to build a reputation as an executive. But some of Jordan's moves are paying dividends. He hired Larry Brown as the coach before the 2008–09 campaign and engineered a slew of trades over the last two seasons involving 21 players. Many of the players he acquired were considered castoffs, and Brown has made good use of them. But how long he will continue to do so is in question. There are murmurs that the well-traveled Brown will head elsewhere after this season.

"I have been successful," Jordan said of his career as an executive. "People look at it under different microscopes. I'm held to different standards than most. The level of success I have is also more noticeable than most."

Right now, it is easy to notice in Charlotte. While they rank 22nd in attendance, the Bobcats are averaging nearly 16,000 fans a game, their best ever and more than a 10 percent jump over last season. No N.B.A. team has improved as much in this category. The Bobcats have also sold three times as many season tickets compared to this point last season and have added 30 corporate sponsors since August.

They're still far away, but they are hoping to duplicate the heyday of the Charlotte Hornets in the 1990s, when the team led the N.B.A. in attendance. Charlotte Coliseum shook. Players could not hear calls from coaches.

"You knew fans were going to be into the game from the jump ball to the final horn," said Dell Curry, a former Hornets guard and now a Bobcats television broadcaster.

But things soured after Shinn became embroiled in a sexual-assault case, and he ended up moving the franchise to New Orleans for the 2002–03 season.

When the N.B.A. returned, many fans did not. Johnson lost millions of dollars annually.

"He was misled," Felix Sabates, another minority owner, said of Johnson. "They forgot to tell him that people had such a bad taste from the Hornets and George Shinn."

As the Bobcats struggled in recent years, some wondered about Jordan's commitment to the franchise and the city. But he stayed and ended up owning the team, paying $25 million less than Johnson did.

Now Jordan sits within earshot of Brown's calls from the sideline. He shakes hands with fans. He says that while he will continue living in Chicago, he will soon have a place in Charlotte.

And he already sounds comfortable in his new role as an owner. Asked about the possibility of a lockout, he said the players had to make concessions. "The model isn't working," he said.

Asked if Jordan the owner would acquire Jordan the player if it meant crossing the luxury-tax threshold, Jordan responded, "It depends."

"If it takes me from the second round to the finals? Of course," he said. "If it doesn't, then why would I do that and risk everything?"

He called ownership a dream come true. "But it's an opportunity I don't want to mess up," he said. "My ego is not big enough to not involve others. I'm willing to learn and I have been learning."

Later this week, the Bobcats will play in their first playoff series, against Orlando. Jordan will be nearby. The boss is in.

MAY 14, 2010

Jokes Aside, Prokhorov Talks of Reviving Nets

BY HOWARD BECK

In a broad, brightly lit Manhattan ballroom, the new owner of the N.B.A.'s worst team made an entrance befitting a Hollywood star. Lights flashed, shutters snapped in rapid-fire fashion and cameras rolled.

Mikhail D. Prokhorov, the suave, swaggering 44-year-old Russian billionaire, strolled up the aisle, took a seat and put on a show. He joked and he jousted, all the while taking great delight in his curious outsider status.

"America," he said in a thick accent, "I come in peace."

The room erupted in laughter.

If Prokhorov is as savvy as he is funny, the Nets should have a very bright future indeed.

The N.B.A. last week approved the sale of the Nets from Bruce C. Ratner to Prokhorov, making him the league's first owner outside of North America. On Wednesday, Prokhorov conducted his first extensive news media tour — a 90-minute breakfast meeting with select reporters, followed by a packed news conference that included 70 reporters and 15 television cameras and finally a radio interview with WFAN's Mike Francesa.

He was glib, funny, exceedingly confident and — on the major issues — mostly guarded. He deflected policy questions with one-liners and coy smiles, whether the topic was LeBron James's free agency, the search for a new coach or the strategy for building a championship team.

The Nets are far from that goal, and might need every ounce of Prokhorov's wit and charisma to revive their fortunes. They lost 70 of 82 games, the worst record in franchise history. Despite having the best odds, they lost in the draft lottery Tuesday, falling from first to third.

But Prokhorov, who built CSKA Moscow into a European powerhouse, projected unwavering optimism about the future. The Nets will move into a state-of-the-art arena in Brooklyn in 2012. They have a bright young star, center Brook Lopez, a flashy point guard, Devin Harris, and, most critically, about $22 million in salary-cap space to spend this summer, when James will headline a spectacular free-agent class.

Over and over, Prokhorov characterized his approach as patient, methodical and reflective. He hinted at a long-term strategy that goes beyond the summer of LeBron.

"My goal is to create a dynasty team, and I'm not in a hurry," he said over a breakfast of eggs Benedict. "We have second year with more free agents coming."

Yet his ambitions seemed boundless. He said he wanted to turn the Nets into "a global team" and aimed to contend for a championship within five years.

On strategy and personnel, Prokhorov was mostly vague. He has committed to keeping Rod Thorn, the widely respected team president, as his head of basketball operations; and Brett Yormark, the chief executive and marketing wizard.

Prokhorov announced, somewhat abruptly, that he would not be retaining Kiki Vandeweghe, the Nets' general manager, who also coached the final 64 games this season. His contract expires June 30.

"Kiki is a very talented guy," Prokhorov said, adding, "I wish him well."

Prokhorov said he planned to attend "25 percent of the home games," a very small fraction of the schedule, because of the demands of running his other businesses, which include banking, media and precious metals. He has appointed a Russian executive, Irina Pavlova, the president of Onexim Sports and Entertainment, to oversee the team and the arena on a full-time basis. Pavlova will live in New York and serve as the conduit between Thorn and Prokhorov.

In business and in his prior stewardship of CSKA, Prokhorov had a reputation for his hands-off style, a point he emphasized many times. Thorn will have the authority to hire a new general manager and coach.

"I give staff the right to make mistakes," he said. "It's very important. Because I am making mistakes all the time."

In the search for a new coach, Prokhorov listed only one requirement — that the person have N.B.A. coaching experience, which would rule out major college candidates, such as Duke's Mike Krzyzewski, as well as the top European coaches. There had been reports of the Nets making a lavish offer to Krzyzewski.

"Coach K, he's a great coach," Prokhorov said, "but I'm looking for the N.B.A.-experienced coach."

The Nets' most important task this summer is rebuilding the roster, an effort that will start with trying to recruit James. Prokhorov said he planned to be in New York when free agency opens July 1 and will be an active participant in the process. Showing a full grasp of N.B.A. tampering rules, he wisely deflected any questions about James.

"I never heard this name," he said with a smile.

It seemed to be on his mind, however. When Prokhorov, who played basketball in college, was asked about his own skills, he quipped, coyly, "Not as good as free agent coming."

He seemed to play down any role that Jay-Z, the minority owner and music mogul, might play in recruiting James. Jay-Z is an icon to many N.B.A. players, and a close friend of James.

"I think it's more than enough that he's very passionate for the team," Prokhorov said, "and I think it's a management job to look for free agents."

Occasionally, Prokhorov turned the tables and asked reporters questions, wondering aloud if he should change the team's name.

"Is it O.K., Nets, or do we need to find something new?" he asked. "I need your piece of advice."

A renowned playboy, Prokhorov joked he could name the team after a girlfriend — "And every time I change, I need to change the name of the team," he said, drawing another round of laughter.

With an estimated worth of $17.8 billion, Prokhorov can buy just about anything. Reviving the Nets will pose a steep challenge.

"I like competition," he said, adding with a chuckle, "nothing can stop me."

April 30, 2013

Q. and A. with Jason Collins

by Frank Bruni

On the day after Jason Collins made history by becoming the first active athlete in any of America's four major sports leagues to acknowledge that he's gay, he hopped on the phone from Los Angeles to talk briefly with me about the reaction to his announcement, and the road he traveled to this juncture. This interview has been edited and condensed.

Where are you right now?

I'm driving from my house, on my way to go work out. I'm one of those people who likes a routine and my routine in the summertime is working out. So yesterday, obviously, being the day that it was, I missed a workout.

What about the reaction to your coming-out has most surprised or impressed you?

I expected some support for my teammates, from my coaches, but to get all the support from every single person I talked to…from the N.B.A. family, the Stanford family. It's been overwhelming, and then beyond that, it doesn't get any bigger than the leader of the free world giving you a call and saying you did a good thing, congratulations — that I did something not only to help myself but to empower others, to help others. It's just remarkable and overwhelming.

Did you have much of a heads-up or expectation that President Obama would call? Where were you when the call came in?

That was out of the blue. I spoke with President Clinton yesterday, but I've had a relationship with the Clinton family. Chelsea and my brother's wife were bridesmaids in each other's weddings. They [the Clintons] came to my graduation party at Stanford. I've known the Clinton family and President

Clinton said he would reach out to the Obama administration. And I spoke with Valerie Jarrett yesterday and I assumed that that was it.

[Then, at his agent's house] we get a call. A woman identified herself and said, "Can you hold for the president?" Sure! A part of me in the back of my mind thought this was going to be the biggest practical joke ever. But then the president gets on the line and his voice is so distinctive, the way he talks. It was amazing.

While most reaction has seemingly been positive, some wasn't. Were you aware that Chris Broussard of ESPN said you weren't a Christian if you're openly and actively gay, and what's your response?

My response is, first, I am a Christian. I know other gay and lesbian members of the community, the LGBT community, who are practicing Christians. This is all about tolerance and acceptance and America is the best country in the world because we're all entitled to our opinions and beliefs but we don't have to agree. And obviously I don't agree with his statement. This is where the discussion begins.

People are my advocate and they're saying, you know, he's a great teammate and it shouldn't and it doesn't matter. It shouldn't matter and it doesn't matter what his sexual orientation is, but it's just about the person, it's about the teammate, it's about this guy is all about the team and making the team better and helping us win basketball games and that's where the conversation should go.

You said on *Good Morning America* that you don't know of any other gay pro basketball players. Could there really not be any others, or is that an illustration of how tightly shut the closet door is in sports?

Statistically speaking, I am probably not the only one. Statistically speaking. But since no one else has raised their hand, you don't know for sure. But statistically speaking, I would say I'm 99.9 percent sure there are others.

So why are none of them out? Why does sports seem to lag behind so many other arenas of society in terms of having openly gay people in it?

You know that you're going to put yourself out there. Coming out is a difficult decision, period, regardless of what your profession is. I describe it as baking in the oven, you just need more time to develop to be comfortable in your own skin, to be comfortable in your own private life. Anytime you're a professional athlete you're already in the spotlight. And some guys like me might have felt, you don't want to be a distraction.

At the end of the day it's all about winning basketball games and your professional conduct and your work ethic. Making your private life public — it's funny, I've been playing a game on my iPad called Domino with one of my teammates. You send it, you go back and forth, sometimes it takes a week to finish the game. Yesterday I make this big statement and I go back to Domino on my iPad and it's my turn in the game. And then I play and I send it and it's his turn. So I made this big declaration but — our relationship, nothing's changed. I hope someday that's what this turns into, being gay.

You said in your *Sports Illustrated* article that over the years, you didn't tell anyone in basketball that you were gay. But were you able to have a gay romantic life outside of basketball? A circle of friends that included gay men?

That question speaks to my private life, and I'm not going to answer. I know the question you're asking. For me, I don't want to talk about specifics in my private life. I've had friendships. I definitely have friends who are gay.

Are you ready for all the scrutiny that comes with the precedent you've set? With the role you've taken on?

I hope so. [Laughs.] It's kind of hard to reverse course right now. I'm just going to be myself. I think that's what's most important, that I live my honest, genuine life. You make a decision to try to make yourself happy in life. You're not going to be able to please everyone.

You said in the article that you'd "endured years of misery." What did you mean by that?

It's tough to live a lie. It's really tough: I describe it as you know the sky is blue but you tell yourself it's red. It's an insane logic. It's tough to continue to live with lies and half-truths. It weighs on you. You put on a mask, but at the end of the day, you're not happy telling yourself a lie over and over again to the point where I am now being honest and truthful and not having to have a censor button, it's liberating.

Some smart commentary after your announcement noted how helpful it could be that the first openly gay major league athlete is also black, because young gay black men can't look around and see as many prominent openly gay black men as openly gay white men. Did you notice and were you struck over the years by that lack of examples?

I was fortunate. Like most people, you look to your family first, and I had an uncle who was gay. My Uncle Mark, who lives in New York. So I had a great role model who I knew I would eventually be able to talk to. And he's been in a long-term relationship with his partner. They recently got engaged. Since I've been in high school, they've been together. So I had that role model in my uncle already. I've been very blessed. I didn't have to look far.

You're a free agent. Let's say you don't get picked up for the next season. Will you ever know for sure whether coming out was a factor?

I'm sure that teams will look at my basketball, look at what I have to offer. My role in the N.B.A. is as a backup center, and I know that I'll be ready at any moment. Seeing the tweets yesterday from my teammates, the Wizards, going all the way back to my teammates from the Nets, to Jason Kidd: They talk about what a great teammate I am.

Is it possible this disclosure — this new honesty, and the freedom it brings — will make you a better player?

I think so. They'll look at me and think: This guy's speaking honestly. My teammates look at me sort of like Yoda a little bit. The old veteran. The old guy who can still get it done. I impart my knowledge. I've earned that right as a 12-year N.B.A. veteran.

Several readers wrote to me this morning not just to express admiration for you, but to point out that you're able to do this because of many men and women who came out when it was much riskier and carried a potentially bigger price. Do you feel indebted to them, and to anyone in particular?

I'm a black gay male, so there are so many people from the civil rights movement and then also from the gay rights movement. And sports figures. The list goes on and on. There are too many names to mention. Martina Navratilova. I'm a huge fan of hers. And even today with Brittney Griner, Esera Tuaolo, Robbie Rogers, Dave Kopay. There are so many people who have come before me both as a black male and then as a gay male, who have sort of paved the road for me.

Now it's time for me to pave the road for somebody else, to be a great teammate, society being the team. It's my responsibility to acknowledge those who came before me, give credit to them, and then there are those who are going to come after me, and it's my responsibility to lift them up.

APRIL 30, 2018

Retired N.B.A. Coach Don Nelson Talks Playoffs, Poker and, Uh, Weed

BY ALEX WILLIAMS

The Hall of Fame legend, now 77 and living in Maui, muses about retirement, getting stoned with Willie Nelson, and growing his own strand called "Nellie Kush." This interview has been edited and condensed.

MAUI — Regrets, he's had a few. But say this about Don Nelson, the retired basketball coach: He definitely did it his way.

On the way to 1,335 regular-season victories (a record), basketball's mad scientist rocked pink fish ties on the sideline, quaffed Bud Lites at news conferences and helped change the way the game is played with "Nellie Ball," a guerrilla-warfare strategy built around speedy, undersize lineups.

With the N.B.A. playoffs underway, we caught up with Mr. Nelson in his cavernous poker room, a Hall of Fame–caliber man cave where he hosts the island's most exclusive poker game with Willie Nelson, Woody Harrelson and Owen Wilson. Inside the paint, outside the box — there is only one Nellie.

Nice beard. Is it new?

It was my wife's idea. She told me she wanted to "get some of that ugly" off my face.

So this is where those big games go down with Willie, Woody and Owen. How big are the pots?

They can get up to $2,000 to $3,000, especially when Willie is in. He never saw a card he didn't like. He raises every time, no matter what. Every time it goes by him, it's $50, $50, $50. I'm conservative. But Willie, man, he's wild. Woody is wild. Owen's pretty good. Woody's a terrible card player.

Pretty good chess player, though.
Oh, very good. Play you fast or slow.

That's a serious shuffleboard table you have here. Do you guys play for money?
Yeah, I'd say so. I've paid for that shuffleboard table at least 10 times over.

I see you're wearing a Warriors hat. Do you like their chances this year?
I haven't studied it enough to give you a good answer. Everybody says Houston is really good. I don't like Houston, personally, but it's just because of a lot of competition over the years — with Dallas, you know. I'm a Warrior guy, so I'm rooting for the Warriors, but Steph has got to be 100 percent to beat that team.

You hung it up in 2010, just before the Warriors turned into a juggernaut. Do you miss coaching?
I really don't. I was pretty well fried by that time. I think I had one year left on my contract when they sold the team.

You missed out on the Warriors' recent championships. Do you think you could have won a title with the Warriors in the '90s if that squad with Chris Mullin, Latrell Sprewell and Chris Webber had stayed together?
No.

Why not?
I didn't think Webber — at that time in his life, anyway — was ready to play winning basketball, or do anything winning at that point. He was a pretty confused young guy. He was about the toughest guy I ever coached. It took him a long time.

You never got your ring as a coach, but you got five as a player for the Celtics in the '60s and '70s. How would you describe your game?

I could ball a little bit. I was a slow runner, so I was a perfect trailer guy. I could rebound, I could pass, I could shoot. I could do a lot of things to fit in, you know, if you need an extra guy. I was just kind of an average guy that fit in with a really great team.

Sounds like a guy who went on to become another great coach, Pat Riley.

Well, I was better than Pat [laughs]. He comes here a lot, too. I was just with him over Christmas.

How did you get hooked on Hawaii?

I used to do some stuff for the armed services with a bunch of the other Celtics and a couple of guys from other teams. We'd go visit the hospitals, then they'd give us a week of R&R in Hawaii on the way back from Vietnam. We just loved that week, and then we'd miss our flight, and end up two weeks. Then another week. I just thought it's the most beautiful place I'd ever seen, and I've been all over the world.

Those hospital visits in Vietnam must have been intense.

It was very, very difficult. Oh my goodness, it was a life-changing experience. You'd walk into the wards, these guys from the front lines, some had just woken up with no legs, no arms. It was the hardest thing I've done. It almost made an alcoholic out of me. You'd visit those hospitals all day and go out and drink all night.

What's your daily life here like?

I've been buying real estate for 20 years here, and building houses and renting them out. So that's our business now. A lot of Warrior fans stay with us. I built this place next to me. It's not a wedding chapel, but they have weddings there. My daughter Lee runs that. She's an interesting story. I had that daughter out of wedlock. I knew nothing about her for 29 years.

How did you find out about her?

I was in Dallas, coaching, and my secretary brought in this letter. It said, "Dear Mr. Nelson. In 1968, you met a young girl in Washington, D.C., by the name of Debby Dial. Nine months later, I was born." I had been on the road with the Celtics, playing the Bullets. We were doing some of that stuff when I was playing, which wasn't the best thing to do. But I did remember that lady's name. I thought, "Wow, this could be true."

So we brought her into Dallas, and there was this 6-foot blond lady who looks like all my other kids, and I'm going, "She's mine." I helped her finish college, met the parents who raised her, because she was adopted. My wife and I have six other kids, but she's the only one who's moved to Maui. Isn't that funny?

And you've got an agrarian venture over here in Maui, too?

I've got a farm, yeah, I do. We grow some pot and flowers and coffee, and I've got a fish farm up there.

Pot?

I've got a medical card. I'm legal here. When any athlete gets old, every injury you have sustained seems to resurrect. It helps me deal with the pain without pain pills, and helps with that stress.

Have you been into cannabis for long?

No, I didn't smoke until maybe three or four years ago. I never smoked when I was coaching. I just started. Willie got me smoking.

He would do it.

He would do it. I didn't think I'd ever be a pot smoker, but hanging out with Willie and Woody and guys like that, you know, everybody smokes in those games. It just became kind of natural. Usually you're smoking with your friends, sitting around, telling stories, you smoke a bowl. It's not that I smoke all the time. I usually just smoke at night during poker games. Like Willie told me, it's hard to be depressed when you're smoking pot.

How do you like cannabis compared to alcohol?

I don't drink anymore, because I like pot better. It's about the same as alcohol, except you don't have the aftereffect. There's no hangover. I mean, I don't drink to excess, anyway. But you know, even if you have a couple of drinks, you're liable to have a headache in the morning.

On your farm, do you grow cannabis for dispensaries?

No, I just grow for myself. You're allowed to grow up to 10 plants, so you have plenty to smoke. I've never sold. I would never do that.

How is the quality?

Oh, it's great. Great stuff. It's called Nellie Kush. It's O.G. and Hindu Kush. Hindu Kush is really good. It comes from India and the guy that brought it over mixed the two of them, so we've got Nellie Kush now.

MAY 16, 2018

Chris Paul:
Point Guard, Activist, Union Boss

BY DAVID GELLES

Ever since Chris Paul joined the National Basketball Association in 2005, drafted fourth out of Wake Forest, he has been near the center of the action.

He won the rookie of the year award in 2006, was named most valuable player at the 2013 All-Star Game, and was a star for both the New Orleans Hornets and Los Angeles Clippers. This season, Mr. Paul — known as CP3, for his jersey number — teamed up with James Harden on the Houston Rockets, creating a fearsome duo that has led their team deep into the playoffs. (They are currently playing the Golden State Warriors in the Western Conference finals.)

Over the years, Mr. Paul's roles and responsibilities around the league have expanded. He is outspoken on social issues, joining LeBron James and other stars in a moving protest against police shootings at the 2016 ESPY Awards. And since 2013, he has served as president of the National Basketball Players Association, the league's union for players.

One of the highest-paid athletes in the world, Mr. Paul is now building his own business empire. He has invested in Wtrmln Wtr, which makes cold-pressed watermelon juice, and Muzik, which makes high-end headphones. And he recently founded a media company, Oh Dipp Productions, which produced a documentary for ESPN about his decision to join the Rockets.

This interview, which was condensed and edited for clarity, was conducted in New York.

What was your first job?
I worked at my granddad's service station every summer from the time I was 7 or 8 years old. My granddad was everything. He had the first African-American-owned service station in North Carolina. In high school, if I

wanted some money to buy something, wanted Jordans, my granddad, would say: "Come work at the service station. Earn it."

When did you know you were going to have a career as a player?

When I went to college, they already had a starting point guard. Then he had an appendectomy a week and a half before our first game of the season. First game comes, we play at Madison Square Garden against Memphis, Coach told me I was starting. We win the game, we go to the second game. Coach says, "Since you started, you'll start again." The rest is history.

How did you prepare for the N.B.A.?

I made my biggest jump between when I declared for the draft and my rookie year, that summer. I worked out for about two months by myself; it was the hardest training I've ever done. Then on draft night, a commentator said that I was going to be too small to play in the N.B.A. That's all I needed to hear. I've always loved to be the underdog. That just pushes me.

Why do you try to steal the ball so often?

After I broke my hand, I was like, I'm done stealing the ball. They can have it, I'll figure out something else to do. But it's just in me. When someone takes the ball into the lane, I just know where that ball is going to be placed. I know the path it has to travel, and I just have to have it. In order to win big, you've got to go for it.

You've been involved with the National Basketball Players Association for 13 years and are now the president. How has the organization changed during that time?

I remember when I started, the meetings were just guys sitting in a room, and we would just listen to people come up and talk at us. Back in 2011 we had like an 18-hour meeting between players and the league. There'd be a lot of posturing, and [the former N.B.A. commissioner] David Stern wanted drug testing for players. He had his shirt undone and was yelling. It used to get a little heated in those meetings.

When we went into the most recent labor negotiations, it was nothing like that. Now the guys in our league understand the business so much more. We understand what our value is and we are much more involved in the business of the game. It's been about taking our union back.

What are your priorities as head of the players association?

The thing we're most proud of is the health insurance for retired players. LeBron James, Melo, D-Wade, Stephen Curry, me, all of us have something in common — at some point we'll all be retired players. I still remember the meeting when we talked to the players about sacrificing a certain amount of dollars for the retired players. It's something no other league has.

Another thing that we're trying to help guys with is financial literacy. I'm around a lot of 20-year-old guys who are thrust into this lifestyle with all this money and nobody knows what to do. The hardest thing is when I see guys who I looked up to when I was kid, I had their jersey, and now they have nothing to show for it.

Michele Roberts is now the first woman to serve as executive director of the players association. How's she doing?

I credit our players for seeing in her something that a lot of people probably questioned initially — you know, to bring in a woman to oversee 450 of the most recognizable male athletes in the world. I can't say enough about her and her selflessness. She never wants any of the credit. Sometimes they say the quietest person in the room may be the one who knows everything that's going on, and she's consistent.

You're outspoken on social issues. Do you think athletes have a responsibility to speak out on issues they care about?

You have to do what makes you comfortable. People can tell when it's not genuine or when it's forced. But for me — being a father, having family and also understanding what I mean to other people that may not have a voice — it's important.

I'm not sure if you've seen David Letterman sit down with President Obama, but Obama said something that was so true. If 20 years from now my son comes to me and says, "Daddy, you knew this was going on and you didn't say anything about it," then I'm just part of the problem. Even if we don't get an opportunity to experience the real change in the culture, at least our kids will.

How do you think about investment decisions and sponsorship opportunities?

When you're younger, you're trying to get a name for yourself, and if such-and-such fast food company comes and says, "Here, we'll pay you such-and-such to endorse it and say this and say that," you're like, "Hey, give it to me. Whatever it is, I'm going to do it." But as I got older, I realized that I can only be in business with things that I believe in. And so that's what happened with investing. And that's why I invested in Wtrmln Wtr. This is something that I actually believe in and it coincides with my lifestyle.

A LinkedIn reader, Varun Paul, asks what you did to make sure you clicked with the Rockets as quickly as possible.

The best way that you build chemistry is time. So me, James, Trevor, a lot of us, we spent a lot of time together that summer playing pickup, going to eat, going out and having real conversations.

What else are you working on right now?

Me and my wife went to visit my son's school in L.A., and we walked in and it was a nice classroom with laptops and iPads and Smartboards, and I got mad. I said, "I don't like that kids on the other side of town don't get this." So that day, we started putting learning centers in underserved communities.

And while that's good and well, at times that can be putting Band-Aids on the real issues. So we did a housing fund and talked about going into some of these housing developments and basically subsidizing some of the housing, putting teachers and medical staff in these different communities. We're always just trying to level the playing field.

What's your advice for new players in the league?

Find your why. It sounds simple, but there's a lot of guys that play professionally, and it may not be for the same reasons that I do it. I play because I couldn't imagine not playing basketball. I always say, "You all are going to pay me to play this game? I'll take it." I love it that much. You may come across a guy who plays professionally and likes the money, who likes the attention or they may like the girls. Our why doesn't have to be the same, but the work ethic should be.

33

Racism and Revenue

Months after Adam Silver took the commissioner's baton from David Stern, his first full-blown conflagration broke out, as potentially ruinous to the league's reputation as the Malice at the Palace had been a decade earlier.

This time, the misanthropy was an owner's, the Clippers' Donald Sterling, who had long been an embarrassment to the sport, competitively and behaviorally. For decades, the league office had strangely allowed Sterling to operate with impunity, as it had done with James Dolan in New York. But when audio of Sterling making crudely disparaging remarks about blacks spread like a virus on the internet, Silver was forced to act, quickly, and largely by his angry, increasingly activist players.

LeBron James wasted little time in issuing a moral conviction. "There is no room for Donald Sterling in our league," he said.

Just weeks before the Sterling story broke, I interviewed Kevin Johnson, who had been appointed by Chris Paul and the players association to lead the search for a new union executive director. Johnson lamented how the union was adrift at a time when its "financial power and leverage should be greater than it's ever been," given a $5 billion global industry.

In the immediate aftermath of the Sterling audio imbroglio, players suddenly had a unifying cause and a smooth politician with the court cred to galvanize James and the players while applying public and private pressure to Silver, who intuitively recognized the need to resolutely meet his first crisis.

Within weeks, the normally combative Sterling was gone from the league. Months later, less-explosive but insensitively expressed sentiments related to race precipitated an ownership change in Atlanta. Without defending Sterling, the always opinionated Mark Cuban expressed reservations about what behavioral precedents the league was setting for owners — perhaps with good reason, as a March 2018 *Sports Illustrated* report shed light on rampant sexual harassment within the Mavericks organization.

The good news for Cuban and the others now on notice that they weren't above it all was the price Sterling got for his championship-less franchise: $2 billion from Steve Ballmer, the former Microsoft CEO.

Sterling may have laughed all the way to the bank, but no tears were shed over his overdue exit.

MAY 23, 2014

Cuban Talks His Way Onto a Limb Occupied by Sterling

BY WILLIAM C. RHODEN

For nearly a month, Adam Silver, the commissioner of the N.B.A., has managed to isolate Donald Sterling, the owner of the Los Angeles Clippers, on an island. With one salvo of explosive comments, Mark Cuban, the owner of the Dallas Mavericks, has put his fellow team owners on that island as well.

In April, Sterling was barred from the N.B.A. for life and fined $2.5 million by the N.B.A. after recordings of him making racist comments about African-Americans were made public.

At a business conference Wednesday, Cuban admitted to being less than enlightened. "I know I'm prejudiced and I know I'm bigoted in a lot of different ways," Cuban said.

Then he made the gaffe.

"If I see a black kid in a hoodie and it's late at night, I'm walking to the other side of the street," he said in a video interview for *Inc.*'s GrowCo Conference in Nashville. "And if on that side of the street, there's a guy that has tattoos all over his face — white guy, bald head, tattoos everywhere — I'm walking back to the other side of the street."

It is one thing to initiate a dialogue about racism but something else to spew tone-deaf ignorance in an interview. The shooting death of Trayvon Martin in 2012, the acquittal of George Zimmerman and the miscarriage of justice that the not-guilty verdict represented are wounds that, for many, have not healed. Some N.B.A. players, most notably LeBron James and his Miami Heat teammates, wore hoodies to protest the stereotyping that led to Martin's death.

"In hindsight, I should have used different examples," Cuban said. "I didn't consider the Trayvon Martin family, and I apologize to them for that."

By implying that not only Sterling, but also everyone else — team owners in the N.B.A. included — has a bias or two and believes in some unexpressed, bigoted stereotypes, Cuban was basically saying, Why isolate one owner?

My initial reaction to Cuban's comments was that he had just given Sterling substantial legal wiggle room. Sterling was being swept down a river by a fast-moving moral current and Cuban gave him a low-hanging limb to grab on to. Or, perhaps, Cuban saw an owner trapped in that gray space between public and private, and simply wanted to extricate him.

"I know that I'm not perfect," Cuban also said Wednesday. "While we all have our prejudices and bigotries, we have to learn that it's an issue that we have to control, that it's part of my responsibility as an entrepreneur to try to solve it, not just to kick the problem down the road.

"I think we're all bigots, and I don't think there's any question about that."

I wonder what Cuban's fellow owners feel about that? Do they think they are bigots?

Is Robert Sarver, the majority owner of the Phoenix Suns, a bigot? In 2010 he had his team wear Los Suns jerseys to protest an immigration law Arizona had adopted.

Is Richard DeVos, the 88-year-old owner of the Orlando Magic, a bigot? He does not support same-sex marriage and once gave $100,000 to an effort to ban it in Florida.

What Cuban is suggesting is that every one of us harbors unexpressed prejudices. Could any of us stand the scrutiny of having all of our private conversations made public? That day may be fast approaching: Social media is ushering in an era of transparency that is shrinking the distance between one's private words and publicly expressed views.

"The thing that scares me about this whole thing is, I don't want to be a hypocrite and I think I might have to be," Cuban said, quite likely referring to the expected vote by the N.B.A. owners to expel Sterling. "Being a hypocrite bothers me more than anything, after my family, so it won't be fun."

Asked how he might be hypocritical, Cuban said, "Well, I just sat here and said I'm a bigot."

More than the legal exercise, Sterling's remarks, expressed in private, and Cuban's, expressed in public, raise questions about the qualifications to own an N.B.A. franchise.

"Cuban's comment calls the question: What standards besides wealth qualify one to own an N.B.A. franchise?" said Linda S. Greene, a law professor at the University of Wisconsin-Madison. "These teams may be privately held, but the ownership of one is a privilege and constitutes a public trust. Therefore, the N.B.A. has a duty to probe deeply both beliefs and actions to ensure that those who steward these unique community institutions are worthy of that trust."

Greene added, "In our post-Sterling world, the possession of billions of dollars may be necessary to the ownership of an N.B.A. franchise, but it will never again be sufficient."

Cuban was a thorn in the side of the former commissioner David Stern. Now he is pricking the consciousness of the new commissioner and the owners. Silver has said he is open to beginning a dialogue about racism. The league's lawyers are probably wondering why Cuban had to start one now.

MAY 29, 2014

Steve Ballmer Said to Sign
$2 Billion Deal to Buy Clippers

BY SCOTT CACCIOLA AND RICHARD SANDOMIR

The former Microsoft chief executive Steve Ballmer has agreed to pay $2 billion for the Los Angeles Clippers, according to a person briefed on the negotiations. If approved by the National Basketball Association, the sale would end a troubling situation for the league and rank as one of the largest deals in sports history.

Mr. Ballmer emerged Thursday night as the last suitor standing in a dizzying bidding process that started when the N.B.A. announced last month that it would try to force Donald Sterling to sell the team. Mr. Sterling had been recorded making racist comments in a private conversation, an episode that touched off a national discussion about race and delivered a public relations blow to the league during its showcase period, the playoffs.

Rochelle Sterling, Mr. Sterling's wife and a co-owner of the Clippers, signed the deal with Mr. Ballmer, and their contract will be sent to the N.B.A. for final approval, the person briefed on the negotiations said. Mr. Ballmer, 58, was already vetted by the league in 2013 when he was part of an investor group seeking to buy the Sacramento Kings, which means the process could be expedited.

But the deal faces possible obstacles.

Mr. Sterling's position remains uncertain. He was said to have authorized his wife to negotiate with potential buyers, but she needed his power of attorney to sign off on an agreement. Mr. Sterling's lawyer, Maxwell Blecher, said Wednesday that Ms. Sterling did not have it. Mr. Blecher also said that, as incentive to agree to sell the team, Mr. Sterling wanted the N.B.A. to drop its charges that he had violated the league's constitution.

Mr. Sterling, who has vowed to fight the league in its efforts to terminate his ownership of the Clippers, is scheduled to appear at a special hearing

Tuesday to answer to charges that he damaged the N.B.A. by making the racist statements. He was barred from the league for life last month.

Commissioner Adam Silver said last week that he would prefer for the Sterlings to sell the team voluntarily. A vote of the league's other owners could force them to sell.

The Los Angeles Times was the first to report that Mr. Ballmer had reached an agreement with Ms. Sterling.

If the Clippers sell for $2 billion, the price would be the highest paid for an N.B.A. team, far exceeding the $550 million that the Milwaukee Bucks recently sold for. Major League Baseball's Dodgers, the Clippers' Los Angeles neighbors, sold for $2.15 billion two years ago.

But a critical difference is that the Dodgers' buyers received much more for their money: the team, as well as Dodger Stadium; an expiring local television contract that the new owners flipped into a long-term, multibillion-dollar payout from Time Warner Cable to start their own network; and a joint venture on the parking lots and land around the stadium with the former owner, Frank McCourt.

In addition to a suddenly ascendant team with a miserable past, Mr. Ballmer would have a training center and a lease at Staples Center that excludes luxury-suite revenue. The team, under new ownership, would benefit from the boons expected in their next local cable contract and the N.B.A.'s next round of national deals. The new local and league contracts will start in the 2016–17 season.

Three bidders had emerged as the top contenders for the team.

One group including Oprah Winfrey; the entertainment mogul David Geffen; Larry Ellison, the software tycoon who runs Oracle and made a losing bid to buy the Golden State Warriors; and Mark Walter and Todd Boehly, two of the principals of Guggenheim Partners, which put together the group that acquired the Dodgers two years ago.

A second group in the bidding for the Clippers included Antony P. Ressler, who runs the private equity firm Ares Management, and the former N.B.A. player Grant Hill. Mr. Ballmer submitted a bid without any partners.

The purchase of the Clippers would open a new chapter in the life of Mr. Ballmer, a technology billionaire who has lately found himself without much of an occupation. He left his chief executive job at Microsoft this year, under pressure from its board of directors to accelerate his retirement after the company had struggled in a number of key new markets.

But unlike his fellow Microsoft billionaires, Mr. Ballmer has done little besides work at Microsoft for the past 34 years. William H. Gates, a Microsoft co-founder and former chief executive, has become a philanthropist, and Paul Allen, another co-founder, owns the Portland Trail Blazers and the Seattle Seahawks.

Mr. Ballmer is relatively unflashy, even though his net worth is estimated at $20 billion by Forbes. He grew up in Detroit, the son of a Ford Motor Company manager, and was known as a commanding, sometimes bullying leader at Microsoft who underestimated major changes in technology that helped lead to the rise of competitors like Google and Apple.

He has made no secret of his passion for sports, particularly basketball. In interviews while he was running Microsoft, Mr. Ballmer said he made a point of attending as many of his son's high school basketball games as possible.

He tried unsuccessfully to bring an N.B.A. franchise back to Seattle in 2013 as part of an investor group seeking to buy the Sacramento Kings. Like many people in the Seattle area, Mr. Ballmer had felt the sting of the SuperSonics' departure for Oklahoma City, where they became the Thunder.

The $1.1 billion paid for the Miami Dolphins in 2009 is the peak price for a N.F.L. team, with the Cleveland Browns, who were sold two years ago, a little behind. N.F.L. franchises share in the most lucrative national television deals of all the major leagues.

No one knows if Mr. Sterling would have put the Clippers on the market in his lifetime unprompted. But the timing for a sale seems fortuitous.

With the Lakers suddenly the losing team in town, the Clippers are considered a prized commodity. They have stars like Chris Paul and Blake Griffin and a brand-name, title-winning coach, Doc Rivers. And just getting rid of Mr. Sterling, who has, by nearly universal opinion, run a laughingstock of a franchise, should make the team more valuable to a willing buyer.

34
Losing Propositions

The clash over what is best for a team as opposed to the N.B.A. existed long before Gregg Popovich. It's still difficult to recall anyone being as blatant in his defiance of league wishes as the Spurs' resident recalcitrant was in November 2012.

In a nationally televised Thursday night game in Miami, Popovich sat two aging veterans, Tim Duncan and Manu Ginobili; prime-career starting guards Tony Parker and Danny Green, while the rising forward Kawhi Leonard and the rotation swingman Stephen Jackson sat out with injuries.

It was the Spurs' fourth game in five nights, but David Stern was stung by the seeming surrender. In one of his final punitive acts as commissioner, he fined the Spurs $250,000, igniting in earnest the debate about not trying to win a game in order to rest players and later — thanks to the 76ers and their Sam Hinkie–devised Process — tanking an entire season in the pursuit of a top draft pick.

No assets were more precious to Stern than his negotiated television deals, the N.B.A.'s lifeblood. Back in the 1990s, he and the Bulls owner Jerry Reinsdorf, typically a staunch ally, wound up in a litigious row over Reinsdorf's refusal to remove his team's games from free national cable television in what Stern saw as unhealthy competition with the league's network deals.

On the night of the game in Miami, Stern issued a terse statement, personally apologizing to "all N.B.A. fans." But Popovich emerged validated, if not victorious. His junior varsity produced a compelling underdog drama, *Hoosiers* at South Beach, the Heat needing a late Ray Allen 3 to win by 5.

In a league whose schedule could be murderous on players' bodies, the resting of multiple starters or stars was sure to be copied. This was another problem inherited by Silver, who took steps to ease the scheduling burden and later more to disincentivize draft tanking.

No one actually believed these issues would ever be totally resolved, not in a sport which sent 16 of its 30 regular-season participants to the playoffs. Or as Popovich barked after the Miami game, "I'm not concerned with finishing first, I'm trying to win a championship, and that's all."

Nor was it lost on anyone that his Spurs took Miami to seven thrilling games in the finals that season, and came back the following spring to literally dismantle the Heat for their fifth overall title. That $250,000 was the best money the Spurs ever spent.

April 7, 2017

When N.B.A. Coaches Rest Their Stars, the Owners Get Restless

by Scott Cacciola

It is neither glamorous nor new, but Commissioner Adam Silver considers it the most important issue for the N.B.A. right now: star players missing games for the sole purpose of rest.

With more coaches sitting players in recent weeks as they prepare their teams for the long haul of the postseason, much to the chagrin of fans and the N.B.A.'s broadcast partners, the issue was a main topic of conversation among the league's owners at their annual meetings in New York this week.

On Friday, Silver said there was agreement among the owners that teams should avoid resting "multiple players" for games that are broadcast on national television. In addition, Silver said, the owners concluded that teams should rest players for home games whenever possible, rather than sit them on the road when opposing fans might miss their only chance to see them play.

"Resting is a complex issue with a lot of factors to consider," Silver said at a news conference in Midtown Manhattan. "But there was a consensus on the need to find the right balance between appropriate rest for our players on one hand and our obligation to our fans and business partners on the other hand."

In recent seasons, the N.B.A. has sought ways to reduce the instances when teams play games on consecutive days, known as the dreaded back-to-back, both to limit wear and tear on players and to lessen the likelihood that coaches will rest players for one of those two games.

As a part of the new collective bargaining agreement between the league and the players' union, which will take effect in July, the 2017–18 season will start about a week earlier than usual to space out games and reduce the number of back-to-backs. But they will not be eliminated completely.

"I'm particularly sympathetic to our players," Silver said, "because my sense is our players take the brunt of it, but they're not the ones who are choosing to rest. Just so it's clear, I haven't heard of instances in the league where players are raising their hands and saying, 'Coach, please rest me.' These are team-led decisions."

Silver's remarks came in the wake of two particularly high-profile occurrences of coaches resting stars.

In December, the Cavaliers left LeBron James, Kyrie Irving and Kevin Love back in Cleveland as the remainder of the team traveled to Memphis for a game against the Grizzlies. Then, in March, Coach Steve Kerr of the Golden State Warriors rested Stephen Curry, Klay Thompson, Draymond Green and Andre Iguodala for a nationally televised game against the team's biggest conference rivals, the San Antonio Spurs.

A number of the Spurs' key players also sat out, but at least two of them — LaMarcus Aldridge and Kawhi Leonard — had significant health problems.

The game against the Spurs was the second half of a back-to-back for the Warriors, who were in the midst of a brutal stretch of their schedule. Like many coaches who have rested players on occasion, Kerr expressed sympathy for the fans who had paid a lot of money ahead of time to see the game — and, most likely, his crew of All-Stars. But he also stressed that the health of his players was of paramount importance.

Spurs Coach Gregg Popovich, who popularized the practice of resting players, recently defended the approach, suggesting that he had preserved some of his players' careers.

"We have definitely added years to people," Popovich told reporters this month. "So it's a trade-off. You want to see this guy in this one game? Or do you want to see him for three more years?"

It has been a persistent challenge for Silver throughout his three years as commissioner. In April 2015, for example, he described rest as an "ongoing discussion" with the players' union. His personal view, he said at the time, was that he would rather the league avoid engaging with coaches and general managers about the issue of playing time.

"I think it's a very slippery slope for the league office to start getting in the business of telling a coach or team what minutes a player should play," he said.

But last month, Silver sent a memo to the league's owners in which he described teams sitting players as an "extremely significant issue for our league" and urged the owners to become more involved in the decision-making process with their coaches. Silver also warned of the potential for "significant penalties."

On Friday, Silver struck a more conciliatory tone, saying the owners had discussed issuing "guidelines" for teams rather than "enforceable rules."

"It's not a function necessarily of owners calling coaches and saying, 'I'm now going to dictate to you or micromanage how you coach the team or how you choose minutes for a particular player,'" Silver said. "But these need to be organizational decisions where there's a fair balance between the competitive issues on one hand and the very real business issues on the other hand."

JUNE 20, 2018

Tank to the Top? Not So Fast

BY MICHAEL POWELL

This was the N.B.A. season in which up became down, the sunny day was abandoned for an embrace of the rainy, and the race to the championship penthouse paled next to the joy of a tumble down the league stairs.

This past winter, nearly a dozen of the league's bottom feeders benched stars, traded off ambulatory role players and made more inexplicable coaching decisions than usual, all in hopes of losing enough to gain a top spot in the N.B.A. draft lottery.

For half a decade now, the league's smart set — those cost-benefit, God-I-love-a-good-spreadsheet analytics guys who proliferate in N.B.A. front offices — have embraced a new creed: The best way to build a champion is to tear a decrepit team to the ground and reseed it with young and cheap talent from the draft.

They are almost certainly wrong.

With one or two exceptions, and those are most often impossible to predict, the tanking parade is a case of the hapless leading the dotards. Don't take my word for it. Akira Motomura, an economics professor at Stonehill College and a man who knows his way around a database, wrote an article two years ago with three other economists for the *Journal of Sports Economics:* Does it pay to build through the draft in the N.B.A.?

I can sum up their findings in two words: Not really.

"We could not conclude that entering the draft was bad for a team," Motomura told me. "But it's not a help."

It gets worse. It's not clear that it's much better to draft fifth than 25th. There was the barest difference in performance, perhaps 5 percent, between players picked at the top of the draft and those selected at the bottom.

Much like marine biologists looking at a particularly unfortunate river bottom, the economists found "dead zones" in the early and middle parts of the draft's first round. These are waters where the decision-making is so mediocre and the talent pool so murky that many teams emerge in worse shape than they entered.

It is not difficult to find a sweet pile of anecdotal data to back up this study. Let's take the 2011 N.B.A. draft. The Cleveland Cavaliers had the first choice and took that whirling scoring dervish Kyrie Irving. That was a good idea.

The Minnesota Timberwolves picked second and took the athletic forward Derrick Williams. That was a bad idea. He is an amiable fellow who at the age of 26 has only had one season in which he averaged in double figures in scoring, and he is currently holding on to his N.B.A. career by his fingertips.

The next three draft picks in that 2011 draft offered a trio of nice, industrial-strength N.B.A. centers: Enes Kanter, Tristan Thompson and Jonas Valanciunas. They are all nice, useful fellows, but none could be considered a difference maker in today's guard-heavy league.

The sixth pick that year went to the Washington Wizards, who chose Jan Vesely. You could be forgiven for asking: Who? Vesely played in the N.B.A. for three years before falling through the league floor. He currently plays for Fenerbahce of the Turkish Basketball Super League.

The best moments of that 2011 draft arguably happened outside of the top 10 picks, and they underlined a more important point: Nothing beats a quality organization. The Golden State Warriors took Klay Thompson with the 11th pick. The Indiana Pacers drafted Kawhi Leonard with the 15th pick and promptly had their pockets picked by the San Antonio Spurs, who traded for Leonard, who would become one of the league's top five players.

The Chicago Bulls held the last pick of the first round that year. With the 30th pick, they took the future four-time All-Star Jimmy Butler.

There is, in fact, a strong Darwinist flavor to the N.B.A. More than in most pro sports leagues, the best N.B.A. organizations and teams remain near the top, year after year. The Spurs, the Warriors, the Miami Heat and the Boston Celtics have consistently fielded winning teams. Yet they rarely appear in the draft lottery unless they've lifted a draft pick from some hapless franchise.

In fact, this study found that a team that achieves high mediocrity — say, 45 wins — is better off bringing in the best possible minds and carefully adding talent, rather than engaging in a tear-down. Those teams trend up more often than drift down.

As Motomura's study noted: "Very good organizations and G.M.s develop successful franchises that win more, even if they pick late in the first round."

Talk of the hapless naturally turns my eyes to my Knicks, the Sacramento Kings and the Phoenix Suns. Any fan of the aforementioned franchises would be advised to seek therapeutic help before persuading themselves their teams will find salvation through the draft.

The Kings are near *sui generis* in their ability to dive into the draft pool and emerge holding something unappetizing. As Al Iannazzone of *Newsday* pointed out, they have had four top-five picks and 11 top-10 choices in the past dozen years and missed the playoffs in each of those seasons.

As for my Knicks, they could self-publish their own how-to book of management dysfunctions.

I don't want to argue against innovation. The Philadelphia 76ers are seen as the great counterexample, a team that embarked on an epic spasm of losing, year after grinding year. That period became known as The Process, the mad vision of their former general manager Sam Hinkie.

You might even say it worked.

The 76ers emerged this year with a 52–30 record and in possession of two lottery-pick stars: Joel Embiid and Ben Simmons. The 76ers' success wound up being the moving snow plate that set off the avalanche of intentional losing the past few years.

Hinkie did not survive to reach the promised land with his team. The owners tired of his prophecies and Hinkie's role in The Process ended in 2016, but not before he penned a 7,000-word resignation letter that quoted physicists and philosophers and offered the following aphorisms: True innovators rarely are honored in their time; the N.B.A. fraternity often celebrates the wrong people for the wrong reasons; and "you can be wrong for the right reasons."

I particularly loved this fortune cookie line: "In this league, the long view picks at the lock of mediocrity."

In that same letter, he noted that his draft-early-and-often strategy, taken together with prescience, had helped the 76ers land such "especially talented" draft picks as centers Jahlil Okafor and Nerlens Noel. As it happens, both of those young men have N.B.A. careers on the intensive care list.

So, you might say the 76ers' draft-lottery strategy turned out to be more right than wrong for reasons that were often more wrong than right.

35
Solely Remarkable

Russell Westbrook notched his 42nd triple double in April 2017, surpassing Oscar Robertson's record 41. The Big O promptly paid tribute to Westbrook with a quote that was also — and perhaps even more so — an homage to himself.

Westbrook, Oscar said, "would have been great in any era."

LOL. Touché. Yes, and it counts.

Most people naturally viewed Westbrook's solo magnificence, following the departure of his tag-team partner Kevin Durant to Golden State, as a testament to the continued evolution of the 21st century athlete — bigger, stronger, fitter, faster and (Greek) freakier. And most probably waved off Oscar as a bitter old man, a chronic nitpicker and naysayer on the modern game.

As he wrote in his 2003 autobiography: "Kids want to dunk and shoot from deep and dribble through their legs a hundred times and there's nobody out there willing to teach them the right way to play."

While conceding that the pro game has been enhanced by across-the-board athleticism and the incorporation of international players with different skill sets, the old-time greats generally scoff at the notion that it is actually better and especially that they couldn't possibly compete with their descendants.

It is and has always been an argument that cannot be won, though points could be scored from either side.

Could Wilt Chamberlain score 100 points in today's N.B.A. game, as he did against the Knicks in March 1962 — the season in which Oscar pretty much invented and averaged a triple-double? Probably not, if only because he wouldn't get anywhere near enough touches in a 3-ball-crazed league. But while many remember Wilt lumbering downcourt and setting up shop in the post, the young version was an athlete to behold. He would have wreaked havoc in an up-tempo game.

What would Bill Russell look like in the modern game? Perhaps a bigger, more adult version of Draymond Green, the all-purpose All-Star.

Sports are cyclical and often what looks brand-new is not. As Kareem Abdul-Jabbar told me, referring to Oscar: "He was a master of the pick-and-roll, which is all they play now. It's also really unfortunate he didn't get to play in the 3-point-shot era because he had amazing range. In Milwaukee, we used to play H-O-R-S-E after practice and he'd be out there, way beyond what would become the arc. But the thing about Oscar that would make him great in any era was his leadership."

Intelligence. Basketball IQ. Confidence. Governance. Those qualities make a difference anywhere, anytime.

Dec. 4, 2014

Wilt the Stilt Becomes a Stamp

by David Davis

Wilt Chamberlain captured America's imagination for two decades. With his 7-foot-1 frame, his commanding presence on the basketball court, his ability to rebound and score and his astounding athleticism, he became one of the most memorable players in N.B.A. history.

Now, Chamberlain, the only man to score 100 points in an N.B.A. game, will become the first player from the league to be honored with a postage stamp in his image. And fittingly enough, the two versions being issued by the Postal Service are nearly two inches long, or about a third longer than the usual stamp.

It would not be right any other way for the player known as Wilt the Stilt and alternately as the Big Dipper. Chamberlain died in 1999 at 63, but his name still resonates in the sport. And even at its atypical size, the new stamp could barely contain Chamberlain's dimensions.

"We still had trouble fitting him into those proportions," said Kadir Nelson, the artist who painted the images.

Nelson created two versions of the stamp. One shows Chamberlain in the act of shooting with his first N.B.A. team, the Philadelphia Warriors, for whom he started playing in 1959. The other depicts him rebounding for the Los Angeles Lakers, his final club, for whom he played from 1968 to 1973.

The stamps will be dedicated Friday, in Philadelphia, his hometown, at halftime of the 76ers' game against the Oklahoma City Thunder.

The ceremony comes at a frustrating time: The 76ers avoided tying the record for the worst start to a season in N.B.A. history Wednesday night when they ended their 0–17 run with a victory at Minnesota.

But for a few minutes Friday night, Philadelphia fans old enough to remember can think back to the days when Chamberlain — first as a Warrior and later as a 76er — engaged in epic battles with the Boston Celtics' Bill

Russell. In 1967, Chamberlain led Philadelphia to an N.B.A. title, the first of two in his career.

But just how did Chamberlain end up on a stamp?

The creation of a postage stamp is a process that takes years and begins with the Citizens' Stamp Advisory Committee, a volunteer group appointed by the postmaster general. The committee evaluates roughly 40,000 proposals annually before recommending about 30 people or subjects for the postmaster general's review.

A Chamberlain stamp was originally envisioned as part of a set of four basketball players who made history, said William J. Gicker, the creative director for the stamp program. A campaign engineered by Donald Hunt, a sportswriter for *The Philadelphia Tribune*, in support of Chamberlain led to thousands of letters and petition signatures being delivered to the committee.

"We were hoping for 2012," Hunt said, "because that was the 50th anniversary of Wilt's 100-point game."

That didn't happen, but by July 2013, Nelson presented the Postal Service with artwork of "early Wilt" and "later Wilt." The citizens' committee approved the images a year later.

"People loved them both," said Antonio Alcalá, a Postal Service art director, "so we decided to do them both."

Nelson said: "I think it was a good move because of his evolution as a player. As a young guy, he was mostly an offensive player. Then he became more of a defensive-oriented player."

In all, about 50 million Forever stamps of Chamberlain, identified simply as Wilt in capital letters, will be printed.

"It's what we consider to be one of our blockbusters, so we do a little bit more than we normally do," said Cindy Tackett, the acting director of stamp services for the Postal Service.

It will be a coup of sorts for Nelson, whose vibrant, expressionistic paintings often focus on African-American experiences.

Nelson was born in Silver Spring, Md., and eventually enrolled at Pratt Institute in Brooklyn, ostensibly to study architecture. He switched his major to illustration, and after graduating he got his first big break helping to draw scenes for the 1997 film *Amistad*, directed by Steven Spielberg.

He then teamed with the actress and dancer Debbie Allen on a children's book, *Brothers of the Knight*, and her friends Spike Lee and Will Smith enlisted him for similar projects. Awards followed.

"I didn't plan to do children's books," he said, "but one thing led to another."

"Children's books introduce art to children," added Nelson, 40, the father of three. "It's usually the first time they look at art. Kids think very visually — everything is larger than life — so it goes hand in hand with their development."

At Pratt, Nelson had painted baseball players from the Negro Leagues, which piqued his interest in the sport's lore. He traveled to the Negro Leagues Baseball Museum in Kansas City, Mo., and met the former player and manager Buck O'Neil.

Nelson's conversations with O'Neil helped lead to a 2008 book, *We Are the Ship: The Story of Negro League Baseball*.

By then, Nelson was receiving regular commissions from the Postal Service. He gets biographical information from its art directors, and then drafts pencil-on-paper sketches. The initial renderings are rough, he said, because "I like to discover as I go and save the spontaneity for the finished piece."

He paints the final version in color using oils. Graphic details, including the subject's name, are added later.

"It's very humbling," he said, "because you're creating a piece of history that's permanent. You want to get it right because you can only do it once."

Nelson revisited the subject of the Negro Leagues in 2010 with two stamps. He then painted a set of four stamps that saluted Joe DiMaggio, Larry Doby, Ted Williams and Willie Stargell. Last year, Nelson illustrated a stamp honoring the tennis champion Althea Gibson. He also painted images of the fiction writers Richard Wright and Ralph Ellison for stamps.

Nelson said that after 15 years of painting baseball scenes from the Negro Leagues he was ready to move on from that subject. Inspired in part by Chamberlain, he acknowledged that the idea of visually exploring the early days of professional basketball and teams like the all-black New York Renaissance was intriguing.

"I really love the history of sports and telling those stories," Nelson said. "I like to see what the game looked like in its early, gritty style."

For the moment, he has Chamberlain, in all his elongated grandeur.

APRIL 13, 2017

The Unreasonable Genius
of Russell Westbrook

BY SAM ANDERSON

The N.B.A.'s regular season ended last night, which means that we can now say it officially: Russell Westbrook is not just an unreasonable maniac — he is an unreasonable maniac of historic proportions. His insanity is now immortal. Back at the season's halfway point, I wrote a profile of Westbrook and his quest to achieve one of basketball's sacred feats: to average a triple-double for an entire season. (A triple-double means registering, in one game, double digits in three different statistics, usually points, rebounds and assists.) This had happened only once in N.B.A. history, in 1962, and it seemed unlikely to ever happen again. "Averaging a triple-double," I wrote, "is like having a helicopter that is also a boat that can also write the Great American Novel"; if Westbrook managed to pull it off, it "would be not only historic and impressive but also a little weird, almost disturbing."

Well, Westbrook did it. And it was, indeed, bizarre and impressive and at times a little disturbing. For 81 games, he flung himself around the court the way only he could, and when the smoke cleared, he had compiled averages of 31.6 points, 10.7 rebounds and 10.4 assists.

On Sunday, Westbrook also broke Oscar Robertson's 55-year-old record for the most triple-doubles — 41 — in one season. The game was a perfect microcosm of the Westbrook experience. His points and rebounds came early and easily, but he was stuck, for an agonizingly long time, on nine assists. (Westbrook's teammates are relatively weak shooters; getting assists can be like pulling teeth.) Whenever Westbrook dribbled the ball up the court, the crowd in Denver stood and cheered for him to get his magical 10th assist — but his teammates traveled or passed or missed open shots, and eventually people started booing them.

Finally, with four minutes left, Westbrook drove and passed to a wide-open teammate at the 3-point line. Unfortunately, it was Semaj Christon, a rookie who was shooting only 17 percent from 3, which meant that Westbrook's chances at history were roughly equal to the chances of rolling two dice and coming up with a matching pair. Christon cocked the ball back and fired — and, improbably, made the shot. Westbrook's numbers came up. He had his 42nd triple-double, the most ever. The crowd exploded.

Westbrook's defining trait is not precision or skill but something harder to describe: some combination of hunger, will and frenzied self-belief. Much of his complexity boils down to one simple question. There is a ball, and everybody wants it — this is the basic situation at the heart of all sports (substitute, depending on the game, puck, shuttlecock, finish line, whatever). So why is Westbrook so often the one who gets there first? If you were to roll a ball out into the precise middle of 50 players, why would Westbrook emerge with it instead of the other 49? What makes Westbrook Westbrook?

Over the course of several months, I asked this question to many different people and received many different answers.

"I think it's just in his DNA," said Wilson Taylor, the Thunder's equipment manager. "That's just who he is. That's just him. He just wants it more."

"Don't fall into the trap of saying 'He wants it more,'" said Bill Walton, like Westbrook a former U.C.L.A. Bruin, a Hall of Famer and one of the greatest loose-ball-claimers in basketball history. "Everybody wants it. But he is more intelligent, more prepared, more creative, more resourceful. He has more heart."

"I might want it just as much as him," Westbrook's teammate Nick Collison said. "But he's just faster than everybody."

"That's just him, mate," Steven Adams told me. "And it looks even more ridiculous because his genetics are phenomenal."

"Because it takes time to shift gears," said Sam Presti, the team's general manager, the man who drafted Westbrook. "There's a penalty — a fraction of a second — to get from fourth gear up into fifth. N.B.A. players are all fast in fifth gear. But every time you shift, you have to pay the tax on time. Russell exists in fifth gear. He's made the clutch obsolete in his model. He saves the time by eliminating doubt. He's in continuous pursuit. That's why he gets there first."

"Because he struggled," said the Thunder's trainer, Joe Sharpe.

Finally, I asked Westbrook himself: "Why does Russell Westbrook get to the ball first?"

"Because Russell Westbrook doesn't care about other players," he said. "Like I've said before, when I get on the court, there's no friends. I don't have any buddies. I only got one buddy, and that's the basketball. My job is to get to the ball before the next guy. You gotta want it, man. You gotta want it more than the other person."

Inevitably, we reach a point where language fails. What makes Russell Westbrook get to the ball is some raw spiritual thing that only Russell Westbrook has: his being, his essence, his life-force, his eternal why-not?-ness.

While watching him play this season, I often found myself thinking of Kendrick Lamar, another native of inner-city Los Angeles, whose song "King Kunta" invokes, again and again, a mysterious quality called "the yams."

"What's the yams?" a chorus of voices asks him in the song.

"The yams is the power that be," Lamar answers. "You can smell it when I'm walking down the street."

The yams, in other words, is the power of life — the primal "I am," a pure declaration of being. It's like the name Yahweh, or, less grandly, Popeye's tautological motto: "I yam what I yam." Russell Westbrook, as much as any other figure in American culture these days, has got the yams. Measure it with whatever numbers you like — triple-doubles, rebounding percentage, player efficiency rating, win shares, VORP — it's all an attempt to approximate some unmeasurable vital force. This season was as powerful a display of the yams as we are ever likely to see, in any medium, ever.

In Denver, after securing his 42nd triple-double, Westbrook didn't stop: He set about furiously rallying the Thunder back from 10 points down, one unreasonable shot after another. At the end, with his team trailing by 2, Westbrook hit a contested heave from 36 feet away to win the game — the least-probable buzzer-beater to cap the least-probable season. In my living room, my mouth flew open involuntarily and emitted a scream I was not in control of. My whole body became a fire hose of noise. It was the only appropriate ending to Westbrook's season: one that was not remotely possible at all. After the game, a reporter asked if Westbrook knew the shot was going in when he released it.

"I knew it had a chance," he said.

This is, perhaps, the best metaphor for Westbrook: He is a pair of loaded dice. He gambles, again and again, in situations when he absolutely shouldn't, and it works out in his favor a crazy amount of the time. So it should be no surprise that Westbrook's numbers all came up in the end.

36

Unicorns, Freaks and 3-Point Frenzy

Phil Mushnick, my old friend and *New York Post* colleague, loves to deride the 7-foot-3 Kristaps Porzingis in his column for loitering out on the far perimeter too much, flinging up 3-balls. I tell him, "That's the game now: Balance the floor, open the lane for the shifty guard, get to the rim or kick out for 3." He says fine, he gets it, but the concept has been carried too far. The game too often is unwatchable.

Fair point. In doing what we do, we overdo. While featuring many incredible new-age athletes, 7-footers with once unimaginable ballhandling skills, the sport has also let loose a generation of bad-shot takers, all in the name of analytics that cannot effectively calculate for game situation, much less what's pleasing to the critical eye.

I covered Game 7 of the 2018 Eastern Conference finals in Boston, LeBron's final triumph with Cleveland, and it was as unsightly a critical game as I've ever seen. When two conference finalists combine to shoot 16 for 74 with a place in the finals on the line, there is something rotten — or terribly robotic — going on.

Basketball is — or should be — an improvisational sport, a game of situational adjustments. When it all starts to look alike, a numbing effect occurs.

This may be more of a generational lament, but for anyone who grew up with James Worthy dunking off a no-look bounce pass on the break from

Magic, the sight of someone eschewing an open lane and clanking a 3 can be tough to take. The range and audacity of the hyper-skilled Stephen Curry and James Harden — with three collective M.V.P. awards between them — are the likes of which we've never seen, but Harden's draining of the shot clock to launch 25-footers during the Rockets' 2018 Western Conference finals against the Warriors was more suited to a video game.

Granted, had Chris Paul not gotten hurt near the end of Game 5, Houston may well have won the series and the title. Harden may in the final analysis be so good that the norms of acceptable shot selection — at least in this souped-up, 21st century N.B.A.—do not apply.

JAN. 18, 2017
Hunting for Unicorns in the N.B.A.
BY JAY CASPIAN KANG

January is hangover month for the National Basketball Association. The pageantry of the league's Christmas Day games has faded, the playoffs are still months away and the exciting unknowns of a new season have mostly been resolved: The Warriors still dominate; the Nets still stink.

Just days after the new year began, two average teams, the New York Knicks and the Milwaukee Bucks, played what set up to be another meaningless regular-season snoozer. But after the game, the reporters crowding the narrow, sterile hallways beneath Madison Square Garden were uncommonly excited. When a Knicks public relations staff member showed up to declare that the home team's locker room was now open for reporters, almost nobody moved: The Knicks had been upstaged that night by a kind of Ghost of Basketball Future, Giannis Antetokounmpo, the 22-year-old, nearly 7-foot-tall Bucks point guard who had just stunned the New York crowd with a buzzer-beater.

It wasn't simply that he made his first game-winner as a pro. He rendered a Knicks defender helpless with one impossibly long, oddly graceful step backward before rising way up to calmly sink a fadeaway jumper. Antetokounmpo is the rare athlete who looks more human in slow-motion replay — that's where you can see the end of his stretchy limbs and the way he moves them as an actual person does. In real time, he seems liquid, his body flowing to the empty spaces on the court. This shot was no different; it looked as if T-1000 from *Terminator 2* had challenged a Wang computer to a jumping contest.

These sorts of revelatory moments, when you can glimpse basketball's future as a game that has abandoned its traditional roles based on body sizes and when a team's players run the floor like five Magic Johnsons, have turned the Bucks — more or less an afterthought since Kareem Abdul-Jabbar left Milwaukee for Los Angeles — into appointment viewing. And as the energized reporters waited in the Bucks locker room for Antetokounmpo to appear, a couple of aging beat writers seemed to be grappling with ways to describe what they had seen. They settled on "Madison Square Giannis."

In the past, a handful of basic precepts defined how the N.B.A. and the shoe-company nation-states dependent on its stars marketed themselves: Big cities beat small ones. The biggest men are harder to market than their closer-to-normal-size teammates. The more television exposure, the better. Winning matters. Also important is "relatability," or the connection between player and consumer, which usually involves the player's personal biography. Larry Bird was the "Hick From French Lick," in Indiana; LeBron James might as well have just walked off a factory line, so completely defined is he by his Rust Belt Ohio roots.

Those old imperatives have never exerted much of a hold over a new, enlightened generation of N.B.A. fans. Ten years ago, the influential basketball blog FreeDarko coined the term "liberated fandom." What FreeDarko celebrated were the quirks and oddities of specific N.B.A. players rather than winning seasons or huge marketing campaigns or even geography. (Disclosure: I wrote a few posts for FreeDarko.) Since then, more N.B.A. fans have detached themselves from tribal ties to local teams. And while the franchises and shoe companies that make up the N.B.A. economy haven't completely caught up with the online buzz generated by the league's most dedicated fans, they have begun to prepare for what feels like inevitable change. Antetokounmpo and fellow young "unicorns" like Kristaps Porzingis of the Knicks and Joel Embiid of the Sixers — their taxonomic ID, co-opted from Silicon Valley, refers to a singular talent without antecedent — will go a long way toward determining whether the pro-basketball industrial complex can make as much money appealing to liberated fans as to their hidebound, local-market counterparts.

"The size of the market doesn't really matter anymore," Dustin Godsey, the Milwaukee Bucks' chief marketing officer, told me, referring to a team's location. "You can be a superstar anywhere."

When the team drafted Antetokounmpo three years ago, he was unknown, born in Greece to Nigerian parents. The Bucks didn't bother putting him on billboards as the face of the franchise. Instead, Milwaukee became the first team, according to Godsey, to provide instant in-game highlights on social media, most of which featured Antetokounmpo streaking up the court and making moves that hinted at his absurd potential. In the three seasons that followed, Milwaukee never finished with a winning record. Antetokounmpo did not make an All-Star Game — that should change this year, his fourth, because he has been averaging something like 24 points, 9 rebounds and 6 assists — but video views through Bucks social feeds tripled over the last year. Online streaming of local games doubled. In response, Godsey's team changed its strategy: Antetokounmpo now appears on billboards in Wisconsin, in TV ads, at events. Whether he has earned this superstar treatment is of no account — he looks good in seven-second video clips.

For the past couple of decades, Nike has practiced caution with its basketball stars. Back in the early 2000s, when Michael Jordan was in his final days with the Washington Wizards, Nike and its Jordan brand aggressively marketed young players like Darius Miles and Quentin Richardson. After they failed to achieve stardom, Nike started to exercise more patience. Today, the company has a tiered system unofficially in place: LeBron James, Kevin Durant, Kyrie Irving and the like are "signature shoe" athletes, and most of the rest get occasional spots in a commercial. Anthony Davis of the New Orleans Pelicans and DeMarcus Cousins of the Sacramento Kings have been two of the highest-scoring players in the N.B.A. this season. They play improvisational, position-free basketball (like Antetokounmpo) and are adored by N.B.A. nerds. Both are signed to Nike but have been relegated to what amounts to a bench role.

"The N.B.A. is changing," Russ Bengtson, an emeritus editor of *Slam* magazine and a senior editor at *Complex*, told me. "The shoe companies need to figure out a way to become super-nimble — the league is full of 'unicorns' now, and by the time a guy becomes a story, the next guy is already coming up. The whole definition of what a star is has changed a bit, and they need to be able to strike while the iron is hot."

As the season rolls into the All-Star break, nearly half the players leading the voting play in ways that defy the old but still widely held archetypes — the high-flying shooting guard, the stoic center, the scrappy white sharpshooter. The marketing efforts haven't fully caught up to the evolution. This month, Nike released a signature shoe for Paul George, who like Jordan and Kobe Bryant is a handsome, high-scoring shooting guard. But George, who plays for the Indiana Pacers, doesn't signal a possible paradigm shift as Antetokounmpo or Embiid or Porzingis does. He may be very good, but he does not fire up the internet. His time as the N.B.A.'s next big thing probably peaked three seasons ago, too.

Because the hype cycle for up-and-coming stars still moves too quickly for them to be marketing stars as well, it's unclear when players like Antetokounmpo, who have no real on-court or business archetypal predecessor, will be able to convert online hype into reliable moneymaking. Nationally, he is still a commercial puzzle — a Nike representative told me the company is going to put him in a digital campaign but wouldn't elaborate on other plans.

Antetokounmpo seems to understand that we haven't yet completely entered the liberated future. In the locker room after his game-winning shot at the Garden, I asked him if he thought his career so far would have been different if he played in New York or Los Angeles. He seemed, at first, perplexed by the question, before he said, "I guess I would have gotten more publicity." But then, like so many up-and-coming superstars, he retreated straight into the sorts of cliché that have become the soundtrack for the marketable athlete. "But anywhere I am," he said, "I am going to be a gym rat and work hard."

Nov. 3, 2017

The Unspeakable Greatness of Giannis Antetokounmpo

BY MARC STEIN

MILWAUKEE — Michael Redd averaged 26.7 points per game at the height of his Milwaukee Bucks career. Redd earned a $91 million contract as a Buck, won an Olympic gold medal while a member of the Bucks and stood as the Bucks' lone N.B.A. All-Star for a span exceeding a decade.

You could thus make the case that Redd, based on his résumé, knows better than anyone else in the basketball universe how it feels to be Giannis Antetokounmpo.

The problem: Redd couldn't suppress a laugh when that idea was presented to him.

As he stood on the floor of the Bucks' first home, in anticipation of watching the Antetokounmpo show at an arena unforgettably known as the Mecca, Redd made the claim that none of his predecessors — from this franchise or otherwise — could truly identify with the prodigy affectionately known as the Greek Freak.

"I've never seen anybody like him," Redd said. "We've never seen anything like this.

"The numbers he's getting right now are almost on accident. Once he learns how to play play — unstoppable. It's almost like he's from another planet."

This is the sort of breathless praise Antetokounmpo routinely inspires in his fifth N.B.A. season. Building on a 2016–17 campaign in which he became the Bucks' first All-Star since Redd in 2004 and won the N.B.A.'s Most Improved Player Award, Antetokounmpo zoomed to averages of 31.3 points, 10.6 rebounds and 5.1 assists entering Friday's play — benchmarks no player in league history had ever hit, in unison, through the season's first eight games.

Yet it is the manner in which he operates, on top of the sheer statistical delirium, that makes the 22-year-old from Greece such a phenomenon.

The N.B.A. is famed for the comparison game it triggers any time a new star emerges, but no one has quite figured out how to size up this 6-foot-11 235-pounder who occasionally needs just one dribble from midcourt to swoop to the rim and does all that scoring without a dependable perimeter stroke to open up the rest of his game.

Is he a budding Magic Johnson — albeit with more athletic ability? Is he the next LeBron James — only blessed with much more size and length? Can we call him a full-fledged point guard now? Is it more accurate to say he's more of a point forward?

What, exactly, is he?

"Point all," Bucks Coach Jason Kidd said, after a lengthy pause in search of the proper summation.

The veteran Bucks guard Jason Terry, referring to his former longtime teammate Dirk Nowitzki, the revolutionary power forward, explained the conundrum this way:

"Dirk, in my eyes, is the best European player to ever play this game," Terry said. "He literally changed the way his position is played. But Giannis doesn't even have a position. He does it all, and he's still learning what to do out there."

A Huge Milwaukee Fan

To the Bucks' delight, "all" includes a trait that tantalizes team officials as much as his 60 percent shooting from the field so far, or anything else the league's hottest individual force does with a basketball in his hands: Antetokounmpo unabashedly loves Milwaukee.

It's a city that, despite a string of successful teams in the 1980s and a squad that fell one win short of the N.B.A. finals in 2001, has never fully shed its "unfashionable" label, which was affixed when the best player in Bucks history — Kareem Abdul-Jabbar — forced a trade to the perennially glamorous Los Angeles Lakers in 1975.

But Antetokounmpo, in a recent interview, went so far as to assert that where he plays directly influences how he plays.

"I'm a low-profile guy," he said. "I don't like all these flashy cities like L.A. or Miami. I don't know if I could be the same player if I played in those cities."

N.B.A. teams saddled with Milwaukee's small-market, glamour-shy profile generally live in fear of big-market behemoths signing away their brightest talents at the first free-agent opportunity. Antetokounmpo is in the first year of a four-year, $100 million contract extension — $11 million less than the maximum he could have signed for — but the Bucks are well aware that teams out there are plotting their recruiting pitches for the summer of 2021.

Visitors to Milwaukee, however, quickly discover that it's no exaggeration to describe Antetokounmpo's future as the least of the Bucks' concerns in their bid to become a credible contender for the first time in nearly two decades. It also doesn't hurt that, by virtue of his speedy ascension to All-N.B.A. status and contention for other top individual honors, Antetokounmpo is on a course to be eligible for a so-called "supermax" contract extension from the Bucks via the league's new Designated Player Exception during the 2020 off-season, which would put him in line for a new deal well in excess of $200 million.

As he tweeted in July, to the presumed glee of every Milwaukeean, "I got loyalty inside my DNA."

An Unexpected Loss

The connective tissue that links this star, team and city runs as dense as you'll find on the N.B.A. map, perhaps surpassed only by Nowitzki's two decades' worth of roots in Dallas or maybe the deep bonds shared in San Antonio by Tony Parker and Manu Ginobili. Milwaukee hasn't simply been the backdrop for Antetokounmpo's fairy tale rise to American stardom; it has been home for virtually his whole family for all but the first few months of his N.B.A. life.

Antetokounmpo admits, furthermore, that the unexpected death of his father just over a month ago has him leaning on his adopted hometown more than ever. Charles Antetokounmpo died of a heart attack on Sept. 29 at age 54.

"I can feel the love from the city every day I step on the floor," Giannis Antetokounmpo said. "For me, what I'm going through now, I appreciate it even more."

Charles and Veronica Antetokounmpo, who moved from Nigeria to Greece as undocumented immigrants in 1991 in search of a better life, secured the necessary paperwork to relocate to Milwaukee along with Giannis's two younger brothers halfway through his rookie season. Kostas Antetokounmpo is a redshirt freshman at the University of Dayton now, but the rest of the family moved into a new downtown complex before this season, with Giannis and Alexandros Antetokounmpo (a high school sophomore) housed on the fifth floor and Charles and Veronica on the fourth.

After years of well-chronicled struggle for the family in a northern section of Athens known as Sepolia, they have found Milwaukee as idyllic as it was portrayed to be in the sitcom *Happy Days*, where not even the frigid winters can detract from the comfort they've experienced as a unit.

Only now, as they confront Charles's death, even more responsibility has been heaped on the ever-widening shoulders of the Bucks' phenom. Veronica Antetokounmpo, meanwhile, has moved up a flight to be with her sons on the fifth floor in the wake of her husband's death.

"Leading your family is a lot tougher than basketball," Antetokounmpo said. "Especially right now. But I've got to be strong for my family.

"Things," he continued, "are going to get better."

Places to Improve

The areas for on-court improvement are obvious for Antetokounmpo even as he stuffs box score after box score. His outside shot still needs copious amounts of work — he is not close to trusting it in times of need — and there is room for growth in reading the game at both ends, consistently making his teammates better and refining his decision-making.

Yet it's also ridiculous, and rather cold, to nitpick what is missing from Antetokounmpo's blossoming game given the level he is consistently hitting with that 7-foot-3 wingspan of his. Doubly so at a time of profound grief.

"He's like a plane that just started taking off," Kidd said. "He's at 10,000 feet."

When he arrived in Wisconsin, via the 15th overall pick in the 2013 N.B.A. draft, Antetokounmpo was measured at 6 feet 9 inches and weighed less than 200 pounds. A half-decade later, he is closing in on 240 pounds, and coaches and teammates routinely refer to him as a 7-footer.

The Milwaukee assistant coach Frank Johnson, noting Antetokounmpo's bulked-up body and added strength, said, "He gets bumped now and he loves it."

As for his perimeter game, Johnson preaches patience, pointing to the countless nights of extra shooting he is getting alongside the mentoring "Coach Sweeney" — the Bucks assistant coach Sean Sweeney. The way Johnson talks about the work-in-progress jumper is reminiscent of what league observers said for years about Shaquille O'Neal's persistent free-throw woes.

"If he had that already," Johnson said, "it wouldn't be fair."

Terry, the Bucks guard, said: "Of course he has to keep working on his outside game. But Giannis just has a peaceful confidence about himself. You can see it. Last year, he didn't have that."

The legendary Kobe Bryant, now in his second season of retirement, had seen enough coming into training camp to challenge Antetokounmpo via Twitter in late August to make a bid for the league's Most Valuable Player Award.

Kobe Bryant ✔
@kobebryant

Follow

MVP

Giannis Antetokounmpo ✔ @Giannis_An34
Still waiting for my challenge... @kobebryant

6:26 AM - 27 Aug 2017

Asked why he set such a high target, as part of his #MambaMentality campaign, Bryant said last week via email that he was moved by Antetokounmpo's "rare physical gifts that are matched by a rare inner passion."

'The Giannis Effect'

Bucks staffers do worry that Antetokounmpo is occasionally too hard on himself, having watched him head straight for the practice floor on the same night as a frustrating loss more times than they care to remember. One example of his blame-me tendencies: He said last week, on the morning after a home setback to the Boston Celtics, that he was still angry "for personal reasons," implying that the 96–89 defeat was all his fault.

But the Bucks do not try to influence Antetokounmpo's thinking too much. They prefer to let him figure things out as they come — except when he decided during the summer that he wanted to have a garage sale as a part of his recent move.

He wanted to stage the sale to pay homage to his Athens youth, when he and his brothers had to peddle knockoff watches and sunglasses to help his parents and siblings survive. The Bucks' front office and Veronica Antetokounmpo ultimately talked him out of it.

"I'm a great seller — that's one of the other talents I have," Giannis Antetokounmpo said. "I wanted to do it so bad. But they told me I couldn't because three or four thousand people would show up."

Sounds like a safe estimate given the Bucks' rising popularity in Green Bay Packers territory and Antetokounmpo's central role in that rise.

At the Milwaukee Brat House near the team's current Bradley Center home, the manager Jennifer Fellin said she saw more patrons wearing Bucks gear now than at any other point in her eight-year stint at the restaurant. It is a fashion trend she attributes largely to the Giannis Effect.

The Antetokounmpo-led Bucks, Fellin asserted, have risen to "cool" status.

"They have breathed new life into the city," Gino Fazzari, owner of the nearby Calderone Club restaurant, said.

Team executives, mind you, are realistic. They know Antetokounmpo will be fiercely pursued by rival teams (and, perhaps more worryingly, stars from rival teams) at the earliest opportunity. They know those future suitors will point to a three-headed Bucks ownership structure that has come under increasing scrutiny in recent months and paint the arrangement as a potential source of instability. They know, even as construction proceeds swiftly on an impressive $524 million arena scheduled to open next fall and complement Milwaukee's gleaming new practice facility across the street, that Antetokounmpo might find it hard someday to resist looking around if the Bucks cannot fortify their roster and rediscover playoff success.

After all, even Bryant and Tim Duncan — two legends whom he hopes to emulate in terms of never switching teams, as Antetokounmpo recently told *Time* magazine — flirted with leaving their teams before opting for the increasingly rare only-one-jersey approach.

"I really don't see Giannis going anywhere," Redd said. "Even in the future.

"With what he's doing on the court, it's going to automatically draw people to come play with him. I know people have that stigma about Milwaukee. But it won't be hard for him to attract talent here. I just want a ring when they get a ring."

Outlandish as the retired Redd sounds at the moment — given, for starters, Milwaukee's lack of a consistent second scoring option as well as a need for more speed and more shooting — Antetokounmpo encourages the lofty talk. He is convincing when he says he thinks he "can take this organization to the next level and bring that championship," undoubtedly projecting so much confidence because he's so aware of how far he has come.

In the month since his father's death, Antetokounmpo revealed that he often found himself looking at a picture on a private Instagram page he maintains. The image shows Giannis, Kostas, Alexandros and their older brother, Thanasis, who currently plays for Panathinaikos in Greece after a brief stint with the Knicks, all sleeping in the same bed.

Giannis estimates that he was 10 or 11 at the time. One bed for the four children was all Charles and Veronica Antetokounmpo could manage. The parents slept in a small nearby den, as Giannis recalled, behind "like a curtain."

"It's an unbelievable story," Antetokounmpo said. "Good stuff."

Memories like that leave little doubt why the only N.B.A. city that the Greek Freak has ever known can feel like the promised land.

"There's a lot of things you can do in Milwaukee, too," he said proudly.

The whole league can see that now.

May 21, 2018

Courtside with Run TMC; Watching the Rockets Miss, Miss and Miss Some More

by Scott Cacciola

OAKLAND, Calif. — The Houston Rockets missed another layup, and Chris Mullin grimaced. He was wearing a black Golden State Warriors T-shirt as a show of solidarity, but it still bothered him that the Rockets were missing so many easy shots. It seemed to wound his basketball soul.

"Wide-open layups," Mullin said, shaking his head. "They're lucky they're only down 12. It'll catch up to them in the third quarter."

Game 3 of the Western Conference finals on Sunday was not yet a rout, but Mullin could sense what was coming. He was once one of the N.B.A.'s premier long-range technicians, but he has always valued layups, and the Rockets were giving the Warriors every opportunity to build on their early lead.

"The Warriors put so much pressure on you to make your open shots," Mullin said, "because they're going to make their shots eventually, and other teams know it."

After watching Game 1 on television from a couch in Iowa and Game 2 from a garage in Alaska, I found myself just a few rows up from the court at Oracle Arena for Game 3 — Section 128, Row 13, Seat 1. Mullin, now the men's basketball coach at St. John's, was to my immediate left. He was joined by his former teammates Mitch Richmond and Tim Hardaway, a trio of guards known in N.B.A. lore as Run TMC.

"We all went on to play in other places," Mullin said, "but we all said it was the most fun when we played together."

Listen, I know the original concept behind my coverage of this series was to watch each game with a knowledgeable coach, far removed from the actual game itself. But after learning that Mullin and the rest of Run TMC would be in the stands for Game 3, we figured that an exception could be made. Our regularly scheduled programming will resume for Game 4.

Mullin, 54, spent a good chunk of the Warriors' 126–85 victory signing autographs and posing for photos with fans who recalled his days as a five-time All-Star with the Warriors. People here were in a celebratory mood.

Mark Wendell, a semiretired construction worker from San Pablo, Calif., just happened to occupy one of the seats directly in front of Run TMC. Wendell, 62, a season-ticket holder during the Run TMC era, could not believe his good fortune. He wore a pin on his baseball cap with Mullin's old No. 17 jersey.

"Are you kidding me?" Wendell said. "Are you kidding me? I come here, and those three guys are sitting behind me? This is just about the greatest thing ever."

Mullin, Richmond and Hardaway played together for just two seasons, from 1989 to 1991, and lost more regular-season games (83) than they won (81). But their up-tempo, small-ball style of play under Coach Don Nelson captivated fans, especially coming as it did when many teams around the league were still running their offenses through back-to-basket centers. The Warriors were anything but dull. They were appointment viewing.

"Nellie was ahead of his time teaching that," Mullin said of the team's high-octane offense. "Now, everyone plays that way."

As for Run TMC's unusually long-running love affair with the Bay Area, Mullin said: "I think there was an appreciation that we played hard and played together. We were just regular guys, you know?"

Alas, the Run TMC experiment was brief. The team had — how to put this politely? — defensive limitations, which was one of the reasons the Warriors traded Richmond to the Sacramento Kings before the start of the 1991–92 season. Richmond went on to become a six-time All-Star with the Kings. The Warriors advanced to the playoffs just twice over the next 15 seasons.

The franchise's post-trade tailspin helps explain why Run TMC — one of the most beloved abbreviations in league history — has been so romanticized over the years by basketball fans, who wonder what could have been had the group stayed intact. Mullin wonders, too. The basketball they played together was fun and fast and free, and he sees elements of it in the way that the modern-day Warriors operate.

"They play without the ball," Mullin said. "They set screens. They shoot a lot of 3s, but they're always moving as opposed to just spotting and standing. I never played standing still. It's the opposite of what the game should be. The game is about motion and flow and rhythm."

As an aside, Mullin loves the 3-point line. He encourages his players at St. John's to take a bunch of 3-pointers.

"Plus, it's the college 3," he said. "It's a joke how short that shot is."

But even by Run TMC standards, the Warriors who obliterated the Rockets on Sunday to take a two-games-to-one series lead appeared to have enviable freedom to line up shots from distant galaxies. Richmond, 52, who now works with Mullin as one of his assistants at St. John's, leaned forward in his seat when the Warriors' Nick Young launched a wild 3-pointer in the first half.

"Heat check!" Richmond shouted.

Mostly, though, Mullin was alarmed by how many open shots the Rockets were missing: layups, runners, uncontested jumpers. The Warriors were not exactly shooting at a historic clip, either, but they already had a 10-point lead in the second quarter when the Rockets' James Harden blew a layup. None of this boded well for the Rockets.

"Gotta make those," Mullin said. "It's demoralizing because you basically did everything right except knock it down."

There were moments when Mullin sensed that the Rockets were preoccupied with dribbling into the lane with the goal of kicking the ball to the perimeter for 3-pointers. He could tell, he said, by the way they were jump-stopping with two feet instead of exploding to the basket — which, on more than one occasion, turned out to be available for layups. Except they kept missing.

The Warriors, meanwhile, began to take advantage. Ahead of halftime, Kevin Durant made a 12-foot jumper.

"Nothing wrong with a nice 2 once in a while," Mullin said.

Durant quickly followed that up with a layup.

"Nothing wrong with layups, either," Mullin said.

When Golden State's huge run came in the third quarter, Mullin snapped his fingers.

"The lead is 30 now," he said, "just like that."

The errors continued to mount for the Rockets. In the fourth quarter, Mullin was baffled when Harden lunged for a steal against the Warriors' Shaun Livingston along the 3-point line. Mullin knew that Livingston was not an outside threat — he attempted five 3-pointers during the regular season — so why, Mullin asked, was Harden guarding him so far from the basket?

Livingston easily evaded Harden with a behind-the-back dribble and drove for a dunk. The building practically shook. The Warriors were in the process of setting a franchise record for postseason margin of victory.

Mullin, who was once similarly capable of energizing crowds, took it as a cue to make a move of his own.

"I might try to beat the traffic," he said.

— POSTSCRIPT —

SCOTT CACCIOLA, 2018: "Rockets-Warriors was the series people were waiting for and we really wanted to do something different., figuring there'd be a million people writing pretty much the same things. The idea was to cover the series away from the arena, watch each game with a basketball expert with some sort of connection to the series, or philosophical connection to the style of play. That took me all over the place, even to Wasilla, Alaska, to watch with a high school coach and his players. But I thought Chris Mullin would also be great because he was part of the Run TMC team, a forerunner to the current Warriors' up-tempo style. I reached out to St. John's, but when I found out that Run TMC was actually going to be at a game, and the Warriors were gracious enough to let me sit with them, especially Mullin, that game became the exception, the only one I covered from inside the arena."

37

Front Office Fame and Folly

More than most, Phil Jackson paid his dues. The N.B.A.'s career leader in coaching championships (11) spent four and a half years in the old Continental Basketball Association, ferrying his players around the Northeast in a van. In May 1984, he lobbied for a salary increase to $30,000 in 1984 and a road per diem increase to $25.

"I will never put a team in monetary stress for a few more bucks," Jackson wrote to Jim Coyne, the general manager of the Albany Patroons. "But I do think you know I am worth that much."

Before Jackson's Lakers lost in the 2008 finals to the Celtics, I interviewed Coyne, who had actually saved the letter from Jackson and faxed me a copy. Coyne had initially reached out to Jackson, he recalled, from a phone booth in an American Legion hall in Lima, Ohio. After Jackson's team won the league title in his first season, he was granted the salary increase by Coyne, but not the per diem raise.

At the time of my interview with Coyne, Jackson was earning roughly $10 million a year to coach the Lakers and had been the organization's undisputed power broker since the so-called retirement of Jerry West from the front office in 2000. West said he was burned out at 62 but insiders maintained he merely wanted out, once Jackson came to town expecting people to kiss his six Bulls championship rings.

West had a few of his own, having presided over the magical '80s before setting Jackson up to overtake Red Auerbach's record nine coaching titles by signing Shaquille O'Neal as a free agent and trading for Kobe Bryant before the teenager had played an N.B.A. game.

West never retired. He pumped life into a moribund Memphis franchise and became a special adviser to the budding Golden State dynasty before returning to Los Angeles with the Clippers. When his health demanded he stop coaching, Jackson made his inevitable front-office killing with the Knicks as another in a long line of would-be saviors in New York, with a $60 million deal that turned out to be James Dolan's contribution to Jackson's retirement fund.

Given a chance to be West, Jackson's reputation went south, as the septuagenarian, clinging to his triangle offense in a league that had changed dramatically since he'd last used it, was an old dog incapable of new tricks. Flattering himself with the belief that he could turn Carmelo Anthony into even a reasonable facsimile of M.J. or Kobe didn't help.

Enjoying the precipitous fall from grace until his death in 2017 was Jerry Krause, the Bulls' general manager who gave Jackson an N.B.A. lifeline as an assistant in 1987, made him head coach in 1989 and, with the exception of Jordan, was the architect of those six title teams. Jackson repaid the favors by casting Krause outside the team's inner circle and seldom, if ever, giving him the credit he deserved.

Sadly, Krause's long-overdue induction into the Hall of Fame didn't occur until months after his death.

June 29, 2017

The Triangle Offense, a Simple Yet Perplexing System, Dies

by Dan Barry

The Triangle Offense, an existential basketball strategy so complex that it was quite simple, and so simple that it was maddeningly complex, died of complications related to confusion on Wednesday. It was ∞ years old.

The Triangle, also known as the Triple-Post Offense, the Sideline Triangle Offense, and the Trade-Me-Coach Offense, reportedly collapsed under the weight of its own pretension in the front office of the New York Knicks at Madison Square Garden. But no one with the requisite training in astrophysics and Zen Buddhism could be located in time to provide resuscitation.

Its demise coincided with the decision by Knicks management to dismiss Phil Jackson, the team's president for the past three years and the Triangle's closest living relative. Mr. Jackson was so attuned to its almost mystical intricacies that he became the "Triangle whisperer" — although critics say that his channeling of the offense could not be understood at any volume of voice.

The Triangle Offense was born on the hardwood courts of the University of Southern California in the 1940s, the offspring of the university's innovative basketball coach, Justin McCarthy "Sam" Barry. It was then raised and refined by one of Barry's many acolytes, Morice Fredrick "Tex" Winter, who attempted to capture its many mysteries in a book called *The Triple-Post Offense*, published in 1962.

Since the publication of Winter's book, others have attempted to explain, clearly and concisely, what the Triangle entails. But many have gone mad in this pursuit; trying to do so is the basketball equivalent to gazing at the face of Medusa.

In 2014, Scott Cacciola of *The New York Times* provided a short primer, saying that the Triangle was "predicated on reading and exposing soft spots in the defense." He continued:

"The triangle — and there is an actual triangle formed by the post, wing and corner players on the strong side of the court — revolves around seven guiding principles that include maintaining proper spacing (about 15 to 20 feet between players), penetration by passing and the interchangeability of positions. Every player ought to be able to score, and from different angles."

In 2015, the writer Nicholas Dawidoff in these pages immersed himself in the "sacred text" that was Winters's book. Part of his search for enlightenment included asking the basketball analyst Jay Williams — who played in the Triangle Offense while with the Chicago Bulls one season — to explain.

"You hand me a piece of paper and say, 'Jay, define the Triangle for me,' it's kind of like a kid with Magic Markers drawing a cartoon. It's all over the page. So many series of actions, I get lost trying to explain it. Now, give me four guys who know how to run it on the court, I can get out there and do it."

Still, even the harshest critics had to acknowledge that Mr. Jackson had carried out the Triangle Offense to astounding effect during his long basketball career. As the coach for the Chicago Bulls and then for the Los Angeles Lakers, his insistence on running the Triangle paid off with a combined 11 N.B.A. titles.

(It is reported that Michael Jordan and Scottie Pippen, of the Bulls, and Kobe Bryant and Shaquille O'Neal, of the Lakers, also played roles in those championships.)

When Mr. Jackson joined the Knicks' front office in 2014, he celebrated the Triangle Offense — new to the city — as the key to basketball success. Hopes were high, given that the once-proud Knicks had for years been adhering to a style of offense technically known as lousy.

But the Triangle Offense struggled to find acceptance in its adopted city, where even the most astute basketball fans did not appreciate the suggestion that watching a Knicks game meant keeping a protractor close at hand. Nor did it help that the Knicks star Carmelo Anthony was reluctant, if that's the word, to embrace the Triangle.

By November 2016, Anthony didn't even want to hear the phrase. "We're just playing basketball," he said after yet another Knicks loss. "We're making adjustments offensively regardless of what we're running. At this point I'm getting tired of hearing about the Triangle. Just getting tired of hearing about it."

The Knicks ultimately proved resistant, even allergic, to the mysterious charms of the Triangle Offense. During the three-year tenure of the Triangle whisperer, the team posted three losing seasons and never reached the playoffs. In order to survive, it seemed, the offense required elements that were in short supply in the Garden: discipline, patience and flowing movement.

In addition to Mr. Jackson, survivors include a player in the post, one in the corner, one on the wing, and two on the weak side. Funeral services, which are private, will include a shaman, several popcorn-scented candles, and the ritual burning of a Chuck Taylor All Star high-top.

Jerry West Just Wants to Feel Wanted

BY MARC STEIN

LOS ANGELES — It wasn't until the Los Angeles Clippers' 74th game of the season, on one of their final home dates, that the excitable owner Steve Ballmer and Jerry West, his hypercritical special consultant, agreed to watch a game together in Ballmer's baseline seats at Staples Center.

"He told me early on, 'You don't always want me sitting with you,'" Ballmer said.

West prefers to watch games alone, or as isolated as he can manage when he takes one in live. This allows him to fume at will, nitpick unreservedly and, most of all, curse freely.

Ballmer, though, didn't offer a reported $4 million-to-$5 million per year and lure West away from the Golden State Warriors to then ask The Logo to muzzle himself. West is encouraged to be as outspoken as he wants with his new team, rants and all.

"We have long conversations — that is true," Ballmer said. "We talk a lot."

Near the end of his first full year as a consultant to Ballmer and Lawrence Frank, the Clippers' president of basketball operations, West will have a seat on Tuesday night that'll make it hard to miss where he works now. The Los Angeles Lakers legend has a chair reserved on the dais at the N.B.A.'s annual draft lottery Tuesday in Chicago — representing L.A.'s other team.

It's largely a symbolic role, often assigned to franchise legends and occasionally even owners' children. But for West — who both turns 80 and celebrates his 40th wedding anniversary on May 28 — the league's made-for-TV production is the boldfaced occasion circled on his calendar this month.

"We have to do a great job this summer," West said of the Clippers over lunch at the Bel-Air Country Club, where he has spent much of his time away from basketball since the 1970s, playing golf and gin.

He insists he doesn't feel 80 — "Not at all," West said — and carded a 78 followed by a 75 last month. Yet on this day, West was far more intent on discussing the two lottery picks the Clippers have in the N.B.A. draft this June.

Do the Clippers hold on to those picks and wait for July 2019 to make their next big free-agent push? Do they try to package one or both in a potential trade this off-season to pursue an established star like San Antonio's Kawhi Leonard?

Frank and Ballmer will ultimately make those calls, but West expects to have significant say.

"I don't just want to be a figurehead," West said. "You want to be a part of the decision-making process. I don't have the final decision here, but I do have a voice."

The Clippers never envisioned worrying about lottery proceedings so soon after they re-signed Blake Griffin to a five-year, $171 million contract last July. Days after West signed on in June, they agreed to trade Chris Paul, the stellar but frustrated All-Star guard, to Houston before Paul could bolt in free agency. But re-upping their star forward, to keep Griffin teamed with the All-N.B.A. center DeAndre Jordan, had the Clippers convinced they would remain a playoff team — even in the stacked Western Conference.

It wasn't long, though, before buyer's remorse set in. Already plagued by a lengthy injury history, Griffin sustained a sprained knee in November. He was the fourth of five projected starters to incur an early season injury, exacerbating a poor start which featured a nine-game losing streak even before Griffin got hurt.

Griffin wound up missing six weeks, but an unexpected opportunity to trade him to the star-starved Detroit Pistons materialized soon after Griffin's late-December return.

Going through with the trade would essentially be admitting that re-signing Griffin was a mistake, an ill-conceived attempt to cling to relevance and respectability after losing Paul.

Do it anyway, West urged.

The Clippers had gone to great lengths just six months earlier to persuade Griffin to stay in free agency, staging a mock jersey retirement ceremony in which Griffin was proclaimed to be "a lifelong Clipper" as part of their recruiting pitch. Trading him so soon after that, for all the financial flexibility it could restore, would also paint the Clippers as heartless.

"Don't be afraid to make that tough decision if you need to," Ballmer recalled West telling him.

"No one wants to do that, particularly with someone like Blake Griffin," West says now. "It was very difficult for everyone, especially Steve, because he really liked Blake personally. But this franchise was really stuck. There was nowhere for it to go. You have to figure out how far away you really are and how we can get there."

If that view makes West cold, too, he is prepared to absorb the criticism, responding with one of his pet phrases: "What is right is not always popular, and what is popular is not always right."

When it comes to making such calculations, West is the antithesis of the modern N.B.A. executive. He openly disdains how much teams rely on statistics in the N.B.A.'s analytics era.

Yet the Clippers will put up with that stubborn streak in exchange for the instant credibility they get from West's presence. It also doesn't hurt that the Clippers' new front-office cabinet features Michael Winger, the highly rated salary-cap guru and strategist, as Frank's top aide.

West does not respond to email or even have an email address, because "he doesn't know how to use a computer," Karen West, his wife, said. But the man whose silhouette and unmistakable left-handed dribble served as the inspiration for the N.B.A. logo has managed to gradually add texting to his repertoire.

"Lawrence and I text each other two or three times a day," West said proudly, after a message from Frank caught his eye.

Before the Clippers called, West's six seasons in a similar advisory role with the Warriors were undeniably fruitful, featuring two championships, a record 73-win season and the successful free-agent recruitment of Kevin Durant. But for all of his achievements and longevity, West still needs to feel needed, say those who know him best.

And he couldn't help but wonder: Did the Warriors, whose then-new ownership group so badly needed the credibility boost West provided upon arrival in May 2011, still need him after the team's president of basketball operations, Bob Myers, had become so adept in assembling a starry, and successful, roster?

For much of his Golden State stint, although it was never advertised, West was the highest-paid member of the basketball operations staff. But Myers, who joined the front office with West's strong backing in April 2011, was promoted to general manager after a one-season apprenticeship and quickly established himself; he earned N.B.A. Executive of the Year honors twice (to match West's career total) in a five-season span.

The longtime *Sports Illustrated* writer Jack McCallum reported in his 2017 book *Golden Days* that West, partly because of Myers's rise in stature, was asked to take a reduction in compensation to stay.

But money was only one factor in West's exit. No matter how hard Warriors officials tried to convince him, publicly and privately, that his input remained vital to their collaborative approach to decision-making, West felt his influence was fading.

"You have to be wanted," West said.

Joining the Clippers, meanwhile, would represent a new challenge reminiscent of West's unexpected move to the Memphis Grizzlies in April 2002, after he walked away from a 40-year association with the Lakers following Shaquille O'Neal and Kobe Bryant's first championship in 2000.

The Lakers back then, like the Warriors now, were set up for success with or without West. Putting the Clippers on a championship course, by contrast, is seen as the ultimate challenge in L.A.

That's not only because of the Lakers' immense shadow but also the stain that lingers from Donald Sterling's 33-year ownership, which for so long was synonymous with ineptitude and frugality to the point of cheapness that it made the Clippers a longstanding laughingstock. Sterling's run finally ended in 2014, with his team competitive at last, when he was barred for life by N.B.A. Commissioner Adam Silver after Sterling was recorded making racist comments.

The Clippers strung together their six most successful seasons before West's arrival, but they also failed to advance past the second round, even after hiring a championship-proven coach in Doc Rivers in June 2013. Mounting frustration prompted Ballmer to strip Rivers of his front-office power in August 2017 and promote Frank to head the department. Atlanta and Detroit likewise went away from that sort of leadership structure over the past 12 months.

San Antonio (Gregg Popovich) and Minnesota (Tom Thibodeau) are the only two teams left in the league that employ a coach who also holds final say over personnel matters. Teams are more apt now to try to replicate the Golden State model, which was built upon the belief that a diverse group of voices — if properly managed — can succeed through collaboration.

"In terms of how to set up a front office, how to think about problems, talent evaluation — Jerry is a superstar," Ballmer said.

The idea to pursue West came from Ballmer's former Harvard classmate-turned-Clippers minority shareholder Dennis Wong, who was once part of Golden State's ownership group.

"He kept saying, 'We need a guy like Jerry West,'" Ballmer said. "I kept saying, 'Show me one guy in the world who's like Jerry West.' Then last season Dennis said: 'Did you know he's near the end of his contract? Jerry West is like Jerry West.'"

Ballmer and West eventually came to terms on a two-year deal. "If he still wants to do it, we can go beyond that," Ballmer said. "Now that I know him better, I can't see him retiring."

Neither can West.

"I'm not a person that does very well when I don't have a reason to get up in the morning," he said.

West admitted he also badly needs the nine-mile drive into the Clippers' offices in Playa Vista for his own psyche, even though he has been part of eight N.B.A. championships as an executive. He typically stays no more than a couple of hours, but merely being able to make frequent visits to the team's nerve center — not an option when he was a Southern California-based consultant to the Warriors — is, he said, "rejuvenating."

"His mood is so determined by work," said his son Jonnie West, an executive with the Warriors who, along with his older brother Ryan West of the Lakers, followed his father into front-office life. "I think he really enjoys the situation he's in. It gives him a puzzle that needs figuring out."

The Clippers finished 10th in the West this season, five games out of a playoff berth, but have high hopes after posting a 42–40 record in spite of their steady stream of injuries. They acquired the promising forward Tobias Harris and the defensive specialist Avery Bradley in the Griffin deal, along with Detroit's first-round pick in June, and can start plotting for the future in earnest after Tuesday night's lottery results.

West, for his part, is convinced that "the mountain is not that high for this team if we make the right moves" under Ballmer and Frank's leadership.

"Frankly, this is Lawrence's first foray into running a front office — and he's fantastic," Ballmer said. "But who can't learn from Jerry West about that? He's kind of the master. So we all get the chance to learn from the master."

Said West: "Leaving the Warriors was probably the most difficult thing for me in my whole life. I didn't want to leave. You get to the point where maybe you don't feel as valued, but it's just something that happened. I hold no malice toward anyone over there.

"It did not end the way I wanted it to, that's for sure. But this is a perfect role for me. People ask me my opinion, and I'm going to give it to them."

— POSTSCRIPT —

MARC STEIN, 2018: "One of my first N.B.A. assignments, at age 20 and nearly five years before I began covering the league full-time, required me to call Jerry West to chase a story involving a draftee named Vlade

Divac and threats by the then-Yugoslavian army to prevent Divac from joining the Lakers. I was terrified to bother the legendary West on a weekend as a summer fill-in for *The Orange County Register*'s Lakers beat man. But sitting down with West for two extended conversations nearly 30 years later as his 80th birthday approached was the complete opposite. I've obviously established my own working relationship with him, but I frankly couldn't wait to spend time with The Logo, who has lost not a single ounce of the fiery *care factor* and candor that have always made him such an interesting figure. He has nothing left to prove in this game, but West is as invested as he's ever been. He simply can't stop competing."

38

Empty (Rose) Garden

In less politically polarizing times, no N.B.A. champion declined an invitation to the White House, much less openly feuded with the president. Nor was the league always so progressive in the face of public relations jeopardy, often reflecting the Republicans-buy-shoes-too sensibility of its leading man, Michael Jordan.

One such delicate situation arose in 1996, when David Stern fined and suspended the Nuggets' Mahmoud Abdul-Rauf for refusing to stand for the national anthem based on his Islamic religious beliefs. Unlike the N.F.L.'s Colin Kaepernick, Abdul-Rauf was in violation of an actual league rule, established in the early 1980s.

Writing in November 2017 about how N.B.A. players were so individually recognizable on mainstream and social media that they didn't have to resort to testing the third rail of American protest, I asked Michele Roberts, the executive director of the players association, what would happen if a player or two did take a knee.

"I'm not going to comment on what hasn't happened yet," she said. "Still, I can't imagine telling players that we support you but if you express yourself on an issue you feel strongly about, we're going to punish you."

As it turned out, the 2017–18 season rolled on without anyone challenging the anthem rule but with a host of players and coaches speaking out forcefully against President Trump, who discovered that the N.B.A. was less of an inviting target than the N.F.L.

Trump had his devoted base but the N.B.A had one, too, and it generally leaned young, urban and liberal. While many Spurs fans in Texas didn't appreciate Gregg Popovich's strong criticism of Trump, many others knew Coach Pop had undergone Air Force intelligence training and served five years of required active duty. He had earned his worldly view.

When Steve Kerr opined about America's state of affairs, he did so as the Beirut-born son of Malcolm Kerr, the university professor who was murdered in Lebanon by terrorists in 1984. When Stephen Curry said the Warriors weren't interested in a White House invitation along the road to the 2018 title, he spoke out as the popular baby-faced 3-point assassin from a deeply religious family in North Carolina.

And months after LeBron James was told to "shut up and dribble" by the conservative television host Laura Ingraham and later had his intelligence derided by Trump, he responded with the money-where-his-mouth-is opening of his I Promise public school.

Roberts said the players understood their cultural influence and didn't need permission to exert it.

"I don't think the players are behaving this way because the league supports them," she told me. "They're acting based on how they feel, though they do appreciate the way the league supports them."

The anthem rule, however, remained on the books.

JUNE 11, 1985

From One Garden to Another

BY GEORGE VECSEY

WASHINGTON — On Sunday, Kareem Abdul-Jabbar was not happy to find out the Lakers were not going home right away. His head extending high above the crowd of reporters, he asked a team official, "Aw, man, why not?"

"The White House," the official said. "We're going to the White House on Monday."

"Oh," Kareem said, not showing much expression one way or the other.

Yesterday, one day after the 111–100 victory that shook loose the Boston Celtics after eight straight disappointments, and one day before the big civic welcome in Los Angeles, the Lakers made a detour to the White House, to be greeted by President Reagan.

After a night of partying in Boston, and pinching themselves to verify that they really had beaten the Celtics in musty, intimidating Boston Garden, they got to spend a few minutes in another garden, the Rose Garden.

If they had enough time to look around in their 15 minutes, the Lakers might have noticed that there were only a few tea roses in the Rose Garden. But the intimate, well-manicured garden at the west end of the White House is a familiar sight to athletes and those who follow sports.

The visit by sports champions is getting to be a regular item on the White House calendar in every season. And the president almost always finds time to call into the locker room of Super Bowl and World Series champions to offer his congratulations.

The brief ceremony takes only a small bit of time and energy from a president, certainly is more fun than thinking about arms control and tax reform, and opens up a whole venue of happy publicity.

Before the ceremony, Pat Riley, the coach, and Abdul-Jabbar were ushered into the Oval Office for a chat. Riley recalled, "I said to Kareem, 'Can you believe it?'"

He said that Abdul-Jabbar had told the president "he wasn't going to switch his affiliation, but he told the president how he takes yoga classes with the president's son and daughter."

And Riley, who had broadcast Laker games between his playing and coaching careers, related: "I told the president, 'From one broadcaster to another, sometimes we turn out all right.'" The president, of course, once served as a sports broadcaster in the Midwest.

Apparently, Abdul-Jabbar did not remind the president that they had also had similar vocational experience. Abdul-Jabbar has appeared in four films: the current *Fletch, Airplane, The Fish That Saved Pittsburgh* and *A Game of Death*, with the late Bruce Lee.

Before his current vocation, Mr. Reagan appeared in *Knute Rockne, All American; The Winning Team; Bedtime for Bonzo* and *King's Row*.

The other party members filed into the Rose Garden. For this important occasion, the team had split, 7–5, between open collars and ties. The five with ties were: Abdul-Jabbar, Mitch Kupchak, James Worthy, Ronnie Lester and the long-haired counterculture figure, Kurt Rambis.

The Laker party stood in the muggy sunshine for a few moments until Riley, Abdul-Jabbar, Bill Sharman, the team president, and David Stern, the commissioner of the National Basketball Association, joined the ranks. Then came the announcement that seems so mundane on television but produces a slight tingle in person: "Ladies and gentlemen, the president of the United States."

Wearing a tan suit, the president strolled across the lush grass, shook hands with every member of the party, and then spoke into a microphone set for his height.

"I thank you all for the greeting," he told some visitors, "but I assure you the Lakers deserve the applause." And he told the athletes: "You showed America what pride and guts and determination, combined with talent, can do. It was Showtime yesterday at the Boston Garden as you defeated another truly great team. You knew that in Boston it was not going to be a tea party."

Smiling at Abdul-Jabbar, the president said: "I see you compared winning the championship to the Dodgers beating the Yankees in the 1955 World Series. Well, Kareem, I remember that Series, too, and you may be, as they say of me, showing your experience. Yesterday, you showed why you were voted the most valuable player. You may be 38, but you played like 25."

The president also praised Magic Johnson for breaking the record of 60 assists in a six-game series "by an awesome 24," and he promised the high-flying James Worthy, "If you're ever looking for a career after basketball, we have lobbying jobs up on the Hill."

Then the president paused and saluted Kupchak and Rambis, the bruising forwards, adding, "Kurt, not everybody would know what to say when diving out of bounds and suddenly landing in a lady's lap," a reference to a play-saving dive Rambis took last Friday in Los Angeles. And the president thanked the players' wives for their work against drug abuse.

These items all smacked of having been culled from newspaper articles and press releases by a diligent staffer, but Mr. Reagan read them well and everyone seemed happy.

Commissioner David Stern thanked Mr. Reagan, and noted that "basketball's purely domestic origins make it America's game" And Abdul-Jabbar, Johnson and Riley brought gifts to the president.

"I was telling the president I'm not a Republican" Abdul-Jabbar said, "but I am one of his constituents, and we ought to suit him up the right way."

He unfurled a gold-and-purple Laker game shirt with a No. 1 on both sides and the name "Reagan" on the back.

Johnson presented an autographed ball, and Riley a Laker gold cap and a T-shirt "for back at the ranch." The president bounced the ball one time on the grass, thanked the players for stooping to the microphone set at his height, and after a few smiles for the camera, he went back to more demanding tasks.

As the Lakers walked to their bus, Riley said he was looking forward to the big rallies in Los Angeles today.

"I'd like to stretch this out as long as I can," he said. "We went a year with the adversity and pain of losing last year. Now we're enjoying the fruits of victory. When you end up with the ultimate prize, you enjoy whatever comes along."

— POSTSCRIPT —

GEORGE VECSEY, 2018: "I loved doing spot columns like this, subjective impressions of something that just happened, linking fact and current events with broader themes. The Rose Garden reception was open to the press. Giants like Ronald Reagan and Kareem Abdul-Jabbar knew how to speak the common language of sports, gave up nothing of their positions, their beliefs. I remember how hot it was, the bright sun on my balding pate. I remember how Riley and Magic and Kareem and Worthy and the rest wanted to be home in L.A. I think I caught the dignity of them all, big people enjoying themselves, win-win, a moment in time."

JUNE 22, 2018

Why the N.F.L. and the N.B.A. Are So Far Apart On Social Justice Stances

BY JOHN BRANCH

WASHINGTON — Over a 16-hour period last September, President Trump took aim at the country's two most popular sports leagues, the N.F.L. and the N.B.A.

In a speech on a Friday night in Alabama, Trump used an expletive to refer to professional football players who were kneeling during the national anthem as a form of silent protest against police brutality, and he said they should be fired. The next morning, he took to Twitter to tell Stephen Curry and the N.B.A. champion Golden State Warriors they were not welcome at the White House.

The N.F.L. hasn't recovered. The N.B.A. hasn't looked back.

After an N.F.L. season fraught with political undertones and cacophonous debate, through Trump's last-minute decision last month to disinvite the champion Philadelphia Eagles to the White House for a customary coronation, the N.F.L. has been unable to extract itself from the sticky web of the anthem controversy.

The N.B.A., meanwhile, has avoided any such entanglement. Its star players and coaches have confidently dived into the political debates without retribution and with the support of the league commissioner and many team owners, if not all of them.

Today, the political and social sensibilities of the two leagues have been exposed like never before, and the fault line between them touches many of the controversies roiling the country: race relations, the gulf between liberals and conservatives, American nativism vs. globalism, and even the best way to respond to Trump's attacks.

What is so different about these leagues that they find themselves in such contrasting situations?

Clues emerged in September. The president's sharp remarks about the protests during the anthem sent N.F.L. owners into a collective panic that persists. The league's fans have been divided, Trump's base has been energized and N.F.L. players have been agitated. The issue is far from settled.

Trump's rebuffing of the Warriors, however, was met head-on by basketball's biggest star, LeBron James, who called him a bum. Other prominent players spoke out, too. The president slinked away, the way a bully does when faced with unexpected resistance.

"I don't think he got what he wanted out of them because it didn't generate very much controversy or passion among his base," said Joe Lockhart, the former N.F.L. executive who was principally involved with devising the league's crisis management of the anthem issue. "He was not able to generate debate within the N.B.A. community. They all seemed to fall in line behind LeBron and Steph Curry."

Shield vs. Player

It has been nearly two years since the 2016 N.F.L. preseason, when Colin Kaepernick, as a San Francisco 49ers quarterback, sat for the national anthem (he later took to kneeling) to protest police brutality against people of color and economic inequality.

Almost instantly, the posture was usurped into a debate about the national anthem. It has not gone away. Kaepernick, now 30, remains out of football, unsigned, as he was all of last season. A collusion case he filed against the league remains unsettled.

Outside experts and historians cited plenty of reasons the N.F.L. and the N.B.A. find themselves on different sides of this cultural divide, ranging from the N.F.L.'s lack of guaranteed contracts to the N.B.A.'s smaller and more unified work force.

"It's clear that we've got two different leagues — two different kinds of owners, two different groups of consumers," said Charles Ross, a history professor and director of African-American Studies at the University of

Mississippi. "But we've got one group of African-American males. To be sure, the black athletes, whether they are in the N.B.A. or the N.F.L., are together."

The key is how those black players are treated, or believe they are treated. The N.B.A. long has marketed its star players, while the N.F.L. tends to focus on promoting teams and the game itself.

The N.F.L. logo — a ubiquitous red, white and blue shield, conveying some message of power or protection wrapped in the colors of the American flag — is the priority. All things are done in reverence to the shield. It is inanimate.

The N.B.A.'s logo has a person on it (the silhouette of Jerry West), and the image is fitting. It is a league of players, athletic and out front, and that is where the N.B.A. puts its public relations focus.

"LeBron James is a bigger brand than the Sacramento Kings," the former N.F.L. player Trevor Pryce said. "Tom Brady is not as big a brand as the Cleveland Browns."

The games are different, of course. Football has more players, covered in armor, fighting in the trenches and trudging across a vast field. The battle metaphors are hackneyed, but the league has associated itself with the military in myriad ways, from accepting money for military flyovers to the pageantry of its national anthem.

Most football players are as anonymous as soldiers on a battlefield. They are not allowed to take off their helmets on the field. Players are rarely introduced by name when the teams pour onto the field, often through fog and fireworks.

Basketball is less of a militaristic pageant, more an intimate stage show. There is no mistaking who the stars are. Performers show as much skin as uniform, and their faces are instantly recognizable.

One easy measure of the difference: James has more than 38 million followers on Instagram and nearly 42 million on Twitter. Brady, the N.F.L.'s biggest star, has 4.1 million Instagram followers and is not active on Twitter.

The best of those N.B.A. players are also power brokers behind the scenes. The executive committee of the N.B.A. players union looks like a future wing of the Hall of Fame, including James, Curry, Chris Paul and Carmelo Anthony.

The president of the N.F.L. players union's executive committee is the veteran offensive tackle Eric Winston, who hasn't started more than two games since 2013.

"There's a fundamental difference between the two leagues," said Lockhart, who before working for the N.F.L. was a press secretary under President Bill Clinton. "The superstar players in the N.B.A. are also the leaders in the union, and they have enormous influence and are a very cohesive group."

He added: "I'm not saying what's better, it's just different. My sense is that in the N.B.A., you could put three or four players in the room and they could speak for the entire league. You couldn't do that with the N.F.L."

Part of that is sheer numbers: The N.B.A. has about 450 players; the N.F.L. has roughly four times that many.

In both leagues, though, more than two-thirds of players are black. The difference is in the balance of star power.

In the N.B.A., most stars are black, as Washington Wizards guard John Wall pointed out last fall in an article on the website The Ringer. Top N.B.A. players have stood up at awards shows to plead for more social activism. They have led on-court protests, wearing T-shirts in support of unarmed black men who have been killed by police officers. (Some W.N.B.A. players knelt and held protests, eliciting both fines, later rescinded, and compliments from the league president, Lisa Borders.)

In the N.F.L., many marquee players — often quarterbacks — are white. Brady, reportedly a Trump supporter, has stayed mostly silent on sensitive issues. ("I respect why people are doing what they're doing," Brady recently told Oprah Winfrey.) In September, Green Bay's Aaron Rodgers urged fans to link arms in a show of "unity and love," careful not to frame it as a protest.

Charles Grantham, the first executive director of the National Basketball Players Association, said the N.B.A., under the leadership of the former commissioner David Stern and others, decided long ago to give the promotional spotlight to the game's stars.

"One of the things that Stern and these guys learned is that you were selling a predominantly black product to white America," Grantham said. "They recognized that and began to promote these stars. Whereas I don't think the N.F.L. has recognized that."

David J. Leonard, whose books include *After Artest: The N.B.A. and the Assault on Blackness*, notes the complex relationship the league has with race, even recently.

In 2005, desperate to improve perceptions of players, the N.B.A. implemented a strict dress code. Some called it racist. Now it's a widely accepted excuse to make a fashion show out of arena exits and entrances, another forum to showcase individual tastes.

The racial script flipped in 2014, when recordings of the Los Angeles Clippers' owner, Donald Sterling, making racist comments were made public. Players threatened protests. Adam Silver, the new commissioner, sent a lasting message. He barred Sterling for life.

"At a certain level, the N.B.A. has found that middle place of embracing progressive politics, embracing hip-hop, embracing critical conversations about racism while not alienating a segment of white America," said Leonard, a Washington State professor of ethnic studies who studies the confluence of race and sports. "They've concluded that there's a segment of the country that's not going to be part of the market because of the nature of the league, the history, the connection to the cities. That's why the N.B.A. has gone global rather than try to keep attracting red-state America."

Sports' Political Map

By most measures, the N.F.L. remains the country's most successful league. Television ratings, while falling, far exceed those of other American sports. With roughly $14 billion in annual revenue, the N.F.L. rakes in nearly twice what the N.B.A. makes. The average N.F.L. franchise is worth $2.5 billion, by one estimation, compared to $1.65 billion for a typical N.B.A. team.

The N.F.L. also straddles the political spectrum more broadly than others. According to the data analysis site FiveThirtyEight last year, "the N.F.L.

had the most search traffic and the least-partisan fan base" among the major American sports.

"It is a purple institution, to use the political frame — the one sport that most everybody loves," Lockhart said. "The N.F.L. wanted to hear from and listen to all its fans. And when you do that, it gets messy."

The turmoil did not please N.F.L. owners, a conservative lot. At least seven N.F.L. owners gave $1 million or more to Trump's inaugural committee. At least one, New England's Robert K. Kraft, has the president's ear.

N.B.A. team owners are wealthy, too, of course, and mostly white, and not necessarily a liberal group. They have donated about twice as much to Republicans as they have to Democrats in national elections since 1989, though the ratio was flipped in 2016, in favor of Hillary Clinton over Trump.

Most eschew the limelight. They tacitly endorse a player-first hierarchy, at least in marketing terms. They mostly let the players — young, diverse, global, social-media savvy and attuned to racial issues — do the talking on topical subjects, following the lead of politically outspoken coaches like Gregg Popovich and Steve Kerr. Rarely is there much blowback about their opinions.

N.B.A. fans, FiveThirtyEight noted, are the most left-leaning of the major American sports. For players, performing for audiences of progressive fans and accommodating owners, the league feels like a safe place to speak out.

Just as important, several experts noted: N.B.A. contracts, generally, are guaranteed; N.F.L. contracts are not. In most cases, teams can cut players without paying the remainder of the contract.

"You can fold them up and throw them around like a paper airplane," Pryce said. "That's about as much as they're worth. Some of that has found its way into the us-versus-them mentality of players and owners. You can stress this 'family' nonsense all you want to, but guess what? Families don't cut each other."

Ross, the Mississippi professor, said N.F.L. players have been warned not to take controversial stands.

"Colin Kaepernick is paying a very, very, very heavy debt," Ross said. "Don't think that in all 32 N.F.L. locker rooms African-Americans are not talking about that. They've made a harsh example out of him. Individuals have to think long and hard about how far they want to take this issue."

A New Anthem Policy

Late last month, the N.F.L. announced a new anthem policy for the 2018 season. It requires players on the field to "stand and show respect for the flag and the anthem," while allowing players to skip it as long as they stay out of sight. Teams will be fined if players do not follow the rules.

It was another top-down attempt at stamping out a controversy. The N.F.L. Players Association said it was not consulted. Trump pounced.

He endorsed the edict that players stand. For those considering staying in the locker room? "Maybe you shouldn't be in the country," he said.

This month, the Eagles were scheduled to celebrate their Super Bowl win at the White House. Trump, expecting a low turnout, abruptly uninvited them the night before. He blamed the Eagles and suggested that their players did not stand for the anthem. (They all did, throughout last season.)

In a statement, the Eagles expressed disappointment at having the invitation revoked, but did not mention Trump's name. Coach Doug Pederson said that he had been "looking forward to going down" to Washington but did not want to discuss it further. Commissioner Roger Goodell said nothing.

The N.F.L. sidled away. The N.B.A. jumped in. Cleveland and Golden State were in the N.B.A. finals, and players including James, Curry and Kevin Durant reminded everyone that their teams would never go to the White House, not with this president, no matter who won the championship.

Kerr, the Golden State coach, crossed league lines to stick up for the Eagles (and the W.N.B.A. champion Minnesota Lynx, who were not invited to the White House, either). He took direct aim at Trump in ways unfamiliar to the N.F.L.

"The president has made it pretty clear he's going to try to divide us, all of us in this country, for political gain," Kerr said.

He added: "The irony is that the Eagles have been nothing but fantastic citizens in their community," citing the work of Malcolm Jenkins and Chris Long. "Those guys are studs."

It was a glaring juxtaposition to the N.F.L.'s tepid response of its own issue. Silver chimed in with support.

"These players in our league, our coaches, are speaking out on issues that are important to them and important to society," he said. "I encourage them to do that."

39

Durant! Durant!

July 4, 2016: Independence Day for Kevin Durant, freed from landlocked Oklahoma City and the solo theatrics of Russell Westbrook.

Durant was 27, an African-American male given a choice between earning his millions in a conservative stronghold of America's heartland or within the coastal progressivism of the California Bay Area. The option of staying on in a take-turns offense with Westbrook or joining a team already renowned for — as the enduring axiom generally attributed to the Hall of Fame coach Larry Brown goes — playing the right way.

Missing the point by miles, critics pounced on Durant's willingness to join a record 73-win squad that had narrowly beaten his Thunder in the Western Conference finals as a cop-out, virtually a free ride to a ring.

I didn't see it that way. If you can't beat 'em, why not befriend 'em? In the era of the N.B.A.'s elite bonding abroad during Olympic and world championship tournaments, Durant had become best buds with Stephen Curry and Andre Iguodala, both of whom attended the Warriors' pitch meeting with Durant in the Hamptons. After nine years overall and eight in laying organization roots in OKC, one finals appearance and an M.V.P. season, what did Durant owe the Thunder?

His move was also an example of how N.B.A. stars had evolved from what I had called the synthetic Jordan era of the late '90s into the early 21st century, when the young wannabes sought to become the Michael of their markets, treated as the one and only. The Celtics' trio of Kevin Garnett, Ray Allen and Paul Pierce helped to reestablish an old-school standard of sharing. The Big Three in Miami carried it to a higher commercial plane.

Two years and two Warriors' championships after Durant landed by the Bay, he was more of a brand name than ever and his bold move looked like checkmate on King James.

Of course, the common argument was that the continued success of the latest Super Team was becoming kryptonite to the league — somehow forgetting the tremendous growth of the game while the Bulls were winning six titles in eight years (and most likely one or two more had a certain No. 23 not taken leave).

In all the complaining about imbalance and the season being a foregone conclusion, typically forgotten was how the Warriors, before Durant, had been built strategically through the draft — and without that obvious first or second pick to tank for.

The message to the rest of the league front offices was simple. Do better.

Feb. 8, 2017

Kevin Durant Is Gone, Durant, Okla., Is Sad

by Scott Cacciola

DURANT, Okla. — Kelly Green, the men's basketball coach at Southeastern Oklahoma State University, battles relative obscurity by using all the tools at his disposal. Until recently, Green highlighted the campus's unique geography to sell out-of-state prospects on his Division II program.

"We're in the city of Durant," Green would tell recruits, "like Kevin Durant."

Green felt much more comfortable using this tangential connection back when Kevin Durant was still playing for the Oklahoma City Thunder. But those ties disappeared when Durant signed with the Golden State Warriors in free agency over the summer, forcing Green to scrap his pitch.

"When Kevin left, I was like, 'Well, now what do I say?'" Green said. "He really screwed up my spiel."

The grief over Durant (the player) is palpable in Durant (the city), a quiet community of about 17,000 people about 150 miles southeast of Oklahoma City that has, in small ways, paid the price for pure coincidence. One teenager sought retribution by campaigning to change the name of the city to Westbrook. Basketball players at Durant Middle School hear the occasional barbs from opponents.

But mostly, people here — like many Thunder fans across the state — are sad that Durant left.

"Honestly," Caleb Heavner, 12, said, "I cried a little bit."

Kevin Durant is set to make his return to Oklahoma City this weekend, when the Warriors play the Thunder on Saturday night. Vestiges of Durant remain here in Durant, most notably tucked among bins of merchandise at Hibbett Sports on West Main Street. Late last month, on a rack near the cash register marked "Clearance: Up to 50% off," six Durant T-shirts from his days with the Thunder were priced to sell at $4.97 apiece. They were not exactly flying out the door.

Natalie Robertson, an assistant manager at the store, said some people had bought Durant T-shirts around the holidays as gag gifts. At least one patron, she said, had announced his intention to use one as kindling for a bonfire, which was perhaps an unorthodox form of therapy.

"But most people are like, 'Why are you still selling these?'" she said.

Considered the magnolia capital of Oklahoma, Durant — traditionally pronounced DEW-rant rather than duh-RANT — was founded in the early 19th century by Dixon Durant, a prominent businessman, minister and civic leader. (Kevin Durant is not in any way related to Dixon Durant.) The city itself is a fairly tranquil place, complete with tourist attractions.

"You know we have the world's largest peanut, right?" asked Asia Willingham, a teacher whose husband, Zach, coaches the seventh-grade boys' basketball team at Durant Middle School.

But that sense of civic serenity was briefly upended over the summer thanks to the handiwork of Ryan Nazari, a 17-year-old high school student from Edmond, Okla. Dismayed by Durant's decision, Nazari started a petition on Change.org that sought to rebrand the city. Durant would become Westbrook, after Russell Westbrook, the Thunder's star point guard.

"Everyone was just really upset over Durant leaving, especially me," Nazari said in a telephone interview. "So why not poke some fun and laugh for a change? The petition was really just a joke."

And then it quickly became popular, collecting nearly 3,000 signatures. Nazari's parents were unaware of their son's extracurricular project until they heard about it on the local news.

"And my dad was like, 'What are you doing?'" said Nazari, who plans to study biomechanical engineering in college.

It might be worth noting that Nazari has never actually been to Durant, where most residents seemed to get a kick out of the petition. They are, however, not changing the name of the city. Nicolas Crouse, a 13-year-old shooting guard at Durant Middle School, has a vested interest in the status quo. His great-great-great-great-great-grandfather, he said, was Dixon Durant.

Like Nazari, Crouse said he was bummed about Kevin Durant. In the dreary aftermath of Durant's decision, Crouse dug out his Durant replica jersey but resisted the urge to cut it into tiny pieces. Instead, he settled on a more peaceful form of protest: He slapped a strip of masking tape across the name on the back and wrote "Westbrook" on it.

If there are others who cannot help themselves, Crouse does not entertain any fantasies that Durant will ever return to the Thunder. Crouse values loyalty.

"He left," he said. "And I can understand that. But I don't really like him anymore."

Heavner, one of Crouse's teammates, attended several Durant-era games at Chesapeake Energy Arena, including one in January 2014 when Durant scored a career-high 54 points in a narrow win over the Warriors. Heavner said he had looked up to Durant. He tried to emulate his shooting stroke.

"He could score the ball with such ease," Heavner said.

As for the N.B.A. All-Star Game this month, when Westbrook and Durant will be reunited as teammates for the Western Conference, Heavner offered Westbrook some unsolicited advice.

"I hope he doesn't pass him the ball," Heavner said.

Green, the coach at Southeastern, where Dennis Rodman was a star player in the mid–1980s, said he would never blame a professional athlete for pursuing another opportunity. It is a business, after all.

"Players get traded, and coaches get fired," Green said. "Billy Donovan, he's doing a great job coaching the Thunder. But one day he's going to take another job or get fired. And that's pro sports."

The hard part for Oklahomans, Green said, was coping with the realization that they could be spurned by a high-profile athlete whom many considered an adopted son. This was a new and disheartening experience for many of the Thunder's more impassioned fans. Remember: When the Seattle SuperSonics relocated to Oklahoma City in 2008 as the Thunder, the franchise became the state's first to compete in any of the four major pro leagues — and Durant was the face of that franchise.

"So when the team came here," Green said, "the feeling was: 'Oh, he'll never leave. He's going to build himself a house out in Edmond, and he's going to live here forever.'"

That did not turn out to be. Jalik Lewis, a 13-year-old point guard at Durant Middle School, dwells on missed opportunities. When Durant was still playing for the Thunder, Lewis thought it would have been cool if Durant had actually visited Durant.

"Because his last name is Durant," Lewis said. "Who wouldn't love that?"

But while Lewis was disappointed by Durant's departure, he does not hold grudges, he said. He prizes his three Durant jerseys, his two Durant T-shirts, his Durant sneakers and his Durant athletic socks.

"Kevin Durant's still the main man," Lewis said. "I mean, I was heartbroken. But it was his decision, not mine. So I'm not going to put him down."

At the same time, Lewis does not expect Durant to be warmly received in Oklahoma City this weekend.

"I think everybody's just going to throw a big fit," he said. "But I also hope that people would have gotten over it by now and be a little more mature."

Here in Durant, there may not be joy, but at least there is a little bit of forgiveness.

June 8, 2017

Kevin Durant Outplays, Outlasts and Outmaneuvers LeBron James

by Harvey Araton

When Kevin Durant rose for a 3-point shot that froze LeBron James in his Nike-sponsored tracks and ultimately drained the remaining tension from the N.B.A. finals late Wednesday night, he all but punctuated the message that this was his time and his title, and that he had leveraged his way onto what remains a perfect postseason team.

James called Durant's audacious launch from the left wing with 45.3 seconds remaining in Game 3 "a bomb in transition," and it was. Once again in the fourth quarter, Durant had outplayed and outlasted James and, in the larger sense, outmaneuvered the league's reigning master of free-agent mobility.

James, in 2010, had perfected a longstanding tradition of pro basketball's best players wielding leverage like a weapon, raising it to a new commercial level while bolting Cleveland for Miami. There, he won two championships with Dwyane Wade and Chris Bosh. He then returned home to northeast Ohio and might well have been defending consecutive titles — not just last year's — over the last week had the Cavaliers not lost Kevin Love and Kyrie Irving to injuries in the first of this fascinating trilogy with the Golden State Warriors.

But Durant's much-debated and derided move to the Warriors from Oklahoma City dramatically rewrote the sport's competitive equation, not unlike a fair number of leading men have done before. James more or less conceded that when he said, in the aftermath of Wednesday's crushing 118–113 defeat, "I played against some great teams, but I don't think no team has had this type of firepower."

He also understands, better than anyone, that the criticism of Durant for bidding Oklahoma City and Russell Westbrook adieu weeks after the Thunder had surrendered a 3–1 Western Conference finals lead to the Warriors last season was overdone and historically ignorant.

The great players in the N.B.A. have always understood how to exploit their muscle, one way or another. From much of the reaction to Durant's decision, you would have thought no other ringless superstar had ever jilted a rising league power, but that large, smiling man sitting behind the ABC broadcast team Wednesday night was a useful reminder otherwise.

Granted, in bolting Orlando for the Los Angeles Lakers in 1996, Shaquille O'Neal didn't enlist with the team that had just ambushed his arena, but, really, what's the difference? What's wrong with a player using his collectively bargained freedom from the much richer owners to choose a team he envisions as a better fit for him in a place he believes is more desirable in which to live?

In the pre-free-agent days, Wilt Chamberlain moved, West to East and then East to West. Kareem Abdul-Jabbar brooded his way out of Milwaukee, to the Lakers, where he teamed with Magic Johnson to win five titles. The folks who would tell you that Kobe Bryant would never have left the Lakers forget that he threatened to on occasion and manipulated the entire draft process to get there in the first place.

No question, Durant's Oklahoma City departure has contributed mightily to a competitively lopsided postseason, with the Warriors, now 15–0, and the Cavaliers blowing through conference play and the Warriors just one victory from an unprecedented four-series sweep. The guess is James and the Cavaliers will fight hard to prevent that in Game 4 on Friday night, the league will survive if it happens and its fan base will eventually look back in awe.

As Adam Silver, the league's commissioner, said last week, "The fan in me would love to see more competition at times, but on the other hand, I've said it before, I think we should also celebrate excellence.

"I also think these things have a way of working themselves out," he added.

It's entirely possible the Warriors are embarking on a run to match or exceed what Michael Jordan achieved in Chicago across the 1990s. They are young and apparently selfless enough, but we'll see how success impacts them and how the more smartly run franchises in the league respond.

The life span of envisioned indestructibility is always in question, as Mike Tyson proved, and later Tiger Woods. For a very long time now, James has been thought to be indefatigable, the basketball specimen impervious to frailty. But, at 32, the do-it-all quality of his play and the magnitude of his effort is finally taking its toll, exacerbated by the energy-sapping burden presented by Durant at both ends of the court, and by the Warriors over all.

Steve Kerr, the Warriors' coach, was speaking of Kyrie Irving and James, who together scored 77 points over a combined 90 minutes in Game 3, when he said: "Both those guys were amazing, 38 and 39. But that takes a lot out of you. We just kept telling the guys, they're going to get tired. Stay in front of them. Force them into outside shots, if you can. Fatigue will play a role."

James had scoffed at the question of fatigue before Game 3, reminding a reporter that he had averaged a triple double in the first two games, snapping: "Do I look tired?"

The proof is in the performance. James's last field goal Wednesday night came with 6 minutes 54 seconds remaining. He missed a very makable stepback 12-footer in the lane at the 1:29 mark and the Cavaliers up, 113–109. His legs didn't respond fast enough to Durant on the game's pivotal possession. Durant outscored him by 14–7 in the fourth quarter (and by 31–11 in the period over three games).

Of Durant, Kerr said: "You can tell he knows this is his moment. He's been an amazing player in this league for a long time, and I think he's — he senses this is his time, his moment, his team.

"When I say his team, I mean it's not literally just his team," Kerr added. "We got a group around him that can help him and create space for him with the shooting and the playmaking, and I think he's having the time of his life out there."

In a nutshell, Kerr was asking, what is so wrong with an era in which the truly great players prefer to share the ball and the burden, as opposed to those post-Jordan years when one roster often wasn't big enough for two franchise stars, and when we said his team, we meant literally just his team?

The Warriors have raised the bar on the drafting, development and acquiring of star-laden talent. And now James is almost out of time and chances to stop Durant, the Warriors' finishing piece, from holding up the trophy and telling him, among others, your move.

MAY 16, 2018

Inside the Hamptons House Where Kevin Durant Hosted N.B.A. Suitors in 2016

BY MALIKA ANDREWS AND MARC STEIN

EAST HAMPTON, N.Y. — The client wanted a 10-day house rental in the Hamptons that offered privacy and proximity to East Hampton Airport. Several important guests would be visiting.

The real estate broker handling the account lined up three options. The first one she showed the client's manager was a farmhouse built in the 1800s. The door frames were deemed too low.

"We would cut to the chase much better if I knew who it was," said the broker, Renee Gallanti, recalling how she was not told at first who the client was for that house-hunting mission in 2016. "At first they tried to give very little information at all. And after we got to the first house and the ceilings were too low, we shifted gears."

The client, she soon learned, was Kevin Durant, the 7-foot N.B.A. All-Star. He was about to become a free agent for the first time — and would soon find himself at the heart of a courtship unlike any the N.B.A. had ever seen.

Durant ultimately picked the Golden State Warriors, a seismic decision for the league, and is expected by many to win a second consecutive title with them next month. Their lineup of Stephen Curry, Klay Thompson, Draymond Green, Andre Iguodala and Durant was nicknamed the Hamptons 5 — a label that has gained popularity during these playoffs and serves as a nod to those who joined team officials in East Hampton in the summer of 2016 to recruit Durant.

But the precise setting for Durant's meetings with his coveters has remained undisclosed until now. It all happened at 189 Further Lane, a five-bedroom, 7,400-square-foot estate one block from the Atlantic Ocean. If a

Warriors fan who truly appreciates the significance of what happened on this property would like to own it as the ultimate souvenir, it's on the market for just under $15 million.

Further Lane is not just any road in the Hamptons. Behind hedges dense and tall, its homes have long sheltered a mix of posh and artsy. Jerry Seinfeld, Jann Wenner and Larry Gagosian have or have had homes down the street that way. Jacqueline Kennedy Onassis's childhood summer retreat, Lasata, is up the road the other way.

"As soon as Rich started walking towards the house, he was elbowing me," Gallanti said, referring to Durant's manager, Rich Kleiman. "He was like, 'This is the house.'"

Durant paid $100,000 for the 10-day rental.

Kleiman and Durant had considered holding the meetings in Manhattan, Los Angeles or Washington, Durant's hometown. But they chose the Hamptons for the sake of privacy and to shorten the commute for Durant's and Kleiman's East Coast-based families. This was especially important to Durant's father, Wayne Pratt, who wanted to participate in all of the meetings.

A Los Angeles broker working with Kleiman contacted Gallanti to help find a short-term rental in East Hampton. Gallanti was unaware that six suitors would be passing through: the Golden State Warriors, the San Antonio Spurs, the Miami Heat, the Los Angeles Clippers, the Oklahoma City Thunder and the Boston Celtics — who would have Tom Brady in tow.

The property at 189 Further Lane is owned by Peter Wilson, a retired lawyer, who had purchased the estate and built the existing house in 2004. The previous house at the address, according to Wilson and his realtor, Patti Wadzinski, was owned by a former mafia member. That house was nearly windowless, they said.

"That house was very, very private," Wilson, 62, said in a phone interview.

The front door of the current home opens into a spacious living room with tan couches on the left and a large round black table with six chairs on the right — suitable for meetings with N.B.A. teams. It was in this room that the elaborate virtual reality presentation that the Warriors prepared for Durant, to give him a glimpse of what life at Oracle Arena would be like, malfunctioned. To their relief, Warriors officials later learned that Durant was happy to take advantage of the extra time to chat with his future Hamptons 5 colleagues and hear more from them directly about how they thought the partnership would play out.

The master bedroom, where Durant stayed, features a raised seating area and double doors that open onto a porch. The room has a queen-size bed, but for Durant's stay arrangements were made to bring in a king size.

There is a large lap pool on one side of the house and a Jacuzzi on the other — both surrounded by vegetation maintained by staff. A cedar bridge connects the pool area to a grass tennis court.

According to Wadzinski, when the mafia member owned the house, what is now the tennis court was a house for the man's girlfriend.

"It's a romance bridge," Wadzinski said, wiggling her eyebrows. "Or now it's a bromance bridge."

That bridge is where Durant stood with his arms crossed for a photographer that appeared on the Players' Tribune website under the headline, "My Next Chapter," announcing his departure from the Thunder and commitment to the Warriors.

Two years later, Durant and his four most influential teammates routinely exchange text messages in a group chat they've labeled the Hamptons 5.

The aftermath was a bit less glamorous for Gallanti and Wadzinski, who worked to preserve the secret nature of the location. Once Durant's party departed, they dug through the trash cans to remove any documents or basketball-related materials that could have revealed what had happened at 189 Further Lane.

Wilson, meanwhile, didn't know at the time what, exactly, was going on inside his home. He is not a big N.B.A. fan. But he has come to understand the magnitude of what happened on his property.

"It can become part of the lure as I try to sell my house," he said.

40
Magic's Man

The state of modern free-agent affairs was the nightmare that Red Auerbach was having when, in 1977, he wrote in *The Times* that the new system empowering players "works against motivation, desire and discipline." He also claimed to have always paid his players fairly based on their contributions — statistical or otherwise — to a winning team.

He must have forgotten all the requested raises he dismissed by coyly asking if a player would prefer a trade to Cincinnati, or some other burg far from Bill Russell's cocoon, where an annual championship run and the financial benefits that came with it was more prayer than plan.

Contractual benefits inserted into the collective bargaining agreement for staying with one's existing team notwithstanding, the opportunity for players to control their destinies had been decided in federal courts decades before. The superstars of the sport had long wielded maneuvering clout — pouting as a substitute for producing was usually quite effective as a trade demand. But now, thanks largely to the paradigm set by LeBron James, superstars were pulling much harder in the eternal tug of war between management and labor.

Magic, Bird and Michael were never moved to exercise that power — or never had to on teams that satisfied their competitive demands. Had Bird or Magic landed in Sacramento, he might not have stayed long.

Many bemoaned the mysterious tactics of Kawhi Leonard in forcing his way out of San Antonio in the summer of 2018. But leverage is only great and deserved when the timing is right, as little Isaiah Thomas sadly discovered when the Celtics wisely but coldheartedly traded him after he'd played spectacularly during the 2016–17 season and hurt in the playoffs, and while mourning the death of his sister.

No question, reading that LeBron would be reaping a $40 million payout from the Magic Johnson–run Lakers by the fourth year of his deal could be disorienting for those old enough to know that Oscar Robertson topped out at $250,000 in 1973–74. Worse, when the N.B.A. in 2014 negotiated new television deals worth $24 billion over nine years, fringe starters and backup centers — think Timofey Mozgov and his $64 million — scored mind-numbing deals.

Was the league, as Auerbach had predicted, on the road to bloated ruin? The sky wasn't — and could never be — cloud-free. Cable cord-cutters were presenting a stiff challenge to the business model of ESPN and other cable networks. Perhaps a reckoning related to soaring ticket prices awaited.

Yet the common industry belief was that live sports entertainment would retain its golden worth for fast-multiplying forums that desired it. The global exploration and expansion was far from complete. And new revenue streams were always on the minds of Adam Silver and the owners: A first-of-its-kind deal made MGM Resorts International the N.B.A.'s official partner after the Supreme Court sanctioned sports betting.

Whatever share of the riches the likes of LeBron and K.D. were extracting, the case could always be made that they were underpaid.

JUNE 7, 2018

LeBron James Delivered. Now Does He Exit?

BY MICHAEL POWELL

CLEVELAND — For four years now, LeBron James has faced brutal June math.

If the man from Akron fails to go galactic in even a single game, if he misses those fallaway jumpers that make defenders close their eyes and shake their heads, if he fails to barrel to the hoop like a B.&O. freight train, if he has trouble levitating to swat away shots, if he is merely human, the Cleveland Cavaliers lose.

Ever since Ohio's native son wandered back from his Miami Beach idyll in 2014, he has, in the N.B.A. championship round, faced the Golden State Warriors, a team that gets more talented each year. James has dragged the weakest Cavaliers team yet to this year's showdown with the Warriors, and now it is perched at the edge of defeat's abyss, down three games to none.

His fans, which is to say a generous portion of the population of Ohio, have a sense of time fleeting.

James will become a free agent, and in his 34th summer, he could well leave for a better-crafted team in another city. Rumors have him going to Los Angeles, Houston, Philadelphia or San Antonio. In 2010, when he left for the Miami Heat, the citizens of Ohio erupted in a collective and pained tantrum, as fans burned his No. 23 jersey and the team's billionaire owner indulged in inane talk of treachery and betrayal.

A replay is difficult to imagine. No doubt some fans will grumble and moan, but he has delivered on his promises. James brought that first championship to Cleveland. It's an intriguing moment when a man and his fans appear to have matured in their relationship with each other.

Before Game 3 of the N.B.A. finals, I wandered the streets and canal walkways of Akron — Rubber City, baby. Then I headed to Cleveland. And again and again, I heard the same sentiment.

James is approaching late middle age in basketball terms. Through a partnership between his foundation and University of Akron, he showered tens of millions of dollars on college scholarships for poor and working-class kids and he speaks up to a president intent on stirring racial embers to no good end.

A man-child has become a man.

"LeBron? I'll talk LeBron all day long!"

Rachel Walker stops to talk with me in a parking lot within sight of the Cavaliers' arena in Cleveland. She's a nurse and she is taking her adult daughter, who is disabled and wearing a Cavaliers hat, to the game.

"He said he would give us a championship — and he did," she said. "He said he would not forget our children — and he never did. You know why the president doesn't go after the N.B.A.? Because LeBron James will go back at him.

"Whatever he does, I wish him nothing but the best."

I cross the street and sit awhile with Terry Smith, a husky and retired veteran of the railroads. He brought his grandchildren downtown to soak up the pregame vibe. "He brought Cleveland a championship, right? He has tremendous scholarship programs for Akron and Cleveland, right? He plays 48 minutes a game, right?"

Almost: James played 46 minutes 52 seconds in Game 3, four minutes more than any other player.

Having added up the tab, he gives me the total: "He has the right to take care of his family and go wherever he wants."

The Cavaliers and their owner, Dan Gilbert, have not exactly held up their side. The five best players on the court Wednesday evening were James, Kevin Durant, Stephen Curry, Klay Thompson and Draymond Green.

Save for James, all were Warriors.

James could not find the mortar range on his jump shot on Wednesday, but he scored 33 points on a variety of drives, flips, hooks and baby jumpers.

He also grabbed 10 rebounds, added 11 assists, had a couple of steals and swatted two more away.

A play in the third quarter was emblematic.

The Warriors' Andre Iguodala, a classy defender and crafty scorer, got the ball near the Cavaliers' hoop. Only James stood in his way. Iguodala faked and faked again. James did not bite, so Iguodala pitched quickly to Green, whose brilliance as a player is diminished only by his adolescent temperament. Green broke into a smile as he rose to dunk, even as James flicked rattlesnake quick hands and slapped the ball off Green's knee and out of bounds.

James immediately took the ball out, came steaming upcourt and tossed a brilliant pass for an assist.

It was like watching a pirate captain swinging from the mizzenmast, dueling all comers: It was great drama, and it works against almost any team not named the Golden State Warriors.

Cleveland's defense, most often a porous swamp, was watertight for much of this night. It held the Warriors' sharpshooting backcourt, Thompson and Curry, to 21 points on 7-for-27 shooting.

Unfortunately, this did not account for Durant. He is 7 feet, with elegantly long arms and the soft hands of a jeweler. To watch his pregame workout was its own treat. This night, he stood 20 feet from the basket and had a coach zip him a pass. He caught it and spun 360 degrees on his heel, came to a stop and just as quickly spun back. He immediately shot the ball.

I watched him do this 15 times in a row, and he did not miss once. I looked around for a security guard. Someone needed to pass a note of warning to James.

"He's an assassin," James said afterward.

And here's where the impossibility of this team comes to bear: On any given night, when Curry is shimmying and shooting and Thompson is his metronomic shooting self, Durant is the team's third option. Coach Steve Kerr acknowledged the glory of it. "Yeah, it's pretty nice; a luxury," he said.

"You know that you can never, ever relax," James said.

Earlier that day, I sat on George Kimbrough's porch in Akron, and listened as the disabled 71-year-old welder talked of how LeBron purchased hundreds of bikes for neighborhood kids and then led summer rides around his hometown, the Pied Piper of Akron. "That man has earned the right to go and find a team worthy of his talent," Kimbrough said, then looked at me and cackled. "Don't talk bad about that man around here unless you want a fight."

I wander down one ravine to another until I reach Overlook Terrace. It is a dead-end street and there are thickets of beech, black cherry and red oak on three sides. The street has four dowager homes, several well into their dotage. Twenty-five years ago, James and his mother washed up here, after losing one apartment or another. An older woman, Mrs. Reeves, gave shelter from the storm. James quickly put up a poster of Michael Jordan over his bed.

Then he and the neighborhood kids nailed a hoop and wooden backboard to a slanting telephone pole and played all day long. A few twisted nails are still visible. Ben Brown lived there then and now, and he recalls James as a friendly little kid — he holds his hand about three feet off the ground.

Brown has a carpet business, Barefoot Carpet, and ducks and chickens and a tomato patch out back. He figures James long ago earned the right to do as he wants. Maybe he stays, maybe he goes. That's up to him.

We chat for a while longer, and he talks of the college scholarships for local children. He also enjoys that a kid from Overlook Terrace does not back down from an orange-haired provocateur president.

A train whistle sounds loud and mournful. It's the Cuyahoga Valley line rumbling through, just behind those oaks.

"I'm happy for him," Ben says. "James inspires me still."

JULY 2, 2018

The Lakers Got Their Man (That's What the Lakers Do)

BY BENJAMIN HOFFMAN

LeBron James, like Wilt Chamberlain, Kareem Abdul-Jabbar and Shaquille O'Neal before him, was drawn to Los Angeles. But can he deliver like they did?

Fans of the Los Angeles Lakers can be forgiven if they are not exactly bowled over by the news that LeBron James, a once-in-a-generation talent, decided to join their team. After all, they have been watching this scenario play out since the late 1960s.

The Minneapolis Lakers of the 1950s became a powerhouse dynasty after acquiring George Mikan when a competing league he was playing in folded. The franchise continued to be relevant thanks to homegrown stars like Elgin Baylor and Jerry West, but starting with the acquisition of Wilt Chamberlain in 1968, the team has shown a knack for knowing when their homegrown talent needs an injection of star power.

James, whom they agreed to terms with on Sunday, is one of four players, each of whom joined the Lakers reasonably close to his prime, who have a legitimate claim at being among the N.B.A.'s 10 best players of all time.

There are those who might try to include Karl Malone, Gary Payton, Dwight Howard and Steve Nash in a list of the team's acquisition highlights, but beyond Howard — a rental who did not work out for a variety of reasons — those players had already lost several steps by the time they arrived.

A look at the Lakers' Big Four acquisitions reveals some similar themes in terms of the players deciding Los Angeles was the right home for them, their previous teams having been fairly powerless to stop them, and, in what could be good news for current Lakers fans disappointed by the team's current five-season playoff drought, they led to championships.

WILT CHAMBERLAIN
Acquired via trade, July 9, 1968

Age at his Lakers debut: 32

Accomplishments: Nine-time All-Star, four-time most valuable player, one-time champion entering his 10th season.

Chamberlain, who in 1968 was the N.B.A.'s all-time leading scorer, was considered the finest offensive player the game had ever seen and was coming off a season in which he had averaged 24.3 points, 23.8 rebounds and 8.6 assists a game. His Philadelphia 76ers had been knocked out of the playoffs in the second round, and the knock against him at that point was that he was not a winner like Bill Russell of the Boston Celtics. He wanted to move along, so he joined a Lakers team that already had Elgin Baylor and Jerry West but had thus far been unable to top the Celtics in the finals.

The trade: The Lakers sent to the 76ers Jerry Chambers, Archie Clark and Darrall Imhoff.

In his coach's (dramatically understated) words: "Over all we're going to be quite a bit stronger," said Butch van Breda Kolff, the Lakers coach. "We had our rebounding problems last year, but I don't envision them this year."

How it turned out: Chamberlain played the final five seasons of his career for the Lakers, going 1 for 3 in finals appearances.

KAREEM ABDUL-JABBAR
Acquired via trade, June 16, 1975

Age at his Lakers debut: 29

Accomplishments: Six-time All-Star, three-time most valuable player and one-time champion entering his seventh season.

Abdul-Jabbar was a force of nature for the Milwaukee Bucks, leading them to an N.B.A. title in just the third year of the team's existence, and he was coming off a season in which he had averaged 30 points, 14 rebounds and 4.1 assists a game. But with Oscar Robertson having retired, the Bucks missed the playoffs in 1974–75 and Abdul-Jabbar badly wanted out of the small city, saying, "I'm not criticizing the people here, but Milwaukee is not what I'm all about. The things I relate to aren't in Milwaukee." The Lakers, beyond playing in the city where Abdul-Jabbar went to college, were a bit of an odd choice, as Gail Goodrich was the team's only truly significant player at that point, and the veteran of the 1972 title-winning team was already 32, but Abdul-Jabbar had them back to winning titles by his fifth season with the team.

The trade: The Bucks sent Abdul-Jabbar and Walt Wesley to the Lakers for Junior Bridgeman, Elmore Smith, Brian Winters and Dave Meyers.

Quotation from one of the guys he was traded for: "Frankly, I think the Bucks really got the best of the deal," Bridgeman said.

How it turned out: Abdul-Jabbar played his final 14 seasons for the Lakers, winning five titles and retiring as the N.B.A.'s all-time leading scorer, a record he still holds.

SHAQUILLE O'NEAL
Signed as a free agent, July 18, 1996

Age at his Lakers debut: 24

Accomplishments: Four-time All-Star and one-time N.B.A. finalist entering his fifth season.

O'Neal, despite being so young, was already one of the most dominant players in the game, and was coming off a season in which he had averaged 26.6 points, 11 rebounds and 2.9 assists a game. He had formed a terrific partnership with Anfernee Hardaway and had already led the Orlando Magic to one finals appearance, and in his final season with that team took them to the Eastern Conference finals. Orlando made the largest offer to O'Neal, but the big center yearned for something new and he chose instead to sign with the Lakers. At the time, he had no way of knowing that the rookie the team had just drafted, Kobe Bryant, would prove to be a perfect complement to him on the court (regardless of how poorly they got along everywhere else).

The deal: He signed a seven-year contract worth $121 million.

Quotation from the man himself (which would prove fairly prophetic): "To me, change is for the good," O'Neal said. "I'm a military child, used to moving every three or four years."

How it turned out: O'Neal stuck around for the full seven years, but by that point the relationship between him and Bryant had severely deteriorated. The team traded him to the Miami Heat for Caron Butler, Brian Grant, Lamar Odom and two draft picks, but not before he and Bryant had led the Lakers to three championships.

LeBron James
Agreed to terms as a free agent, July 1, 2018

Age at his Lakers debut: 33

Accomplishments: Fourteen-time All-Star, four-time most valuable player and three-time champion going into his 16th season.

James had what could be considered his finest season last year, averaging 27.5 points, 8.6 rebounds and 9.1 assists a game and leading the Cleveland Cavaliers to their fourth consecutive appearance in the N.B.A. finals. Unfortunately, everything around him was wrong. The roster was incomplete after the Kyrie Irving trade and a midseason shake-up failed to fix it. James often felt like a one-man show — never more so than an the end of Game 1 of the finals when he watched helplessly as J.R. Smith dribbled out Cleveland's chances of winning — and it became clear that a change of scenery was attractive even after he had ended the city's long pro sports championship drought. In the end, Los Angeles was where he wanted to live.

The deal: He signed a four-year contract worth $154 million.

Quotation from James's social media account: "Thank you Northeast Ohio for an incredible four seasons. This will always be home."

How it will turn out: There is far too much roster maneuvering to possibly predict that, but with Paul George having re-upped in Oklahoma City, building a roster that can compete with the Golden State Warriors will be difficult.

Parting Shots From the Rings Leader

G.O.A.T. arguments are generational. They are loud, sometimes obnoxious. They are also fun and never to be settled.

But Sopan Deb, *The Times*'s culture writer, wrote that he was tired of the endless debate on Michael versus LeBron, which conveniently ignored other deserving all-timers, including Kareem Abdul-Jabbar, whose quotation from an ESPN story Deb included while writing in Marc Stein's weekly newsletter during summer 2018.

"The reason there is no such thing as the G.O.A.T. is because every player plays under unique circumstances," the erudite Abdul-Jabbar said. "We played different positions, under different rules, with different teammates, with different coaches. Every player has to adapt to their circumstances and find a way to excel. This isn't *Highlander*. There can be more than one."

But as Deb concluded: put a gun to his head and he, a Celtics fan, would choose the guy who was the heart and soul of a team that won and won and won — 11 championships in 13 years from 1957 to 1969.

On that closing note, last words of a long and prosperous story to William Felton Russell.

June 24, 2017

Red Auerbach Told Bill Russell, 'I'm the Coach and You'll Fit.'

by Scott Cacciola

There are decorated athletes, and then there is Bill Russell.

As the dominant man in the middle for the Boston Celtics from 1956 to 1969, Russell was a 12-time All-Star selection. He won 11 N.B.A. championships, the last two as the team's player-coach. He won the rare triple of Olympic gold medal, N.B.A. championship and college title. Indeed, he won two of those at the University of San Francisco.

But even as Russell, 83, revolutionized the game with his defensive prowess from the center position, he may have made his greatest impact as a civil rights pioneer. He was the first African-American to coach a major professional sports team. In 2011, he was awarded the Presidential Medal of Freedom.

This month, he appeared on a dais with the Golden State Warriors to present Kevin Durant with the N.B.A. finals' Most Valuable Player Award — an award that is named after Russell.

There is more: On Monday, Russell will receive the Lifetime Achievement Award at the inaugural N.B.A. Awards show, which will be broadcast by TNT at 9:00 P.M. Eastern. Russell, who plans to attend the ceremony, was recently interviewed by telephone from his home in the Seattle area. This interview has been edited and condensed.

In light of your most recent award, what do you feel are your meaningful contributions to the game?
I was a part of a wave of black players that came into the league and played successfully. Before my time, everybody thought of black players as the Harlem Globetrotters. People expected comedy, and they didn't get it. So it was a newly respected level of black players — that we were not Globetrotters

but very good players. You had guys like Oscar Robertson and Elgin Baylor — they could play! And you could not just give them a pat on the head, you know? They eliminated the "you guys" label. In fact, I remember how Jerry West was respected — they used to say that he played like he was black.

I was also the first player recognized for my defense rather than my offense. I think those are examples of how I may have helped change the game.

A lot of today's stars are using their platform to speak out about issues that are important to them, including race relations and gun violence. Are you heartened by the level of social awareness exhibited by some of the players of this generation?

I suppose. I think that every generation throughout the whole society have social issues that they deal with. And this generation is no different. The issues are different, but the fact that they're dealing with them is not different.

What do you think of today's style of play? What do you like about the game, and what don't you like?

It's more one-on-one. I thought it was a team game, and they're getting away from the team aspect and more into one-on-one. And I don't subscribe to that. What we should be working toward is trying to take the team concept to its final conclusion: The best team will be the best team. It's changed.

The Golden State Warriors are probably the best example of that team concept in today's N.B.A. Given your style of play, do you think you could have fit with that team?

When you look back and compare the '50s and the '60s with today's Warriors, I think you'll find that they had a lot in common. In my day, I was just playing basketball — and I could play. I remember when I went to the Celtics, there were questions about whether I could fit in with that group because they were known for being a very offensive team. Red Auerbach, when I got there, he says: "You may be worried about playing with this team. But I'm the coach, and you'll fit."

Some folks tried to encourage me to say that I wanted to play someplace where the team was more defense-oriented. And my attitude was, "I can play and will play defense here." There were very serious questions if I could play pro ball, you know? Some said that I couldn't shoot free throws, couldn't do this, couldn't do that. And I was glad that they said that, because those were the guys that I beat the hell out of.

We're seeing all these centers launching 3-pointers now. If the 3-point line had existed during your era, would you have tried to develop a 3-point shot?
No. Take the game like you find it and play it to the best of your ability.

So you're not jealous of them?
Not at all! That's the only kind of shot they can get off!

42

Update: From Toronto to China

June 14, 2019

New Coach, New Star:
The Raptors Made All the Right Moves

By Scott Cacciola

OAKLAND, Calif. — For six games, Fred VanVleet was tasked with the most difficult defensive assignment of his life: Attach himself to one of the N.B.A.'s greatest scorers as the Toronto Raptors pursued a piece of history. So, for six games, VanVleet chased Stephen Curry of the Golden State Warriors. Six games of back cuts and pull-up jumpers and crossover dribbles and punishing screens.

"A million screens," VanVleet said.

It was like wading into choppy waters and bracing for wave after wave.

But late Thursday night, as the Raptors began to celebrate their first championship after closing out the Warriors with a 114-110 victory in Game 6 of the N.B.A. finals, VanVleet wore a Champagne-soaked T-shirt and a stitched-up gash under his right eye as he reflected on helping topple the league's most majestic team. The Raptors, he said, were not conventional champions.

"It's not the glam stars," VanVleet said, adding: "We got guys who had to get it the long way, who had to get it out of the mud, who had to get it against the grain. And we got a team full of them coming from all different places, all walks of life, all different life stories to get to this point. But we got some talent — we got some talent for sure."

In fairness, the Raptors did have one glam star: Kawhi Leonard, the long-limbed forward who was named the finals' most valuable player after averaging 28.5 points and 9.8 rebounds against the Warriors. But Leonard was eager to share that award with Kyle Lowry, the All-Star point guard who has been one of the few staples of the organization in recent seasons.

"It's been a long time coming," Lowry said.

The Raptors' path to a title was far from a straight line. In each of the past three seasons, they were knocked out of the playoffs by the LeBron James-led Cleveland Cavaliers, and his departure for the Los Angeles Lakers last summer created an opportunity that Toronto was eager to seize. But that opportunity only took shape thanks to years of calculated risks and personnel changes orchestrated by Masai Ujiri, the team's president of basketball operations — a zillion zigzags that ultimately led the Raptors to the very top.

"To do it with the group of guys that we did it with is amazing," said Lowry, who scored 26 points on Thursday. "It's just kind of still surreal."

Ujiri's most obvious gamble, of course, was trading for Leonard last summer — even though Leonard had just one year remaining on his contract, did not list Toronto as one of his preferred destinations and was acquired in exchange for DeMar DeRozan, who was shipped to San Antonio after spending nine seasons with the Raptors.

Leonard, aware that Lowry and DeRozan were close, said he sent Lowry a text message after the trade.

"I said, 'Let's go out and do something special,'" Leonard recalled. "'I know your best friend left. I know you're mad. But let's make this thing work out.' And here we are today."

Ujiri's other big move last summer was replacing Coach Dwane Casey with Nick Nurse, a bespectacled assistant who had spent most of his career overseas and in the N.B.A. G League. Nurse was both unproven (at least as an N.B.A. coach) and undaunted, and those qualities seemed to make him the perfect fit for a team full of strivers.

"Two months of playoff basketball, and they never seemed tired to me," Nurse said. "Mentally, they kept wanting film sessions, they kept wanting to walk through some things, they kept wanting to keep learning and improving."

The Raptors have turned player development into something of a science. Just two years ago, Pascal Siakam (the 27th pick of the 2016 draft) and VanVleet (who was not drafted at all out of Wichita State) were pairing up for a championship run of a lesser magnitude, as key members of Raptors 905 in the G League.

Under Nurse, both flourished this season before becoming breakout stars in the playoffs. On Thursday, Siakam, a 25-year-old power forward who goes by the nickname "Spicy P," had 26 points and 10 rebounds, while VanVleet — in addition to defending Curry — scored 12 of his 22 points in the fourth quarter.

It was an eventful series for VanVleet, a third-year point guard who scored 15 points off the bench in Game 1, lost part of a tooth after getting elbowed in Game 4, then reeled off a collection of crucial plays in Game 6. He made five 3-pointers, including one that gave the Raptors the lead for good with less than four minutes to play.

After the final buzzer, VanVleet and Curry embraced.

"He's a gamer," Curry said. "I obviously saw a lot of bodies on defense, but he was one that took the challenge. And he's a champion now. Well deserved."

The game felt like the end of an era for the Warriors, who played their final games at Oracle Arena (they will move to a new arena in San Francisco next season) while coping with a catastrophic series of injuries. After Kevin Durant tore his Achilles' tendon in Game 5, Klay Thompson tore the anterior cruciate ligament in his left knee in Game 6. Golden State's future — as jarring as this sounds — is suddenly uncertain after three championships in five seasons.

The Raptors have questions of their own moving forward, starting with Leonard, who is bound for free agency: Will he stay or will he go?

But for one night, the organization reveled in the present. Marc Gasol, acquired in a midseason trade with the Memphis Grizzlies, video chatted on his cellphone with his former teammate Mike Conley while pounding a can of Budweiser. Ujiri draped himself in a Nigerian flag. And Danny Green, the veteran guard, was congratulated outside the locker room by Vince Carter, the 42-year-old swingman who, once upon a time, was the face of the Raptors when respectability was an achievement.

These Raptors believed they could do more, then proved it.

"It's unbelievable," VanVleet said.

The Los Angeles Clippers Won Kawhi Leonard and Paul George by Winning

By Scott Cacciola

The Clippers did what they could last season to make an impression in a market long dominated by the Lakers, their roommates at Staples Center in downtown Los Angeles.

Unlike the Lakers, who were a grease fire in LeBron James's first season with the team, the Clippers produced a winning campaign. They played aggressive defense. They treated rebounds like performance art. They went to the playoffs, which was a pleasant surprise, and even won a couple of games there against the Golden State Warriors in their first-round series.

One of their marketing slogans was "L.A. Our Way." Their way was blue-collar aptitude in the shadow of purple-and-gold nonsense.

The aptitude gods rewarded the Clippers over the weekend: Kawhi Leonard and Paul George, two natives of Southern California, are returning home to play for the team.

Leonard, fresh off his championship run with the Toronto Raptors, agreed to sign in free agency after playing a huge role in persuading George to seek a trade from the Oklahoma City Thunder. The Clippers made sure that deal happened by sending an outrageous package to the Thunder that included five future first-round draft picks and two very good players, Shai Gilgeous-Alexander and Danilo Gallinari.

This is worth emphasizing: The Clippers gave up a ton. Gilgeous-Alexander, 20, was the team's starting point guard as a rookie and has all the makings of a future star. Gallinari, 30, was among their leading scorers. And the Thunder are now in possession of an unprecedented number of picks.

But Leonard was not going to the Clippers unless they could pry George loose from the Thunder. So, in that sense, the Clippers were not trading all those assets for George alone. They were trading for George and for Leonard, two of the best players on the planet. It was a deal they had to make, and one that altered perceptions.

Forgotten are the laughingstock seasons when the Clippers won 12 games, 17 games, 21 games. Forgotten are the playoff droughts and the tumult of the Donald Sterling ownership years and the suffering of the franchise's most dedicated fans. Forgotten, too, is the disappointment of the "Lob City" days, which was not all that long ago but now feels like an era from a time capsule.

The fact that the Lakers got spurned in the process — and even lost out on high-profile free agents whom they could have signed as they awaited Leonard's decision — must make it that much sweeter for the Clippers, who have always had second-class status in their own city.

Even last season, when they were making their playoff push, the Clippers were overshadowed by the Lakers and all their attendant drama: their failed midseason pursuit of Anthony Davis (they later got him) ahead of February's trade deadline, the injuries and the losing, the abrupt resignation of Magic Johnson as their president of basketball operations. It was a fire hose of dysfunction.

The Clippers just quietly went about their business, and the same held true in recent days: They had a plan for free agency, and they were going to work to execute it even after the Lakers finally succeeded in trading for Davis, which was a big deal at the time — and still is.

But with one bold strike, the Clippers managed to outshine the Lakers.

The Clippers are better positioned to vie for titles right away. The Lakers lacked depth even before their roster was gutted by the Pelicans in the Davis deal. The Clippers, on the other hand, managed to keep much of their core intact. Leonard and George, two of the league's premier two-way players, join a rotation that already includes Lou Williams, the top bench scorer in the history of the league; Montrezl Harrell, a ferocious post presence; and Patrick Beverley, a defense-minded guard.

In a lot of ways, Beverley personifies the identity of the team: tough, aggressive, fearless. George and Leonard should fit right in. Nothing about the Clippers' approach needs to change. The only difference is that opponents are likely to have even more trouble scoring against them.

For the moment, of course, the refashioned Clippers are an experiment that exists only on paper — flashy and full of championship potential, but with some concerns moving forward.

At the top of that list: George, 29, had surgery after the season on both shoulders, and the timeline for his return is unclear. He could miss the start of the season. When he does return, will he be the same type of high-octane shooter? George has already shown himself capable of returning to top shape after a serious injury. In 2014, he sustained a compound fracture in his right leg. A year and a half later, he was playing in another N.B.A. All-Star Game.

In a twist, the Lakers and the Clippers faced each other on Saturday afternoon at the N.B.A.'s summer league in Las Vegas. James sat courtside with Davis. Four seats down sat Jerry West, the Hall of Famer and consultant for the Clippers who has helped guide the team to its new perch in recent seasons.

At one point early in the game, Darrell Bailey, a superfan who goes by Clipper Darrell, stood in his blue-and-red suit and heckled James: "I'm coming for you, LeBron!"

The Clippers coach, Doc Rivers, laughed. After trying hard to ignore Bailey, James shook his head and smiled. The noise was too much to ignore.

July 12, 2019

N.B.A. Superstar Duos Remake the League

By Sopan Deb

The N.B.A. has fractured into an assortment of tag teams vying for the crown, while general managers keep their eyes peeled for who is next to ask out. Superteams are now dynamic duos. It's not the Avengers fighting Thanos anymore — Batman and Robin are taking on Poison Ivy and Mr. Freeze.

A wild — by any measure — off-season has changed the landscape of the league.

LeBron James and Anthony Davis are in Los Angeles. Kawhi Leonard and Paul George are there, too. Kyrie Irving and Kevin Durant are in Brooklyn.

And let's not leave out the Warriors. Even though Klay Thompson will miss several months of the season with an injury, they still have a powerful pairing of their own: Stephen Curry and Draymond Green.

But the question is: Will any of these duos actually work?

LeBron James and Anthony Davis (Los Angeles Lakers)

There is a strange perception that James had a down year last season in Los Angeles, in spite of his recording more points, rebounds and assists per game than his career averages. Consistent greatness has caused James to, in a way, be taken for granted, and recency bias — meaning a James-led team missing the playoffs for the first time since the Bronze Age — has shaded his personal success.

But make no mistake: Anthony Davis in his prime is the best teammate James has ever had, and we are going to be reminded why James is one of the greatest basketball players in history. Davis is better than Dwyane Wade at 29, Kyrie Irving in his early 20s, and Shaquille O'Neal at 37. He is an exceptional player on both ends of the floor. But it is around the rim where Davis does most of his damage, finishing better than 70 percent within five feet of the basket.

James and Davis will be a lethal pick-and-roll combination.

Kawhi Leonard and Paul George (Los Angeles Clippers)

Fresh off a championship, Leonard will play with the best teammate of his career, as well. (Before you throw a chair, Tim Duncan wasn't in his prime when Leonard was with him on the San Antonio Spurs.) Both Leonard and George have made multiple All-Defensive teams. Top scorers will have to go up against one or both of these two for 48 minutes, not including the professional annoyance that is Patrick Beverley.

Leonard and George immediately turn the Clippers into a juggernaut. Offensively, George and Leonard have different games that should complement each other. George is more of a long-range bomber (9.8 3-point attempts a game last season) and Leonard has the stronger midrange game.

Even if they take some time to feel each other out on that end of the floor, who is scoring on them?

Kyrie Irving and Kevin Durant (Brooklyn Nets)

Durant (Achilles' tendon) is most likely out for most, if not all, of next season. But once he is healthy, the Nets may still have a problem.

Irving and Durant are both ball-dominant, scoring-focused players. In spite of how bizarre his last year with Boston was, Irving put up the best numbers of his career — and showed a willingness to create for others, averaging a career-high 6.9 assists. The ball has a tendency to stick to Irving's hands, though, especially late in games. Because of his exceptional ball-handling ability, Irving thrives in isolation: 63 percent of his field goals last season were unassisted. (In contrast, Durant, another player who enjoys playing in isolation, scored only 51 percent of his makes unassisted.)

Durant can score anytime and anywhere in any number of ways. And he knows it. How will he react when Irving pulls up for a 3-pointer with 20 seconds left on the shot clock, even though Durant is open? Durant and Irving are known to be temperamental when things don't go well. Will they be patient about who is handling the reins on offense? Will they opt for hero ball?

Coach Kenny Atkinson has built a culture of sharing in Brooklyn. But if Irving wouldn't buy in with that culture in Boston, is there any chance he does so with the Nets?

Irving's history tells us: no.

James Harden and Russell Westbrook (Houston Rockets)

No N.B.A. star's stock plummeted following the playoffs the way Westbrook's did after another first-round exit. His critics went after his shot selection, ball dominance and demeanor. But people have forgotten just how good Westbrook is.

He's *great.*

He's undeniably one of the best players in the league, an exceptional playmaker and an elite rebounder. That matters. It was clear that Chris Paul and Harden didn't enjoy playing together in Houston, so something had to change. Westbrook is the change.

Like Irving and Durant, this is a risky pairing: Two alpha dogs who have changed how traditional basketball is perceived, even while being criticized as ballhogs. But each is motivated to prove doubters wrong.

Westbrook's defense is suspect. His shooting is nonexistent, even though his shots aren't. The Rockets' offense, for the last couple of years, has been based on isolations and 3-point shooting. That will have to shift to accommodate Westbrook's open-floor ability (and his weakness from outside).

At a base level, two former most valuable players in their primes are playing together in a wide-open league. The Rockets will be good next year. But good enough? That's the question.

May 15, 2019

Losing the Lottery Might Be the Least of the Knicks' Problems

By Harvey Araton

Just when it appeared that Patrick Ewing would finally win the big one for the Knicks, when you could even conjure up an image of his honorary participation in a championship ring ceremony not too far down the road, the lottery gods chortled and said, "Step aside, Big Fella, you had your turn 34 years ago."

Nobody kidded themselves about the Knicks' statistical chances of landing the No. 1 pick — to be used on Zion Williamson, the would-be generational talent — before Tuesday night's draft lottery. But what transpired during the stage show in Chicago once the Knicks had reached the final round of four felt like a kick in the groin, a blown lead late in the fourth quarter. The promise of Zion was summarily ejected from Madison Square Garden like a taunting fan in the face of its owner, James L. Dolan.

With a 14 percent chance, the Knicks were suddenly the heavy favorite against the competing odds of New Orleans and Memphis at 6 percent and Team LA-Bron, otherwise known as the Lakers, at 2 percent.

Finishing third, behind the Pelicans and the Grizzlies, was not a disaster — and one day it may even be considered a blessing. But not this day, a deflating reminder of how long it has been since the Garden, the self-proclaimed World's Most Famous Arena, actually was the center of the N.B.A. universe.

The draft experts insist the Knicks are still well positioned with the third pick because there are three prospects — Williamson; R.J. Barrett, his running mate at Duke; and Murray State point guard Ja Morant — who rate far above everyone else.

Of course, these experts artificially manufacture a cutoff line for those who "can't miss" every year. Almost always it doesn't work out that way, as

Kawhi Leonard (No. 15 in 2011), Giannis Antetokounmpo (No. 15 in 2013) and Donovan Mitchell (No. 13 in 2017), among many others, would argue.

Heartening are two recent No. 3 selections: Dallas's Luka Doncic, this season's likely rookie of the year, and Boston's Jayson Tatum, drafted from Duke in 2017. Disheartening is the specter of Jahlil Okafor, another Dukie, who would have been a Knick had Philadelphia not spared then-president Phil Jackson from drafting him fourth (instead of Kristaps Porzingis) in 2015.

Projections are fun. Knowledge requires patience. Nothing definitive can be said about this class — Williamson included — until sometime next season at the earliest. But for the moment, the Knicks' failure to land the big prize at least momentarily dulls the sheen of their rising superpower status.

Without Williamson as a centerpiece, they may be hard-pressed to assemble a package that would make them serious contenders for a deal with New Orleans for Anthony Davis, if that was even part of the Knicks' plan. But their lack of appealing assets raises another compelling question: What, exactly, will they be selling Kevin Durant and other impending free agents besides a famously tax-abated building when the season of shameless groveling begins in July?

You watched the Golden State Warriors share the ball so selflessly while beating Portland in Game 1 of the Western Conference finals after the lottery game show and wondered: Durant is really going to leave all that precision to come run with Allonzo Trier?

You watched the Warriors harass the Blazers' often-indomitable Damian Lillard into a 4-for-12 shooting night with seven turnovers, and mused: Durant wants to fall back on defense with the likes of Dennis Smith Jr. and Kevin Knox?

You see how many contributors, in addition to the so-called max (salary) players, it takes to play deep into spring, and you have to stretch the imagination to name just one on the Knicks' current roster who could honestly be considered a solid rotation guy on a serious playoff contender.

Maybe the lure of the Garden and Midtown Manhattan will be enough for Durant to try what LeBron James never considered — the opportunity to resurrect N.B.A. basketball just off Broadway. But it also stands to reason that

Durant, even in tandem with Kyrie Irving, is too smart to take that plunge without at least doing his homework, and asking hard questions of Dolan himself.

If that is the case, then Chairman James will have some explaining to do, given the treatment of aging Knicks stars not only during his volatile era but going way back across the decades.

Rare has been the Knicks luminary who left the Garden without some rancor. Walt Frazier was traded to Cleveland. Willis Reed was canned as coach 14 games into his second season. Bob McAdoo was traded in the dead of the night. Earl Monroe was unceremoniously dropped. Bernard King was cut after diligently rehabbing his surgically repaired knee. Ewing asked to be dealt and, presumably as payback, was never invited back to work — not until the Knicks needed him Tuesday night as they tried to restage the 1985 inaugural lottery that landed him in New York.

A forgiving soul, apparently, Ewing, in a Knicks-blue suit, played along with the endless network hyping of the potential Knicks-Zion marriage. It was shameless and patently unfair to the other teams that tanked for the occasion and especially to Williamson, 18, whose impressionable head was prematurely filled with visions of Big Apple grandeur.

The only time he didn't smile on camera was when he learned where he had landed. Someone might want to inform him that he probably lucked out. The TV networks are sure to follow him to New Orleans the way they chased after LeBron in Cleveland. Nor is being ordained a Knicks savior the world's most desirable appointment. For the most recent historical example, call Porzingis in Latvia and ask how it worked out for him.

OCTOBER 9, 2019

For The N.B.A., a Sticky Situation in China Will Linger

BY MARC STEIN

This was supposed to be a time when the mere mention of the Houston Rockets would inspire questions about their polarizing plan to reunite James Harden and Russell Westbrook and ask them to share one basketball for the next seven or eight months.

You can't help but wonder now how long it will be before we can return to that debate.

A tweet late Friday from Rockets General Manager Daryl Morey containing seven words and one image, in support of pro-democracy protesters in Hong Kong, has plunged the N.B.A. into the most complicated crisis faced by Adam Silver, who is beginning his sixth full season as commissioner.

What began as mostly a China vs. Houston conflict morphed into a full-blown China vs. N.B.A. battle after Silver, at a news conference on Tuesday in Saitama, Japan, reiterated that the league office would not punish or censure Morey — no matter how badly the N.B.A.'s Chinese business partners want that to happen.

"I'm sympathetic to our interests here and our partners that are upset," Silver said. "I don't think it's inconsistent on one hand to be sympathetic to them and at the same time stand by our principles."

Chief among those principles, Silver stressed after failing to spell it out clearly in his first round of comments on the matter, is the right to free speech. "What I also tried to suggest," he said, "is that I understand there are consequences from his freedom of speech and we will have to live with those consequences."

The full scope of those consequences may not be known for weeks or months. Fallout from the Morey scandal continued to mount on Tuesday, when China's state-run CCTV announced that it would not broadcast exhibition games scheduled for this week in Shanghai and Shenzhen. LeBron James's Los Angeles Lakers are scheduled to face the Brooklyn Nets, who are owned by Joe Tsai, the billionaire co-founder of the Chinese e-commerce giant Alibaba.

In discussions I've had over the past few days with a number of well-placed observers, who are familiar with both the Chinese landscape and N.B.A. dealings, there are growing fears that government officials will cancel the two games. Various sponsors, media outlets and the Chinese Basketball Association itself — led by the former Rockets great Yao Ming — have already vowed to have nothing to do with the Rockets for the foreseeable future.

Silver is scheduled to arrive in China on Wednesday to begin face-to-face damage control with some of the aggrieved entities. Among them is Yao himself; Silver has acknowledged that the Hall of Fame center is "extremely" angry.

"And I understand it," Silver said.

That's because the N.B.A. has always known that its efforts to cultivate a foothold in China, which began more than 30 years ago, exposed a league that has long championed social justice to precisely this sort of philosophical quandary. As the great Jack McCallum, one of my foremost mentors, wrote in a 2006 *Sports Illustrated* article on David Stern, then the N.B.A. commissioner: "China presents an even greater conflict for Stern because it has both colossal business potential and a terrible human rights record."

"Believe me, the China situation bothers me," Stern told McCallum at the time. "But at the end of the day, I have a responsibility to my owners to make money. I can never forget that, no matter what my personal feelings might be."

If all of this strikes you as hypocritical, given the N.B.A.'s reputation as the sports league that encourages freedom of expression and activism more than any other, you are absolutely right. Just don't forget that there is a long line of American businesses that similarly refuse to publicly back the pro-democracy protesters in Hong Kong, and instead focus on mining profit from China's estimated population of 1.4 billion.

I was just in China for eight days covering the United States men's national basketball team at the FIBA World Cup. Mere steps from my hotel in Beijing, I had access to Walmart, Starbucks and Kentucky Fried Chicken. McDonald's outlets are everywhere. The N.B.A. is hardly alone in chasing China's disposable income at the risk of impinging on its democratic ideals.

The rub for the N.B.A., of course, is that tag it carries as the "wokest league" on Earth. That is not an identity, contrary to legend, invented by the league's marketing machine — but Silver and other top officials, as well as some marquee players, have undoubtedly embraced and celebrated it.

Every company that boasts purchasing power, everywhere in the world, will flex that muscle upon vendors. Every vendor, everywhere in the world, will eventually yield to its biggest customers. The resulting challenge for Silver's league — more so than for most American businesses, because of its social footprint and the tremendous visibility of its stars — is how to protect those financial interests without trampling on what Silver on Monday termed "values that have been part of this league from its earliest days."

The N.B.A., to this point, is struggling mightily to thread that needle and has been roundly bashed on both sides — crushed by segments of the American news media for not supporting Morey's pro-democracy tweet with more gusto, while a growing number of Chinese institutions appear in a rush to distance themselves from the league. The subsequent geopolitical storm has proved so uncomfortable that Golden State Warriors Coach Steve Kerr, one of the most forthright voices in basketball, essentially declined to comment Monday night when invited by Bay Area reporters to wade into the discussion.

"This isn't the end of the Rockets or the N.B.A. in China," Witold Henisz, a management professor and director of the Wharton Political Risk Lab at the University of Pennsylvania, said Tuesday in a telephone interview. "But it reflects the need for companies to have a political strategy — even companies that you wouldn't think of as having political strategies."

Talking about Hong Kong, Henisz continued, "is not the same as talking about race relations in the United States." Or speaking out in favor of stricter gun control domestically, as Kerr often does, inspired by lingering torment from the assassination of his father, Malcolm, while serving as president of the American University of Beirut in 1984.

There's a sense that the storm is just beginning, too. Is the cancellation of this week's two scheduled games in China as inevitable as it feels? Will broadcasters such as CCTV and Tencent extend bans of N.B.A. coverage into the regular season? How many millions will this whole saga ultimately cost the N.B.A.? And how will a typically outspoken superstar like James, given how closely connected he is to Nike and how significant the China market is to both brand and endorser, handle the uncomfortable questions sure to come his way this week when the Lakers meet the media in Shanghai?

Another question teams back home have rather predictably started asking in the information-gathering conversations so prevalent around the league this time of year: What impact will the lost revenue have in terms of lowering the league's salary cap for next season?

We could surely keep going. So dissecting the potential pros and problems awaiting Houston on the floor — with Harden and Westbrook unexpectedly thrown together again by a July trade that capped perhaps the wildest off-season in league history — will simply have to wait.

"I'm a realist, as well," Silver said at his news conference in Japan. "And I recognize that this issue may not die down so quickly."

Contributors

Jonathan Abrams is a sports journalist and author who covered basketball for *The New York Times* and Bleacher Report.

Sam Anderson is a staff writer for *The New York Times Magazine.*

Malika Andrews, a former sports reporter for *The New York Times,* is now an N.B.A. reporter for ESPN.

Harvey Araton is a former sports columnist and reporter for *The New York Times.*

Arnold (Red) Auerbach (1917–2006) was the coach, general manager and president of the Boston Celtics from 1950 to 2006.

Dave Anderson (1929–2018) was a Pulitzer Prize–winning former sports columnist for *The New York Times.*

Brooks Barnes covers Hollywood for *The New York Times.*

Dan Barry is a reporter and columnist for *The New York Times.*

Howard Beck, a former N.B.A. reporter for *The New York Times,* now covers the league for Bleacher Report.

Ira Berkow is a former sports columnist and feature writer for *The New York Times.*

Sam Borden reported on international sports for *The New York Times.* He now writes for ESPN.

John Branch is a Pulitzer Prize–winning sports reporter for *The New York Times.*

Frank Bruni is an Op-Ed columnist for *The New York Times.*

Chris Broussard, formerly a sports reporter for *The New York Times* and ESPN, is now a Fox Sports N.B.A. analyst.

Scott Cacciola covers basketball and other sports for *The New York Times.*

Steve Cady (1927–1995) was a sportswriter for *The New York Times*.

David Davis is a freelance sports reporter and magazine writer.

Sopan Deb covers culture and the N.B.A. for *The New York Times*.

Maureen Dowd is a Pulitzer Prize–winning Op-Ed columnist for *The New York Times* and a staff writer for *The Times Magazine*.

Tom Friend is a sports journalist who has contributed to *The New York Times* and *ESPN Magazine*.

David Gelles is a business reporter and columnist for *The New York Times*.

Paul Gilbert is a freelance journalist.

Jane Gross is a former sportswriter and national reporter for *The New York Times*.

Adam Himmelsbach is a former *New York Times* contributor and sports reporter for *The Boston Globe*.

Benjamin Hoffman is an editor and reporter for *The New York Times*.

Lee Jenkins was a sports reporter for *The New York Times* and covered the N.B.A. for *Sports Illustrated*. He now works as the executive director of research and identity for the Los Angeles Clippers.

Roy S. Johnson is a former sports reporter for *The New York Times* who is now a columnist and director of content for the Alabama Media Group.

Jay Caspian Kang is a writer at large for *The New York Times Magazine*.

Will Leitch, a former columnist for *New York* magazine, is the founder of Deadspin.

Janet Maslin is a former film and book critic for *The New York Times*.

Victor Mather is an editor and reporter for *The New York Times*.

Malcolm Moran, who covered sports for *The New York Times*, the *Chicago Tribune* and *USA Today*, is director of the sports journalism program at Indiana University.

John Nielsen is a freelance writer who contributed to *The New York Times*.

Michael Powell is a sports columnist for *The New York Times*.

William C. Rhoden is a former sports columnist for *The New York Times*. He now writes for ESPN's The Undefeated.

Liz Robbins covered basketball for *The New York Times* from 2000 to 2007.

Selena Roberts, a former sports columnist for *The New York Times* and *Sports Illustrated*, is also a film documentarian.

Oscar Robertson is a former N.B.A. All-Star and a member of the Naismith Memorial Basketball Hall of Fame.

Richard Sandomir, who covered the business of sports and the media for *The New York Times*, is now an obituary writer for the paper.

William E. Schmidt is a former correspondent and deputy managing editor for *The New York Times*. He now teaches journalism at the University of Arizona.

Matthew Schneier is a reporter for the Styles section of *The New York Times*.

Charles Solomon is a critic and historian of animation who has written on the subject for *The New York Times*, the *Los Angeles Times*, and NPR.

Marc Stein is a basketball reporter and columnist for *The New York Times*.

George Vecsey is a former sports columnist for *The New York Times*.

Alex Williams is a reporter in the Styles section of *The New York Times*.

Mike Wise has covered sports for *The New York Times*, *The Washington Post*, and ESPN.

Acknowledgments

The idea for a book can come in an instant, derived from a conversation that makes a sudden turn from a straightaway and takes off in a direction all its own. The kernel for this one occurred as I addressed colleagues at *The New York Times* during the fall of 2016, upon taking leave of the full-time staff.

Reflecting on my quarter-century at *The Times* as a sports reporter and columnist, with a strong concentration on the N.B.A., I cited some of the basketball-loving folks with whom I'd had the good fortune of working. Ira Berkow. Selena Roberts. Mike Wise. Howard Beck. I could have gone on and on, for I know of no deeper cumulative roster of writing talent on any specific sport at any publication.

Fully aware of how rich *The Times*'s archives were in N.B.A. history, it occurred to me that a collection of work from a newspaper that truly covers the world could best tell the story of an American sports league that had, over the past 40 years, become a global phenomenon.

The next step was to reach out to Alex Ward, The *Times*'s crack editorial director of book development and an erudite N.B.A. fan in his own right. Alex took it from there and partnered with Noah Amstadter and Josh Williams of Triumph Books, who put the project into the able hands of Jesse Jordan. Much gratitude to all these very smart people who made this happen.

Reporters and columnists get the bylines, and the attention, but *The Times* sports department has had great leadership through the period this book covers. Sports editors Lee Anne Schreiber, Joe Vecchione, Neil Amdur, Tom Jolly, Joe Sexton, and Jason Stallman all had a hand in the direction of these works.

A special thanks to Jay Schreiber for his refusal to accept less than the maximum effort from the basketball writing staff every day he was on the case, which was most days. Bill Brink was for years an indispensable voice in the office and in our heads. Fern Turkowitz and Terri Ann Glynn, our amazing office managers, always kept us moving in the right direction.

A nod to all of the editors who helped our copy and kept us off the dreaded corrections page. A special nod to Patty LaDuca, the greatest copy editor in creation, who wrestled this nearly 500-page volume to the mat with her trademark tenacity.

In 2018, as this book was being produced, *The Times* sports family lost two of its most beloved members: Dave Anderson, whose work appears here, and Frank Litsky. We miss them as much as the privileged folks who read them.

—*Harvey Araton*